MIND & SUPERMIND

Vol. II

Other Books by the same Author

1. **Bhagavad-Gītā**: A New Exposition in a broader Spectrum; ISBN: 978-81-246-0525-7 (Hb), 978-81-246-0526-4 (Pb)
2. **Cyclic Universe**: Cycle of the Creation, Evolution, Involution and Dissolution of the Universe; 2 vols.; Contents: vol. 1: The Unsolved Riddle: Eternal, Created or Evolved Universe; vol. 2: Integral Cosmology: Cosmic Creation, Evolution and Dissolution in Cycles; ISBN: 978-81-246-0190-7 (set)
3. **Japa Yoga (Mantra-Yoga)** — Theory, Practice and Applications; ISBN: 978-81-246-0388-8 (Hb), 978-81-246-0389-5 (Pb)
4. **Meditation**: Science and Practice; ISBN: 978-81-246-0211-9 (Hb), 978-81-246-0212-6 (Pb)
5. **Yoga-Nidrā (Yogic Trance)** — Theory, Practice and Applications; ISBN: 978-81-246-0242-3 (Hb), 978-81-246-0243-0 (Pb)

MIND & SUPERMIND

Vol. II

N. C. Panda

PRINTWORLD
Publishers of Indian Traditions

Cataloging in Publication Data — DK

[Courtesy: D.K. Agencies (P) Ltd. <docinfo@dkagencies.com>]

Panda, N.C. (Nrusingh Charan), 1929-
Mind and supermind.
Includes bibliographical references (p.).
Includes indexes.
ISBN 13: 9788124600535 (set)

1. Philosophy of mind. 2. Spiritualism. 3. Philosophy.
4. Psychology. 5. Metaphysics. I. Titles.

ISBN 13: 978-81-246-0053-5 (set)
ISBN 13: 978-81-246-0063-4 (vol. 2)

First published in India in 1996
Second impression, 2013

Printed and published by:
D.K. Printworld (P) Ltd.
Regd. office : *"Vedaśrī,"* F-395, Sudarshan Park
(Metro Station: Ramesh Nagar)
New Delhi - 110 015
Phones : (011) 2545 3975, 2546 6019; *Fax* : (011) 2546 5926
e-mail : indology@dkprintworld.com
Web : www.dkprintworld.com

Contents

VOLUME II

Abbreviations

AB	*Amṛtabindu*
ABSS	*Advaita-Brahma-Siddhi* of Sadānanda
ANB	*Aparokṣānubhūti* of Śaṅkara
APŪ	*Annapūrṇopaniṣad*
AU	*Aitareya Upaniṣad*
AV	*Atharva Veda*
BBB	*The Blue and Brown Books* of Ludwig Wittgenstein, Oxford: Basil Blackwell, 1958.
BDP	*Brahmāṇḍa Purāṇa*
BG	*Bhagavadgītā*
BGŚB	*Bhagavadgītā Śāṅkara Bhāṣyam*
Bhā	*Bhāgavatam*
BP	*Brahma Purāṇa*
BS	*Brahma-Sūtram*
BSRB	*Brahma-Sūtraṁ Rāmānuja-Bhāṣyam*
BSŚB	*Brahma-Sūtraṁ Śāṅkara Bhāṣyam*
BU	*Bṛhadāraṇyaka Upaniṣad*
BUŚB	*Bṛhadāraṇyaka Upaniṣad Śāṅkara Bhāṣyam*

CU	Chāndogya Upaniṣad
CUŚB	Chāndogya Upaniṣad Śāṅkara Bhāṣyam
GP	Garuḍa Purāṇa
HV	Harivaṁśa
IU	Īśopaniṣad
IUŚB	Īśopaniṣad Śāṅkara Bhāṣyam
KLU	Kaivalyopaniṣad
KNU	Kenopaniṣad
KNUŚB	Kenopaniṣad Śāṅkara Bhāṣyam
KP	Kūrma Purāṇa
KS	Kaṇāda-Sūtram
KṢU	Kauṣītaki Upaniṣad
KTU	Kaṭhopaniṣad
KTUŚB	Kaṭhopaniṣad Śāṅkara Bhāṣyam
MAU	Māṇḍūkyopaniṣad
Mbh	Mahābhārata
Mbh-SP	Mahābhārata Śānti-Parva
MGLU	Mudgalopaniṣad
MKG	Māṇḍūkya Kārikā of Gauḍapāda
MS	Manusmṛti
MTNU	Maitrāyaṇa Upaniṣad
MTU	Maitrī Upaniṣad
MUU	Muṇḍaka Upaniṣad
MUUŚB	Muṇḍaka Upaniṣad Śāṅkara Bhāṣyam
NB	Nyāya-Bhāṣyam
ND	Nyāya-Darśanam
NS	Nyāya-Sūtram
NSB	Nyāya-Sūtra-Bhāṣyam

PGLU	*Paiṅgalopaniṣad*
PI	*Philosophical Investigations* of Ludwig Wittgenstein (tr. by G.E.M. Anscombe) Oxford: Basil Blackwell, 1953.
PP	*Padma Purāṇa*
PU	*Praśna Upaniṣad*
PUŚB	*Praśna Upaniṣad Śāṅkara Bhāṣyam*
PYD	*Pātañjala Yoga Darśanam*
PYDTV	*Pātañjala Yoga-Darśana Tattva-Vaiśāradī*
PYDVB	*Pātañjala Yoga-Darśana Bhāṣyam* of Vyāsa
PYDYV	*Pātañjala Yoga-Darśanaṁ Yoga-Vārttika*
ṚV	*Ṛgveda*
ŚBrā	*Śatapatha Brāhmaṇa*
SDSS	*Śrī-Durgā Saptasatī*
SK	*Sāṅkhya Kārikā*
SPB	*Sāṅkhya Pravacana Bhāṣyam* of Vijñānabhikṣu
SPS	*Sāṅkhya Pravacana-Sūtra*
SPSVA	*Sāṅkhya Pravacan-Sūtra — Vṛtti* of Aniruddha
ŚS	*Śiva-Saṁhitā*
SSU	*Sarvasāropaniṣad*
ŚSV	*Śiva-Sūtram* of Vasugupta
ŚU	*Śvetāśvatara Upaniṣad*
SUS	*Sarvopaniṣatsāra*
ŚUŚB	*Śvetāśvatara Upaniṣad Śāṅkara Bhāṣyam*
TBrā	*Taittirīya Brāhmaṇa*

TBU	*Tejobindūpaniṣad*
TLP	*Tractatus Logico-Philosophicus* of Ludwig Wittgenstein. (tr. by D.F. Pears and B.F. McGuinness). London: Routledge and Kegan Paul, 1961.
TSu	*Tattvārtha-Sūtram*
TU	*Taittirīya Upaniṣad*
TUŚB	*Taittirīya Upaniṣad Śāṅkara Bhāṣyam*
UNV	*Uddyotkara's Nyāya-Vārttika*
VāP	*Vāyu Purāṇa*
VC	*Viveka-Cūḍāmaṇi*
VNB	*Vātsyāyana's Nyāya-Bhāṣyam*
VNV	*Viśvanātha's Nyāya-Vṛtti*
VP	*Viṣṇu Purāṇa*
VPDA	*Vedānta Paribhāṣā* of Dharmarāja Adhvarīndra
VS	*Vaiśeṣika Sūtram*
VSS	*Vedānta-Sāra* of Sadānanda
VSU	*Upaskāra of Śaṅkara Miśra on Vaiśeṣika Sūtram*
VTT	*Vācaspatimiśra's Tātparya-Ṭīkā*
YV	*Yajurveda*

List of Figures

7

The Concept of Mind in Western Religions and Philosophy

THE identity of mind and soul prevailed in the Western philosophy during a vast expanse of time in history, starting from the ancient Greek age to the end of the first three decades of the twentieth century. Along with the concept of the mind-soul identity was the accompanying notion of the dichotomy of the mind and the body. The material body was held to be distinct from the immaterial mind.

Plato's Dualism

Plato (428-348 BC), or perhaps Socrates (470-400 BC) and Plato, established the doctrine of the *psyche* as immortal. 'Soul' is an Anglo-Saxon term, the Greek equivalent of which is *psyche* or *pneuma*. The literal meaning of the term 'psyche' is 'breath'. The Latin term *anima* and the French term *âme* are equivalents of *psyche*. When Socrates or Plato used the word *psyche*, it had the same conception as that of the soul. Plato did not regard the soul as the shadow of man, but treated it as the deepest reality of man. He provided the tripartite conception of the soul as reason, will and appetite. One part of our soul searches for truth and loves wisdom. In contrast, another part deals with our appetitive nature, which desires and desires anything that is imaginable. According to the Christian view, it is the spiritual and not the intellectual part of the soul that is most important and most likely to survive death. For the Greeks, on the other hand, reason (*nous* in Greek) is the highest part of the soul. Aristotle holds that only *nous* has any chance of being immortal. Plato, like Aristole, could not successfully manage to link the rational soul or intellect with that part of the soul which is more obviously connected with the body.

Plato puts forward his arguments for the immortality of the soul. He claims that the soul is non-composite, simple, and changeless. A composite thing disintegrates to its component parts. This process is otherwise known as 'destruction', as conceived by Plato. The soul, being a simple entity, cannot be destroyed, and hence is immortal. In contrast, the body is composite, mutable, destructible, and mortal. This is Plato's famous dualism of mind and body.[1] In this dichotomy, the physical body is considered as material and the soul as immaterial, the physical body as modifiable and impermanent, and the soul as unmodifiable and eternal.

In a strict sense, Plato's dualism contrasts the material and the abstract realms. Here we may briefly discuss his concepts of 'universals' and 'particulars'. In the sensible, material world, there are many individual persons, cows, horses, dogs, cats, trees, etc. When we say "this cat" or "that cat ", we refer to individual cats. These are particulars. But the word 'cat' does not mean any particular cat. It is a universl cat that stands for the 'cat' idea of God. Whenever a number of individuals have a common name, they have also a common 'idea' or 'Form'. This is true for all categories of particulars, humans, dogs, trees, flowers, etc. The universal cattiness is not born when a particular cat is born; nor does it die when a particular cat dies. The universal cat is not material; it is an immaterial 'idea' or 'Form' of cat; it has no position in space or time; it is eternal. God has 'ideas' (Greek word EIDOS) or 'Forms' that are perfect and flawless. All particulars of the sensible world are not flawless and each one is the inferior replica of the respective 'idea' or 'Form'. Just as reflection of a tree in a mirror is only apparent and not 'real', so are the various particular trees which are unreal,being only copies of the 'idea' which is the one and the only one real tree. Plato's category of Being is an eternal God in communion with his universal ideas or Forms. His 'ideas' or 'Forms' are the exemplars after which individuals in the world are created. His universals have extra-mental reality. They do not depend upon anything in the world. They have their own eternal realm. Plato says that the philosopher can have knowledge of the universal — the 'idea' or the 'Form' made by God. On the other hand, there can be only opinion on the particulars.

According to Plato, the soul, which is a transcendental entity, dwelt in the realm of Forms before our birth. It will return there after our death. The place where it will return is, however, no place, no region.

Plato's metaphysical dualism that has been presented here is the earliest one in the history of Western philosophy. He attributed true existence to ideas; but he nonetheless recognized the inferior existence of the sensible, material world as a principle opposing the ideas. His metaphysical dualism was parallel with his ethical one. He identified the good with the ideas or Forms and evil with the material counterparts.

Plato paid more attention to contrasting the universals and the particulars than to discussing the status of the soul. He never succeeded very well in integrating the soul into his favourite dualism. Nevertheless, he undoubtedly made a distinction between the material, impermanent body and the immaterial, permanent soul. His soul existed in time but had no extension is space.

Philosophical dualism insists that the soul or mind is a separate non-material substance which can exist independently of a body, although it exists in the body while a person is living. Catholic Christianity does not agree with Plato in this aspect since the former holds that immortality involves having a body, be it one's original body or a new one.

The Platonic soul or mind, being related to the higher and

abiding realm rather than to the evanescent world of sense, is imperishable and so immortal.

The Concept of Mind in Western Religions

This body-soul distinction or body-mind dualism, first formulated as a philosophical doctrine by Plato in ancient Greece, was baptized into Christianity. It was accepted as an inviolable concept in the medieval period. Plato's argument was adopted by Aquinas and became standard in Roman Catholic theology. In this respect, Jacques Maritain, a Catholic philosopher writes:

> A spiritual soul cannot be corrupted, since it possesses no matter; it cannot be disintegrated, since it has no substantial parts; it cannot lose its individual unity, since it is self-subsisting, nor its internal energy, since it contains within itself all the sources of its energies. The human soul cannot die. Once it exists, it cannot disappear; it will necessarily exist for ever, endure without end. Thus, philosophic reason, put to work by a great metaphysician like Thomas Aquinas, is able to prove the immortality of the human soul in demonstrative manner.[2]

Three major religions of the world, viz., Judaism Christianity, and Islam reserve souls to human beings only. They categorically assert that non-human living beings, i.e., animals and plants, are soulless. They deny souls to non-living objects. The Bible says: "God has made the human being out of the dust of the earth."[3] Similar concept has also been given in the *Qur'an*: "See, I am about to create a human being from clay, formed from moulded mud. I have shaped him and breathed My spirit into him."[4] Details of the creation of souls and the precursors of souls, out of which souls have been made, have not been described. But, this much is obvious that God creates a soul for every individual human being when the latter is conceived in the mother's womb. Thus, every soul is not beginningless; neither is it uncreated; it has a beginning in time, and it is a created entity. The creator of the soul is God Himself. Once created, the soul lives eternally. It lives in the body when the person is living. It survives death when the person is dead.

The idea of the immortality of the soul, as envisaged by Plato, supposes an eventual separation of the soul from the body. All the three religions mentioned here, however, support the doctrine of resurrection, as distinguished from Plato's idea of immortality. According to this doctrine, the dead shall rise in bodily form whenever God wills. The Islamic Holy scriptures say: "When Allah wills, He raises the dead."[5] We also get other references to the creation of man and resurrection in the Holy *Qur'an*.[6] In the opinion of the early Church Fathers, the resurrection body has the shape as the physical body.[7] Such an opinion is, however, contradicted by Saint Paul.[8] He reserves this idea to the unique resurrection of Jesus, and he distinguishes the general resurrection from the unique one. St.Paul holds that the general resurrection has nothing to do with the resuscitation of corpses in a cemetery, and that God recreates or reconstitutes the human psychophysical individual, not as the organism that has died but as a *soma pneumatikon*. It is a spiritual body that inhabits a spiritual world whereas the physical body inhabits the material world in which we presently live.

The Day of Resurrection is otherwise known as the Day of Judgement, the Last Judgement, the Last Day, or the Day. On this, God raises all the dead persons. The actions of both the dead and the living persons will be judged by God. The virtuous and the pious will be sent to heaven; the vicious and the impious will be sent to hell. The souls in heaven will enjoy eternal bliss; the souls in hell will be subjected to eternal damnation. About heaven and hell, we get a number of references in the holy *Qur'an*.[9] There is no provision of reincarnation of souls in the religious scriptures of the three religions mentioned here.

The Concept of Mind in Ancient and Medieval Philosophy

Plato's concept of mind-soul identity and mind-body duality has already been described. Aristotle's view on this topic has its own peculiarity. 'Substance' (*ousia*) is his basic ontological unit. He defines 'substance' as "that which is". It involves form, matter, and an internal principle of movement. What is form in one sense can be matter in another. The physical body, although formed, is matter in relation to the soul which is the form of the body. This view of Aristotle was held in the Middle Ages by St. Thomas Aquinas (1225-74) and many Scholastics. Aquinas accepted the soul as man's substantial form, and distinguished intellectual, volitional, and appetitive functions therein. His concept included the soul's immateriality and its creation by God out of nothing.

Neoplatonism is a philosophy which begins from the work of Plato, and interprets him in a special manner. For our purpose here, we will mention the notion of Plotinus (205-70) and that of St. Augustine (354-430) regarding the concept of mind. Both these philosophers were neoplatonists.

In the philosophy of Plotinus, the Egypto-Roman philosopher, reality emerges from an eternal principle of primal unity. The initial emanation from the One is that of the *Nous* or Intelligence, which is the realm of the Forms of Plato. The second emanation is that of the World Soul. It exists in contemplation of the *Nous*. The final emanation is that of matter, which, being devoid of Form, is the closest approach to non-being. The evil in the world and that in man are necessary concomitants of the material principle. Thus man is a combination of the material and the spiritual principles. His body is material, and his mind or soul spiritual.

St. Augustine was a Christian philosopher who was a neoplatonist. His philosophy, among other things, stresses man's temporality, contrasting with God's eternality. Man is a union of soul and body. He extends beyond his life. His body perishes on death; his soul continues to exist after death although it did not pre-exist prior to his birth.

Cartesian Philosophy

The French philosopher René Descartes (1596-1650) was a rationalist rather than an empiricist in approach. He redefined the mind-matter dualism which appeared to him to be a self-evident truth. This so-called truth was rejected in the twentieth century in the forties and afterwards.

Descartes was sceptical of the certainty of the knowledge derived from perceptions through the senses. For him, only one thing was certain, namely, that nothing was certain. But, he asked this question to himself: "If one is doubtful of everything, can one's existence also be doubted?" The answer to this question he got, "*Cogito, ergo sum* (I think, therefore I am)". He asserted that this proposition, and only this one, could stand against the scepticism of doubt. Thus, he undoubtedly posited his self or soul or mind. Next, he posited the idea of God. This is an idea of "a substance that is inifinite, eternal, immutable, independent, all-powerful, and by which I myself and everything else, if anything else does exist, have been created". He could by limitation get the idea of himself from the idea of God, but not the idea of God from the idea of himself, or of other things. He realized that the source of the idea of God must be found in God Himself.

To Descartes a clear difference was discernible between minds and bodies. The body is extended, a *res extensa*, and has reference to space and time, and motion. Descartes defines matter as that which has extension. He elaborates a corpuscular theory of the universe on this basis. This theory holds that all of space is filled with matter corpuscles that are in motion. In contrast, mind is *res cogitans* (thinking thing). It has no extension and no essential need for reference to space and time. Thus, in the opinion of Descartes, thought and extension are two chief attributes of reality, thought being the attribute of mind, and extension being the attribute of body. He further states that minds and bodies are created substances and that God alone, as the self-subsistent Being, is substance in the fullest sense.

Although life involves conjunction of mind and body, both are separate and opposite to each other. The mind or the soul survives death and remains immortal for ever. This is essentially the Cartesian philosophy of dualism.

It is, however, a fact that the body and the mind interact with each other. How can this be explained by the Cartesian philosophy that advocates the exclusiveness of the body and the mind? The views supporting the notion of interaction of the body and the mind are called interactionist theories, or simply interactionism. Although Descartes described the body and the mind as direct and complete opposites, he assumed the pineal gland to be the point of the interaction. The occasionalists could not see how such extreme opposites could relate to each other in any sense, and hence they had to abandon the idea of interaction. The theory of occasionalism introduced God as the intermediary between the soul and the body. When the soul desires something for the body, God moves the latter accordingly; when the body needs something, God informs the soul about it. Nicolas Malebranche (1638-1715), Arnold Geulincx (1625-69), Johannes Clauberg (1622-65) and Louis de la Forge (17th century) are some of the famous occasionalists.

The Concept of Mind in Rationalism

Rationalism is the principle that reason is to be granted the primary role in explanation.

Three philosophers, viz., Descartes, Spinoza, and Leibniz, are noted as the Continental Rationalists. We have already discussed the dualistic philosophy of Descartes. Here we will briefly state the rationalistic philosophy of Spinoza and Leibniz.

Benedict de Spinoza (1632-77) was a Dutch philosopher who was born in a Jewish family. He defines 'substance' as that which can exist by itself. In his opinion, there is only one substance which is the whole of reality. He equates God, Nature, and substance. This God-Nature-substance is absolutely infinite. This Being is one only, eternally existing, its essence implying its existence. God is immanent in the world and lives within each human being. He is not something outside the world.

Spinoza is in agreement with the old Greek mind on the pantheistic outlook. That the world could be conjured up out of nothing was quite absurd for the ancient Greek thinker, for whom something could not come from nothing. Spinoza is the philosophic exponent of the view that God is the world.

God or Nature is its own cause, *causa immanence* and *cuasa sui*. The Supreme Being has infinite number of attributes; but, out of these attributes men know two only, i.e., thought and extension.

Reality is both thought and thing. It follows from this that everything has both its reason and its cause. Parallelism between thought and thing is universal. As an intelligent whole, each thing has its reason; as an extended plenum, each thing has its cause.

Spinoza is of the view that "it is of the nature of mind to perceive things from a certain timeless point of view". But the operations of the passions militate against the mind. As a result, the mind is prevented from realizing a full intellectual vision of the universe.

In the philosophy of Spinoza, God is not different from the world. This creates a problem for explaining the existence of evil. Like Socrates and Plato, Spinoza thinks that ignorance is the prime cause of all evil. He further holds that, evil being negative, and God or Nature being a totality lacking nothing, evil cannot contaminate God.

Leibniz (1646-1716) was a German philosopher. He was one of the three Continental Rationalists of the seventeenth century. His ontological unit was primarily a centre of force.

He named it 'monad'. He differed from Descartes who held extension to be primary for a thing. Monads are extensionless, and hence they do not exist in space. Being partless, they cannot degenerate into something simpler. They are the simplest substances out of which everything else is made.

Each monad is a substance. Monads are, however, not spatio-temporal entities. Leibniz does not assign reality to space and time since he takes them for sensory appearances.

Each monad 'mirrors' the entire universe and hence is a microcosm. The monads are windowless; nothing can go in or out. No two monads can be causally connected. Each one has a career independent of all the rest. Although each monad mirrors the universe, the mirroring is done in a slightly different way. No two monads are exactly alike.

But it is also an observed fact that entities in the universe interact. Then how does Leibniz explain this interaction? He does it by his doctrine of "Pre-established Harmony". Two clocks show the same time without interacting with each other. They are synchronized to run in harmony. And so has God ordained that all monads function in a synchronized way.

All monads are immaterial, indestructible, and therefore immortal. Not only are they centres of force, but also they are centres of feeling, perception, and appetition. Thus each monad is a type of mind.

All monads, however, are not sentient to the same extent. There is a gradual hierarchy of monads from ones infinitely close to insentience to the one with omniscience. The omniscient monad is the perfect Being, that is God.

Every object consists of a colony of monads. In the same analogy, every human being is also a colony of monads. The soul in a person is a monad of higher grade that controls a colony of monads of lower grade.

The Concept of Mind in Empiricism

Empiricism is the doctrine that the source of all knowledge is to be found in experience. It is usually contrasted with rationalism, the doctrine that reason is the sole, or at least the primary source of knowledge. Here we will deal with British empiricism that exerted tremendous influence on the philosophical thought of the world.

Roger Bacon (1214-94) recommended direct inspection rather than speculative argument to establish a conclusion. Thus he preferred experimental science to speculative science.

Francis Bacon (1561-1626) was a great exponent of empirical method or induction. He was against rationalism in all its forms.

John Locke (1632-1704) traced all ideas to experience and argued against innate ideas. The term 'innate' means 'inborn'. Innateness is the doctrine that ideas and principles are present in man from birth. Plato was a strong advocate of this doctrine. Descartes accepted the presence of innate ideas in the mind over and above the ideas whose source was adventitious and fictitious. In the philosophy of Leibniz, there was also place for the innate ideas. Locke attacked the doctrine of innateness. According to him, man begins in the world as a blank slate, a *tabula rasa,* on which experience writes. Man's mind is a dark closet which requires to be furnished from without.

If the origin of all ideas is traced to experience, what is experience made up of, then? Experience provides the mental contents which Locke calls ideas. There are two types of ideas, viz., ideas of sensation and ideas of reflection. The former come from the observation of the outside world through the gateway of our senses. The latter arise when the mind observes itself.

According to Locke, we do not know the world, and what we know are ideas only. He further says that ideas in turn are said to picture or represent the world. Locke is traditionally thought of as a representative realist. In his view, ideas stand for things and words stand for ideas. Whether our ideas exactly correspond to the world of things cannot be ensured by Locke's philosophy.

Our experience provides us only with particular ideas. Abstract and general ideas cannot arise from experience. Locke says that it is the operation of the mind itself that produces general ideas.

Locke was a devout Christian and believed in God and revealed truth.

George Berkeley (1685-1753), the Irish philosopher, was an idealist and empiricist. He denied the existence of matter. He announced "*esse est percipi* (to be is to be perceived)".

Although Berkeley rejected the concept of **material** substance, he fully retained the notion of **spiritual** or **thinking** substances. The thinking substances are the finite human minds or souls and the infinite mind of God. Berkeley[10] conceives of a spirit as one simple, undivided, active being. It is called understanding when it perceives ideas. It is called the will when it operates the ideas.

In Berkeley's philosophy, all reality is mental. He asserts that we perceive qualities, not things. Qualities are relative to the percipient. All sensible qualities are mental, says Berkeley.

Berkeley does not define the word 'mental'. The brain, according to him, is itself of a sensible thing, and it exists only in the mind. Certain traces in the brain are believed by him to be the causes of sensations.

While distinguishing the act of perceiving from the object perceived, Berkeley says that the former is mental while the latter is not. He believes in mental substance. His philosophy upholds the existence of minds and mental events only. He is sometimes known as a subjective idealist. But he can be considered otherwise as a realist. His realism is theistic and immaterialistic.

The opponents of Berkeley could not accept the idea of the intermittent existence of objects. They argued: If Berkeley is correct, things of the world exist when perceived and cease to exist when not perceived. Berkeley replied to his opponents' charge by saying that God always perceives everything. As a matter of fact, this was his argument for the existence of God.[11, 12] Since the existence of a **thing** consists in its being perceived, and since it does not disappear when unperceived by man, there must be an all-perceiving and ever-perceiving mind. That mind is God in whom we live and move and have our being. Hume ridiculed this argument of Berkeley and remarked: "They admit of no answer and produce no conviction".

Thus, in Berkeley's philosophy, reality consists of ideas, finite minds, and an inifinite mind (God). He analysed 'existence' in terms of two desiderata, viz., *esse est percipi* (that which is perceived exists) and *esse est percipere* (that which perceives exists). The perceiving agents, in Berkeley's system, are 'spirits', including souls or minds of human beings, spiritual beings such as angels, and God. According to this subjective idealism, the external world does not exist and the object of the world are mere collections of perceptual experiences, or what Berkeley called 'ideas'. He criticized the representative realism of John Locke and developed his own immaterialistic (theistic) realism.

Berkeley was a bitter critic of the Lockean notion of material substratum. This notion has a long tradition from the time of Aristotle, who conceived of substance as a subject of predication, without itself being predicable of anything. "The pure substance in general" was termed 'substratum' by Locke. Substratum is said to provide something 'substantial' in which a number of qualities or properties may 'inhere'. These qualities or properties become the qualities or properties of an individual 'thing' — macroscopic and microscopic. According to the Lockean thought, both the substratum and the real essence of an individual material object are empirically unknowable. Berkeley repudiates the Lockean notion of substratum and real essence. He categorically asserts the denial of the existence of the external, material world.

G.E. Moore (1873-1958), the British philosopher, popularly known as the common sense realist, published a famous article in 1903. The title of this article was "The refutation of idealism".[13] According to Moore's analysis, the act of knowing requires both a mental act and an object of knowledge which is independent of that act. In every sensation there are two distinct terms, viz., consciousness and the object of consciousness. Thus he insists that in experience object and subject must be distinguished. He castigates awareness that lies at the roots of idealism.

David Hume (1711-76), in his empirical philosophy, has accepted the basic principle of Locke's theory of sensation. He contends that experience is composed of impressions and ideas. We can trace ideas to impressions. Thus the former are derived from the latter that have the greater force and vivacity. It is commonly assumed that our impressions arise from the external world. But this we cannot know from experience, asserts Hume.

All we are aware of in sense experience are impressions. Simple impressions produce simple ideas whereas complex ideas are the results of complex impressions or, alternatively, they result from compounding or manipulating of simple ideas. Present experience has a greater force than the ideas of memory which deals with the past.

The Lockean concept of the ideas of sensation and the ideas of reflection does not exactly correspond to Hume's impressions and ideas as the content of our perceptions. However, in this regard, the two philosophers do not seem to contradict each other.

An impression, for Hume, can proceed from sense experience and also from memory. The mind thinks. By saying this, Hume wants to convey that the mind attends to the ideas within it. He conceives of thinking as picture thinking or imagining. He uses the term 'perception' for all experience, whether in sensation or imagination. He thinks it impossible to experience something which cannot be imagined. Experience consists of a succession of perceptions, says Hume.

Can we know the external world? Hume answers this question negatively. All we can know are successions of impressions or ideas. The impressions may be arising from the physical objects of the external world. But, according to the scepticism of Hume, there is no way for us to know that the impressions have their origin from the physical objects.

Hume criticized Berkeley's theory of mind or soul. Unlike the latter, he did not invoke God to sustain the notion of an objective world independent of our experience of it.[14] He explained the continued existence of bodies by the succession of interrupted perceptions.

Hume discusses the question of personal identity. "There are some philosophers who imagine we are every moment intimately conscious of what we call our 'self': that we feel its existence and its continuance in existences: and are certain, beyond the evidence of demonstration, both of its perfect identity and simplicity".[15] Hume refutes such a claim. He says: "Unluckily, all these positive assertions are contrary to that very experience which is pleaded for them: nor have we any idea of 'self', after the manner here explained. For, from what impression could this idea be derived?" He very forcefully asserts: "For my part, when I enter most intimately into what I call **myself**, I always stumble on some particular perception or other, of heat or cold, light or shade, love or hatred, pain or pleasure. I never can cath **myself** at any time without a perception, and never can observe anything but the perception". Hume contends that the separately existing perceptions have no need of anything like the self or the soul to support their existence. The so-called 'self' is a bundle of perceptions for Hume. He goes on to say: "I may venture to affirm of the rest of mankind that they are nothing but a bundle or collection of different perceptions, which succeed each other with an inconceivable rapidity, and are in a perpetual flux or movement". Thus Hume rejects the ontology of a 'soul' or 'self' and 'substance'.

How does Hume conceive of the mind? He makes a visual picture of the mind by saying: "The mind is a kind of theatre, where several perceptions successively make their appearance". He immediately cautions us by an addendum. "The comparison of the theatre must not mislead us. They are the successive perceptions only, that constitute the mind: nor have we the most distant notion of the place where these scenes are represented, or of the materials of which it is composed".

John Stuart Mill (1806-73) was the chief representative of empiricism in the nineteenth century. He remained in the tradition of Locke. He was committed to representative realism. He defined matter as a "permanent possibility of sensation". He held empirical judgements to be merely probable and necessary judgements to be merely verbal. He interpreted the world in terms of the phenomena available to humankind. Thus the philosophy of Mill approaches phenomenalism, if considered from this point of view.

Mill accepted the principles of associationalism of David Hartley (1705-57) who was an English philosopher and psychologist. The term "association of ideas" was introduced into philosophy by John Locke. According to this notion, complex mental phenomena are derived from simple elements which are joined together according to a small set of principles. Following this concept of Locke, Hartley developed an associationist psychology that later influenced the empirical philosophy of Mill.

Mind in Materialism

The materialists do not recognize anything like the mind-body dualism. They hold that the mind is simply the brain. And hence all processes are physical and none are mental.

Thus the materialists try to solve the mind-body problem by doing away with mind and recognizing matter only. The earliest systematic account of materialism was presented in India by the Cārvāka School in the seventh century BC.

A number of philosophers developed materialistic philosophy in ancient Greece. Thales (610-546 BC) contended that everything came from water and returned back into water. Anaximander (610-546 BC), a friend of Thales, held *apeiron* (an indeterminate and unlimited matter) to be the single eternal prime basis of all natural phenomena. Anaximenes (585-25 BC), Thales' second disciple, considered air as the prime matter. He explained the eternal succession of phenomena as the condensation and rarefaction of air. Heraclitus (530-470 BC) held that fire was the primal matter of all natural phenomena. He said: "This one order of all things was created by none of the gods, nor yet by any of mankind, but it ever was, and is, and shall be eternal fire". Democritus (460-370 BC) was the ancient Greek materialist who theorized the atomic composition of matter. According to him, the universe is composed of basic indivisible elements which he called atoms. A void also exists for the atoms to move in. Democritus claimed that the soul comprised subtle and tender atoms. Thus he opposed idealism and religion and proposed a single materialistic world outlook. Epicurus (341-270 BC), a Greek materialist philosopher, and Lucretius Carus (99-55 BC), an eminent thinker of ancient Rome, made outstanding contributions to the theory of matter.

Epicurus founded a school of philosophy in Athens. This school of epicureanism stressed atomic theory, empiricism and hedonism. This is a materialistic school that understands soul and mind as concentrations of fine, swiftly moving atoms of special sorts. The soul atoms exist throughout the body. Such atoms require the protection of the body for behaving in their characteristic ways. Hence personal immortality is not possible, argues Epicurus. The Epicurean theory of perception is based upon its materialism. Images come to us from the composite bodies through our senses. Perception is possible by means of the outlines of these images. Thus the materialism of ancient Greece does not accept the existence of souls or minds.

In the late sixteenth century, British materialism and all modern experimenting sciences were founded by Francis Bacon (1561-1626). Thomas Hobbes (1588-1679), another British philosopher, was an atheist and materialist. He held that all reality is corporeal, and is controlled by rigid causal laws. All processes can be understood in terms of the least common denominators of matter and motion. All, without exception, are reducible to them. In Hobbes' opinion, the spirit or the soul is 'immaterial material', involving self-contradiction, and hence is nonsensical. The so-called mental phenomena are the externalized properties of the brain which is a physical organ. And hence all mental activities are material or physical activities. Hobbes extended his materialism to questions of language and epistemology. In his view, we work with phantasms of sense in perception and mental operations.

French materialistic philosophy was developed in the eighteenth century. The philosophers who had significant contributions towards this development were La Mettrie (1709-51), Diderot (1713-84), Helvetius (1715-71), and Holbach (1723-89).

La Mettrie was a philosopher and physician. Basing on one aspect of the Cartesian position, namely, that animals are soulless mechnisms, La Mettrie included man in animals who was also deemed by him as a machine. He derived such an inference from the premises of evolutionary evidences of the gradual transition from animal to human form leading through the apes. Man's psychical awareness and its modifications were considered to be the result of physiological causes. It may thus be argued that the intelligence of a person is the function of the character of his brain. La Mettrie further argued: Speech is just physical sound; rational activity depends upon language; thus thought is a physical activity, and it can be explained without a rational faculty. A speech is a loud thinking. Thoughts, besides being physical sounds, are physical images in the brain correlated to sounds. Thus, for La Mettrie, the human soul becomes a collection of images.

Paul Henri D' Holbach agreed with La Mettrie who described man as a machine. Holbach extended this idea further. He said: Not only is man a machine, the world as a whole is a machine; and this machine does not require a mechanist. He emphatically rejected the existence of souls. He recognized the brain as the agent of all mental activities and dismissed the idea of the mind.

Joseph Priestley (1733-1804), an English scientist and philosopher, had materialism in his philosophy. Matter for him was dynamic, but not inert. He hypothesized that the brain thinks. The idea that a soul or a mind thinks was rejected by him. He avoided Cartesian dualism by adopting Hartley's associationist psychology.

Nikolai Chernyshevsky (1828-89) was a pre-Marxian Russian materialist. In his *The Anthropological Principle in Philosophy*[16] he wrote: "Matter is what exists. Matter possesses qualities. Forces are manifestations of qualities. What we call natural laws are modes of operation of the forces". As we see, Chernyshevsky, as distinct from Holbach, stresses the objective nature of matter. He also stresses the material character of natural laws. It may be pointed out, however, that Chernyshevsky's definition fails to stress that objectively existing matter is cognizable by man and reflected by the senses.

The Marxist concept of dialectical materialism was founded by three philosophers, viz., Karl Marx (1818-83), Friedrich Engels (1820-95) and V.I. Lenin (1870-1924). Lenin defined matter as follows: "Matter is a philosophical category denoting the objective reality which is given to man by his sensations, and which is copied, photographed and reflected by our sensations, while existing independently of them".[17] It is to be emphasized here that matter exists objectively, independent of human senses. The Marxists refuted the mechanistic world-view and affirmed the truth of the dialectical materialistic teaching on matter.

Matter and motion constitute the total of reality in the Marxist philosophy. "Motion means the same thing as change, as any transition from one state to another. Motion is the universal attribute, the mode of existence of matter. Nowhere in the world can there be matter without motion, just as there can be no motion without matter".[18]

Lenin, in *Materialism and Empirio-Criticism*, criticised the advocates of energism. Wilhelm Ostwald (1853-1932) contended that reality was energy rather than matter. He claimed that his position superseded the older materialisms. According to this doctrine of energism, energy is the basic stuff that transforms itself into all other forms and properties. Lenin strongly refuted energism and considered energy as a property of matter. In his view, "matter is the vehicle of all change, the substantial foundation of all processes in the world; there is no such thing as motion divorced from matter, no such thing as 'pure motion'."[19]

It has already been stated that materialism proceeded from the fact that consciousness is a function of the human brain, the essence of which lies in the reflection of reality. Dialectical materialism asserts that consciousness is a property not of any matter but of highly organized matter. V.G. Afanasyev specifies this concept by saying that man's consciousness is a special property of highly organized matter, the brain, to reflect material reality.[20] This Marxist concept of consciousness is based on the principle of reflection. The external object is mentally reproduced in the brain of the individual in the form of sensations, perceptions, representations and concepts, and such processes are included in the term 'reflection'. The content of consciousness is ultimately determined by the external world, the human brain and the mechanisms providing the paths that connect the brain and the external world.

Lenin bitterly attacked Machism. Ernst Mach (1836-

1916) propounded a doctrine of subjective idealism which conceives of matter as combinations of sensations. His programme was to get rid of unobservables. Any concept which did not relate to sensations was metaphysical and unacceptable to him. Mach went so far as to say that the world consists only of our sensations. While disagreeing with Mach, Lenin writes: "Matter is primary, and thought, consciousness, sensation are products of a very high development. Such is the materialist theory of knowledge, to which natural science instinctively subscribes".[21] Lenin shows that Machism is contradictory to the basic principles of natural science. Nature existed before man. Earth existed in such a state when there was no living creature whatsoever. Life could not exist in that state. Hence Lenin argues that there existed no sensing matter, no combination of sensations. In this context, the views of Max Planck (1858-1947) and Albert Einstein (1879-1955) may be quoted here. Max Planck attacked Machism in his Leiden Report: "Is the physical picture of the world eventually more or less arbitrary creation of our spirit, or we have to recognize that if reflects real, independent form it processes of nature? Speaking in more specific terms: must we prudently maintain that the principle of conservation of energy operated in nature as far back as when not a single man could think of it, or that celestial bodies would move according to the law of gravitation even then when our Earth with all its inhabitants becomes rubbles?"[22] Albert Einstein wrote: "The belief in the existence of the outside world not depending on the perceiving subject is the basis of the natural science as a whole . . . our notions of the physical reality can never be ultimate. We should always be prepared to change the notions".[23]

To conclude, the Marxist dialectical materialism dismisses anything like the soul or the mind and interprets the nature of consciousness purely on materialistic basis with the basic notion that consciousness is a special property of highly organized brain matter.

Mind in Idealism

The term 'idealism' was first used philosophically by Leibniz at the start of the eighteenth century. It is the general metaphysical doctrine that reduces all physical phenomena to minds or mental phenomena. It includes philosophies which regard the mental or ideational as the key to the nature of reality.

The Greek philosopher Parmenides (515-450 BC) was an idealist philosopher. In his philosophy, thought and being are identical; sense-experience, on the other hand, is full of contradiction and hence is mere appearance; change and motion are impossible; the immutable Being is homogeneous throughout and eternal.

George Berkeley (1685-1753), an Irish philosopher and bishop, was a philosophical idealist. His philosophy of mind has already been discussed under empiricism.

Immanuel Kant (1724-1804) was the German philosopher whose work influenced Johann Gottlieb Fichte (1762-1814) who was the founder of German idealism. Before we discuss the idealism of Fichte, it may be convenient to briefly describe the Kantian notions of mind and relevant epistemology.

Kant cannot be classified as an empiricist, a rationalist, or an idealist. His philosophy holds a balance between two extreme positions, viz., Cartesian rationalism based on innate principles and British empiricism which is based on experience with its denunciation of innateness. The Lockean ideas led inevitably to the scepticism of Hume. Whereas Hume explained concepts in terms of experience, Kant explained experience in terms of concepts. Kant agreed with Hume and other empiricists that all knowledge arises through experience. But, unlike them, he held that only sense-experience is not sufficient for knowledge to take its form. For this, the raw materials of experience are to be transformed into knowledge by some principles of organization. These principles, held Kant, are innate in Descartes' sense.

Mind supplies the general concepts of reason that shapes

experience into knowledge. Following the use of Aristotle, Kant names these concepts of reason as categories. He says that, without categories, we cannot have any communicable experience at all.

According to Kant, the knowing process involves two types of activities, viz., the senses receiving the impact of experience coming from without, and the understanding which assembles the elements of sensation together. Kant distinguishes understanding from reason. Men are equally rational by virtue of the reason they are endowed with; but they are unequal in their understanding which is active intelligence.

Hume had the concept of isolated impressions of rapid succession. In Kant's opinion, these isolated impressions, however rapid in their succession, are not enough for the continuity of experience. He posits some kind of continuity through the framework of the categories, without which he thinks it impossible to have experience of anything persistent.

Kant describes knowledge derived from experience as *a posteriori*, and that independent of experience as *a priori*. Accordingly, the presently called analytic propositions are called *a priori*, and the synthetic propositions are called *a posteriori*. "A triangle has three angles" is an *a priori* proposition. Its truth or falsity can be determined by language analysis only, without recourse to sense-experience. "A cow is a quadruped" is an *a posteriori* proposition, since its truth can be determined by verification through sense-experience only. An analytic proposition cannot be denied without self-contradiction, whereas a synthetic proposition may be denied without self-contradiction. Kant insists on a third type of proposition, viz., *a priori* synthetic. All mathematical propositions, in his view, are *a priori* synthetic. As for example, 5 + 7 = 12. Kant says that it is *a priori*, since it is not derived from experience; further he says that it is synthetic because the concept of twelve is not already contained in the concepts of five, seven, and addition. Kan't view of *a priori* synthetic judgement is not acceptable to modern philosophy, in which both *a priori* and *a priori* synthetic propositions are inclusive of analytic propositions.

In Kant's philosophy, space and time are regarded as two *a priori* particular notions. They belong to pure intuitions, space being an outer and time an inner sense. Kant contends that experience is not possible without a *priori* notions of space and time, which are somewhat akin to the categories in this respect.

Kant does not accept anything like pure experience. He holds that experience is moulded by *a priori* concepts. As to the question of the origin of experience, he says that what gives rise to experience is conditioned by things outside the mind. The sources of experience Kant calls 'things-in-themselves' or 'noumena', in contrast with appearances or phenomena.

On the Kantian theory, the noumenon is unknowable. It is impossible to experience a thing-in-itself, says Kant. All experience occurs with the concurrence of space, time, and categories. When we have impressions, we may at best infer that there are external sources of our impressions. Even such inferences are not strictly valid. We have no independent way of ascertaining that there are such external sources. Let us consider a hypothetical case of the availablity of some way of ascertainment. Still Kant cannot claim that those external sources are causing our sense impressions. When Kant speaks of causality, he is already inside the network of *a priori* concepts that are to operate within the understanding. Thus the external world, as it is, is unknowable to Kant. He talks about noumena, but he is not logically entitled to say that the noumena give rise to phenomena. A similar situation was faced by Locke. By adhering to his own theory, he guarded against inconsistency, and hence did not speak of an external world giving rise to ideas of sensation.

Thus the Kantian philosophy, by introducing noumena, provided some sort of answer to Hume's problem. By positing noumena, Kant also avoided idealism, the doctrine that the outer world is a product of the mind. What was avoided by Kant was done by Fichte, however.

Fichte's doctrine of Ego was designed to counter the Kantian dualism of noumena and phenomena. The Ego, corresponding to Kant's unity of apperception, is active and autonomous. According to Fichte, the world of experience, which is a kind of unconscious projection of the Ego, is the non-Ego. Thus what we know are appearances only, and hence no question arises on the existence of things-in-themselves (noumena). Fichte asserts that it is self-contradictory to talk about noumena.

Ficthe further says that the projection is not only unconscious but also unconditional. Due to the unconditionality of the projection, the projected world, being not experienced, is not determined by the category of causality. The world which is projected from the Ego springs from the practical and moral nature of the latter. Thus Fichte made the practical reason determinative over the theoretical reason. This resulted in an idealism emerging from the moral will.

"One knows, one is perceiving an object". Fichte does not recommend the use of such a statement. Instead, he prefers a statement like "One knows that one thinks one sees an object".

According to Fichte's philosophy, we posit the Ego as well as the non-Ego. He points out that the necessity involved in all of these positings is a teleological and dialectical one. In the history of philosophy, it was Fichte, and not Hegel, who first presented the process of the dialectic as consisting of Thesis, Antithesis, and Synthesis. The activity of reason itself requires that posit, counter-posit, and synthesis, making way for progress.

Fichte conceives of a spiritual and moral order, which he identifies with God Himself. This God is not the Cause or Creator of the world, He is not a separate Being; He is the

Word or Logos, in all that truly is. Since God (Being or Absolute) includes all there is, creation is incompatible with such a concept of the divine Being. God being eternal, all is completed within Him. All humans are now part of the moral order which is one with God; we are even now one with God. Nevertheless, human life and the world in general struggle toward an ideal which, in fact, has already been achieved. Thus Fichte presents us with the paradox of philosophical idealism. His idealistic philosophy became the precursor of Hegelianism.

Schelling (1775-1854) was the German idealist philosopher who was very much influenced by Kant and Fichte. He attempted to spin the world out of the Ego. Both in Fichte and Schelling are seminal materials later used by Hegel for formulating the dialectic method. Schelling noticed polar opposites in Nature and their consequent unity. This concept foreshadowed the Hegelian dialectic.

Not only in Nature, but also in God did Schelling affirm a polarity, involving a merging of absolute and relative, necessary and contingent, eternal and temporal, potential and actual. Such a polarity does not disturb God's essential unity. Schelling could visualize the evolution of divinity through the dialectic method. God, the 'Eternal Contrariety' evolves by means of the opposition between contrasting aspects — between the void of nothingness and the plenitude of being. The progression is upwards; there is helical ascendance through the constant activity of opposition internalized in the divine nature itself.

Hegel (1770-1831) was the German philosopher whose idealistic philosophy was the culmination of the philosophic trends of Kant, Fichte, and Schelling. First, we will mention three distinctive themes in Hegel's philosophy. (1) Reason is the guide to reality. The rational is real and *vice versa.* Thus Hegel identifies the rational and the real. (2) There is constancy of change in the universe. Agreeing with Heraclitus, Hegel could conceive of the change through the activity of opposites. (3) The entire process of the universe is on the path of ascendance to the final state of the Absolute. Thus the divine Reason realizes itself in history.

Hegel was both a rationalist and an idealist while Berkeley was an empiricist and an idealist. In spite of this difference, one aspect was common in their philosophy. The view that only minds and mental events can exist was held by both of them. Hegel's philosophy of dialectic had its source in Kant's table of categories, where the third in each group is a combination of the first and the second, which are opposites. Fichte and Schelling were the other two philosophers who exerted considerable influence on the formulation of the dialectic of Hegel. According to the dialectic doctrine, one view prevails, and a second view opposite to the first one clashes with the first one, resulting in the production of a third view which synthesizes the first two opposite views and rises above the level of the first two, with qualitative and quantitative improvement. The see-saw battle does not stop here. The third synthetic view, in its turn, plays the role of a Thesis, to which an Antithesis develops, and a Synthesis rises. This process of dialectic is always in progression in the history of Nature as well as the human history.

Hegel's dialectic process leads to the Absolute Idea. He constructs a long and arbitrary string of categories until he reaches the Absolute Idea. By this time, a full circle is completed and the totality has reached a unity. Again the category of unity serves as a starting point. The Absolute Idea is the supreme example of unity, in which all contradictions and differences have vanished. After reaching the state of the Absolute, the progression comes to an end. The Absolute is the only reality. Hegelian philosophy proclaims that only the whole is true and that anything partial can only be partially true.

According to Hegel, the Absolute Idea thinks itself. His idealism is objective rather than subjective. His emphasis, however, is on the spirit. He rejects dualism of mind (spirit) and matter. The spirit is the starting point and the final culminating point of the dialectic evolution. The Marxists accepted Hegel's dialectic *in toto* except the spirit. Thus the Marxist dialectic is purely materialistic rather than idealistic. Marxist philosophy borrowed the dialectic of Hegel (with the rejection of the spirit) and the materialism of La Mettrie. Hegel was influenced by Heraclitus, Parmenides, and Spinoza. Heraclitus was a philosopher who pleaded for constant changes and inherent strife in Nature through contradiction. On the other hand, Parmenides opposed any type of change whatsoever. He had the notion of the universe as an immovable sphere. Spinoza had the view that the whole alone is ultimately real. His God is identical with the universe. In his system of philosophy, the individual becomes more and mroe at one with God or Nature and ultimately becomes merged with it. We find the seed of Heraclitus' views in the dialectic method of Hegel. The dialectic process issues from the 'One' of Parmenides, which is undifferentiated. Hegel thinks in terms of the organic whole. The individual gains its full reality through being related to the whole in the analogy of the parts of an organism to the entire system. So does Hegelianism say: We cannot understand any portion of the world unless we see it in its setting in the universe as a whole; the whole is the only reality.

Jonathan Edwards (1703-58) was an American philosopher-theologian. He adopted an idealistic philosophy in which God and space were thought to be identified. That all things exist as ideas in the divine mind was the seminal principle in the philosophy of Edwards. By this he emphasized the supremacy of God; at the same time, he did not deprive the things we experience of their existence. Thus, we find a point of convergence for the ideas of Edwards and Berkeley.

Psychophysical Parallelism

Gustav Theodor Fechner (1801-87) was a German philosopher-psychologist who introduced the term 'psychophysical parallelism'. According to his view, there is one to one correlation of psychical and physical events. The external view of everything is material and quantitative; but internally all is life and soul. Both views are true, although the internal view is more fundamental. Fechner presented the organismic analogy of multiple cells in one living body which is an organic whole. Similarly, reality is a continuum of nested souls or cells from the outwardly inorganic to the inwardly all-inclusive being of God. An individual cell of the body enjoys autonomy, subject to the limitation that it has to serve the general interest of the whole body. And so is the freedom of man compatible with God's control and dominance.

Epiphenomenalism

'Epiphenomenon' is a compound Greek word, coined from the two separate words, viz., *epi* (side) and *phainomenon* (appearance). It means 'side appearance' or an 'incidental appearance'. Epiphenomenalism is a doctrine that consciousness is an incidental effect of neural processes and that it is not a causal agent.

T.H. Huxley (1825-95), the English biologist and philosopher, was an advocate of epiphenomenalism. Being an effective proponent of Darwinian evolution, he contended that all living organisms constitute mechanical systems only. He held that consciousness is epiphenomenal, that is, it is the effect of physical processes of the body and the cause of nothing. Huxley coined the term 'agnostic' to express his position of suspended belief. He was not prepared to accept anything beyond the evidence. In his opinion, evidences available concerning the nature of the universe are not satisfactory. For him, the brain, the spinal cord, and the nerves are parts of the physical body, and their activities result in consciousness, which is thus an epiphenomenon.

Shadworth Hodgson (1832-1912) was another British philosopher who held his philosophical position of epiphenomenalism. For him, determinism and freedom are compatible. Although we determine our own actions, the determining factor is a neurocerebral condition accompanied by awareness. Further, he contends that consciousness always accompanies, but never determines. Thus Hodgson's position is that of epiphenomenalism.

Theodule Ribot (1839-1916) was a French psychologist who supported the development of experimental psychology. He wanted to eliminate all metaphysics from psychology. He eschewed both materialism and spirituality. But he accepted epiphenomenalism of mental processes.

George Santayana (1863-1952), the American-European philosopher, held that spirit is generated from matter and the expression of matter. This spirit, so generated, has no power of its own; it uses the power of the body. Thus Santayana's doctrine of the self is sheer epiphenomenalism.

Neutral Monism

We will discuss the work of two philosophers while elaborating the concept of neutral monism. They are the American philosopher and psychologist William James (1842-1910) and the British philosopher Bertrand Russell (1872-1970).

Neutral monism repudiates dualism, idealism and materialism. On this view, there is only one substance, a single basic stuff called neutral stuff which underlies and accounts for the whole of the natural world and mental phenomena.

In 1904, William James published an article called "Does 'consciousness' exist?" This article became the first chapter of the book *Essays in Radical Empiricism*[24] which was published in 1912. For James, experiences are the basic entities out of which everything is composed. Further he insists that there is no general stuff of which experiences are made. Experiences are made of "of just what appears, of space, of intensity, of flatness, brownness, heaviness, or what not". 'Experience' is a generic term which encompasses experiences of various things. He holds that thoughts and things do have much in common. Both are in time; they have parts; they can be added, arranged, and compared. He asserts that consciousness is not a substance that stands over against experiences and knows them. In his view, consciousness is itself an experience; it is a relation between experiences.

William James introduced the term "the stream of consciousness". As a stream of water flows, so does consciousness. James emphasized the notion that consciousness was not a static thing made up of discrete elements, as conceptualized by the defenders of structuralism, but rather was a confluent, continuous, multifarious succession of images, ideas, feelings, memories, and thoughts. In the continuous flow, the later moments are able to grasp and own their predecessors. His idea of the stream suggests an organic relatedness.

Bertrand Russell, basing upon the views of James, developed and elaborated the concept of neutral monism in his book *The Analysis of Mind.*[25] It is Russell who gave the general notion of a neutral stuff. According to this doctrine, the world is neither mental nor material, but composed of some neutral stuff, which yeilds physical objects when organized in keeping with the laws of physics, and yields minds when organized in accordance with the laws of psychology. He tries to explain memory by speaking of 'mnemic causation' ('mnemic' comes from a Greek word meaning 'memory'), i.e., an experience at one time produces memory images which can be part of an experience at a later time. He elaborates the concept of mnemic causation which occurs when 'the effect of resulting from a stimulus to an organism differs according to the past history of the organism without our being able actually to detect any relevent difference in its present structure".[26]

A.R. Lacey does not accept neutral monism as justifiable. He remarks: "The most obvious objection, I suppose, is that the 'neutral stuff' seems to be given a job it hardly has the strength to perform. To unite things as disparate as conscious experiences and material objects in this way just seems to require too violent a wrench for the result to be able to stand up and contemplated. Idealism says that matter is somehow illusory and materialism (at least in its extreme form) says the same about conscious experiences, but at least they take their stands on something familiar, conscious experiences and material objects, respectively. Neutral monism seems to get the worst of both worlds, asking us to accept that **both** our familiar starting points are illusory, or at least are not what they seem, and that what they are is not something at least familiar in itself, but something quite strange".[27]

Philosophical Behaviourism of Gilbert Ryle

Gilbert Ryle (1900-76) was an English philosopher who wrote a book, *The Concept of Mind*, which deals with philosophical behaviourism. He contends that the Cartesian conception of the mind as essentially private renders it absolutely impossible to know of the existence of any mind but one's own. Through his argument, he tries to prove that the whole Cartesian idea of consciousness is intrinsically absurd. Let it be accepted that X is necessarily conscious of his mental states as they occur. Being conscious of something is itself a mental state. Then X must be conscious of his consciousness of the original state, and conscious of that consciousness, and this goes on *ad infinitum*.

Ryle tries to prove that the origin of the Cartesian puzzle was the category-mistake. Descartes tries to see the University. He meets with the Vice-Chancellor, Registrar, Professors, Students, laboratories, class-rooms, library, playground, and all others in the University. Still he is disappointed for his failure in seeing the real University. How can he see when there is no separate thing as a University? Ryle asserts that there is nothing like a mind except the external manifestations of behaviours which are discernible. He recommends elimination of references to supposed inner states. When we talk about the mental state of someone, we infer the existence of some ghostly inner state, and here lies, according to Ryle, the Cartesian misconception of the mind. He holds that mental terms are not names for private inner states, and that these are to characterize the agent's behaviour. He says: "When we characterize people by mental predicates, we are not making untestable inferences to any ghostly processes occurring in streams of consciousness which we are debarred from visiting: We are describing the ways in which these people conduct parts of their predominantly public behaviour".[28]

The notion that there exists two kinds of stuff, viz., the physical and the immaterial, is strongly rejected by Ryle. He contemptuously discredits the doctrine of the Ghost in the Machine. In his view, to talk about minds can invariably be translated without remainder into talk about actual or potential behaviour of physical processes within it.

Geoffrey Madell[29] has made a fair criticism of the philosophical behaviourism of Gilbert Ryle. Behaviourism is a form of materialism. How far it explains or explains away minds is to be critically analysed. It seems it explains away. It treats the organism like a black box, explains its output or behaviour, and predicts the behaviour as a function of the input and the state of the system.

The Concept of Mind in Language-Analysis

The linguistic philosophers have not positively spoken much on the concept of the mind. As Ludwig Wittgenstein (1889-1951) has defined, all philosophy is a "critique of language".[30] While discoursing on the philosophy of mind, he is concerned, as a philosopher, with the language that is used when one talks about mental acts and states. The linguistic philosopher deals with **what it is to say that** someone is thinking, understanding, willing, feeling, remembering, etc.

Here we may quote the definition of a private language.

"And sounds which no one else understands but which I 'appear to understand' might be called a private language".[31] According to Wittgenstein, language is always public and there is nothing like a private language.[32] He does not say that private sensations like 'pain' or 'pleasure' are nothing, or that they do not exist, or that they are not important; he emphasizes the point that nothing can be said about them. He holds that private sensations play no part in our language-games. He writes:

> "And yet you again and again reach the conclusion that the sensation itself is a nothing." — Not at all. It is not a *something*, but not a *nothing* either! The conclusion was only that a nothing could serve just as well as a something about which nothing could be said.[33]

Wittgenstein says that nothing is more wrong-headed than calling meaning a mental activity.[34] He bitterly rebuts the alleged mental act of meaning and the alleged mental process of understanding. He writes:

> There is a kind of general disease of thinking which always looks for (and finds) what would be called a mental state from which all our acts spring as from a reservoir.[35]

He rejects the notion that an act or process must occur in one's mind prior to one's overt action. We may take the example of 'speaking' which designates a physical process. Some are of the opinion that a parallel mental process designated by 'thinking' must accompany the physical process. Wittgenstein puts forward arguments for the outright rejection of such a notion.[36] We are inclined to say: A man **must** understand an order before he obeys it. Wittgenstein does not accept such an idea of the necessity of a certain intermediary step.[37] In his opinion, understanding is not a mental process.[38] He definitely says that a person's understanding is not a process that occurs in his mind.[39] He views talks on mind as empty verbiage and, in this regard, his remarks are sarcastic:

> If God has looked into our minds, he would not have been able to see there whom we were speaking of.[40]

Wittgenstein pleads against a private language in an uncompromising way. He is of the view that the thesis that 'pain' denotes a private sensation has absurd consequences. Without overt manifestations or expressions of pain, i.e., symptoms like crying, groaning, grimacing, or pleading for help, there would be no conceivable way that anyone could learn the use of the word 'pain'.[41]

We do not find any concept of mind in the philosophy of Wittgenstein. He does not strongly say that there are no minds. Neither does he say that the brain is the mind. He reduces all mental processes and activities to the meaning of the language in use. In one sense, with the inclusion of language analysis, the language philosophers may be regarded as philosophical behaviourists.

Physicalism

Otto Neurath (1882-1945) was an Austrian philosopher who was one of the original members of the Vienna Circle of Logical Positivists. Rudolf Carnap (1891-1970) was a German-born Logical Positivist. This school had a doctrine known as physicalism, which requires the protocol sentences of any hypothesis to be expressed in a physicalistic language.

The Logical Positivists faced a number of problems in the application of their verification principle. One of these problems was how to verify statements about the thoughts and feelings of others. It was solved by a recourse to observing their behaviour. The next problem was the verification of my own feelings. It was largely due to this problem that Wittgenstein did not stick to verificationism. Rudolf Carnap, however, did not find much difference between the first and third persons and opined that it was "only a matter of degree". In his view, the first-person statement too is based on "a kind of observation".

Carnap adopted the physicalist view, according to which all facts and all meaning were about physical entities. Thus he rejected all mental activities and processes and explained them in the physicalist format. For him, human brain-processes and behaviour were also physical instead of mental. He applied the doctrine to all human feelings and he claimed that the same physical fact was empirically observed by the first and third persons.

Functionalism

Functionalism is a late theory in the philosophy of mind. It has been influenced by recent developments in computer science. It does not discuss the 'hardware' of the mind, but is concerned with the 'software'.

The functionalist defines the mind in terms of how it functions. S. Shoemaker, a leading exponent of functionalism, defines it as "the view that mental states are definable in terms of their causal relations to sensory inputs, hebavioural outputs, and other mental states".[42] Similar was the view of C. McGinn who says: "We are to define mental properties in terms of their typical patterns of cause and effect, including their characteristic stimuli, their interactions with other mental states, and their characteristic effects in behaviour."[43]

It is accepted in functionalism that mental phenomena are related to what goes on in the brain or central nervous system. But the theory does not tie itself to the physiological processes. It explains the variable realizability of mental states.

When we compare materialism, behaviourism, physicalism, and functionalism, we find many aspects common, although the emphasis is variable. Shoemaker tells that functionalism is the most respectable descendant of behaviourism. Again he says that, in the strong sense, it seems to fall rather on the materialist or physicalist side of the fence.

Personal Identity

Before the discussion of this topic, we would like to introduce Strawson's concept of 'person'.[44] This is an attempt to compromise between body-soul dualism and the abandoning of souls altogether. Strawson distinguishes between two kinds of properties (he loosely calls 'predicate'), viz., M-predicates and P-predicates. M-predicates are those which can apply to non-conscious material bodies, while P-predicates imply the possession of consciousness, irrespective of the fact whether or not they also involve having a body. We can apply P-predicates only to persons, whereas M-predicates can be applied to both persons and non-conscious bodies. Strawson defines persons as just those which can have both M-predicates and P-predicates. According to this concept, persons are logically primitive, i.e., they are neither embodied souls nor besouled bodies.

Strawson's concept of 'person' does not seem to significantly contribute towards the clearing of the philosophical fog of body-soul dualism *versus* the complete rejection of the soul.

The problems of personal identity are still unsolved in philosophy. A person, X, is born; he lives one hundred years and dies. Does he remain one and the same person over the whole period of his life-time? If he survives his bodily death and is reincarnated as another human being, or an animal, or a plant, does he continue to be the same person? If personal identity is a fact, what is the mechanism for an individual to continue as the same one?

According to some philosophers, there is no problem of personal identity since an individual does not continue to be the same over a period of years. The body constantly changes. A person P_1 known to P_2 thirty years back may not now be recognized at all by P_2 due to physical changes in P_1 during this long period. Even P_1 may not recognize himself from his childhood photograph. Not only physical changes, but also mental changes do take place over a period. Hence all do not agree to the notion of personal identity.

Philosophers in the analytical tradition have produced an enormous variety of fascinating work on personal identity. The publication of Derek Parfit[45] in this regard is worth mentioning. He contends that mental connectedness and continuity are necessary and sufficient for personal identity.

When we consider the issue of personal identity, we should be clear about the entity which continues. The macro-body changes over relatively longer periods. The micro-structures of the body change every few days, and in some cases every few hours or minutes. The chemical elements like carbon, hydrogen, oxygen, nitrogen, phosphorus, sulphur, calcium, etc., in the body are substituted by fresh ones everyday, every second, millisecond, microsecond, or nanosecond. None of the molecules and atoms present in a certain body (the brain and the spinal cord are also parts of the body) today were present some years back, if elemental tagging is considered. Hence it is not a fact that the physical body continues in an unchanged condition.

The mental states also change. The same individual, X, does not possess the same mental state in babyhood, childhood, adolescence, youth, adulthood, and old age. Even the same adult human being may undergo complete mental metamorphosis and may contradict his own old beliefs which were too dear to him.

In spite of the changes in the physical structures and traits as well as mental traits, we cannot whisk away the fact that there is continuity of a person. The genetic material (DNA) remains **almost** in the same identity (barring rare mutations) in spite of a dynamic state of flux at the level of atoms and molecules. This unchanged (for all practical purposes) genotype decides and controls the continuity (whatever is the *ipso facto* continuity) of the physical and the mental traits. But what controls the structural maintenance and functional properties of the genetic (DNA) system is something metaphysical.

We may omit the soul for the present discussion. For the time being, we may also presume that the brain and the mind are different. There cannot be continuity of a person unless there is continuity of his mind (with the scope of changes of mental traits, of course). Although I have forgotten many events of my life, I still do remember a lot. How can I remember unless there is storing and retrieval system somewhere? How can I recognize myself without the mental continuity?

The brain may be idetified with the mind. *Ex hypothesi* it may be provisionally accepted. But the brain tissue is a product of the embryological ectoderm and is constantly changeable through anabolic and catabolic processes. The computer memory can be erased and permanently lost. How can it be conceivable that a changeable brain structure can maintain the continuity of mental records?

Although a lot has been written by analytical philosophers on personal identity, hardly anything has been made clear as to the entity that continues.

Summary Appraisal

The concept of mind in Western religions and philosophy deals with a vast area which has been contracted and compressed to its hard core in this chapter. There is hardly any scope here for the analysis of each and every concept that has been presented here. It is expected that we reach a final conclusion in the end of this chapter. There is no finality and shouldn't be any. Nonetheless, there is no conclusion either.

The Greek philosopher Plato identified the soul and the

mind. Platonic Forms were immaterial; souls or minds were also immaterial. This Platonic concept of the soul (mind) was, *mutatis mutandis*, adopted by the Christian theology. The theologian's soul (equivalent to the mind) was said to be created by God, through the breathing of His spirit, at the time of conception and placed inside the newly formed zygote. Once born, it never perishes. It survives the physical death; on the Day of Judgement, God assigns either heaven or hell to a soul for its permanent abode where it would enjoy eternal bliss or suffer eternal damnation.

René Descartes' dualistic philosophy accepted the soul-mind identity and made a sharp division of the mind and the body. The former is immaterial and spaceless; it is the thinking thing. The latter is material; it is extended in space. Descartes could not be certain about the material world; but he could not doubt his "I" (his soul or mind). Thus goes his famous dictum: "*Cogito ergo sum* (I think, therefore I am)".

The soul is the invisible ghost; the body is the visible machine. Western religions and philosophies accepted this ghost in the machine until the twentieth century. The empiricists talked about experience only. Their philosophy could not fully explain the world and the life. Hume claimed to give a death-blow to the soul. How far his claim is true is still uncertain. But this is certain that he himself became a sceptic about the physical world through his own philosophy of empiricism. The concept of mind is not at all clear in the philosophy of empiricism, which could clarify neither the ghost nor the machine.

The idealists fought against dualism by positing mind only and negating matter. But they did not satisfactorily elaborate the concept of the mind. If matter did not exist at all and only mind existed, how could the ideas about matter originate in the mind? How could one cosmic mind behave differently as different minds? Such and sundry questions could not be answered by the philosophy of idealism.

The materialists did away with mind by positing matter

only. They explained consciousness as the expression of highly organized matter. Thus, for the materialists, the so-called mental activities are only physical activities — external manifestations of highly organized matter such as sense-organs, brain, spinal cord, and peripheral nerves. Materialism has its own difficulties which will be discussed in the last chapter.

To obviate the difficulties of idealism and materialism, William James thought of a third alternative. Inspired by the idea of James, Bertrand Russell presented the doctrine of neutral monism. Wherefrom Russell got this neutral stuff is not known. This imaginary stuff behaved like physical or mental, depending upon circumstances. Russell's neutral monism, however, could not satisfactorily solve the problems of the philosophy of mind.

Gilbert Ryle talked about philosophical behaviourism. He did not recognize anything like the mind and mental activities. He translated all mental processes and activities into external behavioural symptoms. Ryle's doctrine could not solve all the problems of the philosophy of mind in a satisfactory way.

Wittgenstein was interested in the analsysis of language and, through that, he explained away the mind. He tried to dissolve the issue instead of solving it. But the issue was insoluble although not insolvable. It can hardly be said that Wittgenstein really brought about a dissolution.

Strawson's primitive 'person' is another fiction whose true nature can hardly be identified. The 'software' discussion of functionalist philosophers like Shoemaker and McGinn, after the model of the computer, is another variety of attempt to dissolve the issue. It seems, conscious attempts have been made to avoid the ghost in the black box. Somebody denies the existence of the black box. Someone else is reluctant to mention anything about the black box, but wants to describe the inputs and outputs. Someone disowns the inputs, and recognizes the outputs in terms of behaviour only. Somebody limits his activities in finding out meaning of the language applied for the behaviour. In spite of all these attempts, the black box remains unexplored.

We may justifiably discard the Platonic identity of mind and soul. We may not accept the Cartesian dualism. But we must clarify the concept of mind which takes cognizance of the recent developments in physical and biological sciences, neurophysiology, psychology, psychiatry, *yoga* science, computer science, etc. To run away from the ghost and derecognize the black box harbouring the ghost is escaping. Are we not engaged in this sort of escapism?

Notes

1. Phaedo.
2. Maritain, J., 1953, *The Range of Reason*, p. 60.
3. Genesis, 2:7; Psalm, 103:14.
4. *Iblis Story*, 15:28 ff.
5. Sura, 80:17-22/16-22.
6. *The Holy Qur'an*, 23:12-16; 71:17f/16f.
7. Irenaeus, *Against Heresies*, Book II, Ch. 34, para 1.
8. Saint Paul, *I Corinthians*, 15.
9. *The Holy Qur'an*, 22:19-23/20-24; 56:11-56; 69:13-37; 76:11-22.
10. Berkeley, G., 1710, *Principles of Human Knowledge*, p. 27.
11. *Ibid.*
12. Berkeley, G., 1713, *Three Dialogues between Hylas and Philonous*.
13. Moore, G.E., 1903, "The Refutation of Idealism", In *Mind*, Vol. 12, no. 48.
14. Hume, D. (1st publ. 1739-40) *Treatise on Human Nature*, Book I, Part IV.
15. *Ibid.*, Book I, Part IV, Sec. 6.
16. Chernyshevsky, N.G., 1950, *Works*, Vol. 14, p. 675 (in Russian).
17. Lenin, V.I., *Collected Works*, Vol. 14, p. 130.
18. *The Fundamentals of Marxist-Leninist Philosophy*, 1974, p. 80.
19. *Ibid.*
20. Afanasyev, V.G., 1980 (1st publ. 1963), *Marxist Philosophy*, p. 59.
21. Lenin, V.I., *Collected Works*, Vol. 14, p. 75.
22. *Max Planck and Philosophy*, 1963, pp. 19-20 (Russ. edn.), Quoted in:

Fundamentals of Marxist-Leninist Philosophy, 1985, pp. 79-80.

23. A. Einstein, *Collection of Scientific Works*, Vol. 4, 1966, p. 136 (Russ. edn.), Quoted in: *Idem.*, p. 80.
24. James, W., 1912, *Essays in Radical Empiricism.*
25. Russell, B., 1921, *The Analysis of Mind.*
26. *Ibid.*, p. 86.
27. Lacey, A.R., "Mind and Body: Non-reductionist Theories", In *An Encyclopaedia of Philosophy*, Ed. by G.H.R. Parkinson, 1988, p. 392.
28. Ryle, G., 1986 (1st publ. by Hutchnson 1949), *The Concept of Mind*, p. 51.
29. Madell, G., 'Behaviourism', In *An Encyclopaedia of Philosophy*, Ed. by G.H.R. Parkinson, 1988, pp. 432-39.
30. *TLP*, 4.0031.
31. *PI*, Sec. 269.
32. *PI*, Secs. 256-58, 261.
33. *PI*, Sec. 304.
34. *PI*, Sec. 693.
35. *BBB*, p. 143.
36. *PI*, Sec. 307, 431; *BBB*, p. 148.
37. *PI*, Sec. 146, 307; *BBB*, p. 130.
38. *PI*, Sec. 154.
39. *PI*, Sec. 138-9, 151, 155, 179-80, 183-4, *BBB*, pp. 146-47.
40. *PI*, p. 217.
41. *PI*, Sec. 257, 347.
42. Shoemaker, S., 1984, *Identity, Cause, and Mind*, p. 337.
43. McGinn, C., 1982, *The Character of Mind*, p. 33.
44. Strawson, P.F., 1959, *Individuals*, Ch. 3.
45. Parfit, D., 1984, *Reasons and Persons*, pp. 202, 253, 256.

8

The Concept of Mind in Psychology

PSYCHOLOGY, as an independent discipline, is not very old. Previously it was a component part of philosophy. It was established as an independent experimental science in 1879.

In the ancient age, Western philosophy and religions equated mind and soul, and distinguished it from the body. This concept has been deep-rooted since the time of Plato. St. Augustine (354-430) and St. Thomas Aquinas (1225-74) believed that there was a complete division between the soul or mind and the body.

René Descartes (1596-1650) established the dualism of body and mind in philosophy. He was a rationalist for whom innate ideas were not derivable from experience. He considered animals as soulless and automatic machines. According to his speculation, the pineal gland inside the skull was the site through which the body and the mind interacted. Descartes is said to be the father of psychology.

British empiricists, viz., Locke, Berkeley, and Hume, were against the continental rationalism. Locke accepted the objects of the external world. He rejected innate ideas. He conceived of the mind at birth as a *tabula rasa* or a blank slate. It is equivalent to saying that there is no mind at the time of birth. In Locke's empiricism, matter generates mind. He accepts experiences which are received by the mind from the source of the objects of the external world. He accepts the existence of abstract ideas in the mind, although he rejects innate ideas. In contrast, in the empiricism of Berkeley, mind generates matter. He accepts experiences, minds, and the existence of God. He knows nothing more than his experiences. Anything outside the experiences of individual minds must be within the mind of God. For Hume, there are only experiences. He denies the existence of mind or soul. He also denies the existence of God. He is sceptical of the existence of matter. Thus Hume's psychology is the first one which is without mind. Subsequently, it was J.B. Watson, the founder of behaviourism, who denied the existence of mind. He rejected the ideas of mind or consciousness to be the subject-matter of psychology.

The short discussion given here with reference to the transition of psychology from the period of Plato to that of Hume or Watson would be helpful in understanding the definition of psychology which has undergone a complete metamorphosis. According to the earlier concept, psychology is the study of mental activity. Such a definition is unacceptable to modern psychologists who deny the existence of mind. For the acceptance of the modern psychologists, we may define psychology as the scientific study of human and animal behaviour. In 1919, J.B. Watson defined psychology as the division of natural science which studies human behaviour — the doings and sayings, both learned and unlearned — as its subject-matter. It may be pointed out here that Watson excluded consciousness from the subject-matter of psychology.

Here we will briefly discuss the developments of some important systems or schools of psychology and the concepts of mind or no-mind therein.

Associationism

Associationism is the psychological doctrine that we connect things in memory, in thought, and in all mental life, simply because they were connected in our original experience with them. Because of the fact that our first encounters with things are by means of our senses, associationism holds that all the complexity of mental life is reducible to sense impressions, which are the elementary components of consciousness, as connected in experience. Associationism maintains that higher order mental or behavioural processes result from the association of simpler mental or behavioural elements. Its roots can be traced back to Greek philosophy. Plato (427-347 BC) talked about similarity and contiguity without further elaboration. It was Aristotle (384-322 BC) who first gave the concept of association in his epistemology. In an essay on memory, he identified three 'relations' between elements. These were similarity, contrast, and contiguity which lead to associations. Later philosophers did not pay much attention to this concept until British empiricists renewed their interest in it. Thomas Hobbes (1588-1679) was the first to suggest that Aristotle's 'relations' could lay the foundation of an associationistic model of human cognition. Hobbes spoke of 'association' of ideas which he considered to be the "train of thought". He outlined an empirical psychology in which sensation was emphasized as the source of ideas. He explained the interconnections between the elements of experience through free and controlled association. John Locke (1632-1704), George Berkeley (1685-1753), and David Hume (1711-76), the three leading British empiricists with their strong anti-nativist bias, were in need of some principle by which they could explain complex mental life by mere appeal to experience. Locke tried to show that experiences could be transformed into ideas through laws of association, viz., contiguity and similarity. George Berkeley judged perception of the depth or the distance of objects by associating two dimensions. He considered contiguity and similarity as the laws of association. David Hume indicated that, in addition to similarity and contiguity, ideas could become associated due to causality.

Associationism did not represent an identifiable school of thought. It was a movement that grew directly out of British empiricism. David Hartley (1702-57), who was a contemporary of Hume, was the father of British associationism. He was a medical practitioner. Locke's theory of association and Newton's theory of vibration had direct impact on Hartley's psychology.

First, we should give a clarification of the concept 'association'. It is any learned, functional connection between two or more **elements**. For this purpose, elements are ideas, acts, images, stimuli and responses, memories, etc. Philosophers and psychologists were occupied for many a year in theoretical exercises for precisely identifying these **elements** and specifiying the mechanisms underlying their connection (i.e., in formulating associative laws).

Hartley borrowed the concept of vibration from the science of Newton. Being himself a medical scientist, he correlated Newtonian physics and physiological science to bring out the dependence of sensations and bodily motions upon the brain, spinal cord, and nerves. When a nerve is stimulated by an external object, small vibrations are produced in it. Such vibrations generate sensations. Vibrations in the brain and the spinal cord are still smaller than those in the peripheral nerves. Such exceedingly small vibrations in the central nervous system generate ideas. Thus, in Hartley's psychology, both sensations and ideas are dependent on vibrations that occur in nerves for the former, and in the brain for the latter. He holds that vibrations for ideas are always smaller than those for sensations.

In Hartley's opinion, association may occur among sensations and ideas. There may be either simultaneous (synchronous) association or successive association. The former type produces trains of thought whereas the latter gives rise to fusion of simple ideas into complex ones. Association serves as the base for mental compounding.

Hartley recognizes only one law of association, viz., the law of contiguity. When two sensations reach the brain either simultaneously or successively, they cause vibrations which become connected with each other due to their contiguous nature.

Thus Hartley related sensations and ideas with vibrations produced in the peripheral nerves and the spinal cord and the brain. He provided physiological explanation for mental activities in terms of vibratory motions in the brain. In his opinion, each mental idea invariably has its physiological correlate or vibration in the brain. This view of Hartley is known as psychological parallelism.

Associationism had its heyday in the eighteenth century with the efforts of James Mill (1773-1836) and his son John Stuart Mill (1806-73). James Mill was very close to Hartley in describing the elements of mind. For him, sensations and ideas are the primary states of consciousness. Sensations are antecedent to ideas which are derived from the former. Like Hartley, James Mill accepted only one law of association, viz., the law of contiguity. In his opinion, this law is applicable only to ideas, and not to sensations. This law functions both successively and simultaneously. Successive associations are more frequent and numerous. Simultaneous or synchronous associations play their role in building perceptions of objects.

Through the principle of 'mental mechanics', James Mill explains the genesis of complex ideas. The complex idea of any real object is formed by the addition of the original simpler ideas which are put together by association.

The associationism of John Stuart Mill proved to be more effective than that of his father. Like his father, he also holds that sensations and ideas are the basic elements of mind. In his opinion, ideas are weaker than sensations, and in this regard, he comes close to Hume. In 1843, he announced three laws of association, viz., similarity, contiguity, and intensity. In 1865, he revised his previous opinion, and announced four laws of association — similarity, contiguity, frequency, and inseparability. He omitted intensity from his previous list. He held that ideas could coalesce according to any of these laws.

John Stuart Mill substituted his father's 'mental mechanics' with his own concept of 'mental chemistry'. In chemistry, two atoms of hydrogen and one of oxygen combine to produce one molecule of water. In this example, the product possesses newer properties which were not present in any of the reactants. J.S. Mill says that the whole is not only the sum of its parts, but also it contains something new. In the analogy of this example, a complex idea is not simply the sum of simple ideas; it is rather more than that. This he termed 'mental chemistry'.

In the theory of perception of John Stuart Mill, we find his psychological theory of matter. For him, sensations are fugitive and transitory; the possibilities of sensations are, however, permanent. He defined matter as the permanent possibility of sensation.

Alexander Bain (1818-1903) brought about the culmination of associationism. He was the first modern physiological psychologist.

Although Leibniz and Hartley discussed psychological parallelism in greater detail, Bain subscribed to this concept in his own way. He holds that every human activity has both physical and mental aspects and that both these aspects run parallel. Cause and effect are more or less quantitatively equivalent in the physical aspect; this quantitative equivalence is absent in the mental aspect, however.

Descartes and Hartley had popularized physiological psychology before Bain. The physiological psychology of Descartes was rather primitive, and that of Hartley speculative. It was Bain who put physiological psychology on a scientific track. He described the sense-organs and their functions. He added an 'organic sense' to Aristotle's five senses. This organic sense was said to be involved in hunger, thirst, or other internal mental traits. He described the reflex arc. He also described the functioning of muscles in opposite pairs.

Bain accepted two fundamental laws of association, viz., contiguity and similarity. The retentiveness of sensations is brought about by the law of contiguity. The law of similarity works for constructive association which operates in thinking, creative imagination, and memory.

In Bain's psychology, action may be spontaneous or deliberate. Reflex action and instinctive action are spontaneous. These so-called spontaneous actions are, however, controlled by the nervous system. The voluntary actions are regulated by our will which plays important role in our mental life.

Herbert Spencer (1820-1903) was an evolutionist. He propounded evolutionary associationism. He recognized similarity as the only law of association. According to Spencer, association generates hereditary qualities which become cumulative in successive generations. When a particular association is often repeated in an individual, he transmits it to his offspring in whom the particular trait becomes an instinct. These instincts, in course of time, become the basic traits from which cognitions and memory are carved out. Thus, according to Spencer, there is an evolutionary hierarchy through which simpler states lead to complex ones.

After Spencer, British associationism came to an end. Then emerged modern associationism through the work of experimental psychologists who applied various principles such as contiguity, similarity, etc., in their fields of investigations like learning, remembering, forgetting, etc. We will briefly discuss the concepts of some modern associationists, viz., Hermann Ebbinghaus (1850-1909), Ivan P. Pavlov (1849-1936), V.M. Bekhterev (1857-1927), Edward L. Thorndike (1874-1949), and Edwin R. Guthrie (1886-1959). These modern associationists were experimental psychologists who studied the association of stimulus and response with reference to learning, memory, etc.

Hermann Ebbinghaus (1850-1909) was a German

psychologist. He conducted experiments on learning and memory, and used statistical technique in psychological experiments. He invented over 2,000 nonsense syllables, consisting of two consonants separated by a vowel, such as ZAK, KAX, etc. He used these nonsense syllables instead of words in his experiments on learning. In his experiments on remembering, he reported his memory span as seven. In other words, he could recall syllables up to a maximum of seven. He conducted experiments on forgetting and derived his forgetting curve. He found that spaced repetition was more efficient than continuous repetition for remembering. He was the first psychologist who applied the principles of association in psychological tests. His experiments have served as models for verbal learning, and they are still useful today.

Ivan Petrovich Pavlov (1849-1936) was a Russian physiologist. He obtained a degree in animal physiology and also a medical degree. All his research was in physiology. In 1904, he was awarded the Nobel Prize in physiology for his brilliant work on glandular and neural factors in digestion.

Pavlov became famous for his discovery of the conditioned reflex. In 1902, he developed a surgical technique for canulating the salivary gland of a dog so that quantitative collection of saliva could be made. The presence of feed before a dog served as a stimulus for the secretion of saliva which was a response. Pavlov subsequently rang a bell while offering the feed. In a third phase, he rang the bell only without offering the feed. Still the response of salivation was unhampered to the stimulus of the bell-ringing. This was the famous conditioned reflex of Pavlov.

Pavlov made a complete shift of the concept of association from speculative philosophy on ideas to experimental study of stimulus and response. His discovery has served as a great impetus to modern psychologists on learning.

Vladimir Bekhterev (1887-1927) was a Russian physiologist who was a contemporary of Pavlov. He was also instrumental in shifting associationism from ideas to overt responses. He worked on the psychology of motor conditioning. He applied electric shock to the paw of a dog or a goat or the hand of a person. This was unconditioned stimulus. The animal or the person exhibited response through withdrawal of the shocked paw or finger. This was unconditioned response. In the second phase of the experiment, the shock was simultaneous with the ringing of a bell. In the third phase, the shock was discontinued, and only the bell served as the stimulus. The withdrawal response thus obtained was the conditioned motor response.

Like Pavlov, Bekhterev liked the idea of physiology-based psychology. He, however, did not ridicule psychology in favour of physiology unlike Pavlov. Bekhterev studied psychology under Wundt at Leipzig; but he did not accept the subjective approach of Wundt and Titchener in psychological explanations. The psychology of Bekhterev used associationistic principles in objective way.

Edward Lee Thorndike (1874-1949) was an American psychologist who had a professional career in Columbia University for about half a century. His celebrated work was his Ph.D. Dissertation — *Animal Intelligence: An experimental Study of the Associative Process in Animals,* which was published in 1898. In this work, he formulated his theory of learning based upon the principles of association. Like Ebbinghaus and Pavlov, Thorndike brought the principles of association out of the philosophers' 'ideas', and experimented with them. He propounded the psychology of connectionism which was neither a system nor a school.

For Thorndike, psychology was the study of stimulus-response connections or bonds held together by associations. He also emphasized upon the utilitarian aspect of psychology. Thus, Thorndike was both an associationist and a functionalist. In his opinion, all behaviour could be analysed in terms of stimulus-response connections, and all behavioural processes were quantifiable. He liked to remain unaware of mind-body problems.

Thorndike held that the principles of connections were the same as the principles of learning. Some of these principles are enumerated here.

Thorndike placed a hungry cat inside his puzzle box, invented by him in the 1890s. Through the bars of the box the animal could see a food reward placed outside. But it could not obtain the food until some mechanism was manipulated to open the box. The mechanism was usually a lever that was to be pushed. The cat exhibited a variety of responses like clawing, biting, jumping, etc., before pressing the lever which was the appropriate response. In course of practice, the right response was learned and the wrong ones were eliminated. This type of learning he called trial-and-error. Later he preferred to call it "learning by selecting and connecting".

Thorndike did not favour the *tabula rasa* concept of John Locke. In his opinion, stimulus-response associations account for selection of behaviour in addition to acquisition of behaviour. All external events experienced by a person are not written on the blank slate. The analogy of a sensitive photographic plate duplicating everything to which it is exposed is also not correct. Some experiences are selected and some others are not.

The Psychology of Wundt

Wilhelm Maximilian Wundt (1832-1920) was a German philosopher who turned to be a psychologist. He, however, had received his original degree in medicine. He founded a psychological laboratory in the University of Leipzig (now Karl Marx University) in 1879. This was the first psychological laboratory in the world.

Wundt initiated experimental research in psychology and supervised the research of the first generation of experimental psychologists. Hence he has been rightly called the father of experimental psychology. He founded psychology as an independent discipline in 1879. Since that time, psychology has been separated from subjects like philosophy, physiology, biology, etc.

The ideas of a number of philosophers and psychologists influenced Wundt. He accepted the views of John Locke that all knowledge came from experience. Thus Wundt defined psychology as the study of immediate experience. John Stuart Mill gave the concept of mental chemistry. Accordingly, Wundt analysed immediate experience as two primary elements, viz., sensations and feelings. Alexander Bain and Herbert Spencer spoke of association of ideas. Wundt accepted association as the basic principle of connecting elements of consciousness. Johann Herbart's doctrine of apperception, Hermann Helmholtz's physiology, and Fechner's psychological methods did exert influence on Wundt.

Wundt divided experience into immediate and mediate. The former was mental and the latter physical. He defined psychology as the science of immediate experience. Mediate experience was not included in his definition. He had the notion of the atomistic nature of consciousness, the elements of consciousness being sensations and feelings. These two types of elements combine to yield psychical compounds. The combination takes place through association. In this connection, he formulated "the principle of creative synthesis". This principle is rooted in the concept of mental chemistry of John Mill.

In the opinion of Wundt, experience is composed of three main types of elements: sensations, images, and feelings. The structuralists retained these three categories of Wundt in their psychology.

Introspection was Wundt's method of studying consciousness or immediate experience. He did not separate introspection from experimentation.

Wundt held mind and body to be parallel, but not interacting. Such a doctrine is known as psychophysical parallelism. In his opinion, mind can be studied directly, without any dependence upon the body.

Structuralism

Structuralism (introspection psychology) was founded at Cornell University by Edward Bradford Titchener (1867-1927). He was British by birth, became a pupil of Wundt, and finally worked as a Professor of psychology at Cornell University in USA. He defines psychology as "experience dependent on an experiencing person". It is the study of consciousness distinct from mind. He makes a distinction between mind and consciousness. Mind is the sum total of a person's experiences from birth to death whereas consciousness is the sum total of a person's experiences at any given time.

For Titchener, all science has its starting point in experience. He differed from Wundt on the division of experience into immediate and mediate. Both of them considered consciousness as the subject-matter of psychology. For both, introspection (self-observation), experimentation and observation were the primary methods of psychology.

Both Wundt and Titchener accepted psychophysical parallelism, with a clear distinction between mental and physical events. Neither was the cause of the other. There was no interaction between them. They ran parallel to each other. Changes in one were not accompanied by changes in the other.

Wundt accepted two elements of conscious experience, viz., sensations and affections. Titchener added one more, viz., images, to it. The analysis of these elements was the main task of structuralism. This school of psychology is no longer living.

Psychology of William James

Three psychologists, viz., William James (1842-1910), Granville Stanley Hall (1844-1924), and James McKeen

Cattell (1860-1944) were the forerunners of functionalism. Here we will make a brief presentation of the psychology of William James.

William James was an American philosopher-psychologist who had received a degree in medicine. He became a Professor of Psychology.

James was a pragmatist. His philosophy is known as pragmatism. His attitude of pragmatism was reflected in his psychology. In James' opinion, psychology must study functions. It is the general opinion of James that the validation of any knowledge must be in terms of its utilitarian consequences.

James strongly criticized Wundtian introspectionism and the elementarism of structuralism. Like Wundt and Titchener, James thought that psychology was concerned with consciousness. But James laid emphasis on the functional utility, and not on the analytical character. He defined psychology as the science of mental life. By 'mental life', he meant consciousness.

According to the James-Lange theory of emotion, stimulus leads to response which, in turn, leads to experience. Seeing a bear is a stimulus which generates both external reactions (such as running away) and internal reactions (such as adrenaline secretion, acceleration in heart beat, increase in blood pressure, etc.). These reactions constitute response. Then the person becomes afraid and this is his experience. This posits the interaction of mind and body.

James-Lange theory of emotion has been replaced by Cannon-Bard theory. This new theory rejects the notion that emotional behaviour precedes emotional experience. It states that response and experience occur simultaneously.

By instinct, James meant unlearnt patterns of reacting. They are self-preserving. One can modify one's instincts by habit.

James equated 'self' to 'personality', a concept of modern psychology. As conceived by him, this is the empirical self which consists of a hierarchy of three aspects, namely, material self, social self, and spiritual self. The physical body and the personal possessions of a person constitute his material self, which is placed at the bottom. The social self is placed in the middle level. The social recognition a person gets and opinions other persons hold about him go to shape his social life. In addition, James recognizes the 'pure ego' or "I" as the knower.

Memory or the ability to remember something is considered by James as a special property of the brain structure. He divided memory into two types, viz., primary memory (short-term) and secondary memory (long-term).

Like Wundt, James recognizes both mind and body. But the former is a parallelist whereas the latter an interactionist.

James is famous for the concept of the stream of consciousness. In his opinion, psychology is the study of consciousness, and not the study of mind or soul which is manifested through consciousness. He further says that consciousness is a continuous flow, ever dynamic, and never static. This is the concept of the stream of consciousness of William James. In contrast, Wundt and Titchener took consciousness to be in a static state, and this static consciousness could be analysed or broken down into several elements.

We summarize James' concept of consciousness as follows:

> Consciousness ever flows and ever changes. It is a continuous stream. The same idea or thought is never obtained twice. Consciousness deals with objects other than itself. Thoughts about objects are always unitary although objects may be complex. Several stimuli may produce several sensations

simultaneously. But a few sensations are selectively brought to consciousness.

Functionalism

Theories of evolution prepared the seed-bed for the germination of functionalism. Jean Lamarck (1744-1829), a French naturalist, proposed early ideas on evolution. Herbert Spencer (1820-1903) presented his ideas on evolution prior to 1859, the year of the publication of *Origin of Species* of Charles Darwin (1809-82), an English naturalist, who developed a general theory of evolution and natural selection of species. Alfred Russel Wallace (1823-1913), an English naturalist, developed his theory of evolution independently of Darwin. Francis Galton (1822-1911), an English geographer and anthropologist, invented the statistical measure of correlation. He laid the foundation of psychometrics and made significant contribution to psychological statistics.

In 1885, Spencer published his famous book *The Principles of Psychology*. Charles Darwin published his *Origin of Species* in 1859, and *Expressions of the Emotions in Man and Animals* in 1872. Francis Galton published his book *Hereditary Genius* in 1869. These three persons, viz., Spencer, Darwin, and Galton, exerted tremendous influences on the formulation of functionalism.

William James (1842-1910) is regarded as the forerunner of functionalism. His two-volume work *Principles of Psychology*,[1] published in 1890, was the antecedent force that was responsible for the birth of functionalism. The seminal principles of James' psychology with reference to functionalism may be stated here. Behaviour, involving both body and mind, is adaptable. An organism must be able to adapt to its environment in order to survive psychologically. This view of James is the central theme of functionalism. Another view of James that consciousness is the product of evolution is pertinent to functionalism. James' pragmatism which stressed that the validation of any knowledge is to be done in terms of its consequences or usefulness has been made use of by functionalists.

In 1894, the school of functionalism was founded by John Dewey (1859-1952) and James Rowland Angell (1867-1949) at the University of Chicago. Harvey A. Carr (1873-1954) was the developer rather than the founder of functional psychology. This school reached its peak in popularity under the leadership of Carr. The two schools of structuralism and functionalism were antagonistic to each other.

John Dewey attacked the elementalism of the structuralists. In his opinion, psychological activity should not be broken down into elements, and should be considered as a whole. Thus he preferred molar analysis to the molecular analysis of the structuralists. The second point he made is that behaviour should be studied in context of its function, particularly adaptative function.

James Rowland Angell contributed three concepts to functional psychology. (1) A functionalist studies how a mental process operates and what it accomplishes, whereas a structuralist analyses consciousness into its different contents or elements. (2) A psychological function is an adaptive process. Such adaptation to the environment helps the organism in its survival. (3) Mind and body cannot be separated since they belong to the same whole. They constantly interplay. Functionalism deals with the totality of the relationship of the organism to its environment.

Harvey A. Carr developed the school of functionalism and established its prominence. Adaptive behaviour or action is the key concept in the psychology of Carr. His psychology deals with mental processes rather than mental contents.

In the opinion of Carr, for a response to occur, there must be some stimulus, and all activities are initiated by some sensory stimulus. Sensory stimuli affect both motives and behaviour. Behaviour is intrinsically adaptive and purposive, and it tends to modify the stimulus situation.

Unlike structuralism, functionalism did not completely

die out, although it is no longer a living psychological school. The main tenets of functionalism have since been absobred into the mainstream of psychology.

Behaviourism

In 1913, John Broadus Watson (1878-1958) founded a psychological school known as behaviourism when he was Chairman at the Department of Psychology at John Hopkins University. It did not spring up all on a sudden. Four streams of thought acted as antecedent forces that led to the birth of behaviourism.

It would be good to present a brief sketch of these antecedent forces before a discussion on behaviourism is made. These four forces are: philosophy of objectivism: animal psychology, Pavlovian conditioned reflex, functionalism.

Philosophy of objectivism: Aristotle, the Greek philosopher, in his book *De Anima*, considered functions like digestion, movement of limbs, etc. as acts of body. Descartes considered animals as machines deprived of souls. Although he interpreted the actions of the human body mechanistically, he assigned a soul to each human being. Hence he did not categorically say that human beings were automata. Julien de la Mettrie (1709-51) viewed man as a machine. Such a materialistic view purged out sprituality and went in favour of objective data and direct observation by rejecting subjective data and introspection. Pierre Cabanis (1757-1805) pointed out that the brain was the organ of consciousness in the analogy of the stomach as the organ of digestion. He maintained a mechanistic position in his philosophy. August Comte (1798-1857) founded a movement called positivism. According to this view, only positive knowledge which comes from objective observation is valid. Positivism rejected introspection and mentalistic as well as subjective approaches. Descartes, La Mettrie, Cabanis, and Comte were all French philosophers.

Animal pshychology: Charles Darwin published his

famous book *Expressions of Emotion in Man and Animals*[2] in 1872. He demonstrated close relationships between expressed emotion of human beings and animals. In 1886, George John Romanes (1848-94) published his studies on animal behaviour in his book *Animal Intelligence.* Romanes introduced anthropomorphism in his animal studies, in other words, he attributed human traits, motives, and abilities to animal behaviour. This he did in order to provide a continuity between human beings and animals. C. Lloyd Morgan (1852-1936) was another important researcher who published several books on animal behaviour. Rather than talking about intelligence, thinking, and memory of animals, he described their habits. Thus he rejected the anthropomorphism of Romanes, and still showed the continuity between human beings and animals. He laid emphasis on the trial-and-error method of learning that was common among animals and humans. Jacques Loeb (1859-1924) was a German biologist who worked in USA. He conceived of tropism or forced movement as the major explanatory factor in animal behaviour. Tropism is the direct function of a stimulus. As an example, light serves as a stimulus to moths that show tropistic behaviour by their irresistible and mechanical movement towards light. This is an example of phototropism. E.L. Thorndike, W.S. Small, and R.M. Yerkes were some of the other psychologists who significantly contributed to animal psychology. All these researchers in animal psychology did influence Watson to formulate his behaviouristic psychology.

Pavlovian conditioned reflex: We have already discussed the conditioned reflex of Pavlov and the motor conditioning of Bekhterev. Behaviourism was influened by the conditioning experiments in two ways. First, these served as methods for the objective study of behaviour. Second, they became an experimental paradigm of learning.

Functionalism: J.B. Watson did his Ph.D. work under the supervision of Angell at Chicago. Angell was one of the founders of functionalism. Thus Watson was exposed to functionalism and influenced by it. Due to this influence, behaviourism adopted objectivity in psychology and rejected conscious experience which was a subjective and mentalistic concept.

Bebaviouristic psychology is a purely objective, experimental branch of natural science. It rejects introspection. It excludes the study of consciousness from psychology. It accepts behaviour, both simple and complex, as the subject-matter of psychology. Watson maintains: The only appropriate subject-matter for scientific psychological investigation is observable, measurable behaviour. A proper scientific approach is one that limits behaviour to specific peripheral, muscular, and glandular responses and regards consciousness and mental states as epiphenomena. Thus the Watsonian approach is antimentalist, and regards cognitive experiences such as thinking and feeling to be mere epiphenomena that accompany peripheral behaviours.

Watsonian behaviourism embodied a strict environmentalism in which genetic factors were assumed to be responsible for few (or none) of the observed differences between individuals. In 1914, Watson published his book *Behaviour: An Introduction to Comparative Psychology*. In this book he recognized instinctive behaviour as hereditary tendency. In 1925, in his book *Behaviourism*, he rejected the concept of instinct at the human level and became a staunch supporter of environmentalism. Thus, on the issue of nature *versus* nurture, Watson altogether rejected nature and accepted nurture as the determiner and moulder of human potentialities. He may be quoted as follows: "Give me a dozen healthy infants . . . I'll guarantee to take anyone at random and train him to become any type of specialist. I might select — a doctor, lawyer, artist, merchant-chief, and yes, even into a beggarman and thief regardless of his talents, penchants, tendencies, abilities, vocations, and race of his ancestors".[3]

Watson laid emphasis on earlier training during infancy and childhood. His experimental results convinced him that adult personality disturbances were due to faulty training during earlier years of life and exposure to unconducive environment. In his opinion, human behaviour is determined, and it is not the product of free will. Thus, according to this view, a criminal is not responsible for his actions, since he does not possess a free will. The society can avoid the making of a would-be criminal through reconditioning — exposing him to a conducive environment, and imparting proper education to him.

Watson rejected the existence of mind, and hence question does not arise regarding the concept of mind in Watsonian psychology. He did not consider memory as a faculty of mind. He explained remembering on the basis of learning of skill or habit, forgetting on the basis of disuse of the learnt habit, and relearning on the basis of regaining the habit through further efforts. Many other psychologists contributed to behaviourism. Here we will mention the radical behaviourism of B.F. Skinner (1904-   ) and his operant conditioning. He described human behaviour and development as a process of responding to rewards and punishments in the environment. He rejects anything like mind and rules out such unobservables as drives, motives, and emotions. He also rules out the trait and type notions. In his view, there is no need for a concept of personality. His notion of personalityless personality is a set of responses strengthened by reinforcers. He does not recognize creativity.[4] He thinks a mother is not creative by having a baby, and a hen is not creative by laying an egg. A mother, according to him, is a place, a locus in which a very important biological process takes place. He establishes an analogy between a poet writing a poem and a mother conceiving a foetus. A woman is a place where a baby is formed; a poet is a place in which poetic ideas happen.

We have already discussed Pavlovian classical conditioning. In classical conditioning, an organism learns that two stimuli tend to go together. The term 'operant conditioning' was coined by B.F. Skinner. It is often equated with 'instrumental conditioning' in spite of a subtle conceptual difference between them. In operant conditioning, an organism learns that some response it makes leads to a particular consequence. When a response operates on the environment, it may have consequences that can affect the likelihood that the response will occur again. Such an operant conditioning is called instrumental, because the key feature of this form of learning lies in the fact that some action or behaviour of the learner is instrumental in bringing about a change in the environment that causes the likelihood of the action to occur again in the future.

The environmental change consequent on an instrumental response may be a reward or a punishment. If the behaviour pays off, it is likely to be repeated. An environmental stimulus that is the consequence of an instrumental response and that makes that response more likely to occur again is known as a reinforcer or a reinforcement. The reinforcer may be positive or negative. When the presentation of the reinforcer strengthens the preceding response, it is a case of positive reinforcement. When the removal of the reinforcer strengthens the preceding response, it is a case of negative reinforcement. In contrast, a punisher is a stimulus that reduces the probability of the recurrence of the res ponse, when the onset of the stimulus is contingent on the response. The reinforcer is always contingent upon the instrumental response.

To sum up the concept of mind in radical behaviourism, Skinner lays all emphasis on nurture and altogether ignores nature. Further, he rejects the existence of mind and all unobservables with reference to mind. Thus, there is no mind is Watsonian and Skinnerian psychology.

Gestalt Psychology

Gestalt psychology is a German school founded in the 1910s by Max Wertheimer (1880-1943). Wolfgang Kohler (1887-1967) and Kurt Koffka (1887-1941), the colleagues of Wertheimer, were the cofounders of this school. The Gestaltists maintain that the whole dominates the perception and that it is experienced as different from simply the sum of its several parts. Perceptual wholes are more than the sum of its parts. The character of the perceptual whole is unanalysable. Thus the Gestaltists view psychological phenomena as organized, structured wholes (Gestalten). In contrast, the structuralists hold that psychological phenomena can be introspectively 'broken down' into primitive perceptual elements. This view of the structuralists was challenged by the Gestaltists who argued that the structural analysis left out the notion of the whole, unitary essence of the phenomena.

The behaviourists maintain that learning is an association between stimuli and responses. The Gestaltists reject such a notion and regard learning as a restructuring or reorganizing of the whole situation, often involving insight as a critical feature. This insight is a process by which problems are solved. It characterizes a sudden reorganization or restructuring of the pattern.

According to the then prevailing notion of the physiology of the brain, the cerebral cortex was considered as a static, well-differentiated system. The Gestaltists could not accept this view and argued for a co-ordinated physiology in which the cortex was conceptualized as the locus in which incoming stimuli interacted in a field of forces. This is the concept of isomorphism in Gestalt psychology. According to this hypothesis of isomorphism, there is a relationship between excitatory fields in the cortex and conscious experience. In this concept, the correspondence between the physical stimulus and the brain is accepted.

Gestalt psychology is antithetical to atomistic psychology in all of its varieties such as atomism and elementarism. It is also equally hostile to behaviourism and structuralism.

As regards the mind-body problem, the Gestaltists considered isomorphism to be the real solution. This is parallelism rather than the psychophysical parallelism of Wundt and Titchener. It may rather be termed as psychophysiological parallelism. It assumed one-to-one relationship between perceived or mental field and the brain field.

As a separate theory, Gestalt psychology hardly exists today. Many of its discoveries and insights have been incorporated into contemporary psychology, particularly in the field of perception. At modern times, cognitive psychology has been very much influenced by the Gestaltists who rejected piecemeal analysis. Bower and Hilgard[5] have rightly commented: "They were, in fact, the intellectual forefathers of much of what is today called cognitive psychology, which is now a dominant viewpoint in American experimental psychology".

Freudian Psychoanalysis

Psychoanalysis is a school founded and developed by Sigmund Freud (1856-1939). Other schools of psychology developed in universities in an academic environment; but psychoanalysis had its origin in the clinical practice of Freud who was a psychiatrist doctor.

Freud divided mind into two parts, viz., conscious and unconscious. The unconscious, in turn, has two levels — the unconscious proper and the preconscious. The concious is the aspect of mind that encompasses all that one is momentarily aware of. The general meaning of consciousness is a state of awareness. In psychoanalysis, the conscious is a domain of mind that contains the sensations, perceptions, and memories of which one is momentarily aware. The preconscious is a domain of mind that refers to knowledge, emotions, images, etc. which are not momentarily in consciousness but which may be retrieved by a simple exercise of memory. The unconscious is a domain of mind encompassing the repressed, primitive impulses and desires, the memories, images and wishes that are too anxiety-provoking to be accepted into consciousness. It is populated by two varieties of psychic entities, those that were once conscious but had been exiled from awareness, and those that were never in consciousness. According to Freud, only a small part (10 per cent in some estimate) of mental life is in consciousness, and that the unconscious is the largest part of mind. He gives the analogy of an iceberg. The upper small portion of the iceberg represents consciousness whereas the larger submerged part of the iceberg stands for the unconscious. The preconscious acts as a bridge between the conscious and the unconscious. We also come across the use of 'the subconscious' in the psychoanalytic theory. It is a level of mind through which material passes on the way towards full consciousness. This term has been overtly popularized, but it, being imprecise, is eschewed by most purists who prefer 'the preconscious' to 'the subconscious'.

Unconscious experiences are, however, not non-conscious. Some activities like the secretion of body hormones, the secretion of urine in the kidneys, the secretion of insulin in the pancreas, and the mitotic as well as the meiotic cell-divisions in the body are non-conscious. The unconscious processes are experienced since they do not lie in the depth in a static condition for ever and now and then they assume a dynamic role. Unconscious experiences influence our memories, motives, and emotions.

To describe the personality structure, Freud gave a tripartite model consisting of three interlocking parts: the id, the ego, and the superego. The id is the primitive, animalistic, instinctual part, which can be thought of as a sort of storehouse of biologically based urges: the urge to eat, drink, excrete, and, especially, to be sexually stimulated. The sexual energy that underlies these urges is called the libido. The libidinal energy demands immediate gratification. The id corresponds to the deepest component of the psyche, the true unconscious. It remains as an entirely self-contained unit, completely isolated from the world about it. It is represented as the ultimate hedonist; it decides everything on the basis of the pleasure principle only. If left to itself, that is, without the restraining influence of the ego, it would satisfy its fundamental urges immediately and reflexively as they arose. In satisfying its urges, it has hardly scant regard for rules, morals, and realities of life. It is bent on achieving its carnal pleasure without the 'ought' and 'ought not' aspects of the issue.

The ego constitutes the 'executive function' of a person. It bridles the id, restrains it, and manages it. As Freud says, the id operates on the pleasure principle whereas the ego works "in the service of the reality principle". The ego tries to find out realistic ways that take account of the social norms, and, in doing so, it delays satisfying the id motives. While satisfying the urges of the id, the ego channelizes behaviour into more socially acceptable outlets. The ego helps a person work for a living, get along with people, meet social demands, and adjust to realities of life.

The superego corresponds to what we call the conscience. It sets its own ideals; it prescribes its own ethical and moral code. It seeks for higher values, without being practicable sometimes. It develops in response to the prohibitions learned from parents and other authorities. But for the influence of the superego on the ego, the latter would permit the id to satisfy its urges in ways that would be condemned as 'wrong' and 'immoral' by the former. The ego mediates between the id and the superego by a compromise action that partly accepts the ideals of the superego and allows the id to satisfy its urges according to socially acceptable norms. Thus the ego functions as an executive to adaptively maintain psychic balance. Freud conceptualized that the superego was concerned with the ideal, the id with the pleasurable, and the ego with the actual or the practical.

All the three components, viz., the id, the ego, and the superego, of the psychoanalytic psyche are mere metapsychological constructs. Spatially and anatomically they are not located anywhere. They are neither material nor immaterial structures. The three concepts should be used only as descriptive characterizations of three distinct systems of actions and behaviours.

In a normal and mentally healthy person, all the three

components of the Freudian tripartite model of mind are well-integrated and work in harmony. There are, however, variations in different individuals. The id may dominate in some individuals whereas the superego may dominate in some other individuals.

The concept of 'instincts' is vitally important in Freudian psychology. An instinct is an innate biological force that predisposes an organism to act in a certain way. Animals were supposed to act instinctively since they were thought to be deprived of souls, intellect, and power of reasoning. Darwin's theory that human beings are descendants of animals and that there are no sharp distinctions between animal species and *Homo sapiens* opened the door for the use of the concept of instinct in explaining human behaviour. William McDougall[6] was the strongest advocate of the instinct theory in psychology. He believed that human behaviour was the result of inherited instincts which were compelling sources of conduct, subject to modification, of course, by learning and experience.

According to Freudian psychology, the term 'instinct' carries the meaning as any of a number of unlearned, inherited tendencies that are hypothesized to function as the motivational forces behind complex human behaviours. Frued spoke of life instincts (*eros*) and death instincts (*thanatos*) that determine behaviour. These are two basic energies which motivate the behaviour. The life instincts are expressed in sexual behaviour whereas the death instincts underlie aggressive acts. Both these instincts are unconscious, and still are powerful motivational forces.

Thus, according to Freud's psychoanalytic theory, human actions are determined by inner forces and impulses which often operate below the level of consciousness. All human behaviour stems from two opposing groups of instincts — life instincts and death instincts. The energy of the life instincts is libido, which involves mainly sex and related activities. The death instincts may be directed inward or outward. In the former case, it may be suicide or other self-destructive behaviour. In the latter case, it is expressed in the form of aggression towards others. Sex and aggression are the two basic human motives, as held by Freud. Freud believes that both these basic motives start functioning early in a child's life. Sex energy (libido) starts functioning from birth. Frued holds that the major factor underlying personality development is sexual instinct. During the period from birth to the age of five or six years, a child passes through three stages of psychosexual development, viz., oral, anal, and phallic. These three stages together constitute the infantile stage. During each of these three stages, the pleasure-seeking impulses of the id focus on a particular sensitive zone of the body and on activities connected with that zone. The first year of an infant's life is the oral stage of psychosexual development. During this stage, pleasure is derived through suckling and putting the thumb or anything into the mouth. The second year of life is the anal stage, in which gratification is derived from withholding or expelling faeces. The phallic stage covers the age-range of three to six. During this state, children derive pleasure from fondling their genitals; they observe the anatomical differences between males and females; and they direct their emerging sexual impulses towards the parent of the opposite sex. This phallic stage is followed by a latency period (six or seven to eleven or twelve years of age), during which sexual impulses tend to be repressed and sublimated. The genital stage is the last one that begins in adolescence. Interest in the opposite sex is developed in the genital stage. Freud considers the first three stages of psychosexual development (the first five or six years of life) to be decisive for the formation of personality. He further states that fixation would take place if a child's needs at one of the psychosexual stages are either unsatisfied or oversatisfied. As a result, personality development is arrested or fixated, and the child would show continued attachment to an old stage even after moving on to a new one. Wherever fixation occurs, behaviour patterns from the fixated stage would persist often into adulthood. Regarding the death instincts, Freud also traces their initial functionings to early infanthood, during which aggression is exhibited through biting or hitting.

Freud elaborates his concept of repression which is an outcome of the failure of the expression of the life instincts and the death instincts. Sex is usually more severely repressed than aggression.

Repression is a defence mechanism and process in which certain memories and motives are not allowed to enter awareness but are operative at an unconscious level. Forgetting is very often motivated. As Freud states, forgetting in all cases is proved to be founded on a motive of displeasure. People have a tendency to have failure of retrieval of anxiety-provoking or threatening information from long-term memory. It is generally observed that people remember pleasant events more often than they do unpleasant ones. This is due to the fact that unpleasant memories are repressed. The process of repression is unconscious and automatic. No person chooses to repress an idea or impulse; it just happens whenever we feel that the idea is painful and anxiety-arousing and we want to escape from it. In such situations, the anxiety triggers repression, resulting in the burial of the unacceptable material in the unconscious.

In Feud's view, defence mechanisms originate in conflicts among the id, the ego, and the superego. Repression is one such defence mechanism which reduces anxiety and guilt. Because the id's unconscious demands are instinctual, infantile, and amoral, they are often blocked by the ego and the superego. This process results in conflicts. Due to this conflict and the persistence of unsatisfied demands, anxiety and guilt are aroused. Thus arises the need to protect the ego from frightful anxiety, and so defence mechanisms are set up. A person forgets by pushing down unpleasant thoughts into the unconscious. He forgets and then forgets that he forgot. But the worst thing in this is that the unpleasant thoughts are not rendered inert and immobile even though they are buried in the fathomless depth of the unconscious. The repressed memories continue to seek expression, and, in this endeavour, they may emerge in the form of 'accidents', 'slips' or neurotic symptoms.

Here we have presented a few salient features of the Freudian theory of psychoanalysis. We don't intend to have an exhaustive discussion of Freudian psychology in a brief chapter like this, and it is also not necessary for our specific purpose in this book. However, the basic question which remains unanswered may be restated: What is Freud's concept of mind? He perhaps didn't have any clear and precise concept of mind. R.L. Gregory[7] assumes that Freud was adopting some kind of brain-mind parallelism, with mind affecting brain systems.

The terms 'id', 'ego', and 'superego' are descriptive and functional without reference to really existing entities. The terms 'the conscious', 'the preconscious' and 'the unconscious' are also similar in nature. If mind is physical and equivalent to the brain and the spinal cord along with peripheral nerves, Freud's terms, mentioned here, must refer to some spatial and anatomical entity in the nervous system. That is, however, not the case in Freudian psychology. If mind is immaterial like the so-called soul, it is difficult to conceive of the locational specificities of these Freudian terms. Of course, Freud himself has rejected the existence of souls, and hence any occasion does not arise to establish association of soul and Freud's tripartite model. Regarding the location and the anatomy of mind, Freud writes: "I shall entirely disregard the fact that the mental apparatus with which we are here concerned is also known to us in the form of an anatomical preparation and I shall carefully avoid the temptation to determine psychical locality in any anatomical fashion. . . Strictly speaking, there is no need for the hypothesis that the psychical systems are actually arranged in a *spatial* order".[8] Freud's concept of memory is also vague. He says that memory traces are laid down beyond the apparatus receiving perceptual stimuli. The perceptual system, for him, has no memory whatever.

Thus Freud's psychical terms like id, ego, and superego, and 'the conscious', 'the preconscious', and 'the unconscious' are purely descriptive and functional. But these terms describe the functions of non-entities that are in void, and non-entities in void are logically non-existent.

The Freudian tripartite model could be locational, had the Indian concept of mind been accepted. Freud was not exposed to Indian Psychology which has not yet been known to the world in the modern format. Further, Freud discarded the concept of 'self' and reincarnation. So Freud's thought and Indian thought on psychology are incompatible. According to the Indian concept, both brain and mind are material, but separate. The former is made of gross matter and is a component part of the gross body. In contrast, the latter is made of subtle matter and is a component part of the subtle body. The brain is a sophisticated electronic machine much more wisely evolved than any man-made machine. It is used as an instrument by the mind. The brain of a person is disintegrated when he dies. But his mind persists to exist even after death. The mind vanishes only when the *jīva*-hood terminates and the 'self' becomes indistinguishable from *Brahman* or *Ātman*. This is the state of liberation (*mokṣa*). Mind or *manas* is an important component of the inner organ (*antaḥkaraṇa*). The subtle body and the empirical self are inextricably bound to constitute the *jīva* that transmigrates through several births and deaths. The subtle body which is also material survives death and serves as the reservoir of all mental impressions of successions of lives. If we accept the Indian concept of the subtle body and the inner organ, we recognize its components such as *manas, ahaṅkāra, buddhi, citta*; we also take cognizance of related concepts like *saṁskāras, vāsanās, sattva, rajas, tamas*, etc. Freud's tripartite model of psychology can be explained and can be rendered locational if we accept the concept of the subtle body of Indian psychology. The presence of the empirical self (*jīvātmā*) throws light of consciousness on the insentient mind that is made conscious. The mind uses the brain as its instrument, and thus the brain functions mechanically although not foolishly.

Freud's depth psychology does not refer to any really existing depth. His 'mind' has no spatial dimensions like length, breadth, and depth. He says that the mind buries some ideas in the deeper levels of the unconscious. In the absence of the dimension of depth, the descriptive psychology of Freud baffles any language of description.

The life instincts and the death instincts are important aspects of Freudian psychology. The sex energy, libido, is active from the time of birth and plays the most important role in shaping the personality of the individual throughout the life. The instincts are innate and inherited. If these concepts of Freud are accepted as facts, we face some problems which are hardly solved. The innateness or hereditary nature of instincts is not questioned here. But it is sheer reductionism if all types of instincts are reduced to *eros* and *thanatos*. A baby's suckling instinct is self-preserving and might not have anything to do with sex. Why should it not be called a feeding instinct? Even in the genital stage of personality development in adolescence, psychological attraction towards the opposite sex is a mechanism for the preservation of the species. All instincts are meaningful and they are never rooted in mere hedonism. To interpret *Homo sapiens* or any animal species in terms of sex only, as has been done by Sigmund Freud, is over-simplification and total misrepresentation. Any powerful instinct can also be modulated by one's will; reason can bring instincts under partial or full control. This idea is relatively more true in human beings than in animals. Environment and training can change instinctual behaviour. Freud does not contradict these modifying influences on instincts. Nevertheless, he lays over-emphasis on the sex instinct which is almost invincible or irresistible for him.

Freud did not live in the age of computer. He did not spell out how ideas and urges were recorded in the unconscious and the conscious. We do not find even the rudiments of cognitive psychology in his descriptives. But we do find elaboration of storage of memory, retrieval, *saṁskāras* and *vāsanās* (recordings in the conscious and the unconscious mind) in Indian psychology.

To conclude, Freud did not do away with mind; but his concept of mind was limited to verbal description only. He did not say that the brain and mind were different. He did not say that the brain and mind were identical. He did not believe in the existence of God and soul. Neither did he believe in reincarnation. We can definitely say that Freud's concept of mind is purely hypothetical, without any reference to any material or immaterial entity. It is a tripartite model, a descriptive one to explain overt and covert human behaviour.

Jung's Analytical Psychology

Carl Gustav Jung (1875-1961) was born in Switzerland. With a degree in medicine, he worked as a clinical psychiatrist. Freud's famous book *Interpretation of Dreams,*[9] published in 1900, deeply influenced Jung. In 1907, Freud invited Jung to visit Vienna where the former was working. Both were academically interacting. Jung got much support from Freud who considered the former to be his heir apparent. In spite of close association between Freud and Jung during the period from 1907 to 1913, personal and theoretical differences between them started emerging. As a consequence, Jung broke with Freud in 1914 and thereafter they never saw each other. Jung founded his own school called analytical psychology.

In 1928, Jung published his book *Analytical Psychology.*[10] Like Freud, Jung divided psyche into the conscious and the unconscious. Jung identified the ego with the conscious aspect of psyche; but his concept of the 'self' involved both the conscious and the unconscious psyche.

Jung credited each individual with a personal unconscious, which formed out of the individual's conscious experiences that had been repressed. He had a notion of 'individuation'. Each healthy person gradually comes into contact with the unconscious part of his/her personality, and thereby the unconscious is integrated with the 'conscious ego'. Through this integration, all major components of the personality eventually work in concert to form a purposeful self. According to Jung, this process of harmonizing one's conscious and unconscious components of psyche is effected in a unique way for each individual, leading to a unique pattern of behaviour. This process is known as individuation. Jung recognized this process as the means by which each human being becomes an individual distinct from others.

Jung's notion of 'collective unconscious', which is controversial in psychology, has made him famous. The collective unconscious is part of the unconscious mind of every person, and it goes beyond the personal experiences of every individual. In the opinion of Jung, all the past experiences of the human race cumulatively form the collective unconscious. Primitive fundamental images, impressions, or predispositions, common to earlier members of the human race, are stored within the collective unconscious. These stored images, impressions, or predispositions inside the collective unconscious were termed by Jung as 'archetypes'.

What is an archetype? It is hard to define this word. It is better to conceptualize it. Archetypes are subjective reactions that originated in our ancestors in response to certain universal experiences. The human race has been observing the sun rising and setting, seasons moving in cycles, order prevailing in Nature, beauty and benevolence expressing in Nature that seems to be nourishing like a mother and protecting like a father. Consequent upon subjective reactions of the ancestors to the universal experiences, the human race conceived of gods, goddesses, and God. The recurrent phenomena in Nature might have given rise to the concept of rebirth and resurrection. Human beings, from time immemorial, have been observing the horrors of malevolent Nature that expresses anger through earthquakes, volcanoes, deluge, thunder, and pestilence. The human race conceived of devils, ghosts, and evil spirits as a subjective reaction to the universal experiences. By observing both males and females in the society through aeons, the human race conceived of *animus* (a male archetype present in females) and *anima* (a female archetype present in males). Nature constantly plays tricks through which old things disappear, new things appear, and disappeared things reappear. The human race subjectively reacted to these experiences and conceived of tricks and magic, spells and miracles. The forceful and chaotic Nature, the potent Nature with devastating activity has been frightening man through ages, and, as a reaction, the human race has been harbouring the concept of the hero. We have inherited many such tendencies towards subjective reactions, and these tendencies are our archetypes. Each archetype involves strong emotion. From this, Jung infers that the emotion-generated behaviour of a person may be explained by identifying the key archetype that influences him.

The main reason for which Freud's affection for Jung faded was the academic difference between the two theorists. According to Freud, childhood psychosexual development is the prime force that shapes the behavioural pattern in adulthood. He emphasized sexual impulses and motives as the motor of human behaviour. They serve as the prime source of the libido's energy. In contrast, Jung placed less emphasis on sexual and aggressive impulses in moulding human behavioural pattern, and more emphasis on people's future-oriented goals, hopes, and plans. He held that "only a continuous life" was the driving force that fuelled the libido. This life urge is the striving to live so that the survival of one's species be insured. Another important difference between Jung and Freud was that the latter rejected the former's concept of the 'collective unconscious'.

If we critically review Jung's concept of the collective unconscious, it seems to be both right and wrong. From our observations of the innate (unlearned) behaviours of different species of animals, we do infer that instincts, useful for the survival of the species, exist and operate in each species, including the human animal. Similar is our conclusion for sub-races, communities, and tribes in the human species. Here we quote three definitions of 'instinct' given in *The Penguin Dictionary of Psychology*[11]: (1) An unlearned response characteristic of the members of a given species. (2) A tendency or disposition to respond in a particular manner that is characteristic of a particular species. (3) A complex, co-ordinated set of acts found universally or nearly so within a given species that emerges under specific stimulus conditions, specific drive conditions, and specific developmental conditions. Again, we quote here some unresolved problems concerning these definitions. (a) To what extent are the instincts biologically pre-programmed, or, do they result from environmental factors? (b) Are instincts general motivators, or, do they function within individual species? To what degree can we incorporate specific behaviours within an instinct? Basing on accumulating evidences, ethologists stress species-specificity of instincts.

In this connection, Jung says: "This collective unconscious does not develop individually but is inherited. It consists of pre-existent forms, the archetypes, which can only become conscious secondarily and which give definite form to certain psychic contents".[12] In trying to explain the inheritance of the collective unconscious, Jung suggested that the archetypal forms were "present in the germ-plasm".[13] Rupert Sheldrake refutes Jung's concept of the inheritance of the collective unconscious. Sheldrake writes: "But it is very doubtful that anything with the properties of the archetypal forms could be inherited chemically in the structure of DNA, or in any other physical or chemical structure in sperm or egg cells".[14]

We believe that Jung is right in the formulation of his concepts 'the collective unconscious' and the individual unconscious. But he does not seem to be right in saying that the collective unconscious and the individual unconscious are inherited. Freud did not recognize the collective unconscious. But he also erroneously thought that the individual unconscious was inherited.

What is the solution of this problem? Perhaps no solution can be reached so long as we try to hold that memories must somehow be stored within the brain. Instincts are deeply buried memories (*vāsanās*) in the unconscious. And hence a search for physical memory traces within the brain would inevitably be fruitless.

In the *Sāṅkhya-Yoga* system of Indian philosophy and psychology, there is provision for a universal mind (*Mahat* or *Buddhi*) and individual minds (*antaḥkaraṇas*). The former is one only and the latter are as many as there are individuals. Both *Mahat* and *antaḥkaraṇas* are not immaterial, their material nature being too subtle to be perceived by our senses. Each *antaḥkaraṇa* is a computer which is ever linked up with *Mahat* or *Buddhi* which is the unviersal computer. Long-term memory traces are stored in the *antaḥkaraṇa* rather than in the brain. The brain is the instrument of the *antaḥkaraṇa* or the mind and both are hooked up throughout the life. The brain disintegrates and decomposes when a person dies. The *antaḥkaraṇa* which is in the subtle body (*sūkṣma śarīra*) survives death and is transmigrated. Transmigration ceases when the memory traces in the *karmāśaya* (karmic reservoir) and the *vāsanā* traces are completely erased. This psychology, as given in the *Sāṅkhya-Yoga* system, has been adopted in principle by the *Vedānta*. Both Freud and Jung can explain their psychology if they accept these Indian concepts. Otherwise they would be speculating and hypothesizing in a vacuum background.

Nativism *versus* Empiricism

In the history of philosophy and psychology, the issue of nativism *versus* empiricism has been in dispute since the seventeenth century. The French philosopher René Descartes (1596-1650) who was a rationalist was a strict nativist. The nativists hold that our ability to perceive the way we do is inborn or innate. The three German nativists, Immanuel Kant (1724-1804), Johann Herbart (1776-1841), and Hermann Lotze (1817-81), put forward the doctrine of nativism by saying that our capacity to perceive time and space is inborn. It may not be strictly correct to say that Kant was a nativist. He held that knowledge must be understood as a product of both sense and understanding. He drove a balance between empiricism and nativism and gave importance to both experience and innate ideas. Through his concept of *a priori* judgements, he recognized the innateness of ideas. But, he also recognized the importance of sense experience, and, in that connection, he spoke of *a posteriori* judgements.

The issue of nativism *versus* empiricism is the same as that of nature *versus* nurture. In modern terminology it is heredity-environment controversy. Nature refers to innate or inborn processes that influence behaviour and perception. In the contemporary use of the term 'nativism', we refer to orientation to psychology or philosophy that stresses the genetic, inherited influences on behaviour and thought in contrast to the acquired, experiential influences.

Nurture constitutes the totality of learning, the total exposure to environment. In general, nurture refers to the effects of the environment on behaviour and perception. Empiricism disregards nature and gives full emphasis on nurture. The three British empiricists, viz., John Locke (1632-1704), George Barkeley (1685-1753), and David Hume (1711-76) maintain that we learn our ways of perceiving through experience.

Back in 1688, William Molyneux posed a query to his friend John Locke: Would a congenitally blind adult, upon suddenly recovering vision, be able to distinguish between a globe and a cube without touching them? This is the classical Molyneux's question. The questioner answered his own question with a vigorous negative. Locke unsurprisingly agreed. This simple question drove straight to the heart of the debate over nativism *versus* empiricism. It is still an issue of active interest in modern psychology. Is the brain biologically pre-programmed particularly with respect to questions concerning perception, language, and social behaviour?

Here we will refer to a few sensitive-period experiments. A sensitive period is defined as the time in the early development of a person or an animal, during which the environment has its greatest effect on behaviour or on the brain processes underlying behaviour. In the prolonged absence of environmental stimuli during the sensitive period, the relevant brain cells are damaged permanently or undergo irrevocable changes such as disuse atrophy. Even if environmental stimuli are restored at a subsequent stage, the concerned brain activity does not generally come to normalcy.

A.H. Riesen[15] has published the results of some experiments on sensory deprivation. He raised animals with translucent contact lenses over their eyes from birth. He removed the special lenses after the sensitive period had passed. He observed that the experimental animals had great difficulty in perceiving form. Subsequent special training and visual experience improved the form perception of the animals to some extent; but the animals' behavioural responses to visual stimuli never became normal. To a greater or lesser degree, the animal's visual form perception became permanently impaired as a result of the sensory deprivation during the sensitive period.

The experimental results of M.V. Senden[16] may be briefly reported here. His studies were on individuals who were blind from birth with cataracts on both eyes. In the adult age their vision was restored by surgery. On the removal of the eye-bandages, the patients were very much confused by the bewildering array of visual stimuli. It resulted from the prolonged deprivation of their sensory experience. But they were able to distinguish a figure from the ground, to fixate figures, scan them, and to follow moving figures. These abilities appeared to be innate.

Next we discuss if there is a critical period in childhood for language development. Psychologist Eric Lenneberg[17] proposed a critical period hypothesis. He maintains that a child's brain, before the age of two years, is not mature enough for language acquisition to take place. He further says that, after puberty, the brain loses the flexibility for the acquisition of a first language.

Lenneberg's critical period hypothesis may be analysed in the context of the tragic story of Genie, the "wild child". In 1970, officials of California discovered a thirteen-year old girl, Genie, who had been reared as an animal in confinement. She was forced to live in almost total isolation from the age of twenty months to that of thirteen years. She was deprived of any opportunity for language development and normal development in other areas during this long period in her childhood.

Susan Curtiss,[18] an expert in language development, worked with Genie in the post-isolation period. To the question, "Did Genie develop language after the age of thirteen years?" the answer is both yes and no. With training, she did develop some language. But she could not become fluent and failed to attain efficiency in language use. Curtiss, basing on the results of her study on Genie, proposed a modified critical period hypothesis. It is usual for nearly all right-handed people to use the left hemisphere of the brain for language. But, Genie used the right side of her brain for language. Like all normal people, the functions of the right hemisphere of the brain such as face recognition were well developed in Genie. Thus it is clear that Genie's left hemisphere functioned poorly as a result of prolonged disuse, and that her right hemisphere 'adopted' the functions of the left hemisphere, although below the normal level of efficiency. Curtiss inferred from the results of her studies that there might be critical period for the development of the left hemisphere of the brain. We also come across an interesting article on the civilizing of Genie, written by Pines.[19]

Before concluding the nativist and empiricist viewpoints, we would like to discuss the results of a few further studies on visual deprivation and subsequent disuse atrophy of some areas of the brain as the effects thereof. Infant chimpanzees were reared in total darkness until they were sixteen months old. They were found to have serious perceptual deficiencies when they were tested upon first exposure to light. They had neuronal deterioration in various parts of the visual system. In the absence of any light stimulation, nerve cells in the retina and the visual cortex began to atrophy.

Riesen[20] conducted experiments on monkeys, chimpanzees and kittens that were made to wear translucent goggles from birth to anywhere from one to three months of age. In these animals more complex visual activity was seriously affected although simple perceptual abilities were unimpaired. They failed to follow a moving object, discriminate forms, and perceive depth. Riesen's findings have been supported by research, recording single-cell activity in the visual cortex. These investigators were Blakemore,[21] Barlow[22] and Mitchell[23].These studies have shown that the responses of the cells in the visual brain are altered in specific ways that relate to the visual features to which the developing animal is exposed during the sensitive period.

What do the sensitive-period experiments say? Do these support the empiricist or the nativist view? Environmental alterations during sensitive periods do change perception and brain-cell responses. Hence the empiricist claims that nativisim is disproved. The nativist says that brain-organization is patterned by genetic codes and hence is innate. Perception is also innate since it depends on the brain-organization. The nativist does not ignore the plastic changes observed in controlled experimentation due to sensory deprivation during sensitive periods. He explains the plastic changes by saying that this happens due to loss or attrition of the inborn brain-connections that need environmental input (nurture) for their maintenance.

It seems both the nativists and the empiricists sit on the

extreme fences in opposite directions. Genetic preprogramming and predetermination cannot be denied. Both physical and mental traits are regulated by genetic codes. And that's what we call nature. The environmental influences constitute nurture. Genetic abilities are generally potentialities. A potential trait has to be expressed in order that it becomes a trait as we know. Nurture helps in the expression of what is potential. What is expressed is the outcome of the interaction of nature and nurture. The comprehension of this interaction puts a full stop to the nature-nurture dispute.

Cognitive Science

Cognitive science emerged in the 1950s and 1960s in part as a critical reaction to behaviourism. The behaviourism of J.B. Watson and the radical behaviourism of B.F. Skinner produced an outgrowth which may be termed stimulus-response psychology (or S-R psychology for short). It is called the "black box" approach since it is not concerned with what goes on in the organism. The S-R psychologist builds a science of psychology based strictly on what goes into the box and what comes out, without worrying about what takes place inside. He avoids the study of mental processes that intervene between the stimulus and the observable response. He studies animals and humans as input-output systems, the input being sensory stimulation, reward and punishment, and the output being behaviour. The cognitive approach to the study of psychology was a reaction to the S-R approach.

The branch of psychology that deals with cognitive processes is known as cognitive psychology. Cognitive processes are mental processes involved in knowing about the world. Perception, attention, memory including encoding, storing, and retrieval of information coming through the senses, imagery, thinking, language-use, reasoning, problem-solving, and creativity are terms that describe hypothetical stages of cognition.

Cognitive science is not cognitive psychology only. It is a multi-disciplinary science involving investigators in psychology, neurophysiology, computer science, linguistics, anthropology, and even philosophy. The development of computer science and cognitive science have run parrallel. As a matter of fact, the brain is studied as a model of the computer and *vice versa*. The cognitive scientist studies cognition, all processes of which intervene between stimuli and responses.

We know very little about the ways cognitive processes (perception, thinking, language use, memory) are represented in the brain. The present situation of our ignorance should not make us pessimistic, since future research may provide the key to open the hitherto closed cover.

Memory: What we call memory has three stages, viz., encoding, storage, and retrieval. Information is put into memory, and that is encoding; it is maintained in memory, and that is storage; it is recovered from memory, and that is retrieval.

We classify memory into two types, viz., short-term memory (STM) and long-term memory (LTM). Short-term memory lasts for only seconds or a few minutes at most. Long-term memories last from hours to a lifetime. Before we discuss more about these two types of memory, we would introduce the concept "the sensory register".

Before information gains access to STM, it can be held for a brief time in the sensory channels (visual, auditory, olfactory, gustatory, tactile) themselves. This storage function of the sensory channels is called the sensory register. Most of the information briefly held in the sensory register, without being passed on to STM, is lost; it simply decays from the register. The visual sensory register holds information for up to about one second. The auditory sensory register stores information somewhat longer — up to about four or five seconds.

The sensory register transmits information to short-term

memory. Information can be stored in STM for up to about thirty seconds. The storing capacity of STM is very much limited; about 7±2 items can be stored in STM. Electrical activity in certain circuits or networks of nerve cells in the brain is represented by short-term memory.

It is possible to increase the storage capacity of STM by chunking. For example, it may be difficult to remember a telephone number 703895 when someone on the telephone line mentions his/her number. It becomes relatively easier to remember this number by grouping the digits into two chunks of three digits each such as 703 895. After prolonged practice, one can remember 7±2 chunks. About 80 items, grouped into a number of chunks, have been remembered through practice, and this is so far the world record.

Anything and everything to which we are exposed are not stored in STM. Someone goes to a grocery shop, buys articles and comes back home. On questioning, he/she is unable to tell the colour of the eyes of the grocer. Unless attention is paid on an object or event, STM does not store it. Much of whatever is stored in STM is lost unless it is transmitted to long-term memory. The loss is due to the displacement of the stored information by incoming items of information. Before the information is lost from STM, it can be retrieved and used within the short period of storage.

Short-term memories become long-term ones through a process known as consolidation. Transient patterns of nerve-cell activity in the brain, representing STM, if allowed to continue for a period of time, are consolidated into longer lasting brain changes which underlie long-term memory.

In the temporal lobe of the brain are structures known as hippocampus and amygdala that are critically involved in the consolidation of STM into LTM. Temporal lobe patients have relatively normal short-term memory. Their already formed long-term memory remains intact even if the hippocampus and the amygdala are damaged; already formed long-term memories are not stored in the hippocampus and the amygdala; they are stored elsewhere in the brain. But consolidation of short-term memory into long-term one is prevented if the hippocampus and the amygdala are damaged. Hence new information stored temporarily in STM cannot be transmitted to LTM for consolidation and thus are lost in a few seconds.

We have not known any specific area in the brain where long-term memory is stored. It has been observed that damage to small regions of the brain (ablation) does not usually wipe out well-established long-term memories. It is inferred from this observation that particular memories may be stored throughtout fairly wide regions of the brain. If one region of the brain is damaged, the memory function of that region ceases, but other normal regions of the brain carry out their memory activities in the usual manner, and hence memory is not impaired. However, if the brain damage is extensive, or any disease process alters the structure and function of the brain (as in Alzheimer's disease) consolidated long-term memories can be lost.

Under normal circumstances, long-term memories, once formed, are relatively permanent. They can last for days, months, years, or even a lifetime. The storage capacity of LTM has no known limit.

Some theorists believe that, once information is stored in LTM, it is there for good. According to this view, no stored information is ever lost from LTM. But, it is a fact that we forget. Forgetting is explained by saying that we have trouble in retrieving, or getting access to what has been stored. Some others explain that we forget due to confusion and interference brought about by new things which have been learned and put into LTM. There are also other causes of forgetting. But, according to the concept of the life-long storage of information in LTM, no information is ever lost from the long-term memory of the brain, irrespective of the fact whether we can retrieve or not.

Long-term memory contains words, sentences, ideas, concepts, imagery, and life experiences. Our memory may be semantic or episodic. We know meanings of words. We know how words can be related to one another and used in sentences. We know grammatical rules for their use in language communication. Anything we do in connection with our language use has been stored in our LTM. It is this kind of memory which makes our use of language possible. It is called semantic memory.

Our life is full of experiences. The incidents that have happened at particular times and places and that we have directly or indirectly experienced are remembered by us. All these are stored in our long-term memory. This type of memory is known as episodic memory.

How are information encoded, stored, and retrieved? Very little is known about these memory processes. Where is the site in the brain where information are stored? This question can hardly be answered at the present level of our knowledge. Maybe, science will discover the physiology of memory in future. But, it is to be confessed that our present knowledge on this aspect of memory is crude and scanty.

According to one hypothesis, memory processes are associated with the altered functions of brain cells in whole regions of the brain. In order to find out some clue, some investigators have studied the widespread changes that occur in the brain's electrical activity during learning and memory. Others have taken a more structural approach. They believe that memories are stored by changes in brain's electrical circuits or networks, i.e., by changes in the ways brain cells or neurons are inter-connected. According to this view, long-term memory is represented in the brain by the changed circuits. Since memories are not narrowly localized in the brain, any particular memory is represented by a large number of changed circuits. When something activates a circuit, the memory represented by the acitvity in the circuit is retrieved.

There is one hypothesis which involves synapses and neurotransmitters to exaplain the physiology of memory. Connections between neurons (nerve cells) are known as synapses. When a nerve cell is active. a chemical known as neurotransmitter is released at the synaptic connection. The receiving nerve cell is either excited or inhibited due to the action of the neurotransmitter. This function of the neurotransmitter has already been established in the physiology of nerve conduction. It is hypothesized that a neurotransmitter can also trigger a chain of events that alter the manufacture of proteins in the receiving cells. Certain proteins which are embedded in the membranes of nerve cells are involved in regulating the excitability of the cells. More of these proteins are synthesized when a circuit is active. On the activation of circuits and consequent synthesis of membrane proteins, the cells of the circuit become structurally and permanently changed to form a memory module for LTM. This is the process of memory storing. The retrieval process involves in the activation of a neuron in the circuit or network which acts as a unit.

In consonance with the hypothesis that long-term memory is linked to protein-biosynthesis by neurons, research has been conducted on several lines for exploring the biochemical bases of long-term memory — encoding, storage, and retrieval. The earlier work that has been referred to in the previous paragraph focused on changes occurring at synaptic connections between brain cells. Later research work probed into changes in the biochemical nature of the brain cells themselves.

The nucleus of each cell contains deoxyribonucleic acid (DNA) which is a double helix. This DNA molecule is a long chain of genetic codes that constitute the blueprint of the individual organism. This DNA never leaves the nucleus of the cell. Three types of ribonucleic acid (RNAs) are transcribed by the DNA that serves as template. The RNAs leave the nucleus and migrate to the cytoplasm of the cell. Body proteins which are specific to the species and individuals inside the species are synthesized in the cellular cytoplasm and this biosynthesis of body proteins is regulated by the RNAs. Many researchers[24-26] have suggested that RNA composes the biochemical basis of memory. This hypothesis has not yet been confirmed to be a fact. All body cells including the nerve cells of the brain contain RNA. If the RNA of brain cells is involved in memory, RNAs of body cells other than brain cells should also function similarly. We know some peculiarity in the membranes of neurons; but we are not aware of any speciality in the RNA of neurons. We hope further research would throw more light on this important issue.

Language: Next we will discuss the physiology of language use. We do not know how language is encoded in our memory and how it is retrieved. We do exactly know the co-ordinating processes that are involved inside the brain for the effective use of language. We have some knowledge about the physiology of the brain in connection with language use. We will restrict our discussion to this narrow area.

The brain has two hemispheres, left and right. The left hemisphere is specialized in understanding language, formulating language for communication, and thinking with language symbols. To deal with images, spatial relationships and pattern recognition is the specialized function of the right hemisphere. Of course, none of these are the exclusive functions of one hemisphere or the other. The left hemisphere is not totally devoid of some spatial abilities. Similarly, the right hemisphere has some ability for the use of language.

In the upper temporal lobe of the left hemisphere is a locality known as Wernicke's area. It has been named after the German neurologist Carl Wernicke. In the lower frontal lobe of the left hemisphere is a locality known as Broca's area, named after Paul Broca, a French physician. The main language functions of the brain are localized in these two areas.

We understand spoken and written language due to the involvement of the Wernicke's area. This area plays a vital role in the formulation of sentences and in organizing spontaneous speech. By the help of this area, one finds words for expression and one links the words into meaningful sentences. If the Wernicke's area is damaged, the ability to comprehend language is seriously impaired, and problems arise with reading, writing, repeating a spoken word, and naming common objects. A patient with lesion in the Wernicke's area or damaged Wernicke's area can speak fluently, but the speech conveys little meaning.

If Broca's area is injured, or if this area develops pathological lesions, the speech of such a person becomes non-fluent and ungrammatical.

Wernicke's area and Broca's area are connected by a bundle of nerve fibres, called the arcuate fasciculus, which runs through the white matter under the cortex. This serves as the communication pathway between the two langauge-areas of the brain.

There is a cortical region known as the angular gyrus. This region plays an important role in the processes involved in reading. Persons whose angular gyrus has been damaged may understand speech of others and may verbally communicate with others; but they lose their ability of reading.

We may now sum up the physiological processes of speaking. Wernicke's area transmits what is to be spoken to Broca's area through the arcuate fasciculus. Broca's area contains the programmes for the complex patterns of muscle movements needed for speaking. The programmes of the Broca's area are then relayed to the region of the motor cortex that sends message through the nerves to the lips, tongue, and vocal cords which accordingly move to produce the speech sounds.

A person, X, replies to the question of another person, Y. Input from the auditory cortex of X goes to Wernicke's area, where the language of the reply is organized. The Wernicke's area sends the reply through the arcuate fasciculus to the Broca's area that, in turn, sends message to the motor cortex. Thence goes the nerve-impluses to the lips, tongue, and vocal cords.

You read a passage aloud. In this case, input from the visual cortex reaches the Wernicke's area via the angular gyrus. The Wernicke's area sends the language for reading to the Broca's area through the arcuate fasciculus. From the Broca's area information is relayed to the motor cortex. And thence the message is transmitted through nerves to the lips, tongue and vocal cords.

Thinking: Everyone of us is accustomed to the use of the two words — 'thinking' and 'thought'. But cognitive scientists are puzzled over the definition of thinking. Some of them avoid the term in professional discourse. Some others characterize it as "the ability to manipulate the environment symbolically". Some others call it "all that goes on in the mind between input and output". Morgan, King, and co-authors[27] say that "we mentally, or **cognitively**, process information" when we think. More formally, they say that "thinking **consists** of the cognitive rearrangement or manipulation of both information from the environment and the symbols stored in long-term memory".

Thought and language: Some theorists assert that verbalization is necessary for thought. Especially the linguistic philosophers seem to be of the opinion that language is essential for intelligent or conscious thought. It is a fact that we do use language in many of our thinkings. But, the reverse is not true, that is, non-verbalized thought is possible and is also a fact.

Words, their meanings, and the rules of grammer to join the words together into phrases and sentences have been stored in our semantic long-term memories. When we think with language, we draw on this store to use language as a tool of thought.

There is bipolarity on the relationship of language to thought. At one pole are those who assert that thought and words are coextensive. Hannah Arendt,[28] a philosopher, writes in her book that thought without speech is inconceivable. There are others who agree with Benjamin Whorf,[29] a linguist, who argues that our thoughts are confined to and moulded by the syntax and the vocabulary of our **native** language.

There is almost a consensus of a group of cognitive scientists on the use of vocal speech symbols, or verbal language, in thinking. Other language systems which are non-vocal have also been found as tools of thought. A number of investigators, experimenting on born-deaf persons, have come to the conclusion that non-verbal language like visual-gestural sign languages used by deaf people do also serve as tools of thought.[30] Even if deaf children are not taught gestural sign language, they develop their own, indicating that human beings have an innate programme for language, be it verbal or gestural.[31]

Concept: Concepts are said to be important language symbols used in thinking. We will analyse this statement in some greater detail.

A concept is a building block of thought. It is a symbolic construction that represents some physical object, imaginary mental object, quality, quanitity, action, event, and spatial or temporal relation. Every word we use in language is a name (label) of a concept. Each noun is a name of a concept. A universal term like 'man' is a name of a concept; at the same time, a particular term like 'Shakespear' is also a name of a concept since it refers to a particular person about whom we have some descriptions. All abstract nouns like 'kindness', 'cruelty', 'anger' are names of concepts. All adjectives are names of concepts. Words like 'beautiful', 'ugly', 'clever', 'foolish' are names of concepts. Quantitative words such as 'much', 'many', 'one', 'two' are names of concepts. Pronouns like 'I', 'we', 'he', 'she', 'they' are names of concepts. Verbs such as 'reading', 'eating', 'running' are names of concepts. Prepositions such as 'in', 'on', 'under', 'above', 'with', 'without', are names of concepts. Conjunctions such as 'and', 'or', 'if' are names of concepts. Exclamatory words such as 'alas', 'ah', 'oh', are names of concepts. Words referring to imaginary objects or beings such as 'unicorn', 'angels', 'fairies', 'demons', are names of concepts. There is no word in a language which is not the name of a concept.

Our ability to form concepts enables us to classify things into categories. Due to our concept of 'red', we sort out objects as red and not-red. Due to our concept of 'fluid', we classify objects as fluid and not-fluid.

This discussion on 'concept' reverses the proposition that "concepts are language symbols used in thinking". Concepts are not symbols for language; words are rather symbols for concepts. Every word in a language is a label for a concept. We form concepts by thinking. Conceptualization is a thinking process. We express our concepts by speaking language. By using language, we think aloud. We do not speak silently by thinking.

Anthropological studies have shown that in some tribal language there are only two 'colour' words like 'white' and 'black'. In spite of this fact, the people of such language judge all colours as is done by people with language having many words for seven or more colours. This provides an evidence that, for colour at least, it is possible to think without words.

Non-verbalized thought: Now we take up abstract concepts such as those involved in mathematics and physical sciences. A number of scientists such as Faraday, Francis Galton, and Albert Einstein have spoken in favour of non-verbality of thought. They have reported that they solved scientific problems in visual images and only afterwards translated their thoughts into words. Psychologist Roger N. Shepard[32] of Stanford University demonstrates the existence of non-linguistic thinking. Hadamard,[33] in his study of creative thinking, refuted the thesis that verbalization is necessary for thought. Roger Penrose,[34] the famous Rouse Ball professor of Mathematics of Oxford University, is in accord with these thought-modes. He writes: "Almost all my mathematical thinking is done visually and in terms of non-verbal concepts. . ." He further adds: "This is not to say that I do not sometimes think in words, it is just that I find words almost useless for mathematical thinking."

Many mathematical and scientific concepts are invented before they are given names. Words such as 'quark', 'graviton', 'quantum', 'tachyon', etc., are coined later than the birth of the respective concept in the mind. That there can be no thought without verbalization is thus refuted at least for abstract concepts in mathematics and physical science.

Some psychologists maintain that much of our most important and creative thinking takes place in images rather than in words. We use stored images that we have experienced in the past and recorded them in our long-term memory. Not only do we reproduce images from our memory, but also we create new images out of our experienced ones.

Language is not well suited to encoding information such as visual and spatial relations. A scientist, a mathematician, a poet, an architect, a sculptor, a painter, a musician, and such other creative scientists and artists think in images while they create ideas. By admitting the role of imagery in creative thinking, we do not belittle the fact that previous verbalized thinking exerts tremendous influence on thinking in imagery.

Other Processes of Thinking

We have already discussed concept-making as a thinking process. Problem-solving, decision-making, reasoning, and creativity are some of the other important processes of thinking.

Problem-Solving as Thinking Process: Out of two or more conflicting and complicating situations, we wish to reach our goal, and thereby solve our problem. Our thinking for the solution of a problem is thus goal-oriented and motivated by the need to reduce the discrepancy between one state of affairs and another.

While we try to solve a problem, we use information available to us from our long-term memory. We also make use of our "here-and-now" perception of the problem situation before us.

A child is asked to solve the arithmatical problem, 25 x 15 =?. A school student is required to solve an algebraic problem, $\frac{8x}{4}+15=19$. For the solution of such problems, a set of rules is to be followed, and if followed correctly, the solution to the problem is guaranteed. This is the algorithmic type of solution. An algorithm is a learned, memorized, working plan or procedure.

Most of the problems we face in life cannot be solved by some set rules, because we do not have algorithms for them. One encounters the problem of unemployment. The wife of a person sues him for a divorce. An earthquake has taken a toll of the lives of sixty thousand people. A country faces the problem of over-population. Such problems and many others cannot be solved by algorithms. In such cases, we try to find a solution by heuristics, that are special strategies devised for the solution of each problem. The strategies which we employ are usually based on our past experience with problems. We also think to innovate old strategies and to create new strategies.

Decision-Making as a Thinking Process: Decision-making is a kind of problem-solving in which we choose out of several alternatives we are presented with.

When there is only one path before us and we must go ahead on that path out of compulsion, we do not make any decision in such a situation. Sometimes, we have two alternatives, and both the alternatives are bad. In this situation, we think and recognize the alternative which is a lesser evil. We decide to follow the path of the lesser evil.

Very often, two or more alternatives are available for us. Life abounds with situations in which we must choose between alternatives. Our decision-making becomes heuristic. We try to estimate that likelihood of outcomes of the different alternatives and decide the one with the most outcome favourable to us. This process is the estimation of subjective probability. In such a thinking activity, we decide if the current situation is similar to one we have encountered before. In other words, we decide whether the current situation is a representation of something we have already experienced. In such a process, we use the heuristic of representativeness to arrive at subjective probabilities.

Creative Thinking: The creative thinker may be an artist, a writer, or a scientist. He/she creates something "new under the sun". The emphasis here is on the word 'new'.

Most creative thinkers feel that their major innovative ideas and discoveries have not been deliberate constructs of their conscious mind but have come to the surface, mysteriously and spontaneously, from the depth of their unconscious mind. The creator of the idea has been doggedly trying and consciously perspiring to get the vision, but without success. He/she instantly gets the symbolism of the vision. The new idea springs into being from the uncons- cious, and the conscious mind has very little role to play to generate it. Such sudden appearance of new ideas is called insight.

It has now been well recognized by cognitive psychologists that information is processed outside the conscious mind (in the unconscious) and that the products of that processing emerge into consciousness. Creative thought or any thought is not a mental process but its product.

Prominent cognitive scientists like George A. Miller of Princeton, and Ulric Neisser of Cornell hold that all conscious thinking is the result of unconscious thinking.[35] They say that we do not know the real reasons of our thinking about any matter as we do.

Creative thinking is done by the unconscious mind, and the thought, once generated, emerges to the conscious mind. With most of our everyday routine acts such as driving, dressing, swimming, cycling, typing, dancing, piano-playing, etc., the unconscious mind is also involved. Donald Norman,[36] Director of the Programme in Cognitive Science at the University of California at San Diego, speaks in favour of this idea. We **will** the act; in other words, we select the act at the conscious level, and then the subconscious completes the details. All the unconscious automatic mental processes operate according to this plan.

The unconscious mind is involved in tennis playing or in beating a musical drum. The same unconscious mind works for creativity like writing a poem, painting, or creating the idea of gravity or relativity. What is the difference then? The difference is clearly markable. Any automatic action is a problem-solving response in which the precise algorithms, by using which the goal can be reached, have already been known and repeatedly practised. The creative idea is also a problem-solving response. We use heuristic search methods to find out a solution. But, the contrasting feature is that we have no previous knowledge on the thought to be created and the goal to be reached. The cognitive scientists put the question: How is it possible for the mind to create a concept it has never known? We don't think that the answer to this question has so far been obtained. It is realized that the product of the unconscious cerebration emerges into the light of consciousness; but what happens in the darkness of that black-box before the emergence of the creative thought remains unknown.

Those who create ideas do have the realization that creativity takes place in the unconscious. Hermann Helmholtz,[37] a German physiologist and physicist, describes his own scientific discoveries as proceeding through three stages. viz., saturation, incubation, illumination. In 1908, the French mathematician Henri Poincaré[38] added a fourth stage, viz., verification, to his creative process. The stage of incubation which takes place in the unconscious is productive of creative ideas.

Reasoning as a Thinking Process: Reasoning or logical thinking is of two types, viz., deductive and inductive. In deductive thinking, we deduce from the general to the particular, general to general, or particular to particular. When the conclusion follows from the premises **necessarily**, the process is called deduction. We may take an example:

All men are mortal.
Socrates is a man.
Therefore Socrates is mortal.

It may be mentioned here that logic is the theory of the conditions of valid inference. The inference may be formally valid, but factually untrue. This would be clear from the following example:

All Prime Ministers of India are males.
Indira Gandhi is the Prime Minister of India.
Therefore Indira Gandhi is a male.

In this second case, the inference is formally valid, but it is factually untrue since the major premise is not factually true.

When the conclusion follows from the premises with a degree of probability less than certainty, the process is called induction. The widespread distinction between induction as an inference moving from specific facts to general conclusions, and deduction as moving from general premises to specific conclusions is no longer held in philosophy. It is a fact that this distinction distinguishes one kind of induction from one kind of deduction. But it cannot distinguish all kinds of inductions from all kinds of deductions. Induction is **probable** inference whereas deduction is necessary inference.

Every night is followed by a day. Everyday is preceded by a night. All men are mortal. All crows are black. All these statements are inductive. The sun may explode and disintegrate. If that happens, the first two statements would be wrong. Any statement which is not self-contradictory may be a possibility. Some day an immortal person may be born. Its theoretical possibility cannot be ruled out. If that ever happens, the third statement would be wrong. Animal breeders and geneticists may induce artificial mutation in black crows, and thereby they may be successful in breeding a white crow. If that ever happens, the fourth statement would be wrong.

After conducting a large-scale investigation, doctors concluded that smoking causes lung-cancer. They studied one hundred million smokers and one hundred million non-smokers to come to this conclusion. Someone who is 95 years old and a chain-smoker refutes the conclusion of the doctors. Such refutation is based on misunderstanding. Many smokers suffer from lung-cancers whereas some smokers don't. Many non-smokers do not get lung-cancer; but some non-smokers do get it. It may be a fact that more than 95 per cent of smokers are prone to lung-cancers and less than 5 per cent of non-smokers are also prone to it. The whole concept of induction would be topsy-turvy if we exclude 'probability' from our judgement.

The Greek philosophers like Plato and Aristotle and many Western philosophers like Spinoza and Leibniz believed that the way to explore the nature of reality was by means of rigorously deductive thinking. This concept on reason and reality was later discarded. Deductive thinking is not a means by which our minds can effectively interpret the larger part of the reality around us.

Immanuel Kant, in the eighteenth century, has shown that pure reason, when applied to topics such as God, soul, and immortality which are external to our possible experience, can lead to contradictory conclusions. In the earlier part of the twentieth century, Alfred North Whitehead, Bertrand Russell, Rudolf Carnap, and all logical positivists have made a shift of the issue. According to their view, the laws of logic deal with the relationship among statements we make but have no direct bearing upon reality other than the reality of thoughts. In the opinion of Russell, logic and mathematics are valuable tools for handling the knowledge we acquire, but neither one can produce new knowledge, except about itself. He further says that all the important inferences outside logic and mathematics are inductive rather than deductive. His observation on the exceptional nature of law and theology, the inferences of which are neither deductive nor inductive, is noteworthy. According to him, law derives its first principles from the statute books, and theology from the scriptures, both statute books and scriptures being unquestionable.

Reasoning is an important activity of the thinking brain. Cognitive science has not yet explored the details of the neural mechanisms involved. Aristotle's statement. "Man is a rational animal", may be disputed, since it is not factually so. Of course, if man should be a rational animal, he has the capability of being so.

Summary

After finishing the chapter on the concept of mind in psychology, it becomes awkward to say that the conceptual field is more confusing and less clear. If we start psychology with René Descartes, his dualism of matter and mind is hard to be acceptable at the present level of our knowledge. Many schools of psychology have come and gone. We have discussed associationalism, structuralism, functionalism, behaviourism, Gestalt psychology, psychoanalysis, analytical psychology, and cognitive psychology. In no system could we get a clear concept of mind.

The school of behaviourism did not accept anything like mind which was a "black box" for the behaviourists. They recognized the stimulus that went into the "black box"; they recognized the response that came out of the "black box". The stimulus and the response were observable for them. The activities of the "black box" were unobservable and hence, in their opinion, unspeakable.

The psychoanalytic school seemed to recognize mind. It

analysed the conscious mind and the unconscious mind. It spoke of the id, the ego, and the superego. But all these terms did not represent anatomical entities; neither were they physical entities of any kind. If they would be considered as psychological entities, they were speculative ones and, in the strict sense, non-entities. These were descriptive terms to explain psychological phenomena. Thus Freud's depth psychology was alright for description, but it lacked the dimension of 'depth'. There was no spatial reference to upper, middle, and lower loci in any longitudinal axis of an entity with spatial dimensions of length and breadth. Freud did not say that the brain and the mind were identical; neither did he say that they were different. His over-emphasis on psychosexual development has made his psychology highly controversial and totally imbalanced. Some philosophers and psychologists have considered 'brain' as a structural term and 'mind' as a functional term. As they think, these two terms refer to the same 'entity'; but the sum total of the functions of that structural entity is referred to as the 'mind'. The cognitive psychologists who reacted against the behaviourists have started their work since the 1960s. They try to open the "black box", and they identify its structures and functions in a wider perspective of psychology. For them, mind is not different from the brain. If these two terms convey different connontations for them, the structure is the brain whose functions refer to the mind. In a nutshell, the older concept of mind does not find a place in modern psychology.

Notes

1. James, W., 1890, *The Principles of Philosophy*.
2. Darwin, C., 1872, *The Expressions of Emotions in Man and Animals*.
3. Watson, J.B., 1925, *Behaviourism*. Quoted in Sing, A.K. 1991, *The Comprehensive History of Psychology*, pp. 225-26.
4. Skinner, B.F., 1972, "A lecture on 'having' a poem", In *Cumulative Record*, A Selection of Papers (3rd edn.), pp. 352-54.
5. Bower, G.H. and Hilgard, E.R., 1981, *Theories of Learning*, p. 325.
6. McDougall, W., 1908, *Social Psychology*, p. 282.

7. Gregory, R.L., 1984, (1st publ. 1981) *Mind in Science*, p. 488.

8. Freud, S., 1978, (1st publ. 1900) *The Interpretation of Dreams*, transl. by James Strachey. Cha. 7B, pp. 684-92.

9. Freud, S., 1900, (Stand. edn. 1953) *The Interpretation of Dreams.*

10. Jung, C.G., 1968, (1st publ. 1928) *Analytical Psychology: Its Theory and Practice.*

11. Reber, A.S., 1985, *The Penguin Dictionary of Psychology*, pp. 360-61.

12. Jung, C.G., 1959, *The Archetype of Collective Unconscious*, p. 43.

13. *Ibid.*, p. 75.

14. Sheldrake, R., 1985, (1st publ. 1981) *A New Science of Life: The Hypothesis of Formative Causation*, p. 27.

15. Riesen, A.H., 1966, *Sensory Deprivation*, In E. Stellar and J.M. Sprague (Eds.), *Progress in Physiological Psychology* (Vol. I).

16. Senden, M.V., 1960, *Space and Sight* (P. Heath, tr.).

17. Lenneberg, E.H., 1967, *Biological Foundations of Language.*

18. Curtiss, S., 1977, *Genie: A Psycholinguistic Study of a Modern-Day "Wild Child".*

19. Pines, M., 1981, The Civilizing of Genie, In *Psychology Today*. 15 (Sept.), pp. 28-34.

20. Riesen, A.H., 1965, Effects of Early Deprivation of Photic Stimulation, In S. Osler and R. Cooke (eds.) *The Bio-Social Basis of Mental Retardation.*

21. Blakemore, C., 1974, Developmental Factors in the Formation of Feature Extracting Neurons, In F.O. Schmitt and F.G. Worden (eds.) *The Neuro-Sciences: Third Study Program.*

22. Barlow, H.B., 1975, Visual Experiences and Cortical Development, In *Nature*, 258: 199-204.

23. Mitchell, D.E., 1977, The Influence of Early Visual Experience on Visual Perception, In C.S. Harris (ed.) *Visual Coding and Adaptability.*

24. Flexner, L., 1967, Dissection of Memory in Mice with Antibiotics, In *Proceedings of the American Philosophical Society*, 111: 343-46

25. Hyden, H., 1969, Biochemical Aspects of Learning and Memory, In K. Pribram (ed.) *On the Biology of Learning.*

26. McConnel, J.V. Shigehisa, T., and Salive, H., 1970, Attempts to Transfer Approach and Avoidance Responses by RNA Injections in Rats, In K.H. Pribram and D.E. Broadbent (eds.) *Biology of Memory.*

27. Morgan, C.T., King, R.A., Weisz., J.R., and Schopler, J., 1986, (1st publ. 1956) *Introduction to Psychology*, 7th edn.

28. Arendt, H., 1977-78, *The Life of the Mind*, Vol. I: *Thinking.*

29. Whorf, B.L., 1956, *Language. Thought, and Reality.*

30. Furth, H., 1971, Linguistic deficiency and thinking: Research with deaf subjects 1964-69, In *Psychological Bulletin*, 75: 58-72.

31. Goldin-Meadow, S. and Feldman, H., 1977, The development of language-like communication without a language model, In *Science*, 197: 401-03.

32. Shepard, R.N., 1978, "Externalization of Mental Images and the Act of Creation", In *Visual Learning, Thinking, and Communication*, edited by B.S. Randhawa and W.E. Coffman.

33. Hadamard, J., 1945, *The Psychology of Invention in the Mathematical Field.*

34. Penrose, R., 1989, *The Emperor's New Mind*, p. 424.

35. Hunt, M., 1982, *The Universe Within: A New Science Explores the Human Mind*, p. 276.

36. *Ibid.*, p. 277.

37. *Ibid.*, p. 295.

38. *Ibid.*

9

The Concept of Mind in Science

THE word 'mind' is used in science. But it is a functional term which structurally refers to the nervous system, especially the brain. At the outset, we will present a brief discussion of the anatomy and the physiology of the nervous system.

Systems within the Nervous System

The nervous system is divided into two sub-systems, viz., central nervous system (CNS) and peripheral nervous system (PNS). The CNS is composed of the brain and the spinal cord. The brain is located inside the skull. The spinal cord is an elongated bundle of nerves running down the hollow of the bony spinal column.

The PNS consists of all the cranial and the spinal nerves, including their branches. Twelve pairs of nerves branch out from the brain itself. They are called cranial nerves. Organs like the eyes and the ears are directly connected with the brain by the cranial nerves. Thirty-one pairs of nerves branch out from the spinal cord. They are called spinal nerves. The hands, the legs, and the peripheral parts of the rest of the body are innervated by the spinal nerves and their branches. Both the cranial and the spinal nerves come in pairs, usually one of the pair leading to the left side, and the other to the right. A schematic diagram of the nervous system in the body is presented in *fig.* 9.1.

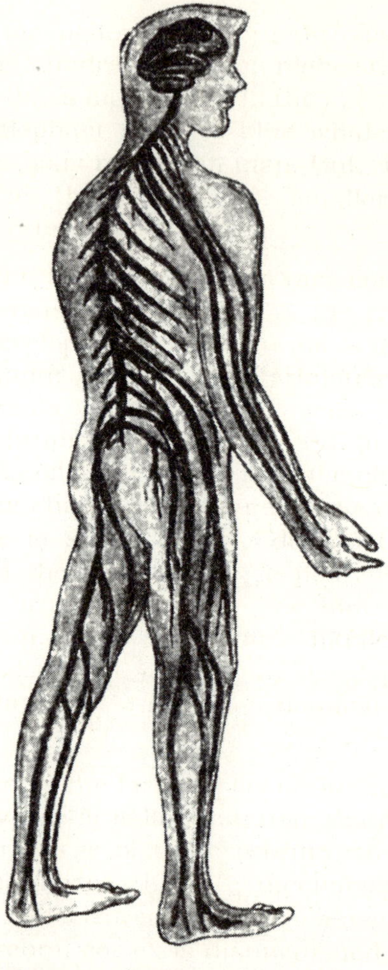

fig. 9.1: A schematic diagram of the nervous system.

A nerve looks like a bundle of white nylon fibres. It conducts electrical impulses and thereby transmits messages. Depending upon the direction of the transmission of the message, nerves are classified as sensory (afferent) and motor (efferent) nerves. When messages travel from the body and senses to the CNS, the concerned nerve-pathway is sensory or afferent. When messages are transmitted from the CNS to the body parts that are to react, the concerned nerve pathway is motor or efferent.

A nerve cell is called a neuron. Motor neurons which are the work crews of the PNS cause things to happen. Those motor neurons that cause voluntary muscle movements belong to the somatic or skeletal system. A person lifts his hand, or walks, or climbs stairs. The muscle movements involved in such actions are voluntary. There are involuntary muscle movements as in the beating of the heart, the movement of the stomach wall, the intestinal wall, the bladder wall, etc. The involuntary muscle movements are not ordinarily under our voluntary control. They happen without our knowing about them. Motor neurons that regulate involuntary muscle actions belong to the autonomic system. The autonomic system either accelerates or retards the muscle actions. The sympathetic nervous system speeds the muscle actions whereas the parasympathetic nervous system slows down.

It has already been mentioned that the autonomic nervous system is divided into two sub-systems — the sympathetic and the parasympathetic. Both these sub-systems are apparently antagonistic to each other. The sympathetic system accelerates the heart-beat which is retarded by the parasympathetic system. Due to sympathetic stimulation, more of adrenaline is secreted, resulting in vasoconstriction and consequent hypertension. Parasympathetic stimulation does the reverse to the cardiovascular system.

The sympathetic system is activated in emergencies and stresses. In stressful conditions, pupils dilate, heart-beat speeds up, breathing deepens, digestion slows, blood pressure rises, more blood flows to the limbs and brain, and blood sugar rises. The sympathetic system raises a war and mobilizes the body for maximum use of energy.

The parasympathetic system apparently opposes the sympathetic system and reverses the emergency or stress physiology. It tries to normalize our internal organs and glands. It tries to restore peace in our body system and thereby stores and conserves energy.

Both the sympathetic and parasympathetic systems work for the interest of the organism and, in this work, they complement each other. Hence, as far as the total organism is concerned, the two sub-systems are not antagonistic. Under stress, the sympathetic system dominates; during times of relaxation, the parasympathetic system becomes dominant.

The nervous system, including the CNS and the PNS, is the body's operation and communication network, all of which is controlled by the brain. The brain, directly or indirectly, controls our conscious efforts as well as our unconscious ones. I wish to pick up a pen and I do it. This is my conscious effort. My heart beats, without interruptions from my intra-unterine life to my death. My blood circulates through my blood vessels without my conscious effort for it. My lungs expand and contract and thus my breathing becomes a continuous process from my birth to my death. My stomach, intestines, and pancreas work for the digestion of my food without my conscious efforts. My endocrine glands secrete hormones as and when they are required, and for such actions I do not consciously try. My internal body temperature is regulated through a number of mechanisms without my conscious efforts. When bacterias or viruses attack my system, my body combats the invasion without my conscious efforts. But, in all these complex automatic functions of the body, my nervous system plays a role, without which none of these meaningful and yet unconscious function would successfully operate.

Functions of the Spinal Cord

The spinal cord located within the column formed by the vertebrae is basically a transmission cable of nerve fibres. In the analogy of telephone wires, these fibres provide communication between the brain and the various parts of the body. When a telephone wire is severed, communication is disrupted. When nerves in the spinal cord are damaged, the brain cannot send a message to muscles to act. If the damage to nerve in the spinal cord is slight, disruption in nerve communication is temporary like a short-circuit in the electric transmission wire. A nerve with a minor injury may repair itself. When damage to a nerve in the spinal cord is severe, it cannot be healed, and any technique has not yet been known to repair medically. In such a case, communication between the brain and the peripheral parts of the body is bound to cease. Muscles, without getting message from the brain to act, are paralyzed. The area of paralysis is below the level of the injury to the spinal cord. The higher up the injury in the spinal cord, the more of the body paralyzed.

The bony vertebral column provides a good protection to the spinal cord, which is hardly damaged unless some serious accident occurs, or weapons or bullets cause the injury. In addition to accidents and weapons, certain diseases, like poliomyelitis, and genetic disorders can destroy motor nerves in the spine.

The spinal cord possesses some decision-making power. Whenever something happens to the body and urgent measure is to be taken for the protection of the body, the spinal cord immediately takes action and informs the brain. Thus the spinal cord is an important reflex centre.

We may give an example of a reflex action. A lady is ironing clothes. Her right hand touches the hot iron. Immediately, without thinking, she pulls her hand away. This is a reflex action accomplished by a reflex centre in the spinal cord before the brain feels the pain. For reflex actions, the decision and the command of the brain are not required by the spinal cord, which itself takes action, and simultaneously informs the brain.

The basic unit of integrated neural activity is the reflex arc. It is illustrated in *fig* 9.2. The arc consists of a sense-organ, an afferent neuron, one or more synapses in a central integrating station, an efferent neuron, and an effector. In man and other mammals, the afferent and the efferent somatic neurons are connected in the brain and the spinal cord. For spinal reflex arcs, the afferent neurons enter the spinal column via the dorsal roots, and the efferent fibres leave via the ventral roots. The dorsal roots are sensory whereas the ventral roots are motor. The afferent neurons have their cell bodies in the dorsal root ganglia.

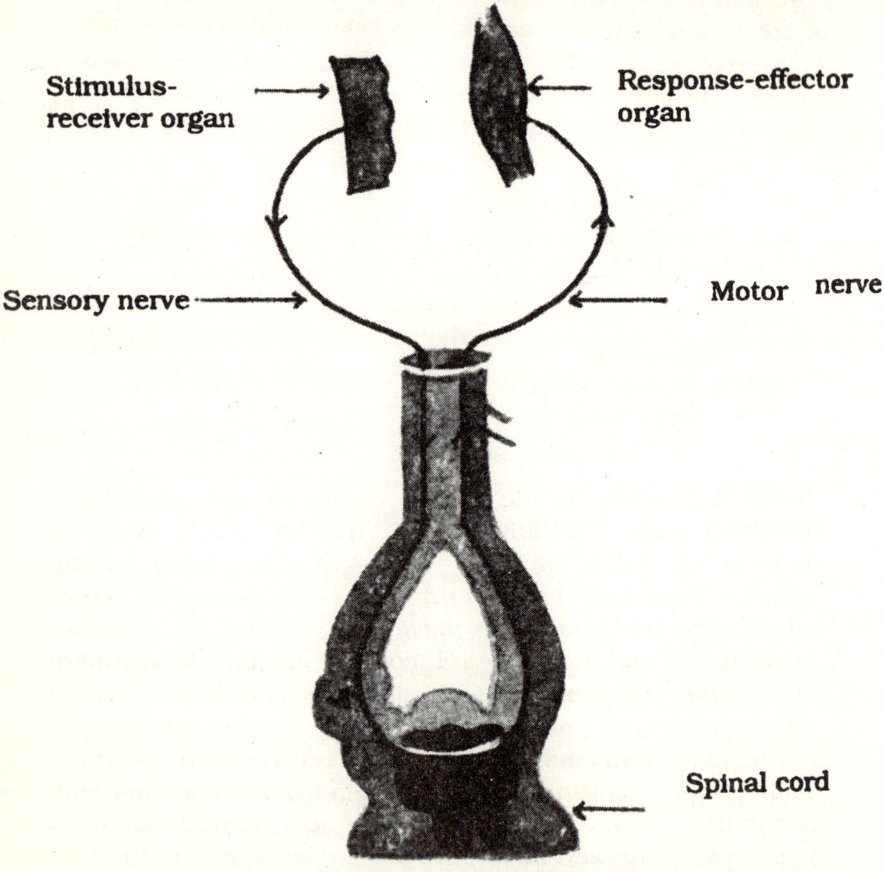

fig. 9.2: The basic units of a reflex arc.

Neurons and Synapses

A nerve-cell is known as a neuron. It has some special

features to distinguish it from other body cells. A diagrammatic picture of a spinal motor neuron with myelinated axon has been presented in *fig.* 9.3. The neuron has a main cell body or soma with a nucleus in the centre. Many processes called dendrites extend out from the cell body and arborize extensively. There is a thickened area called axon hillock on one side of the cell body. A long fibrous axon originates from this hillock. Before the termination of the long axon, it branches. Each branch or sub-branch is enlarged to form a terminal button or synaptic knob. Each knob contains a

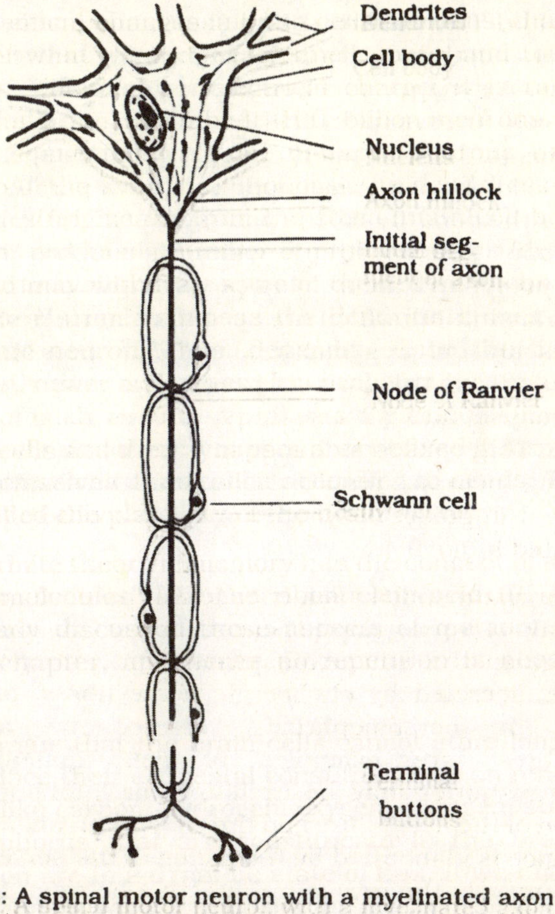

fig. 9.3: A spinal motor neuron with a myelinated axon.

number of vesicles that secrete special chemicals known as neurotransmitters. Except at the origin and the ending, the axon of a myelinated nerve fibre is enveloped by a sheath of myelin which is a protein-lipid complex. The myelin sheath is discontinuous, with constrictions about 1mm apart. All neurons are, however, not myelinated. Some mammalian neurons and most neurons in invertebrates are unmyelinated.

Signals are transferred from one nerve cell to another. This is done through electrical events and certain chemicals. The electrical impulse cannot pass from one neuron to another due to lack of continuity between any two neurons. A synaptic junction is one where the axon of one nerve cell (presynaptic cell) terminates on the soma or dendrites (or both) of another nerve cell (postsynaptic cell). Synaptic knobs of a presynaptic cell are separated from the soma or the dendrites of the post-synaptic cell by a synaptic cleft about 200 angstroms wide. Signals are transferred from a presynaptic neuron to a postsynaptic neuron through neurotransmitters which are special chemicals secreted by vesicles present in synaptic knobs. The neurotransmitter diffuses across the narrow space between the two cells at the synapse and affects the dendrites of the receiving neuron. This causes a change in the electric charge of the receiving neuron, resulting in the transmission of an electrical impulse. A synapse has been diagrammatically presented in *fig.* 9.4.

A neurotransmitter is a chemical substance secreted by terminals of a presynaptic neuron for the transmission of a message to the immediate postsynaptic neuron. Acetylcholine, secreted by cholinergic nerve fibres, and epinephrine or norepinephrine, secreted by adrenergic nervefibres, are examples of neurotransmitters. A neurotransmitter may be excitatory or inhibitory. At the junction of the nerve fibre and the effector organ, a chemical substance is elaborated by the action of the nerve impluse. An example is the myoneural junction between the termination of a nerve fibre and a muscle. Such a chemical

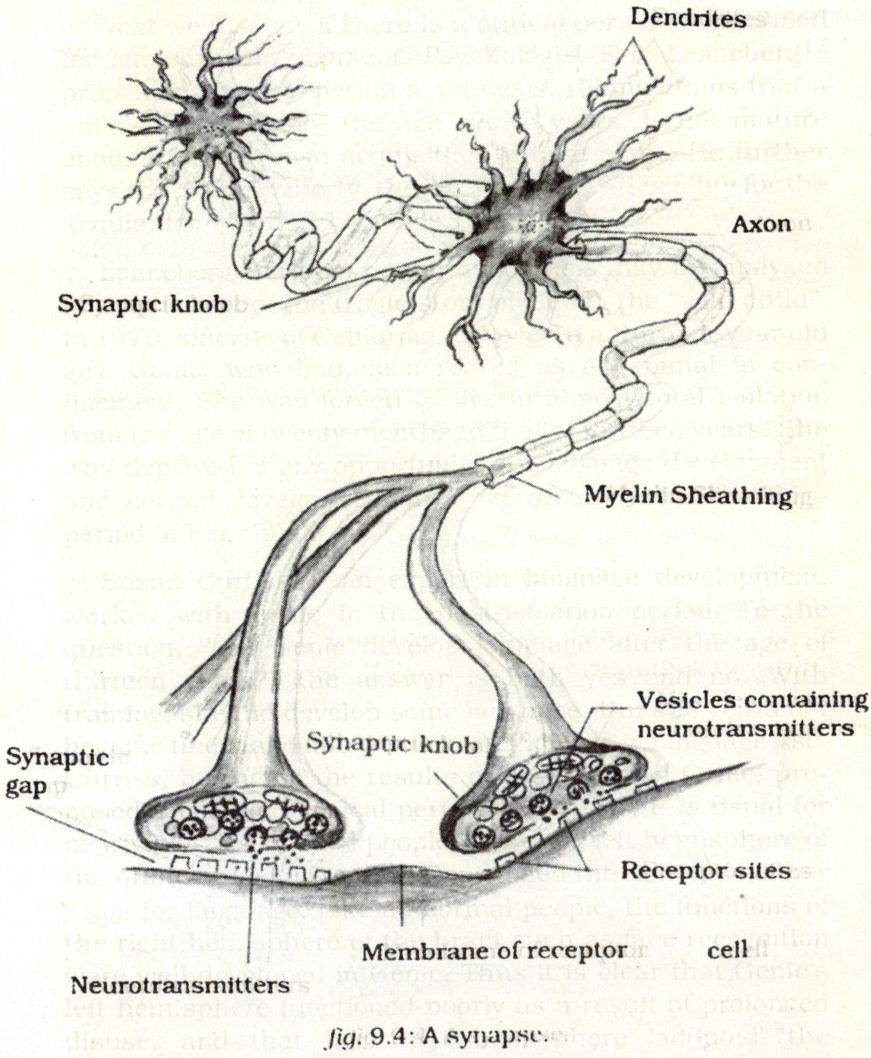

fig. 9.4: A synapse.

substance, known as a chemical mediator or a neuro-hormone, is responsible for the transmission of the nerve impulse from the nerve fibre to the muscle or any other effector organ. Acetylcholine is the mediator at all synapses between preganglionic and postganglionic fibres of the autonomic nervous system, at the myoneural junction, at all postganglionic parasympathetic, and at some post-ganglionic sympathetic endings. Norepinephrine is the chemical mediator at most postganglionic sympathetic endings in the autonomic nervous system. Thus nerve endings are biologic transducers that convert electrical energy into chemical energy. What has been said here about the chemical transmission of messages in the autonomic nervous system and at the myoneural junctions also holds good for the central nervous system.

The Electrical Activity in a Nerve

An electric current flows in a conducting wire such as a copper wire. Essentially the same thing happens in a nerve fibre. But the mechanism is more complicated in the nerve than in the conducting wire.

The nerve cell membrane is polarized at rest, with positive charges lined up along the outside of the membrane and negative charges along the inside. This charge distribution on both sides of the membrane is due to the differential distribution of sodium (Na^+), postassium (K^+) and

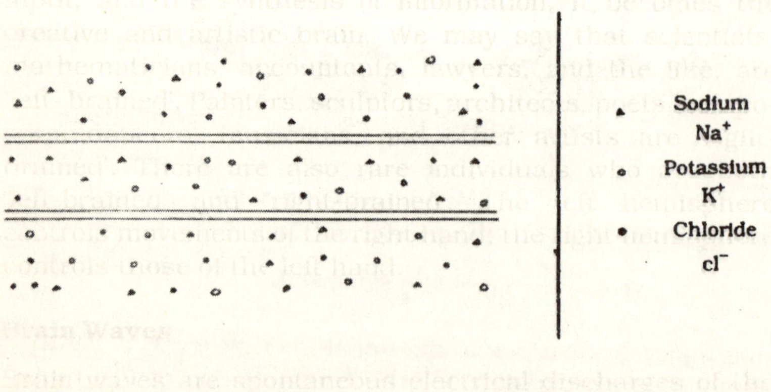

fig. 9.5: The charge distribution outside and inside the nerve-cell membrane.

chloride (Cl^-) ions. Sodium ions are in higher concentration in the solution outside the nerve cell membrane; potassium ions are relatively more in the solution inside the nerve cell membrane. A net positive charge outside is due to the preponderance of sodium and potassium ions over chloride ions. A net negative charge inside is caused by excess of choride ions over sodium and potassium ions (*fig.* 9.5).

Processes start functioning to initiate a nerve impulse. The first process to generate a signal lies in the nerve cell membrane becoming 'leaky', so that sodium ions enter inside and potassium ions pass outside. To compensate for this migratory activity of sodium and potassium ions across the cell membrane, a "metabolic pump" very slowly pumps sodium ions back out. Similarly, another metabolic pump, on a somewhat smaller scale, pumps potassium ions back in. This unequal pumping contributes to the potassium excess on the inside. And thus a charge imbalance on both sides of the membrane is created.

A nerve signal is a region of charge reversal travelling along the fibre. At its head, sodium gates open to allow the sodium ions to flow inwards. At its tail, potassium gates open to allow the potassium ions to flow outwards. In spite of the metabolic pumps acting to restore the *status quo*, the nerve fibre is depolarized in a region. At this stage, the charge becomes positive inside and negative outside in that region. The signal consists simply of a region of charge reversal moving along the fibre. The sodium and potassium ions move along very little; they just move in and out across the cell membrane; but the electric charge moves along the nerve fibre. This self-propagating nature of the nerve impulse is due to circular current flow and successive electrotonic depolarizations ahead of the action potential (*fig.* 9.6).

The sequence of events just described moves regularly along an unmyelinated axon to its end. The conduction of an impulse in myelinated axons follows a similar pattern of circular current flow. However, there is a difference between

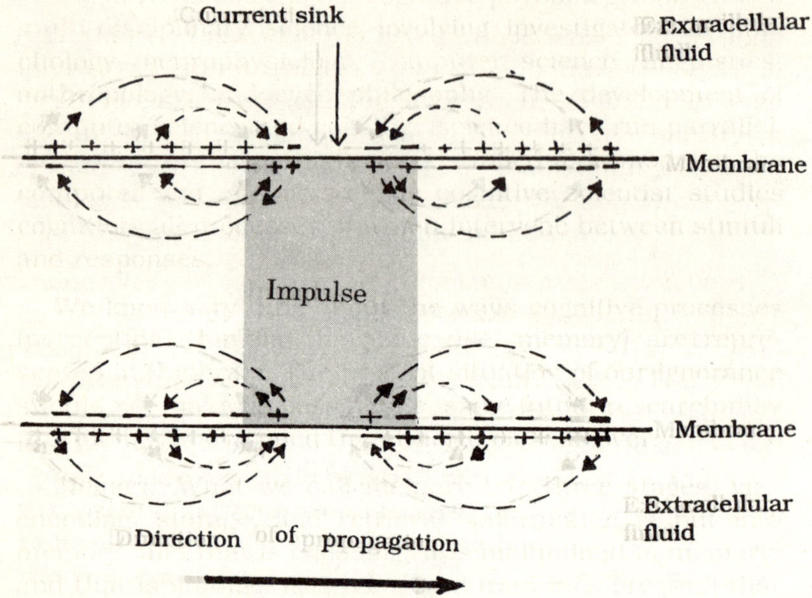

fig. 9.6: The propagation of the nerve-impulse.

the conductions of nerve impulses through unmyelinated and myelinated nerve fibres. The current flow through myelin is negligible since it is relatively an effective insulator. Depolarization in myelinated axons jumps from one node of Ranvier to the next. This jumping of depolarization from node to node is called saltatory conduction (*fig.* 9.7.). Nerve signals travel in myelinated axons at a speed of about 120 metres per second. This conduction speed in myelinated axons is about 50 times faster than that in the fastest unmyelinated axons.

An axon of a nerve can conduct an impulse in either direction. But, in a living animal, impulses normally pass in one direction only. They pass from synaptic junctions or receptors along axons to their terminations. Synapses, unlike axons, permit conduction in one direction only. Such unidirectional conduction is called orthodromic.

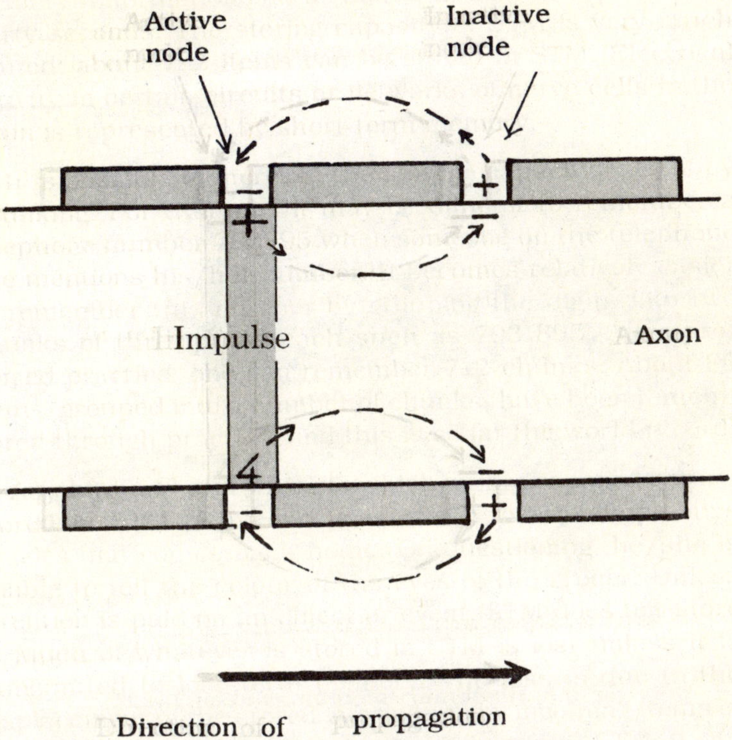

fig. 9.7: Saltatory conduction in myelinated axons — the jumping of depolarization from one node of Ranvier to another.

The Macro-Structures of the Brain

The brain is located inside the cranium which is a double-layered bony box with trusses connecting the two layers of the cranial bones. It is well-protected unless it is damaged by accidents, bullets, or weapons.

Neuroscientist Paul MacLean divides the brain into three parts, viz., hindbrain (rhombencephalon), midbrain (mesencephalon), and forebrain (prosencephalon). The structures of these three parts of the brain have been illustrated in *fig.* 9.8.

The hindbrain is the primitive brain which is almost

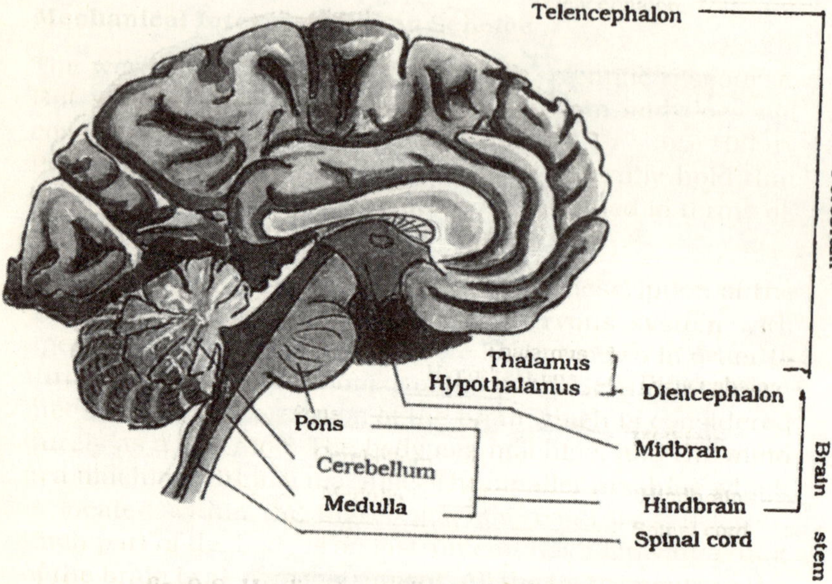

fig. 9.8: Hindbrain, midbrain, and forebrain.

common in mammals and lower vertebrates. Structures at the very top of the spinal cord and portions of the brain stem constitute the hindbrain, which contains the medulla, the cerebellum, and the pons. In the posterior and ventral part of the cerebrum are located two ball-like structures, one on each side. These are the cerebella. The cerebellum is larger in man than in animals. Its thin outer layer contains grey matter and its thick inner layer contains white matter. The cerebellar cortex has convolutions for the increase of the surface area of the grey matter. The pons and the medulla are ventral to the cerebella which hide the former two structures, when viewed from the top. The medulla is immediately anterior to the spinal cord.

The hindbrain of man resembles the total brain possessed by reptiles such as lizards and snakes. In

MacLean's terminology, it is the reptilian brain. It is mainly devoted to life support. Actions such as breathing, heartbeat, and muscle movements are regulated by the hindbrain. Basic drives such as eating, mating, and self-protection are also under the control of the hindbrain.

The limbic system is extended in the core of the hindbrain, the midbrain, and the forebrain, its major part being a component of the midbrain. Formerly, the midbrain was known as the rhinencephalon which was known to be responsible for the perception of smell. But it was later discovered that the olfactory function of the midbrain was restricted to a small area only. The major portion of the midbrain is now called the limbic system. It is not so well developed in reptiles; but it is prominent, both structurally and functionally, in mammals. Each cerebral hemisphere has a limbic lobe which consists of a rim of cortical tissue around the hilum of the cerebral hemisphere and a group of associated deep structures — the amygdala, the hippocampus, and the septal nuclei.

The limbic system regulates behaviour, involving complex emotional responses. The neocortex and the limbic system are poorly connected. Hence, emotions are hardly turned on and off at will. Following stimulation of the limbic circuits, there is prolonged after-discharge. This explains, partly at least, the prolonged nature of emotional responses.

The reticular formation has one part in the midbrain and another part in the hindbrain. It occupies the midventral portion of the medulla and the midbrain. It is made up of myriads of small neurons arranged in complex intertwining nets. It is responsible for the general state of alertness of the brain. Whenever the reticular formation is active, the brain is in a waking conscious state. The state of inactivity of the reticular formation corresponds to the unconscious state.

The forebrain consists of the telencephalon or cerebrum and the diencephalon or the thalamus and the hypothalamus. In addition, it contains the corpus callosum, hippocampus, and many other parts as well. The human species has a far higher ratio of brain-to-body weight than the others. It is hundreds of times higher than in the rats, and five to ten times higher than in the apes. A few animals such as the elephant and the blue whale have an even higher brain-to-body ratio than man. But, in spite of their large brain size, they have a far smaller proportion of uncommitted cortex.

The cerebrum is the most important component of the forebrain. Whereas the hindbrain is the most ancient in evolutionary development, the forebrain is the newest. The cerebrum is more developed in primates than in non-primate mammals. The human species has the most developed cerebrum in the animal world. In size, the brain of the monkey is one-fourth of that of the chimpanzee, and the brain of the chimpanzee is one-fourth of that of man. This difference in size is mainly due to the differential development of the cerebrum. The possession of a very developed cerebrum by man makes him unique in the animal kingdom. His reasoning, intellectuality, and creativity are ascribed to this highly developed cerebrum. In the human adult, the forebrain dominates in size and complexity.

The cerebrum is the largest part of the human brain. In relation to body size, it is larger in man than in animals. In spite of the large size of the cerebrum, the largeness is inadequate, and hence there is mechanism for further increase of the surface area without increasing the volume. The human cerebral cortex is distinguished by its greater quantity of convolutions or gyri. The cortex is folded and refolded to produce vallyes (fissures and sulci) and ridges in it. This process increases the surface area of the cortex and allows a maximum amount of grey matter to be packed within the limited capacity of the skull. The brains of lower mammals have relatively smoother cortexes due to less cortical convolutions, resulting in less surface area and less grey matter. The cerebrum has comparatively thin (about 2.5 mm in thickness) outer surface layers of grey matter and larger inner layers of white matter. The nuclei of the nerve cells that are predominantly present in the cortex impart the grey colour. The white matter consists of long nerve fibres carrying signal from one part of the brain to another. The axons of the nerve fibres are myelinated. The myelin sheath is white in colour, and hence is the colour of the white matter.

The cerebrum is divided down the middle into left and right cerebral hemispheres by a deep cleft, or fissure, called the longitudinal fissure. The front portion of the cerebrum is known as the frontal lobe, and the extreme back portion is the occipital lobe. In between the frontal and the occipital lobes are the parietal lobe at the top and the temporal lobe at the sides. All these lobes are present in both the hemispheres. We use the term 'neocortex' for the evolutionarily most recent and most complex of neural tissue, the brain's grey outermost layer. The frontal, parietal, temporal, and occipital lobes of the brain consist of neocortex.

The prefrontal lobe pertains to the anterior part of the frontal lobes of the brain. About 40 per cent of the human cerbral cortex is in the frontal lobes. With the exception of the motor area immediately in front of the central sulcus and Broca's area, much of this cortical region has no primary sensory or motor functions, and is therefore regarded as the association cortex. The association cortex of the frontal lobe, being farthest forward in the head, is known as prefrontal cortex. The prefrontal cortex is interconnected with a number of cortical areas in the brain. It has connections with the visual, auditory, and somato-sensory cortical areas, and with other association cortex in the parietal and temporal lobes. It has also connections with the thalamus, and many non-cortical structures of the brain.

The superiority of *Homo sapiens* over all species of animals is attributable to the higher development of the cerebral cortex. Man is unique for his ability to use spoken and written language. He has the ability to think, imagine, and conceive. He can analyse and integrate his experiences to solve problems. He can plan ahead and foresee the future. All this is possible due to the functions of the highly evolved cerebral cortex which man possesses.

Much of the rear part of the brain is specialized and is committed to bodily functions. In contrast, the forebrain (chiefly the frontal and temporal lobes) is relatively non-specific and freed from bodily functions. It is very much larger in the human species than in other animals. The process called thinking is the result of the interaction of its various areas in highly complex ways.

What we call "uncommitted cortex" is the forebrain's grey matter uncommitted to bodily tasks. It is uncommitted to sensory and motor functions and therefore available for higher mental processes.

The Micro-structures of the Brain

The central nervous system contains two main classes of cells, viz., neurons or nerve cells, and non-neuronal cells. Neurons are the brain's excitable cells; these are the ones that 'fire' to send signals. The rest of the brain cells are non-excitable; they support the neurons' work. The bulk of the non-neuronal cells are collectively known as neuroglia (or glia). In addition to neurons and glial cells, the brain has several other kinds of cells. Blood vessels — arteries, veins, and capillaries — that serve the brain tissue are made of cells. Inside the brain, there are canals and cavities that hold cerebrospinal fluid that acts as shock-absorber to protect the brain. The lining cells of these canals and cavities are special ones.

Neurons and glial cells in the surrounding nerve glue are present in the brain in the proportion of 1:5 to 10. What do these glial cells do? We do not know all functions of the glial cells, but we have been able to know a few. During the development of the brain before birth, certain glial cells aid neurons in their migration to their ultimate sites in the nervous system. In this function, glial cells act as ladders or scaffolds. New glial cells are also formed after birth. By adulthood up to half of the brain's volume consists of glial cells. Astrocytes and oligodendrocytes are the two major types of glial cells. The former are star-shaped in form. Glial cells, previously thought to be inert and passive, have been known to interact constantly with neurons to affect the electrochemical processes that underlie the transmission of nerve-impulses. It has been conjectured that the glial cells play a role in the healing process of an injured brain tissue. Astrocytes function in the maintenance of blood-brain barrier, which allows some substances into the brain and keeps others out. Oligodendrocytes function in the formation of the myelin sheath that wraps around the axons of myelinated nerve fibres.

The neurons are the most important cells in the nervous system. They send and receive information through electrical and chemical activity. A nerve impulse is purely an electrical signal. Hence the transmission of a message through a nerve fibre is the same as the conduction of an electrical signal. Unlike the other body cells, the neurons constantly change themselves to adapt to newer situations demanding changes in the communication network and memory functioning (*fig.* 9.9). Such adaptive changes in the structuring and functioning of the brain cells is known as brain plasticity. The brain is not simply a fixed collection of wired-up neurons. The inter-connections between neurons are changing all the time, without changes in the locations of axons and dendrites. Changes in old neuronal network and establishment of new neuronal network can be effected through active changes at the synaptic junctions. The actual changes occur at places called dendritic spines, which are tiny protuberances on dendrites. The synaptic knobs of presynaptic neuron and the dendritic spines of a post-synatpic neuron make 'contact' for the transmission of nerve impulses. Here 'contact' is not actual touching, but leaving a narrow gap (synaptic cleft) which is narrow enough for the relaying action of the neurotransmitter. The right gap is about forty-thousandths of a millimetre. Under certain

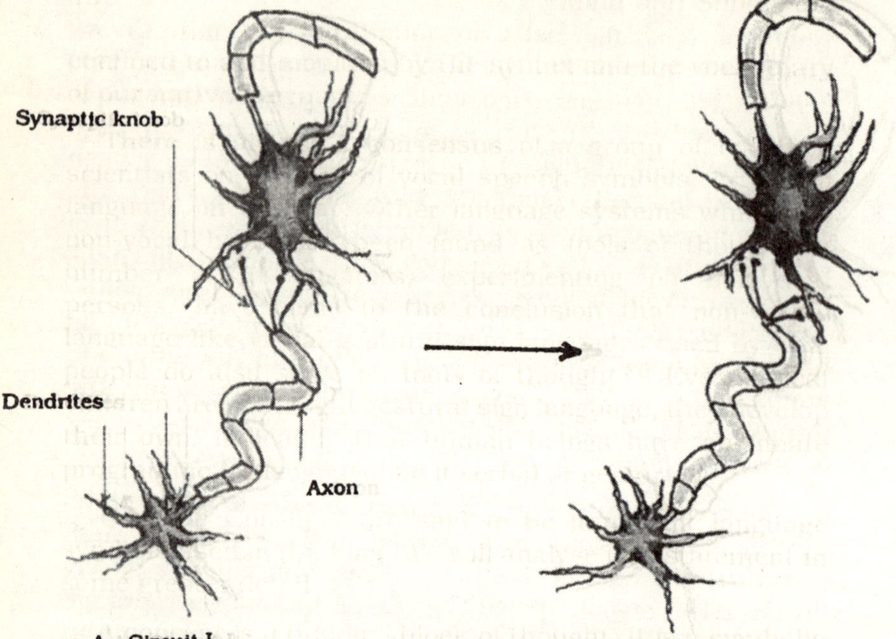

fig. 9.9: Brain-plasticity, showing adaptive changes in the structuring and functioning of the brain-cells.

conditions, the dendritic spines shrink away and break contact. Under certain other conditions, new dendritic spines appear at newer sites in the dendrites and grow to make new contacts. Some theorists of long-term memory hold that such changes in synaptic connections provide the means of storing information. Each neuron has hundreds to thousands of connections with other neurons. Some neurons in the cerebrum have a great many more links. The soma of a neuron has many dendrites and each dendrite can increase or decrease the number of dendritic spines. More than 100 billion (1 billion = 10^9) neurons work together in the brain in ever-changing relationships. We can comprehend the gigantic complexity in the network of the brain especially when we consider the plasticity of the brain.

How many nerve cells do we have in our brain? This

number fluctuates from person to person and from age to age. On the average, a person has over 100 billion neurons in his/her brain at the time of birth. Some others estimate the figure as at least 150 billions. All these neurons have been formed in the prenatal period. Their number continues to decline throughout the life. Neurons die and the dead neurons are never replaced during the life. Our other body cells, like the nerve cells, are worn out or die; but unlike the nerve cells, the non-neuronal cells are replaced when they are worn out or die. Nerve cells are not born during post-natal life; neither do they regenerate to repair themselves when they are injured and damaged.

By the time a person attains twenty years of age, his nerve cells die by thousands a day, and all the dead neurons are never replaced. Even if 5,000 neurons die a day, the number of living neurons at the age of 90 would be 99.983385 billions, if we presume that 100 billion neurons were present at the time of birth. Cognitive processes slow down as we grow older. But the effect of aging on the mental abilities of persons fluctuates to widely varying degrees.

Functions of the Brain Structures

Any individual structure of the brain does not function in an isolated way. There are many structures that play specific roles. There are other functions that are taken up by a number of structures. However, the brain parts work harmoniously in an integrated way. The parts are inter-connected and they interplay.

MEDULLA OBLONGATA

The medulla oblongata has centres for the automatic reflex control of respiration, heartbeat, and blood pressure. These are called the vital centres since damage to them is usually fatal. The heart organ itself has its own autonomy and thus continues to beat throughout life. Had the heart been controlled by the will for its beating, it could have been incompatible with life. The acceleration or retardation of the heart, as demanded by special situations, and so also the respiration are regulated by the cardioregulatory centre and the respiratory centre, respectively, present in the medulla oblongata. There are also other medullary autonomic reflexes. Swallowing, coughing, sneezing, gagging, and vomiting are reflex responses integrated in the medulla oblongata.

CEREBELLUM

The cerebellum functions in the co-ordination, adjustment and smoothing out of movement. Afferent impulses reach this organ from the motor cortex, proprioreceptors, cutaneous tactile receptors, auditory and visual receptors, and even visceral receptors. It contains vestibular centres. It has an area that is involved in the regulation of head and eye movements. We develop skills in dancing, driving, painting, istrumental music, playing tennis, etc. In all such skills, precise movement and co-ordinated movement of body parts become indispensable. The cerebellum is responsible for such co-ordinated movement. When we begin to learn bicycling, we **think** to move our body parts in a balanced and co-ordinated way. In such **thinking**, the cerebral control for muscle co-ordination and balance is obvious. But we acquire the skill, and it becomes our 'second nature'. At this stage, the cerebellum takes over the control. The cerebellar control is unconscious; it is an automation for the body's co-ordination and balanced movement.

We observe the "crossing over" behaviour of the cerebrum. The left half of the cerebrum controls the right half of the body and its right half controls the left half of the body. This is, however, not the case with the cerebellum. The left and the right cerebella largely control the left and the right side of the body, respectively.

Each ear has three parts, viz., external ear, middle ear, and inner ear. The external ear, the middle ear, and the cochlea of the inner ear are concerned with hearing. The three semicircular canals, the utricle, and probably the saccule of the inner ear are involved in the maintenance of equilibrium. The three semicircular canals are perpendicular to each other so that they are oriented in the three planes of space.

Each cerebellum receives information from the respective side of the vestibular organ of the inner ear. It also receives sensory and other inputs from the spinal cord, brain stem, and forebrain. After processing the information, it sends outputs to many parts of the brain for making body movements precise, co-ordinated and smooth.

LIMBIC SYSTEM

The limbic system is our emotional switchboard. Along with the hypothalamus, it is concerned with the control of biologic rhythms, sexual behaviour, feeding behaviour, the emotions of rage and fear, and motivation. The limbic structures in the forebrain are connected with the "limbic midbrain area" by a nerve circuit through the hypothalamus.

The behavioural components of sexual mating, involving intense emotions, are regulated, to a large degree, by the limbic system and the hypothalamus. It is the limbic system that is associated with motivation. Stimulation of the reward or approach system provides a potent motivation for learning. The reverse is the case for the punishment or avoidance system.

Almost all plants and animals show biologic rhythms, i.e., cyclic variations in many of their functions. The best known circadian or diurnal rhythms in mammals and man are the daily fluctuations in body temperature, adrenocortical function, sodium and potassium excretion, urine volume, sleep-wakefulness cycles, and many others. The "biologic clocks" controlling some of these rhythms are located in the limbic system.

The amygdala is the aggression centre. Its stimulation causes hostile, angry emotions. Animals and human beings exhibit rage, fighting, or attack reaction by the stimulation of the amygdala. Stimulation of the hypothalamus and amygdaloid nuclei produces the fear reaction. Fear and rage reactions are instinctual; they are related protective responses to threats in the environment.

The hippocampus deals with smells and short-term memories, and lays down or consolidates long-term memories to be stored perhaps in several places in the cerebral cortex. The power of smells to evoke strong memories and emotions is mediated through the hippocampus.

HYPOTHALAMUS

The hypothalamus is a portion of the anterior end of the diencephalon. There are neural connections between the hypothalamus and the posterior lobe of the pituitary gland. The anterior lobe of the pituitary gland and the hypothalamus are not neurally connected; but they are vascularly connected, i.e., blood vessels connect both the structures. Most of the afferent and efferent nerves to and from the hypothalamus are unmyelinated. Many of these nerves connect the hypothalamus and the limbic system. The "limbic midbrain area" and the hypothalamus are connected by some nerve fibres.

The hypothalamus is a seat of emotion — pleasure, rage, fear, aggression, despair, hunger. It has certain role to play in sleep. Lesions in the posterior hypothalamus cause prolonged sleep, and stimulation of the dorsal hypothalamus in conscious animals causes them to go to sleep. These observations have led to speculations that the hypothalamus contains "sleep centres" and "wakefulness centres". Other research on sleep does not, however, assign a primary role to the hypothalamus in the physiology of sleep. There is a continual flow of signals between the hypothalamus and various regions of the cerebral cortex. This indicates the interaction of the cerebral cortex and the hypothalamus.

Appetitive Behaviour — Hunger. The hypothalamus regulates appetite through the interaction of two centres, viz., feeding centre and satiety centre, both of which are located in it. The satiety centre functions by inhibiting the feeding centre. Its cells become active when their protoplasmic concentration of glucose reaches a threshold maximum. The cells of the feeding centre respond to a minimum level of glucose in their protoplasm. Cells of both the satiety centre and the feeding centre function as glucometer although in an opposite way. It may be noted here that they are not responsive to the blood glucose level; but they are responsive to their protoplasmic glucose level. It has already been mentioned that the limbic system is also involved in the neural regulation of appetite. Lesions in the amygdaloid nuclei produce moderate hyperphagia.

Appetitive Behaviour — Thirst: There is a thirst centre in the hypothalmus. The cells of this centre are osmoreceptors that are stimulated by an increased osmotic pressure of the body fluids to initiate thirst and drinking.

Sexual Behaviour. The hypothalamus regulates sexual behaviour. It has afferent connections with sex organs whose cells are sensitive to circulating oestrogen or androgen. The anterior ventral hypothalamus has an integrating centre for the regulation of sexual behaviour. In addition, the pyriform cortex in the male is also involved in the integration. According to one theory, the hypothalamus has a "sex nucleus" at the lower region of the thalamus at the base of the cerebrum. When the physical attraction of the opposite sex is very appealing, the cerebral cortex influences the hypothalamus through its nerve connection; as a result, the sex nucleus of the hypothalamus sends a chemical message (gonadotropic releasing factor) to the pituitary gland which, in turn, triggers the release of gonadotropic hormones. Finally, sex hormones from gonads are secreted in higher concentrations. Both the hypothalamus and the limbic system have roles to play in the regulation of sexual behaviour.

Defensive Reactions — Fear and Rage: Centres for fear and rage are not localized in the hypothalamus. Instead, integrating centres for the regulation of fear and rage are diffuse in the hypothalamus as well as the limbic system. Both these behaviours are defensive reactions of human beings and animals.

Endocrine Regulation: Nerve fibres connect the hypothalamus and the posterior pituitary, that secretes two hormones, viz., oxytocin and vasopressin. The hypothalamus regulates the secretion of these two hormones via its nervous control of the posterior pituitary. In contrast, the anterior pituitary secretion is controlled by chemical agents carried in the portal hypophyseal vessels from the hypothalamus to the pituitary. These chemical agents or "brain hormones" secreted by the hypothalamus are called "releasing factors". The median eminence of the hypothalamus secretes six releasing factors that control the secretion of six hormones by the anterior pituitary. These six hormones are : adrenocorticotropic hormone (ACTH), thyroid-stimulating hormone (TSH), growth hormone (GH) or somatotropic hormone (STH), follicle-stimulating hormone (FSH), luteinizing hormone (LH), and luteotropic hormone (LTH) or prolactin. The pituitary gland located in the ventral floor of the brain is the royal endocrine that regulates all the other endocrine glands of the body. The thyroid, the adrenalcortex, the ovary and the testes are all controlled by the pituitary, which, in turn, is controlled by the hypothalamus. The hypothalamus is also controlled by the cerebral cortex. Thus, the brain exerts influences on the total endocrine system of the body.

The hypothalamus plays a definite role in the physiology of stress. A hostile environment acts as a stressor. The limbic system adversely responds to stressful conditions and produces anxieties. The cerebral cortex becomes aware of the stresses and strains and informs the hypothalamus about the stressful conditions. Hans Selye, the famous Canadian physiologist and Nobel-Laureate, termed the body's response to stressors the "general adaptation syndrome". This syndrome consists of three stages: (1) the alarm reaction, (2) the stage of resistance, and (3) the stage of exhaustion. In the stage of resistance, the hypothalamus secretes a hormone-like chemical substance — corticotropin-releasing factor (CRF) that flows to the pituitary gland through a specialized system of blood vessels. The anterior pituitary responds to the CRF and secretes adrenocorticotropic hormone (ACTH) that induces the adrenal-cortex gland to secrete more corticosteroid hormones.

Steroid hormones secreted by the cells in the outer layers, or cortex, of the adrenal-cortex gland allow the body to deal adaptively with stressors for long periods of time during the stage of resistance. But, if the stress is not removed within reasonable period, and consequently if steroid hormones are allowed to exert their influences for a prolonged period, the body is subjected to harmful effects due to long exposure to steroids. The second stage is followed by the stage of exhaustion, the final stage of the general adaptation syndrome. Now the stressful person exhibits psychosomatic disorders. Due to stress alone, a person may die of heart disease or cancer. Due to stress, one may suffer from hypertension, asthma, eczema or other skin diseases, peptic, ulcer colitis, etc.

Even if a stressor environment is hostile, the cerebral cortex may be utilized by Yogic technique to restrain the hypothalamus and the limbic system so that the body does not react to the stressful condition. This is possible, practicable, and demonstrable.

Temperature Regulation: Reptiles, amphibia, and fish are poikilothermic or cold-blooded. Avians and mammals are homeothermic or warm-blooded. A group of reflex responses integrated in the hypothalamus operate to maintain body temperature of homeothermic animals within a narrow range in spite of wide fluctuations in the environmental temperature. Thus, the body's thermostat is located in the hypothalamus.

All the hypothalamic controls that have been described

here are not due to our conscious efforts. We are unconscious of all these controls which happen mechanistically.

RETICULAR FORMATION

The reticular formation occupies the midventral portion of the medulla and midbrain. It has one part in the midbrain and another part in the hindbrain. An afferent system, called the reticular activating system (RAS), is in the brain stem reticular formation. Electrical activity in this system is responsible for the maintenance of a conscious, alert state that makes perception possible. Whenever the reticular formation is active, then the brain is in a waking conscious state. When the reticular formation is inactive, the brain is in an unconscious state.

SLEEP

We sleep at certain times and then wake up. Sleep is necessary for our health — both physical and mental. Sleep strengthens our capacity to remember. It has restorative powers. During waking and working hours, certain hormones are used up. While we sleep, new hormones are formed by our endocrine system. The growth hormone or somatotropin is one such hormone secreted more during sleep by the anterior pituitary. The growth of the body cells may be speeded up during the sleeping hours. The body purges itself of the catabolic byproducts accumulated during waking hours.

What has been said is about the necessity of sleep. But, what is the mechanism of the induction of sleep? What role does the brain play in inducing sleep and causing wakefulness?

Structures in the limbic area and brain stem are involved in sleep and wakefulness. The brain stem controls when and how long we sleep. Structures in the brain's limbic system regulate the cycles and stages of sleep.

During waking and working hours, the body-cells make

some chemicals that, in certain concentration, induce sleep. Some peptides have been known to be among these chemicals. These peptides increase the production of antibodies in the system, and thus bolster the immune capacity of the body. Thus good sleep helps fight illness and infection.

A person loses consciousness during sleeping. But the brain is not inactive during the sleeping hours. In the 1920s and 1930s, scientists began studying electro-encephalographs (EEG) which recorded the brain waves of sleeping people. It was revealed that the brain buzzes with activity during sleep.

In the early 1950s Nathaniel Kleitman and his assistant, Eugene Aserinsky conducted pioneering research on sleep. They used an electro-oculogram (EOG) which recorded eye movements even when the lids were closed. In 1952, they found that, at a certain stage in sleep, eyeballs began to dart back and forth. During this period of frantic eyeball movement, intense brain activity was registered by the EEG. They also observed that most of the body's muscular activity halted, as shown in an electromyogram (EMG), a record of electrical impulses in muscles.

The period of sleep when all the three changes happen simultaneously, viz., a surge in brain activity, increased eye movements, and near paralysis of muscles, is named as REM (rapid eye movement) sleep. Its other name is paradoxical sleep. This is paradoxical because our brains work furiously although we sleep at this time. REM sleep is light. Dreaming mostly occurs during the period of REM sleep.

In addition to REM sleep, we also get NREM (non-REM) sleep, which is longer in duration than the former in each sleep cycle. The NREM sleep is "quiet sleep", characterized by measured breathing and little body movement. Our senses are least responsive during this period. Those who snore do it during the NREM period.

The NREM sleep has four stages. Each stage has a

distinctive brain-wave pattern, which can be detected by the EEG. In stage 1, light sleep begins. Sleep is still light in stage 2. There is onset of deep sleep in stage 3; and deep sleep prevails in stage 4. Each sleep cycle lasts up to about 90 minutes and is mostly NREM sleep.

The NREM and REM sleeps are different. During REM sleep, there is rapid eye movement; muscles of the arms, legs, and trunk are paralyzed; there is no snoring, but there is dreaming. In contrast, during NREM sleep, there is little or no rapid eye movement; the arms, legs, and trunk are able to move, although there is little body movement during this period; there may be snoring during the NREM period.

Nathaniel Kleitman, the famous sleep researcher, has proposed that sleep is our natural condition and that we continue to stay asleep unless and until we are stimulated into wakefulness by sensory experiences and by muscular activity.

THALAMUS

The thalamus consists of two oval-shaped lobes that lie at the core of the brain, above the brain stem and beneath the cerebrum, in the area often called the forebrain limbic system.

The thalamus acts as an important processing centre and relay station. It receives incoming signals from the senses, determines their source, evaluates their importance, and then passes them on to the cerebral cortex. It acts as a secretary to the cerebral cortex. Thus it serves as the key communication link between the senses and the cortex. It has three functions: (1) It receives information from the senses. (2) It integrates the received information. (3) It telegraphs messages to the cerebral hemispheres, where awareness and recognition occur.

A special mention is necessary on the role of the thalamus in our perception of pain. The ability to feel pain is critical to our survival. Had we been pain-blind (insensitive to pain), it would have been impossible for us to survive. Pain may be acute or chronic. For feeling any type of pain, the thalamus in our brain plays a key role.

There are two main nerve pathways for signals to move from pain receptors to the central nervous system. One pathway sends signals quickly; the other more slowly. The express route is made up of large nerve fibres that transmit pain messages at about 350 kilometres per hour.

In certain situations, the pain message is to be transmitted through the express route in order to save life. As for example, a finger is accidentally burnt. Pain receptors urgently send the pain message through the express route to the spinal column, which immediately triggers a reflex action so that the finger is jerked away. The spinal column informs the cerebal cortex about the pain, and this information is conveyed to the cortex through the thalamus.

A few minutes after the burning of the finger, the first felt pain is replaced by a dull throbbing sensation. At this stage, pain receptors send messages by the slow route which is made up of small nerve fibres.

The destination of pain travel by both routes — fast or slow — is the thalamus. The pain message is processed in the thalamus which then sends it to the cerebral cortex, near the front of the brain. Real cognition of the pain is done at the cortical level. The cerebral cortex perceives the pain, identifies its nature and intensity, and also its specific location.

CEREBRAL CORTEX

The top of the human brain is entirely covered by the cerebral cortex (*fig.* 9.10). It includes the motor cortex, supplementary motor area, somatosensory cortex and four lobes. The cerebral cortex is divided into left and right hemispheres by a longitudinal fissure, a deep groove down the centre of the brain front to back. Other grooves divide

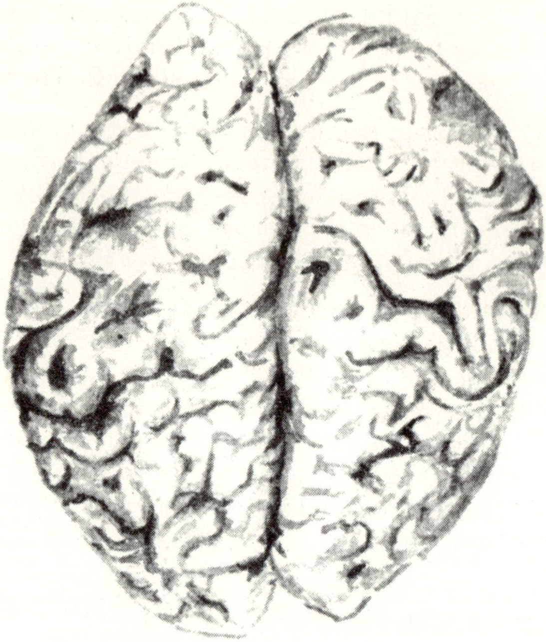

fig. 9.10: The top of the human brain, covered by the cerebral cortex.

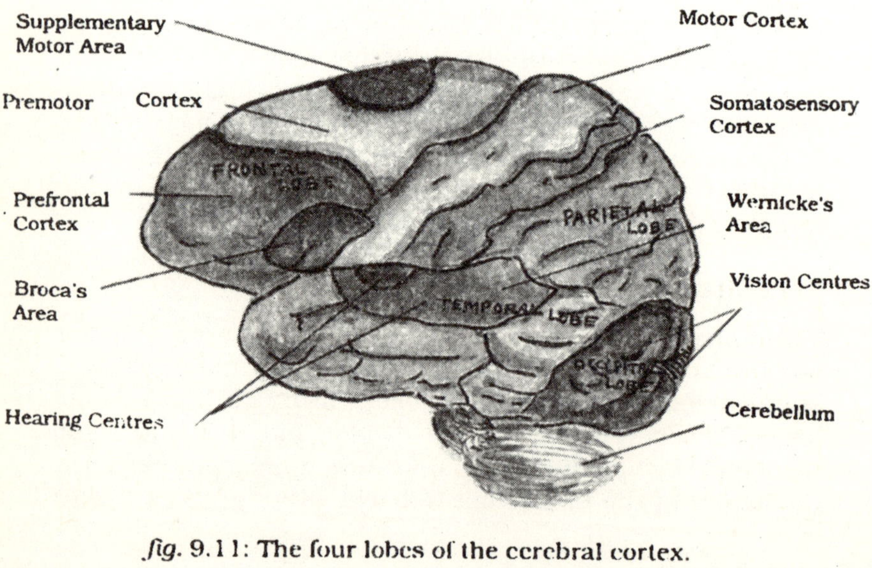

fig. 9.11: The four lobes of the cerebral cortex.

the surface of each hemisphere into four lobes. The four lobes are the frontal (including the prefrontal cortex), parietal, temporal, and occipital (*fig.* 9.11). The anterior part of the cortex is the frontal lobe and the posterior part is the occipital lobe. The parietal lobe is at the top, located in between the frontal and the occipital lobes. The temporal lobes are at the two sides.

A bundle of fibres known as the corpus callosum connects areas of the cortex of one hemisphere with corresponding areas in the other hemisphere. We will discuss the importance of this structure later.

Sensory Functions of the Cerebral Cortex

We have five sense-organs, viz., visual, auditory, olfactory, gustatory, and tactile. With the exception of the olfactory sense-organ, the other four send their sensory inputs to the primary sensory area of the cerebral cortex.

The visual cortex is a region within the occipital lobe, right at the back of the brain. It receives the visual input and interprets it. The right side of the visual cortex is associated with the left-hand field of vision of both eyes. The reverse is the case with the left side of the visual cortex. It may be noted that the image on the retina is inverted. This inverted image is further inverted in the visual cortex so that a direct image is obtained. This is brought about by the crossing over of nerves (*fig.* 9.12). We may divide the retina of each eye into two hemispheres, viz., nasal hemiretina and temporal hemiretina. The axons (nerve fibres) from each nasal hemiretina change the side at the optic chiasm, that is, the fibres from the nasal hemiretina of the left eye go to the right side, and those from the nasal hemiretina of the right eye go to the left side. Fibres from the temporal hemiretina do not change their sides at the optic chiasm. After leaving the optic chiasm, the left optic tract formed by the axons from the right nasal hemiretina and the left temporal hemiretina reaches the left lateral geniculate body. Similarly, the right optic tract formed by the axons

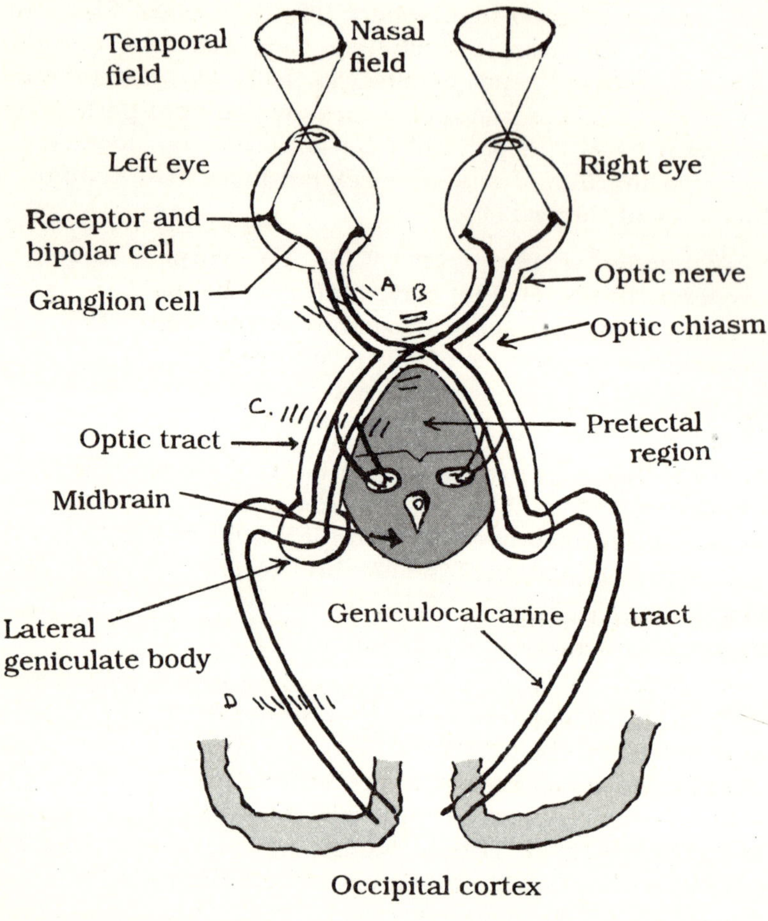

fig. 9.12: Crossing over of the fibres of the optic nerve.

from the left nasal hemiretina and the right temporal hemiretina reaches the right lateral geniculate body. Both these geniculate bodies are located in the thalamus. From each geniculate body, a geniculocalcarine tract, synapsed in a highly specific fashion by the fibres coming from the left and the right retinas, passes to the occipital lobe of the cerebral cortex.

The primary sensory area of the cortex for hearing is located in the temporal lobe. Signals from the ears cross over to the opposite side of the brain. The right auditory cortex is located in the right temporal lobe and makes auditory perception of sound mainly received from the left. The left auditory cortex is located in the left temporal lobe and makes auditory perception of sound mainly received from the right.

The gustatory receptors are located in the tongue and the oral mucous membrane. Taste signals are carried through three nerve pathways, viz., facial nerve, glosso-pharyngeal nerve, and vagus nerve. All the taste nerves unite in the medulla oblongata to form the tractus solitarius which reaches the thalamus. Taste impulses are relayed from the thalamus to the taste projection area in the cerebral cortex at the foot of the postcentral gyrus.

The skin is a giant sense-organ that covers the body. The skin senses are otherwise known as somatosenses. They are of four types, viz., pressure or touch, cold, warmth, and pain. The skin contains receptors for each of the four types. Tactile receptors on the skin send touch signals that finally reach the somatosensory cortex located in the parietal lobe. Various parts of the surface of the body have specific corresponding regions in the somatosensory cortex. The right somatosensory cortex deals with cutaneous sensations from the left-hand side of the body, and *vice-versa.*

Olfactory receptors are present in the nasal epithelium of each nasal cavity. They are connected, without synapse, directly to the olfactory bulbs of the brain, which are just below the frontal lobes. The olfactory bulbs are in turn connected with the olfactory cortex on the inside of the temporal lobes. The olfactory primary sensory area extends to the non-cortical limbic system and especially to the hippocampus. The right olfactory cortex deals largely with the right nostril and the left with the left nostril.

Motor Functions of the Cerebral Cortex

The motor cortex is on the gyrus just in front of the central sulcus. This cortical region sends nerve fibres to the brain stem and spinal cord. From these latter areas appropriate synaptic connections with specific peripheral nerves are made. Thus nerve impulses are transmitted from the motor cortex to the muscles. Various regions of the motor cortex are devoted to movements of specific parts of the body (*fig.* 9.13). The motor cortex contains complex circuits of nerve

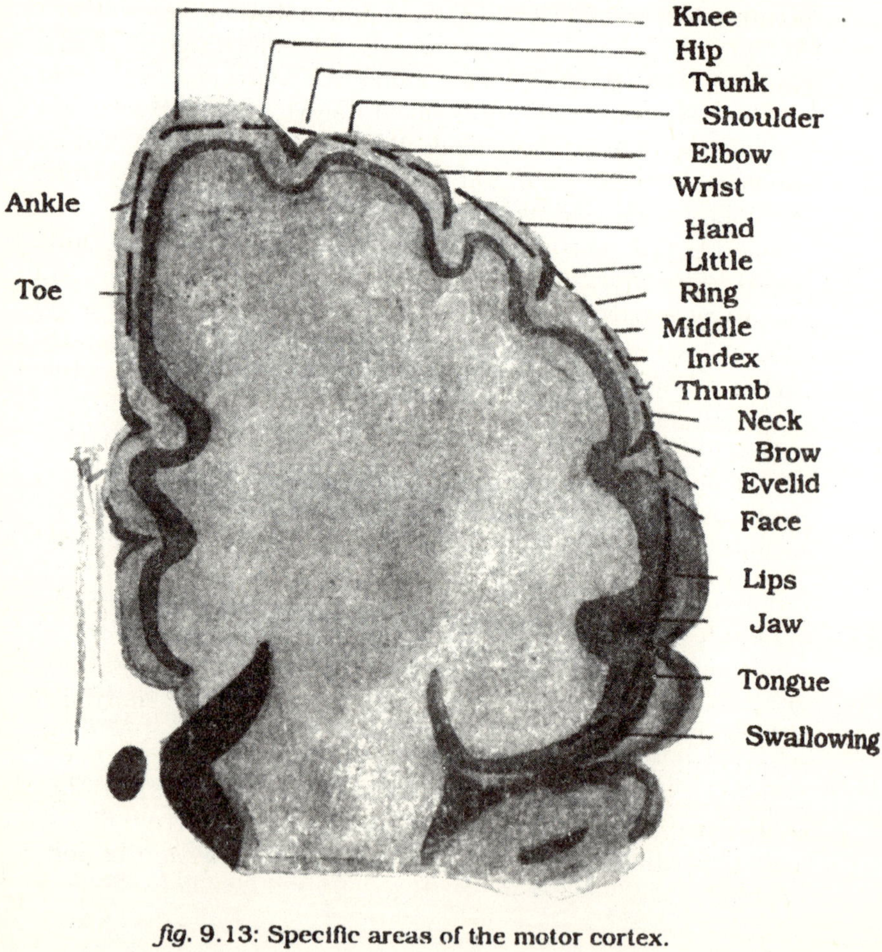

fig. 9.13: Specific areas of the motor cortex.

fibres, all of which are involved in muscle movement. It is closely linked to the cerebellum which is an automation for the co-ordinated and balanced movement of muscles.

Fibres from one side of the cortical motor area cross to the other side of the body below the head on their way to the spinal cord. For this reason, any damage to a region of the motor cortex due to stroke, physical injury, or pathological lesion is exhibited by weakness, loss of dexterity, or spastic paralysis on the side of the body opposite the damaged cortex. A person with left-sided damage has movement difficulties on the right side of the body below the head, and the reverse is the case with right-sided damage.

Functions of the Association Areas of the Cerebral Cortex

We have already described the functions of the sensory areas and motor areas of the cerebral cortex. In addition, there are other areas known as association areas. We have been using this term for want of a better one. All the cortical lobes, viz., frontal, parietal, temporal, and occipital, have association areas. The bulk of the cerebral cortex lies outside the primary sensory areas and the principal motor area.

The association cortex is the site where the most abstract and sophisticated activity of the brain is carried out. By dint of the activity of the association cortex, we are able to speak, remember, think, imagine, plan, evaluate, solve problems, make decisions, and create ideas.

Language: In the vast majority of right-handed people and in most left-handed people, the speech centres are on the left-hand side of the brain. The Broca's area and the Wernicke's area are the two speech centres. Broca's area is situated in the lower rear part of the frontal lobe. Wernicke's area is a region of association cortex situated in and around the upper rear part of the left temporal lobe. Broca's area is involved in the formulation of sentences, and Wernicke's area in the comprehension of speech and written language. Both these areas are connected by a bundle of nerves called arcuate fasciculus. A damage to this bundle leads to failure of vocalization and comprehension.

The Wernicke's area finds words to express and to link them into meaningful sentences. The programme of the Wernicke's area is then sent through the arcuate fasciculus to the Broca's area which makes programmes for the complex patterns of muscle movements needed in speech. The programmes of the Broca's area are then relayed to the region of the motor cortex that is in charge of controlling the lips, tongue, and vocal cords which actually produce the speech sounds.

Memory: Three processes operate in memory. These are the encoding, storage and retrieval. Encoding is the process of receiving sensory input and transforming it into a code which can be stored. Storage is the process of putting coded information into memory. Retrieval is the process of gaining access to stored, coded information and reproducing the original information whenever it is needed.

When we get a sensory input from the environment, it is held for a very brief time (some seconds) in a sensory register associated with the sensory channels such as vision, hearing, smelling, tasting, and touch. Information may be passed on to short-term memory (STM). The short-term memory is represented in the brain by transient pattern of nerve-cell activity. Here it is held for twenty to thirty seconds and is lost unless it is transferred to long-term memory (LTM). In the process of the transfer of memory from STM to LTM, attention is focused on it, it is repeated over and over, and it is somehow linked up with other information already stored in memory. This activity is known as rehearsal. The way of rehearsal may be more important than its amount. Items of information are organized into categories for being stored in LTM.

The site where LTM is stored is not a localized centre. Particular memories are stored throughout the cerebral cortex. Two structures in the brain, viz., the hippocampus and the amygdala, are essential for consolidating STM processes into LTM ones. Both the hippocampus and the amygdala are situated in the temporal lobe and are parts of the limbic system. If these two structures are damaged, STM cannot be consolidated as LTM, resulting in the failure of **new** long-term memory. But, what has already been stored in LTM, prior to the damage of these two structures, can be retrieved.

What is actually the memory store? There are actual electro-chemical changes in brain cells (neurons) that form a record of what we see, hear, smell, taste, and touch. A memory is stored as an electrical charge; it is rather a circuit. The brain has about 100 billion neurons. Each neuron is connected with one or more neurons through synapses. At the synaptic junctions, the dendrites, which are tentacles originating from the soma (main cell-body) of the neuron, produce a number of protuberances (dendritic spines) and may withdraw some of them. The knobs of the presynaptic neuron juxtapose the dendritic spines of the postsynaptic neuron. Thus, depending upon the input of information, newer and newer electrical circuits are formed. Each one of such circuits represents a particular memory. The brain cells and their synapses are not fixed in form; they change themselves and realign according to needs. This is what is called the plasticity of the brain.

An alternate theory of memory has the concept of special "memory molecules" like the ribonucleic acid (RNA). We have already discussed these aspects of memory in the previous chapter, and hence no repetition is necessary here.

Some argue that the brain cells cannot store long-term memory since their elemental constituents go on renewing. Elements like carbon, hydrogen, oxygen, nitrogen, sulphur, and phosphorus that are constituents in the brain-cell composition are in a dynamic state of flux. If we tag them by radioisotopes, we find that they are replaced by elements of the same species over a period of time. Maybe, a single carbon or nitrogen atom present in the brain cells three months back is not available at present. All the atoms have been substituted by those of the same species of elements; in spite of this fact, the present atoms are different from the previous ones with reference to individuality. The question is: How can the long-term memory is intact when the basic constituents of the sites of memory have been totally replaced?

One solution to this problem may be obtained by the concept that the electrical circuits representing particular memories are not altered in spite of the substitution of elements belonging to the same species.

Thinking: We have already discussed various thinking processes such as conceptualization, problem-solving, decision-making, creative thinking, and reasoning in the last chapter on cognitive psychology. All these activities of the brain are carried out by the association cortex.

Left and Right Brains

It has already been said that the cerebrum is divided down the middle into left and right cerebral hemispheres. The two hemispheres are connected by a bundle of nerve fibres called the corpus callosum (*fig.* 9.14). The left hemisphere is more 'logical' and the right one more 'creative' in most persons. The left half of the brain controls the right side of the body and the right half of the brain controls the left side.

The left hemisphere functions in understanding language, formulating language for communication, and thinking with language symbols. The main language functions are localized in the upper temporal lobe and the lower frontal lobe. The former locality is known as Wernicke's area, and the latter Broca's area. How these two language centres function has already been described. Strokes typically affect one side of the brain. If the left side of the brain is affected, the right side of the body is paralyzed, and *vice-versa*. People with strokes in the left

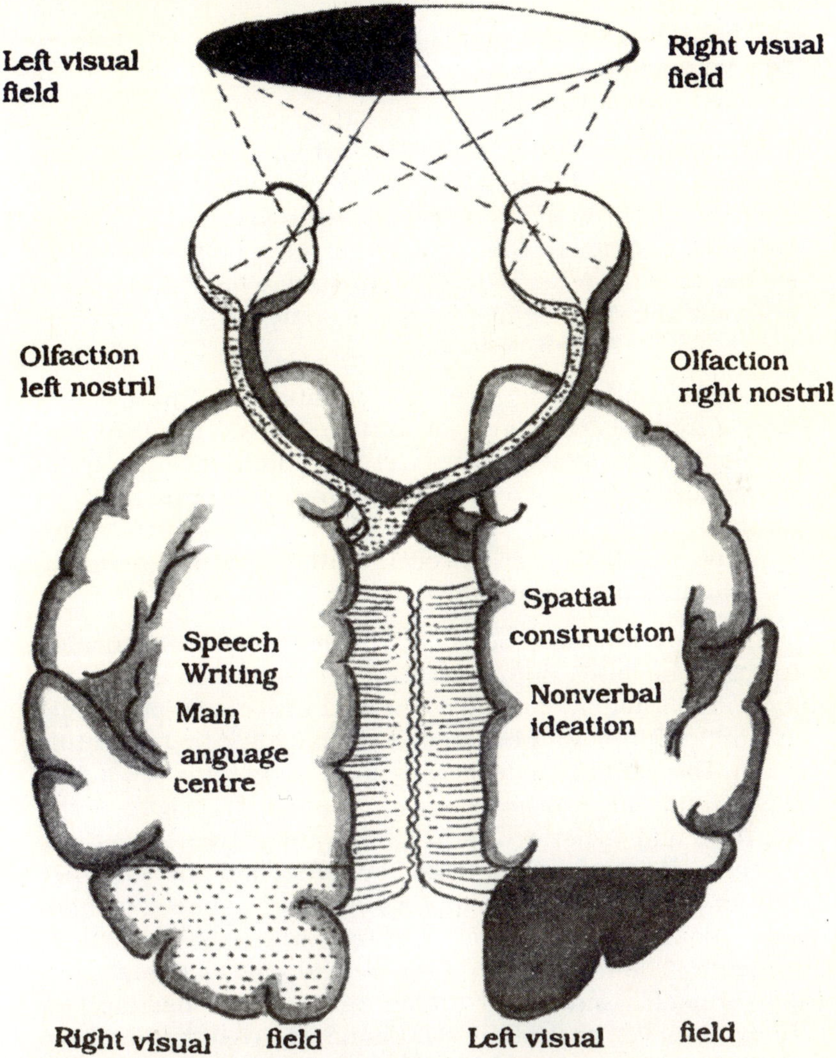

fig. 9.14: Left and right cerebral hemispheres, connected by the corpus callosum.

hemisphere and paralysis in the right side of the body are much more likely to have serious language problem than are people with right hemisphere stroke and paralysis of the left side of the body.

The right cerebral hemisphere is usually specialized to deal with images, spatial relationships, pattern recognition, and non-verbal ideation.

Although the cerebrum is divided into two halves, they do not function in complete isolation. They interact with each other through the nerve connections via the corpus callosum. None of the abilities of one hemisphere are exclusive of the other. The left hemisphere has some spatial abilities; the right hemisphere has some language abilities too.

The left and the right cerebral hemispheres are not very specialized at the time of birth. Any damage to one hemisphere in infancy is not very harmful since the other hemisphere can take over the functions of the damaged one almost successfully. As the child ages, the two hemispheres develop more of specialization, and, as a result, their adaptability diminishes.

In the adult age, some hemispheric specialization of function is quite apparent. The left brain is analytical, logical, mathematical, and concerned with cause-and-effect scientific thinking. It becomes the analytical and scientific brain. The right brain deals with images, patterns of sensory input, and the synthesis of information. It becomes the creative and artistic brain. We may say that scientists, mathematicians, accountants, lawyers, and the like, are 'left- brained'. Painters, sculptors, architects, poets, composers, dancers, musicians, and other artists are 'right-brained'. There are also rare individuals who are both 'left-brained' and 'right-brained'. The left hemisphere controls movements of the right hand; the right hemisphere controls those of the left hand.

Brain Waves

Brain waves are spontaneous electrical discharges of the brain as recorded by an electroencephalogram (EEG). In terms of the number of cycles per second (frequency) and the amplitude of the wave, four types of waves have been identified. These rhythms are: alpha, beta, delta, and theta.

Alpha waves have a frequency of 8 to 12 cycles per second and amplitude of up to 40 microvolts. Beta waves have the frequency of 14 to 28 cycles per second. Delta waves show a frequency of 2 to 3 cycles per second. Theta waves have a frequency of 5 to 7 cycles per second. As expected, the wavelengths bear an inverse relationship with the frequencies.

Alpha waves are associated with an alert state that is devoid of concrete visual imagery. It is accompained by feelings of tranquillity and a lack of tension and anxiety. The appearance of alpha waves is intermittent. A typical individual gets alpha about 5 to 30 times per minute. A person, while getting alpha waves, is in a state of relaxation and drowsiness.

Beta waves are fast-paced. They occur in an individual when he attempts to solve a problem or when he worries about something. They are usually accompanied by feelings of tension. We get beta waves in states of extroversion, concentration, logic-oriented thinking, worry, and tension.

Delta waves occur only when the individual is asleep or unconscious. They are generally associated with deep sleep.

Theta waves appear in states of dreaming and creativity. Children and young adolescents very often get theta waves.

A state of relaxation prevails in meditation. It is characterized by the predominant appearance of alpha waves and occasional runs of theta waves. These theta waves are different from those seen in sleep. Occasionally in deep meditation or transcendence, the alpha-theta pattern is suddenly followed by a spurt of rhythmic beta waves which are synchronized high-amplitude waves unlike the normal small-amplitude ones. The meditator is introverted. Beta waves appear in extroversion. The reason for the occasional spurts of beta waves in deep meditation has not yet been ascertained.

Persons are usually unaware of their brain-wave patterns and unable to control them consciously. *Yogīs*, however, consciously control their brain waves and produce alpha waves at their will. Persons can be trained to produce alpha waves. Experiments were conducted in 1958 by Joseph Kamiya to know if biofeedback training (BFT) could induce the production of alpha waves. Experimental subjects were placed in a darkened room and were instructed to close their eyes. Kamiya monitored the brain waves of these subjects who were asked to guess whether they were in an alpha or a non-alpha state whenever they heard a bell ring. After each guess the subjects were told the success or failure of their guess. A few sessions of this training enabled the subjects to discriminate between alpha and non-alpha states. After the subjects were sufficiently experienced, no more feedback was necessary and they could voluntarily switch alpha rhythms on or off. Kamiya's[1] later investigations in 1968 changed the experimental technique. The subjects heard a feedback tone whenever they could produce alpha waves. By this technique, the learning process could be speeded up. Many other investigations have confirmed the practicability of the conscious control of brainwaves and paved the way for its possible therapeutic use.

Several investigations have shown that adept *Yoga* and Zen meditators can override their autonomic nervous system, and can also control their brain-waves. Hirai and Kasamatsu[2] of Tokyo University found a high correlation between brain-wave control and the proficiency rating of Zen masters. In many successful *Yoga* or Zen meditation, alpha activity becomes prominent.

It has been experimentally established that BFT can be successfully utilized for the control of brain-waves, especially for the production of alpha activity. Alpha activity is associated with relaxation which entails decrease in muscle tension. Thus BFT would be helpful in overcoming chronic anxiety and tension. This biofeedback-mediated relaxation therapy is known as "electronic *Yoga*".

A meditator, adept in *Yoga* or Zen, does not need the biofeedback technique. Through his *Yoga* or Zen technique, he can produce his alpha activity that would reduce his muscle and mental tension and remove his anxiety.

Conscious Control of the Autonomic Nervous System

The smooth muscles of the stomach and the intestines have their own autonomy for contraction. The cardiac muscles continue their systolic and diastolic movements throughout the life of an individual and, for doing so, they exercise their own autonomy. The liver, the pancreas, the kidneys, and the urinary bladder have autonomy to function. If a situation demands, the function of a certain autonomic organ like the heart or the lungs may be accelerated; in a reverse situation, the function of such an organ may be retarded. This speeding up or slowing down action may be done chemically or neurally. The autonomic nervous system has the neural mechanism to regulate the involuntary functions of the body.

Life without the autonomic nervous system would be one crisis after another. If an individual consciously takes care of all his body functions and fine-tunes everything, it becomes theoretically and practically impossible. Every moment he has to precisely regulate his heart beat, respiration, body temperature, blood pressure, insulin secretion, urine secretion, liver function, co-ordination of all centres of the nervous system, and myriads of such functions. He cannot do all these things and hence he cannot live. To make living possible, all these functions are performed without the awareness of the individual and hence without his conscious control.

For a *yogī*, however, all involuntary actions can be made voluntary if he wills. He can override the autonomic nervous system and control all his body functions, even though some functions are otherwise involuntary. He can increase or decrease his heart rate at his will, bring metabolism to a near halt, and raise or lower body temperature. His blood pressure will be low or high as he commands.

Mechanical Interpretation in Science

The word 'mind' is very often used in scientific discourse. But science does not subscribe to dualism and does not consider mind as distinct from the brain.[3] To quote Hillary Putnam, "Identity theories of the Mind generally hold that Mind is to be regarded as, or at least described in terms of, functions of the brain regarded as a machine".[4]

In this chapter, we have given a short description of the anatomy and the physiology of the nervous system with special emphasis on the brain. We have done so in order to throw light on the functioning of the mind. Science makes a mechanistic interpretation of the brain which is considered purely as a machine. The body is a machine, and the mind is a machine within a machine. The smaller machine which is located within the bigger machine controls the latter. Each part of the body is an instrument. Each individual unit of the brain is also an instrument. All the instruments in the body work synchronously for a common end. As science says, there is no driver to operate the machine. It automatically works by following mechanical laws. It has been designed and programmed to work, although it has no designer and programmer. It has itself evolved to the present state with its present structure and function. Everything happens in the body-machine and the brain-machine mechanically. This is the mechanical interpretation of science.

What we call consciousness or awareness is the group of the exhibited properties of the brain. Basically, these properties are electrical in nature. After all, the brain is a living electronic machine. Thus, all our mental activities are rooted in the interactions of the electromagnetic field.

The computer is also an electronic machine. Most of its features are similar to those of the brain. Can we regard the brain as a naturally evolved computer? Is the computer an artificially made brain? We will discuss the issue of the brain *vis-a-vis* artificial intelligence (AI).

Artificial Intelligence

Artificial intelligence (AI) is the branch of computer science which uses computers for solving problems that require some heuristic technique and some intelligence to solve. For the solution of problems, the computer uses the available data stored in its knowledge bank, and draws inference with the help of the rules supplied to it.

Before any discussion on AI, we may present some preliminary information on the computer. A computer is an electronic device which accepts digital information, processes it in a pre-defined fashion, according to the set or sequence of instructions provided to it, and produces the desired binary output.

Computer Architecture

The functional components of an electronic data-processing (EDP) system are four. They are: Input devices, output devices, central processing unit (CPU), and storage devices. The input devices convert the data to be processed into a format acceptable to the computer. The datas are then passed on to the central processing unit (CPU) of the computer for being processed. The CPU is the heart of the computer. Actual processing of the data is done here. It consists of arithmatic and logic unit (ALU), control unit and working storage (memory). The output devices get the processed datas from the CPU and translate them from the format used by the computer back into a form that people can understand.

The central processing unit (CPU) of a computer has different types of registers, viz., accumulator, storage registers, instruction register, address register, and general purpose register. An accumulator is a register that temporarily holds intermediate results during an arithmatic or logic operation. It is located in the arithmatic and logic unit (ALU). Storage registers are located in the ALU. They hold datas that are to be sent to or taken from the primary memory. Instruction registers are located in the control unit. They are used for decoding the instructions. Address registers are also located in the control unit. They hold addresses of memory locations containing the datas called for the instructions. Each memory location in the primary or auxiliary memory is assigned a binary number with which it is identified. This is known as its address. General purpose registers are used for both arithmatic and addressing functions.

A bus is a communication path between the processing unit and peripherals. It is a group of wires that carry bits. The processing unit, the memory, and the input/output ports in a computer are linked to one another by three major buses. These are the address bus, the data bus, and the control bus.

There are two types of storage devices, viz., working storage (primary storage or main memory) and the auxiliary (secondary) storage. The working storage is present inside the CPU. It is the primary memory of the computer. It holds the programme instructions for the programme to be executed, the input data to be processed, and the intermediate results of calculations done while processing. The primary memory located inside the CPU is usually limited in size. The larger the size of the primary memory, the costlier becomes the computer. The secondary or auxiliary storage is often found physically outside the computer system. This off-line storage capacity can be unlimited. Being outside, it can be voluminous. It is cheaper to connect an auxiliary storage to a computer.

Alphanumeric Codes

A computer does not understand words, phrases, and sentences. It does not recognize the ten decimal digits (0, 1, 2, 3, 4, 5, 6, 7, 8, 9). It recognizes the two binary digits, "0" and "1". Again, for this purpose, these two binary digits are not like the ones written here. If the magnetized state is 1, the unmagnetized state is 0. If the state of electrical conduction is 1, the non-conduction state is 0. If the "on" state is 1, the "off" state is 0. The computer refers the two binary digits, 0 and 1, to the non-existence and the existence, respectively, of one aspect only. Thus, "0" stands for the non-existent state and "1" for the existent state. In computer language, a "BIT" stands for a binary digit, either "0" or "1". A binary representation of 4-bits is called a "nibble", and that of 8-bits a "byte".

Binary codes that are used to represent all the letters of an alphabet, the ten decimal digits, mathematical symbols, and punctuation marks are known as alphanumeric codes. The binary coded decimal (BCD) representation of the ten decimal digits is as follows:

Decimal	*BCD*	*Decimal*	*BCD*
0	0000	5	0101
1	0001	6	0110
2	0010	7	0111
3	0011	8	1000
4	0100	9	1001

Memory Devices

For a discussion on the basic principles of memory devices used in digital computers, we will refer to the magnetic core memory and the semiconductor memory.

The basic storage element in a magnetic core memory is the tiny doughnut-shaped ferrite. A large number of ferrite rings are strung together in a grid-like structure of wires. This constitutes a core plane. Core planes are stacked one over the other, so that the memory size becomes bigger. Electric current flowing in one direction magnetizes the core in one direction, while current flowing in the opposite direction magnetizes the core in the opposite direction.

Thus two different magnetic states are obtained, one state representing the binary digit "0", and the other one representing the binary digit "1".

Magnetic core memory was used in the computers of the first and the early second generations. It is bulky. With such bulky memory type, we could not have got a table-top microcomputer with a primary memory of one megabyte capacity. It would be difficult to imagine computers with larger memory capacity, had there been no improvement in the storage devices over the magnetic core memory. The biggest advantage of the magnetic core memory lies in the fact that it is non-volatile. The contents of the magnetic core memory are not lost when the power supply to the computer is switched off.

The basic component of the semiconductor memory is the semiconductor transistor. We may briefly describe semiconductors and transistors which may serve as preparatory to a discussion on the semiconductor memory.

Metallic conductors have a large number of free electrons available as charge carriers. Non-metallic insulators have practically no free electrons available to conduct electric current and hence are non-conductors. Materials whose electrical conductivity is intermediate between metallic conductors and non-metallic non-conductors are classed as semiconductors. There are many varieties of semi-conductors; but the ones frequently used in electronics and transistor manufacture are germanium and silicon.

Silicon has four valence electrons in its outer shell. This outermost electron shell of an atom is of interest in electronics, since it contains the loosely held valence electrons, which are easily dislodged to become electric current carriers. But none of these four electrons in the outermost shell of the silicon atom is loose. The silicon crystal structure shows covalent bonds. In this structure, adjacent silicon atoms share their valence electrons in a strong covalent bond, so that effectively four orbital electron pairs are associated with each nucleus. The four electrons in the outermost shell of a silicon or a germanium atom are bound so strongly to the nucleus that no free electrons are available to conduct an electric current. A pure silicon or germanium crystal is practically a non-conductor of electricity. The picture, however, changes if a small amount of an impurity is introduced into the silicon or germanium crystal. Atoms of antimony or arsenic that have five electrons in the outer shell are introduced into the silicon or germanium crystal. This procedure is known as "doping". The fifth electron of the impurity atom does not find a place in the symmetrical covalent-bond structure, and hence roams about in the crystal as a free electron. Thus doping renders the originally non-conducting silicon or germanium crystal into a current-conducting one.

Before the invention of transistors, bulky thermionic valves were used in the early computers. Valves utilize the flow of free electrons through a vacuum or gas. In contrast, transistors operate by the movement of charge carriers through a solid substance, a semiconductor. Valves have filaments that need heating power, whereas transistors have no filaments. Transistors are far smaller than valves, may be operated in any position, are mechanically rugged, and have practically unlimited life.

A transistor may be in a conducting or non-conducting state. These two different electrical states are recognized by the computer as the two binary digits, "1" and "0" respectively.

Transistors are used in a computer to store digital data for operational purpose. They are used in the semiconductor storage device for the input and the output of data. They are the basic components of the semiconductor memory. The semiconductor memory is compact, economic, and reliable. But it has the disadvantage of being volatile. The contents of the memory vanish with the switching off of the power supply to the computer.

With the development of integrated circuit (IC), computer hardware has been revolutionized. It is a circuit composed of many transistors reduced in size to fit on a chip. In computer science, a chip is defined as an integrated circuit or integration of many electronic circuits on a single silicon wafer slice, mostly called as the silicon chip. The IC technology has so much developed that hundreds of thousands of such transistors can be integrated on one silicon chip of the size of 6mm square.

We have so far discussed two storage technologies. Possible future storage technologies are many, two of which may be mentioned here. One of these is the concept of bubble memory. Magnetic bubbles are formed when a magnetic material is uniformly applied to a thin magnetic film. The presence of a bubble represents a logic "1" and the absence of a bubble a logic "0". This provides a binary basis for representing data. The advantages of the bubble memory over the semiconductor chips are the higher capacity and non-volatility.

A digital biochip has been conceived as some organic molecule. The molecule may also be a genetically engineered protein which may serve as a memory device. If the organic molecule would turn the flow of electrons ON or OFF, the ON might present the binary "1", and the OFF the binary "0". A protein molecule, genetically engineered, may serve as an analog biochip which would be capable of graded responses and would perform special computations.

Hardwares of the Brain and the Computer

In a general way, the hardwares of the brain and the computer can be well compared. All the five senses with their nerves connected to the brain constitute the input device. The motor nerves and the effector organs make the output device. The brain has its central processing unit with control unit and memory. The computer possesses all these units. Thus, at the gross level, both are comparable.

Both the brain and the computer function electrically. Only when a person dies does the brain de-electrify itself. Even when a neuron is not activated, it emits pulses, but only at a slow rate. When a neuron "fires", it emits a whole sequence of such pulses in quick succession. The brain has integrated circuitry. In principle, the computer has similar electrical components — wires, transistors, and integrated circuits. Both are electronic machines, of course, with differences in their complexities.

The brain has nerve cells or neurons. The neurons of the computer are transistors, tiny bits of semiconductor crystals. Depending upon the applied voltage, a transistor can be non-conductive or highly conductive. It can, therefore, be used as a micro-switch which is either 'on' or 'off'. Two transistors can be wired together in such a way that when one is 'on', the other is 'off'. A control device may ask these transistors to reverse their switches, that is, 'on' becomes 'off', and 'off' becomes 'on'. Such a device is known as a 'flip-flop'. Thus we get either one of the two states — on-off or off-on. It is the same thing as the "0" and "1" of the binary digits. Thus the flip-flop can serve as an elementary information-storage unit. Flip-flops can be interconnected with other flip-flops to form a 'register'. Thus, in principle, any amount of information can be stored by means of the binary system. Decimal digits, all characters of any alphabet, mathematical and other symbols, and punctuation marks can be coded into binary numbers, and again these can be decoded. Larger numbers merely require more flip-flops, and there is no other problem. In a nutshell, the hardware of a computer is its anatomy and the software is its physiology. Regarding the brain, we do not exactly know how information are coded and decoded. Perhaps, the brain also does by the same binary system. The two electronic machines — the brain and the computer — operate on the basis of electromagnetic interactions, binary digit system, Bhoolean algebra, and symbolic logic.

The computer is a fixed collection of wired-up transistors. But the brain is not a fixed collection of wired-up neurons. The interconnections between neurons go on changing, all the time, depending upon the brain's need of new circuits. It is a fact that the complicated 'wiring' (nerve-circuitry) in the brain is established in broad outline at birth. But, the synaptic junctions where communication between different neurons takes place continually change as the needs demand. This phenomenon is known as brain plasticity which is lacking in the computer. Synaptic knobs of the axon of a presynaptic neuron juxtapose dendritic spines of a postsynaptic neuron, leaving a narrow gap (synaptic cleft) which is about forty-thousandths of a millimetre. Dendrites are short tentacles protruding from the soma of a neuron, and dendritic spines are tiny protuberances on dendrites. These dendritic spines are not fixed in location and number. New spines may grow at new sites in a dendrite, and old spines may shrink away from old sites. This plasticity makes a big difference between the brain and the computer. The brain is a computer which is capable of changing all the time.

The cortex alone contains about ten billion (10^9) neurons. If the interior of the brain is included, the total number of neurons in an average brain becomes one hundred billion (10^{11}). The total number of transistors in the largest computer (manufactured up to 1993) is 10^9. Of course, computers with still more number of transistors may be manufactured in the future.

A logic gate in a computer has a few input and output wires (three or four). In contrast, a neuron may have a huge number of synpases on it. As an example, the purkinje cells (special neurons in the cerebellum) have about 80,000 excitatory synaptic endings. On an average, a neuron is connected to hundreds of others by 1,000 to 10,000 synapses or relay points. The total number of interconnections and pathways through the brain must be in the order of trillions. Due to the astronomical number of pathways in the human brain, any neuron or group of neurons can contact a vast number of others via the innumerable circuits. The computers made by human beings have not approached this complexity.

There are about 10^{15} synapses in the brain. If we assume two states (excitatory and inhibitory) for each of these, we get $2^{10^{15}}$ possible brain states. This enormous number is much larger than the number of states in a big supercomputer.

The transistors in a computer are connected serially. The neurons in the brain form networks by parallel connections. The parallel connections give a large number of advantages when compared with serial connections. Of course, the parallel networks of the brain can, in principle, be simulated on a serial computer. Some computer scientists have already made some attempts in this direction. It is very difficult to do so, and hence the simulation is incredibly slow.

A typical neuron operates on the time scale of milliseconds (10^{-3} seconds). In contrast, the microcircuits in a computer operate on the time scale of nanoseconds (10^{-9} seconds). Thus neurons of the brain communicate information a million times slower in comparison with the wires in the computer. In spite of this slowness in conduction, in about 100 milliseconds (100 steps in neuronal firing time) the brain's performance in sense-perception and cognition is remarkable. The brain is able to do so by its massive parallelism. In the case of the brain, billions of neurons simultaneously function in parallel. A serial computer has the advantage of higher speed, but it computes only one step at a time.

Unlike the computer, the brain is highly redundant as a consequence of its massive parallel architecture. Is this redundancy nonsense and unnecessary waste? The answer is an emphatic 'no'. The brain has been intelligently designed to be redundant. The functioning of the brain would be very slow had there been no parallel network. Another big advantage of the redundancy is that the brain is fault-tolerant. If a single circuit wire breaks, an entire serial computer stops working. Thousands of neurons (100,000) die everyday in every person due to aging; still everybody is capable of normal thinking until very old age. Immense quantity of facts is stored in millions of circuits. Even if some part of the brain is damaged, the other parts still function as memory store. People meet with accidents in which the brain may be partly injured. Due to certain illness, pathological lesions may develop in certain area of the brain. In all such contingent situations, the brain is fault-tolerant. The whole network continues to function even if part of the network is destroyed. It is the redundancy of the brain — its excess of parts and circuits — that keeps it running smoothly. Although some specific areas of the brain specialize in some specific functions, many functions are duplicated in several regions of the cortex. Instead of single tracks or channels, there are many alternate pathways by which impulses can get from one point to any other.

Can the Computer Think?

We have compared the hardwares of the brain and the computer. The computer can do calculations faster than the brain. For official and commercial purposes, the computer can be used for better expediency and efficiency. Work can be facilitated by the manipulation of the computer memory which may be more dependable and handy. Such uses and many more are everyday practicalities. It is envisioned that computers will play more extensive roles to serve humanity. This is about the service of the computer for the welfare of man. The computer is a machine made by man to serve as means to human ends. All these points are neat and tidy and we have no disputes over them. The real debate is on the proposition that the computer is going to take over the mental capabilities of man. It is claimed that the computer will learn, think, make decisions, solve problems, write poems, do painting, architecture, and sculpture, make inventions and discoveries, do reasoning and show sentiments and emotions. The computer will soon surpass human intelligence and produce anything comparable to the thinking of a living mind. This is the issue over which disputes are brewing.

The silicon chips constitute the brain cells of the

computer. The metal wires are the nerve fibres of the computer. Would it be correct to think that non-living materials like sand and iron or copper would be able to take over the functions of the living brain? This question has been answered both positively and negatively.

Robert Jastrow, Director of the Goddard Institute for Space Studies, and Professor of Astronomy at Columbia University says: "In another fifteen years or so — around 1995, according to current trends — we will see the silicon brain as an emergent form of life, competitive with man."[5]

Edward Fredkin, Professor of Electrical Engineering and Computer Science at MIT says: "Eventually, no matter what we do, there'll be artificial intelligences with independent goals. It's very hard to have a machine that's a million times smarter than you as your slave."[6]

Marvin Minsky of MIT, the computer scientist and artificial intelligence authority, says: "The machine will begin to educate itself . . . (and) in a few months it will be at genius level . . . A few months after that its power will be incalculable . . . If we are lucky, they might decide to keep us as pets."[7]

Heinz Pagels, esteemed physicist and science writer, gives his opinion on this controversy in the following way: "Ever since computers came into existence, their capabilities have been compared to those of humans, especially with regard to mental abilities. These comparisons are rather facile because human beings and computers are very different; it is like comparing a screwdriver to a human hand".[8]

Roger Penrose, Rouse Ball Professor of Mathematics, University of Oxford, rejects the view that our thinking is basically the same as the action of some very complicated computer. He remarks on consciousness as follows: "Consciousness seems to me to be such an important phenomenon that I simply cannot believe that it is something just 'accidentally' conjured up by a complicated computation. It is the phenomenon whereby the universe's very existence is made known. One can argue that a universe governed by laws that do not allow consciousness is no universe at all. I would even say that all the mathematical descriptions of a universe that have been given so far must fail this criterion. It is only the phenomenon of consciousness that can conjure a putative 'theoretical' universe into actual existence!"[9]

Rochel Gelman, psychologist at the University of Pennsylvania, thinks that the brain is an unparalleled evolutionary creation. She says: "The human mind, as I see it in my work, is a wonderful, a magnificent structure created by evolution. Nothing resembles it or comes close to it — not the mind of the smartest ape and not even any AI program."[10]

Thus there is division of opinion over the issue of equating the computer with the brain. Most AI people do not place any importance on the difference between the living brain and the non-living computer. The computer is made of semiconductors and wire whereas the brain is made of living cells. This difference is not significant to most AI people who can conceive of newer developments in computer science and technology that would impart capability to the computer to outbeat the brain. Most cognitive scientists differ from the AI scientists. The former consider the differences between computer hardware and the brain's neuron network, and cannot predict even the equality in the intelligent functionings of both.

The circuitry of the computer is basically linear. Each flip-flop is connected to a preceding and a succeeding one. The flip-flop has only two conditions, on-off or off-on. The computer deals with information serially, in a single line. In contrast, the brain-cells (neurons) function via millions or trillions of parallel channels. Every neuron has thousands of linkages to other neurons. The AI scientist argues that computers with parallel circuitry will be manufactured with equal complexity or even more. Many cognitive scientists are sceptical of such claims. They do not say that there cannot be improvement in computer technology. This much they say that the computer cannot perform the creative and intelligent functions of the brain.

Brain Versus Computer

A computer is superior to the human brain in certain respects, but much inferior in some other respects. The calculations of the computer are much faster than those of the brain. A computer can figure out in minutes or seconds what a human being would need months to calculate. Secondly, a computer can store a lot of information in its memory and can retrieve whenever required. The capacity of the brain's memory is not limited for all practical purposes during a person's life. But the retrieval of information from the memory is more dependable in the case of the computer. Even the storing of information in the computer is more handy. Computers are tireless and quick to draw and fetch.

A human being gets information about the world through the five senses. A second agency is not necessary for the input of information into the brain. The brain constructs new concepts or understandings from this direct input. Man has to feed information into the computer through binary coding. The computer cannot directly perceive the world and get knowledge about it. Further, man makes a programme for the computer. This programme is a set of instructions to the computer which functions as instructed. For the processing of information, for the various manipulations of the input data, and for retrieval, computers apply a fixed set of algorithms to the data provided by their human operators. The brain does not need an external programme whereas computers cannot function without it.

The human brain performs heuristic problem-solving whereas the computer cannot. Computers function at a low intellectual level. They do not exercise discretion since they do not have it. If a problem crops up during the process of seeking a solution, the computer cannot alter the algorithmic pathway. It foolishly completes the programmed algorithm even if an intervening problem demands a modification in the programme.

The brain functions intelligently. When the environment changes, the organism changes and adapts itself to the changing environment. This is possible due to the intelligent functioning of the brain. The brain is responsible for the interaction of the organism and the environment. The computer's algorithmic processing does not involve changes, adaptability, and interaction.

The computer works towards known end states which have been fixed by the human programmer. It does not set a new goal for itself. That is not the case of the brain of a human being, however. A person sets his/her goal and works to attain it.

The brain is self-correcting. If there is a fault in its hardware or software, it ordinarily rectifies the defect without extraneous help. If there is a fault in a transistor, in the wiring, or in the programme, the computer cannot correct itself.

The computer processes data according to information fed and programme given. Garbage in, garbage out. If the input data are correct, if the programme is right, the output information is right. We cannot expect correct output from a computer if wrong data are fed or the instructions to the computer are defective. That is, however, not the case with the brain. The brain has the capacity to scan and screen right and wrong data and refuse data if they are wrong. The brain also can sense a wrong or impossible result. The functioning of the brain is not purely mechanical.

A computer cannot do creative work. It cannot write a poem. It cannot compose a music. It cannot produce a painting. It cannot think creatively. It cannot reason. It cannot solve intricate problems that need heuristic methods for solution. It cannot feel pleasure and pain. It cannot have love and hatred. It cannot have compassion. It cannot experience. It cannot be conscious of itself and the external world. It cannot have the sense of "I". It cannot be able to understand and recognize, and to organize experiences into new concepts. It cannot create and test hypothesis about reality. It cannot solve heuristic problems. It is devoid of desires and emotions. It is not able to cope with all the phenomena of higher intelligence.

Many AI researchers do not agree to what has been said here. They assert that whatever the mind can do can be done by the computer in the future, if not today. They foresee that the future computers can do all forms of creative work which the human brain is doing today. They claim even further. They visualize a situation in which the computer's creative performance will be better than man's.

The claim of the AI researcher is not totally baseless, but seems to be exaggerated. The computer is now able to play chess. The computer gives the structural formula of an unknown chemical compound, provided results of mass-spectroscopy are available to it. With sufficient input data, the computer can give the medical diagnosis of a disease. We do observe the effectiveness of artificial intelligence in a number of areas. We do expect still better performance when computer technology is still more developed.

The information-processing by a computer is linear, proceeding step by step. Any artificial intelligence, expected from a computer, may be able to simulate, partly at least, the logical processes of the left half of the brain. In contrast, the intuitive functioning of the right half of the brain is non-linear and non-logical. It is hard to think of artificial intelligence that can simulate the functioning of the right half of the brain. A large part of creative work is non-logical and unconscious. Many cognitive scientists are disinclined to accept the notion that computers can do creative work. The extraordinary multiplicity of parallel pathways in the brain is conducive to the production of creative thought, which may be impossible for computers to simulate.

In spite of this scepticism about the 'intelligence' of computers, some reputed thinkers are still in favour of equating the computer with the brain. H.R. Pagels writes:

> The existence of these machines would also put an end to much discussion about the mind-body problem; because it will be very hard not to attribute a conscious mind to them without failing to do so for more human beings. Gradually the popular view will become that consciousness is simply 'what happens' when matter is put together the right way into a neural network, the same way that a working television set is 'what happens' when electronic components are put together the right way.[11]

Brain-Mind Identity

Many natural-scientists, psychologists, and philosophers do not consider brain and mind as two separate entities. George John Romanes (1848-94) who was a neighbour and personal friend of Charles Darwin was a naturalist. He wrote in favour of mind-brain identity in his book *Mind and Motion* where he states: "Any change taking place in the mind, and any corresponding change taking place in the brain, are really not two changes but one change."[12] Hilary Putnam,[13] an American philosopher, dilates the basic principle underlying the brain-mind identity theories. According to these theories, the brain is regarded as a machine, and mind is held to be the functions of the brain-machine. If one has to locate the mind, one has to do so by locating the brain functions. The brain functions are to be ascribed to various aspects of the mind.

Murton Hunt, in his book *The Universe Within*[14] writes in favour of brain-mind identity. He does not support the idea that mind is a sort of stuff different from the brain. It is rather a series of processes of immense complexity, the integration of millions or billions of neural events. The mind is not something apart from the brain, but is the brain's programmes, the brain's total set of symbol manipulations. Hunt regards the brain as phenomenon and mind as epiphenomenon. Accordingly, mental processes which we call thoughts, or more broadly mind, are secondary or collective effects of the brain's biological processes, and thus are epiphenomena.

William Uttal,[15] a psychobiologist, holds that mind is to the nervous system as a rotation is to the wheel. Rotation is a mass effect of organized movement and not an independently existing thing apart from the wheel. And so is mind not separate from the brain.

Hunt cites the analogy of digestion and the stomach. Mind is to the brain as digestion is to the stomach: the brain is what **is**, the mind is what the brain **does**. We do not say that digestion is a spirit that inhabits the stomach. "And why then suppose that mind is a spirit or incorporeal stuff that inhabits the brain?"[16] — asks Murton Hunt.

That brain is structural and mind is functional, both referring to the same entity, is the dominant view in science. However, there are dissenting views expressed by some famous scientists. The distinguished neurophysiologist and Nobel Laureate Sir John C. Eccles is a highly vocal advocate of the view that mind exists apart from the brain. Sir Karl Popper and Sir John Eccles[17] argue that mind, as associated consciousness, has some control over the brain. They say that mind and brain are separate, with weak, slow-acting interaction.

William James, in his book *Principles of Psychology*,[18] discusses mind affecting brain. He holds that mental images of mind control the brain. He further states that consciousness has significant, if small, causal effects on perceiving, thinking, and behaviour.

Here we may refer to the most direct experiments relating the brain to the mind by electrical stimulation with microelectrodes of the brains of conscious human subjects.[19,20] Most of these subjects were epilepsy patients who underwent brain surgery. Patients receiving stimulation of the temporal lobe describe past events which they had experienced. This was a play-back or 'flash-back'. This was not recall of past events, but actual experiential response. Penfield and Roberts[21] indicated a dualist account of consciousness. They concluded:

> Every individual forms a neuronal record of his own stream of consciousness. Since artificial re-activation of the record, later in life, seems to recreate all those things formally included within the focus of his attention, one must assume that re-activated recording pattern of neuronal activity may be considered much more than a record, for it was once used as the final stage of integration to make consciousness what it was.
>
> How far the conclusion in favour of dualism is justified is debatable. But the findings of the experiments are to be seriously pondered over.

Thus opinion is divided on the issue of the identity or separateness of the brain and the mind. The dominant view in science, however, is reductionistic, both the terms referring to one and the same entity. When we refer to the entity by the term 'brain', we mean a structural entity. When we use the word 'mind', we mean the functional aspect of the very entity. We will analyse the tenability of this concept in the concluding chapter.

Notes

1. Kamiya, J. 1968, Conscious control of brain waves, In *Psychology Today*, I(11): 56-60.
2. Hirai, T. and Kasamatsu, A., 1966, An electroencephalographic study of the Zen meditation, In *Folia Psychiatrica et Neurologica Japonica*, 20: 315-36.
3. Gregory, R.L., 1981, *Mind in Science*, p. 484.
4. Putnam, H., 1975, *Mind, Language, and Reality: Philosophical Papers*, 2 vols.

5. Jastrow, R., Quoted by Hunt, M., 1982, *The Universe Within*, p. 318.
6. Fredkin, E., *Idem.* p. 318.
7. Minsky, M., *Idem.* p. 318.
8. Pagels, H.R., 1989, (Ist Publ. 1988) *The Dreams of Reason*, p. 91.
9. Penrose, R., 1989, *The Emperor's New Mind*, pp. 447-48.
10. Gelman, R., Quoted by Hunt, M., p. 82.
11. Pagels, H.R., 1989, p. 92.
12. Romanes, G.J., 1985, *Mind and Motion*, In G. Vesey (ed.) 1963, *Body and Mind*, p. 183.
13. Putnam, H., 1975.
14. Hunt, M., 1982, pp. 80-81
15. Uttal, W.R. Quoted by Hunt, M., p. 81.
16. Hunt, M., pp. 81-82.
17. Popper, K. and Eccles, J.C., 1977, *The Self and Its Brain*, parts I & II.
18. James, W., 1890, *Principles of Psychology*, p. 470.
19. Penfield, W., 1975, *The Mystery of Mind.*
20. Penfield, W., and Jasper, H.H., 1954, *Epilepsy and the Functional Anatomy of the Human Brain.*
21. Penfield, W., and Roberts, L., 1959, *Speech and Brain Mechanisms*, pp. 51-53.

10

Mind and Supermind

IN this concluding chapter, we will present the concepts of mind and Supermind, as given in the Indian scriptures. We will further try to justify the Indian concepts without which the integrated, holistic approach would be fragmented, and many problems will remain unsolved.

Supermind

There is only one Cosmic Mind and we call it Supermind. For each individual entity, either living or non-living, there is an individual mind. At the micro and quantum level, all individual minds and the Supermind are connected. The substratum of the universe is an unbroken whole. In contrast, at the macro or gross level, all minds seem to be separate and a host of entities in plurality exist and function. Their existence and functioning are empirical and phenomenal. They are not real entities in the Vedāntic sense. They are not self-subsisting. They are to be scaffolded for their existence in certain state. They don't remain unchanged for any two adjacent moments, however infinitesimal their time-span may be. Without constant changes, they cannot exist. No entity of matter and energy in the universe can stay in absolute rest. They are always in motion, i.e., in change of time and space. Hence all matter and energy entities are temporal and spatial. All of them are impermanent. The *Vedānta*, however, does not preach nihilism. *Brahman* is the fundamental Consciousness that transcends space and time. It is unchanging and ever existing in the same unchanged state. Anything which is spaceless (*anākāśam*)[1] and timeless (*akālam*)[2] is bound to be non-functional and attributeless. *Brahman* or B continues to remain as B; hence it has no beginning and neither has it end. This unitary, homogeneous, and fundamental Consciousness is the foundation of the multiplicity of the empirical and phenomenal world. It is Existence (*Sat*), Consciousness (*Cit*), and Bliss (*Ānanda*). The English word 'Bliss' is not a proper one to convey the meaning of *Ānanda* here. *Ānanda* is an unchanged state free from ecstasy and agony. It is not a mental state since *Brahman* has no mind (*amanaḥ*).[3] Thus it may be noted here that the concept 'Supermind' does not refer to *Brahman*.

What is the Supermind, then? The *Vedas* use the term *Virāḍ* or *Virāj* for the Supermind. The *Puruṣa-Sūkta* of the *Ṛgveda* says: "From him (the manifested *Puruṣa*, which is figuratively one-fourth of the total) *Virāṭ* (the nominative form of *Virāj*) was born; again *Puruṣa* from *Virāṭ* was born (i.e., all the matter and energy entities of the universe came into being)."[4]

In *Sāṅkhya* philosophy, the first evolute of *Prakṛti* is *Mahat*[5] which is analogous to the Vedic *Virāṭ*. *Mahat* is the cosmic Intellect (*Buddhi*), distinguished from the individual intellect (*buddhi*). It is made up of three strands, viz., *sattva*, *rajas*, and *tamas*.

The precursor of *Virāṭ* or *Mahat* is *Māyā* or *Prakṛti*. *Virāṭ* or *Mahat* has both beginning and end. It is born when a world-period begins; it ends when the world-period terminates. It is used as the Cosmic Mind or Supermind by *Īśvara* (God); but it belongs to *Māyā*, and not to *Īśvara*. The reflection of *Brahman* or the fundamental Consciousness in *Māyā* is *Īśvara*. Thus *Māyā* serves as the limiting adjunct (*upādhi*) of *Īśvara*, who acquires attributes (*guṇas*) and becomes functional (*kriyā*) by virtue of the possession of the *upādhi*. *Māyā* is the power (*Śakti*) of *Brahman* and co-eternal with *Brahman*. Thus *Brahman*, *Īśvara*, and *Māyā* are co-eternal, although they are not three different entities, the fundamental reality being *Brahman* alone.

In Śaiva philosophy, reality is bipolar — Śiva and Śakti. The male pole is Śiva and the female one is Śakti, both being ever united. In this philosophy, both Śiva and Śakti are conscious. *Vedānta* considers *Māyā* as insentient; it is rendered sentient through the reflection of *Brahman* in it.

In the *Śākta* or Tāntric philosophy, the *Devī* or Divine Mother who is the progenitor of the entire universe is conscious. All living and non-living entities in the universe from microparticles to giant-sized stars gain consciousness and intellect because of the presence of the pervading *Śakti* who is *Citi* or Consciousness.[6]

In spite of some subtle differences in the different Indian schools of philosophy, there is convergence of opinion on *Māyā*, *Prakṛti*, or *Śakti* who is regarded as the Mother of the universe. A *Śākta* treatise like the *Śrīdurgā-saptaśatī* designates *Śakti* as the *Māyā* of Viṣṇu[7] (sustainer God who pervades).

Many authors on Hindu philosophy consider *Brahman*, *Īśvara*, Śiva, or Śakti as the Supermind or the Cosmic Mind. It is, however, not true if one goes deep into the subject. The Supermind (*Virāḍ* or *Mahat*) is the first created product out of *Māyā* or *Prakṛti* and it serves as the mental apparatus of *Īśvara*.

No Universe Without a Supermind

Many scientists and philosophers consider the universe as beginningless and endless, although they allow changes inside the world system. This idea has been revised, at least by many, during the second half of the twentieth century, consequent on many discoveries in astrophysics and cosmology. The present notion admits at least the birth of the universe, if not the death. The universe appeared as a cosmic egg that exploded with the production of a tremendous quantity of heat. In the first few seconds after the Big-Bang the formation of some particles and light elements took place. The universe expanded and it is still expanding although at a comparatively slower rate. Some scientists say that the universe will some day (in the very distant future) stop expanding and start contracting. The contraction will be accelerated in due course of time and will end in a Big Crunch. Some say that this will be the heat death of the universe. Some others foresee an oscillating universe or a pulsating universe, the expansion followed by contraction, these two alternate phases continuing for ever. The *Vedānta* philosophy has a somewhat different opinion. The whole universe will be dissolved in *Māyā* and this process is known as dissolution. Again, when *Īśvara* desires, a cosmic egg will appear from *Māyā* and this will be the beginning of the subsequent creation. The world cycle of creation and dissolution go on *ad infinitum*. These cycles did not have beginning in the past; they will not have end in the future.

Some thinkers may discard the Vedāntic concept by saying that this is speculative and metaphysical. Hence, we may suspend the consideration of the Vedāntic notion of the cyclic universe, involving God, *Māyā*, *Virāḍ* or *Mahat*. Even if we do that, we don't rid ourselves of problems. The Big-Bang was previously thought to be fortuitous and chaotic. The present universe was considered as one of the innumerable chances. One random event happened and so our universe exists today. Some other random events could have happened also, and, in that case, our present universe and we could not exist today. This version of cosmology, involving no design, no preplan, and basing on chance alone, is no longer acceptable to a number of cosmologists. They think that the Big-Bang and the events that followed have been precisely preplanned and designed. They discard the view that the appearance of our universe and its subsequent functionings are purely fortuitous. The argument of design is also a forceful one in the *Vedānta*.[8] If design is accepted, it implies the existence of an intelligent designer with a Supermind.

Paul Davies, British professor of Physics and a renowned expositor, admits the prevailing order in Nature:

> Nature displays a hierarchy of structure. From the smallest known constituents of the atom to the large scale arrangement of the galaxies, we observe systems with characteristic organization and size, each level of structure interlocking with the others in a highly ordered way. What determines the scale of these structures and their relation to one another?[9]

Looking at the cosmic coincidences, Paul Davies expresses his thoughts in a deep philosophical way by the following words:

> . . . accidental numerical relations between quantities as unconnected as the fine structure constants for gravity and electromagnetism, or between the strengths of nuclear forces and the thermodynamic condition of the primeval universe, suggest that many of the familiar systems that populate the universe are the result of exceedingly improbable coincidences.
>
> Turning to the subject of cosmology . . . we encounter further cosmic cooperation of such a wildly improbable nature, it becomes hard to resist the impression that some basic principle is at work.[10]

Heinz Pagels[11] presents some instances of the fine tuning of our universe. The force of gravity has been set at an ideal level. Had it been higher by just a bit, the stars would have consumed their hydrogen fuel more rapidly than what they now do; our sun might burn itself in less than a billion years; and this time would have been hardly sufficient for the evolution to continue up to the emergence of the human species. The other alternative might be thought of, that is, gravity would have been nudged downwards a notch. In that case, our sun would have cooled down to a temperature, too chilly to sustain life.

The ratio of photons (particles of light) to nuclear particles (protons and neutrons) falls within a most convenient range. This ratio plays a critical role in determining the rate at which the cosmos expands. Had this ratio been one hundred times wider than what it is now, the universe would have expanded so rapidly that stars and galaxies might not have formed, in which case there would be no place for life to live.

The preponderance of hydrogen is another convenient characteristic of the universe. This element (its lightest isotope, whose occurrence is the most frequent, is made up of one proton and one electron) comprises about 74 per cent of the observed matter in the universe. The proton is a stable particle whereas the neutron is not. A neutron decays into a proton, an electron and an antineutrino. The neutron is slightly more massive than the proton. Let us take a hypothetical case in which the proton would be more massive than the neutron, say by a small fraction of one per cent. Then protons would decay into neutrons. In that imaginary universe, protons would be unstable, and eventually that universe would not contain enough hydrogen to serve as the fuel of the burning stars. We do not expect life to evolve in a universe in which protons are unstable.

The Big-Bang explosion was not chaotic. Everything of it was finely tuned. Had it been uncontrolled, we would have got an inhomogeneous and anisotropic universe. But the universe is isotropic, that is, it looks much the same in all directions. The galaxies are evenly distributed over the entire sky, without being lumped into one place and scarce in others. The microwave background radiation, that is the heat left over from the primordial Big-Bang, is equally spread across the universe. Had the universe been anisotropic, matter would not have formed into galaxies, stars, and planets. The formation of galaxies, stars, and planets could have been prevented by the vast quantities of heat produced by an anisotropic universe. The enormous quantity of heat could have exerted strong radiation pressure. Could there be evolution of life then? It might be that some miracle(?) could have happened and *Homo sapiens* could appear. But how could he reside without a place?

The universal constants play very important roles in order that the universe may function meaningfully. We have encountered six fundamental universal constants, viz., the velocity of light in vacuum ($c = 3.00 \times 10^8$), the charge on a proton ($e = 1.60 \times 10^{-19}$), Planck's constant ($h = 6.63 \times 10^{-34}$), Newton's gravitational constant ($G = 6.67 \times 10^{-11}$), the weak force constant ($g_w = 1.43 \times 10^{-62}$), and the strong force constant ($g_s = 15$), all these numerical values being given in SI units. All these constants have been intelligently contrived for designing the macro- and the micro-structures of the universe. Had one constant been missed or altered, we could not get a universe as we have, and *Homo sapiens* could not be evolved.

In physics, astrophysics, and cosmology, we meet the large number 10^{40}. A few examples concerned with this large number are cited below:[12]

$$\alpha_G^{-1} \sim 10^{40}$$

Here α is the electromagnetic fine structure constrant and G is Newton's gravitational constant. Thus α_G^{-1} is the inverse of the gravitational 'fine structure' constant.

$$N \sim 10^{80} = (10^{40})^2$$

Here N is the number of protons located inside the Hubble radius.

$$N^* \sim 10^{60} = (10^{40})^{3/2}$$

Here N^* is the number of stars in a galaxy.

$$t_H/t_N \sim 10^{40}$$

Here t_H is the Hubble time (H^{-1}) which is 5.00×10^{17} in SI units: and t_N is the proton (nuclear) Compton time, $h/m_p c^2$, which is 4.41×10^{-24} in SI units.

$$t_N/t_P \sim 10^{40}$$
$$t_H/t_P \sim 10^{60} = (10^{40})^{3/2}$$

Here t_P is Planck time which is 5.39×10^{-44} in SI units.

$$\alpha_w \sim (10^{40})^{1/4}$$

Here α_w is the weak fine structure constant which is 3.05×10^{-12} in SI units.

$$S \sim (10^{40})^{1/4}$$

Here S is the cosmic photon/proton ratio which is 10^9.

$$N^*_g \sim N_g \sim (10^{40})^{1/4}$$

Here N^*_g and N_g are the number of stars in a galaxy and the number of galaxies in the universe, respectively.

We get early references on large-number coincidences from the reports of Eddington[13,14] and Dirac.[15,16] Dirac has noted that most physical and astrophysical dimensionless constants are of the order of the magnitude of integral powers (positive and negative) of the number 10^{40}. In his opinion, there is hardly any likelihood of the accidental correspondence of the apparently unrelated, enormous numbers. Hence he suggested some unknown causal connection. Rees *et al.*[17] discussed the topic of large number coincidence by analysing the two alternatives of coincidence or consequence.

The four fundamental forces are the gravitational force,

the electromagnetic force, and the two nuclear forces — weak and strong. We cannot imagine a universe without these four forces or interactions. The protons and neutrons inside the nucleus of the atom are bound by the strong force. Without this strong force, atoms could not be formed. Our sun and the other stars burn through a sequence of nuclear reactions, the initial step being the fusion of two protons (hydrogen ions) to produce a deuteron, a positron and a neutrino. This is a weak interaction process involving the inverse of beta decay, in which a proton converts into a neutron. Without the weak force, stars could not burn, we could not get energy from the sun, and the evolution of life would have been impossible. No chemical reaction could be possible without the electromagnetic interaction, and hence the emergence of life could be inconceivable. The galaxies, stars and planets would fly away from one another, had there been no gravitational interaction. Even the cells of the human, animal or plant body could not be held together without the influence of gravitation.

Even if the four fundamental forces are present, the universe would have been different from what it is now, and life could not emerge if the strong force constant, weak force constant, weak fine structure constant, electromagnetic fine structure constant, and gravitational fine structure constant could have been slightly altered.

We have taken a few examples of the numerous cases of the fine-tunings of the universe. It may suffice to say that the universe has been over-designed.

We have already quoted from the book *The Accidental Universe* written by Paul Davies who could appreciate the order and design existing in the universe. He has presented an extensive catalogue of physical coincidences and indicated apparently accidental cooperation. He has hinted at a hidden principle that seems to be at work, organizing the cosmos in a coherent way. Of course, he has not proposed such a principle. It is apparently anomalous, of course, to recognize design and harmony and at the same time interpret them as accidental. This was perhaps done in order to avoid criticism. No scientist could publicly declare the existence of a designer even if he/she privately realized in the core of his/her heart. In the history of religion *versus* science, religion antagonized science and adhered to the so-called revealed truth. Then came a phase in which science antagonized religion through observed and carefully tested truths. Now this second phase is over. We are at the threshold of a third phase in which empirical truths alone cannot explain all phenomena of Nature. Scientific discoveries of the twentieth century badly need the fusion of empirical science and spirituality which is not necessarily religion. Religions have dogmas. But science is not free from them although in a different way. Due to our preconceived ideas and dogmas, we are psychologically hesitant to associate science with spirituality. The result is the birth of some queer ideas in science. One such illogical idea is the 'anthropic principle'.

One may usually assume that *Homo sapiens* has 'accidentally' evolved in the 'accidental universe', that all the physical constants and coincidences are fortuitous, and that no intelligent designer, co-ordinator and controller is involved in bringing about order in the universe.

Theological interpretations outrightly reject such chance or accidental notions and posit a creator who has designed and created the universe and is still controlling it. The Bible is geocentric as well as anthropocentric. God created man in His own image and created everything else for the pleasure of man. The best creation of God is man and everything else has been created with an anthropocentric object.

Some scientists have challenged the traditional theological interpretation and also the chance interpretation of the physical sciences. They declare that the structure of the physical world is inseparable from the inhabitants that observe it, in a very fundamental sense. They do recognize the existence of a guiding principle which works to fine-tune the cosmos to incredible accuracy. In their opinion, this guiding principle is not a physical principle, but an anthropic principle.

The anthropic line of reasoning can be traced back to the year 1955, when the mathematician Gerald Whitrow[18] of Imperial College, London, published an article in the *British Journal for the Philosophy of Science*. In this article he argued: "The universe is three-dimensional, because life could not exist in other dimensions". In 1957, the Princeton Physicist Robert Dicke published an article in *Reviews of Modern Physics*,[19] where he suggested the concept of the anthropic principle although he did not name it so. He said: "The fundamental physical constants such as the gravitational constant and the charge on the electron are 'not random but conditional by biological factors'; the universe is such and such, because life must emerge and organisms must exist in order that these constants are to be measured."

In 1974, Brandon Carter,[20] an English cosmologist, coined the term 'anthropic principle'. "What we can expect to observe must be restricted by the conditions necessary for our presence as observers". This is the weak anthropic principle as formulated by Carter. He defines the strong anthropic principle: "The universe must be such as to admit the creation of observers within it at some stage."

Support for the strong anthropic principle may be found in quantum physics and also in the philosophy of positivism. The quantum physicist asserts that the process of measurement demands the participation of a conscious observer at a fundamental level. Accordingly, there cannot be an object without the participatory observation of a subject. The universe came into existence to be observed by the human observer. The philosophical school of logical positivism demands that only that which is perceived enjoys true reality. For a logical positivist, a universe which did not admit observers is meaningless. According to this notion, the only truly **real** universe is that which is perceived. In order that this universe is to be real, it must adjust its properties for being conducive to the emergence of life and evolution of conscious beings.

One may go through the comprehensive discussion on the anthropic principle in the book *The Anthropic Cosmological Principle*, written by John Barrow and Frank Tipler.[21] This book contains much history of the design argument. The teleological statement, "our universe must contain life" has been emphasized by the authors.

John Barrow writes: "Many observations of the natural world, although remarkable *a priori*, are seen in this light as inevitable consequences of our own existence".[22]

Joseph Silk is another advocate of the strong anthropic principle. He states: "Gravitational instability and fragmentation must lead from giant clusters to galaxies to stars, and ultimately to planets and an environment suitable for the development of life. This unbroken chain is essential in any cognizable universe, and may therefore provide the key to understanding the significance of the fundamental dimensionless numbers of astrophysics and cosmology".[23] A universe that is not cognized does not exist. Silk supports this notion and suggests: "It is cognizability that will *explain* in numbers, not *vice versa*."

Wheeler[24] presents his famous concept by what he terms "our participatory universe". According to this concept, the existence of an observer (*Homo sapiens*) at some historical stage is directly responsible for the creation of the universe.

Barry Collins and Stephen Hawking,[25] while furnishing an anthropic explanation of cosmic isotropy, addressed the question: "Why is the universe isotropic"? To their question they answered: "Because we exist".

We get a classic survey of the early literature on the anthropic principle in an article published by Carr and Rees.[26] According to Carr's interpretation, at least in some of his papers, God might have chosen to create just the kind of cosmos in which living beings could evolve. Richard

Swinburne[27] wondered at the fine-tuning of the universe and argued in favour of the existence of God. John Leslie,[28, 29] like Swinburne, has also deduced the existence of God from the observational premises of the fine-tuning of the universe.

Some thinkers reject the notion that there is anything like the anthropic principle. Heinz Pagels claims that the anthropic principle is not testable.[30] Stephen Jay Gould[31] does not find evidence to support any belief in the anthropic principle, and he rebuts any argument in favour of such a principle by saying that it is "historically moth-eaten". B.J. Carr, for whom a theological interpretation of the anthropic principle is not unacceptable, remarks in guarded language: ". . . one would have to conclude either that the features of the universe invoked in support of the Anthropic Principle are **only** coincidences or that the universe was indeed tailor-made for life. I will leave it to the theologians to ascertain the identity of the tailor."[32]

Paul Davies does recognize the coincidences of the **accidental** universe. But he is not convinced with the explanation provided by the anthropic principle. He writes:

> From the strictly physical point of view it seems mysterious, to say the least, that the existence of conscious beings can actually bring about the celebrated coincidences. Clearly any direct causal connection is impossible. Special physical conditions may produce man, but man can hardly be attributed the credit for establishing his own environmental requirements.[33]

The foregoing discussion on the anthropic principle strongly indicates one fact that the universe is designed, well co-ordinated, and fine-tuned. The inference that the design and harmony are caused by man's appearance on the earth is illogical and irrelevant and hence unacceptable. How can a future event (the appearance of *Homo sapiens* on the earth) cause all the phenomena of the universe starting from the Big-Bang? If it is teleological, we accept the version of the Bible that invokes God as the Creator and Designer. How can we reject God and accept the anthropic principle?

The ideas of geocentrism and anthropocentrism are pre-Copernican and are rooted in the Bible. Science has established the fact that the earth is not the centre of the universe and that everything in the universe is not tuned to the interest of man. If we think statistically, we cannot eliminate the chances of extraterrestrial life. Somewhere in the universe, there might have evolved conscious beings, much more advanced than man on the earth. Further, man is not the terminal point in the evolutionary ladder, the summit or the highest rung has not yet been reached, there is nothing like a last rung, and we do expect that evolution is an ongoing process by which species more evolved than man would appear on the earth in the future (provided mankind does not commit suicide). Anthropocentrism is implied in the anthropic principle. Facts and arguments do not allow one to accept anthropocentrism. The scientists who advocate the anthropic principle have been very much influenced by the Biblical thought that God created everything of the universe for the comfort of man. Science rejected God, or remained unconcerned with God, but accepted the idea that the whole universe is fine-tuned to the interest of man. It would be outrageously unscientific to accept the anthropic principle.

But the design, the co-ordination, the harmony, and the fine-tuning that we observe in the universe cannot be whisked away by saying that they are mere chances or accidents. There may be accidental designs in rare instances. But it is almost impossible to think of universal designs and fine-tuning without a Designer with a Supermind. The universe is a product. Man is a recent product in consideration of the long history of the universe (15-18 billion years). If the primordial cosmic egg was designed, the Big-Bang was designed, and all later events in the cosmos were designed, we must search for the Designer who transcends the universe, although still immanent. That designer must be prior to the universe.

If we accept a Designer who has the Supermind, how is He different from God of the Bible then? This Designer is the Presiding Deity of the cosmic evolution. This is a major point of difference from the theology of the Bible that rejects evolution. We accept the Designer; we accept His Supermind; we accept the cosmic evolution which is cyclic — evolution followed by involution, or in other words, manifestation and evolution, followed by dissolution. The cycle of unmanifest ⟶ manifest ⟶ unmanifest had no beginning in the past and shall have no end in the future. These cosmic cycles operate under the guidance and supervision of an intelligent Divine Being who is both immanent and transcendent. We do not accept the one-time creation out of nothing; and we do not accept man as the best and final finished product in the creation, around whose interest everything revolves. We do expect somebody better than man to be evolved. And we do not exclude the possibility of the presence of conscious being more evolved than man in our galaxy and other galaxies even at present. These are our basic concepts which are at variance with geocentrism and anthropocentrism. The anthropic principle is neither scientific nor theological.

The Vediç and Vedāntic literature conceives of divine deliberation[34] prior to the cosmic manifestion and evolution. The word 'creation' is not used in the Vadāntic concept since *de novo* creation is rejected, *creatio ex nihilo* being a logical absurdity. The Vedāntic cosmology allows something to be manifested out of something latently existing in an unmanifested condition. But the manifestation and subsequent evolution followed by the involution and subsequent dissolution are not mechanistically operative. The *Vedānta* holds that everything of the universe — all matter and energy — is insentient. It further holds that *Māyā*, the power of *Brahman*, which is the material cause of the universe is also insentient. Anything insentient cannot think, plan and design. *Virāḍ* or *Mahat* which is the first product of *Māyā* or

Prakṛti is the Supermind of *Īśvara* (God). The Supermind is also insentient. Although insentient, it is the apparatus of sentience. *Īśvara* uses the Supermind as the Cosmic Computer. But the Maker and Programmer of the Cosmic Computer is *Īśvara* Himself. The Cosmic Intelligence is *Īśvara* who desires to have a universe. This desire precedes the appearance of the cosmic egg. In every cosmic cycle, this divine desire is always precedent to the cosmic manifestation.

According to the *Advaita Vedānta*, *Īśvara* is not an entity second to *Brahman*. *Brahman* reflected in its power *Māyā* constitutes *Īśvara*. Thus *Māyā* serves as the limiting adjunct (*upādhi*) for *Īśvara*. *Brahman* is the fundamental Consciousness which is attributeless and actionless. *Īśvara*, the reflected Consciousness in *Māyā*, has attributes and is active. He is the Cosmic Intelligence who has full control on *Māyā* through which He performs all actions. In a hypothetical case of the total absence of *Māyā* (*Śakti*), *Īśvara* cannot posses attributes and cannot perform actions. And this *Māyā* is not an independent (*svatantrā*) entity. It is the power (*Śakti*) of *Brahman* in the analogy of the light and heat of the sun. Thus, in the final analysis, it is *Brahman*, the non-dual fundamental Consciousness, that is all.

Īśvara offers Himself to be functional in three ways. He is an architect and a builder, and for such creative actions He is known as Brahmā.[35] He is the sustainer, controller, and administrator of the universe, and for such executive actions He is known as Viṣṇu.[36] Destruction is co-existent and co-extensive with creation. It is more apparent in the micro-world than in the macro-world. Every moment micro-particles are created and annihilated. *Īśvara* functions, as the destroyer and devourer. For annihilative functions, both in the micro- and the macro-world, He is known as Rudra.[37]

According to the *Vedānta*, *Īśvara* entered[38] into everything that was created, subsequent to the explosion of the cosmic egg. This word 'entered' used here has a symbolic meaning only. There is no place where *Īśvara* is not present,

He being omnipresent and all-pervading. Remaining within, the one *Īśvara* assumes many forms according to whatever form He enters into.[39] Dwelling in all created entities, both living and non-living, He controls all activities of all entities from within, and hence is known as *antaryāmī* (inner controller).[40] His presence inside an entity induces action in accordance with the cosmic laws. Thus *Īśvara* is the executor and controller (*praśāsaka*)[41] of everything of the universe. He pervades all entities of Nature and is the Presiding Deity (*adhyakṣa*)[42] of everything. Without this function of the presiding of the fundamental Cosnciousness, insentient Nature does not have the ability to work. There must not be confusion over the control of *Īśvara* through His presiding function. He is not the doer whereas Nature (*Prakṛti*) does everything.[43] The subtle difference between becoming a doer and controlling the actions of other doers through presiding may be appreciated. The photon, the proton, the electron, the star, the galaxy, the virus, the amoeba, or every human individual does its, his, or her actions. All of them are not inert and passive; neither are they mere instruments. Nature evolves through the presiding supervision of *Īśvara*.[44]

The *Vedas* declare order (*ṛta*) in the universe.[45] Scientists observe order in the universe. There is no dispute over the order. How this order is brought about is the real bone of contention. The *Sāṅkhya* is atheistic and gives an atheistic interpretation. According to it, *Pradhāna* (insentient Nature) evolves without the guidance and control of an omniscient Lord. Of course, this *Sāṅkhya* concept accepts the mere presence of innumerable *jīvas* that are sentient entities, *albeit* inactive. The atheistic interpretation of science avoids a Divine Being as the controller and co-ordinator of the world phenomena. Śaṅkara, the celerated exponent of the *Advaita Vedānta*, holds that the orderliness of the universe is not possible without a ruler-*cum*-co-ordinator and so he adduces inferential evidences for the existence of *Īśvara*.[46] He poses the question: How is it possible for the insentient Nature (*Pradhāna*) to exercise ruling (*praśāsana*) and controlling (*niyantraṇa*) power?[47] He holds that the universe cannot function as a *saṁsāra* (the universe with orderly motion, co-ordination, and harmony) without a Supreme Controller (*Parameśvara, Maheśvara*).[48]

For the purpose of our discussion here, we may take a few examples such as Pauli's exclusion principle, the behaviour of a photon in the double-slit experiment, and the mutual cooperation of a pair of electron and positron in the experiment of Alain Aspect and his collaborators.

In 1925, Wolfgang Pauli formulated the 'exclusion principle', which says that no two nearby electrons can be exactly in the same state. For this discovery Pauli won the Nobel Prize in 1945. The exclusion principle is one of the primary laws of quantum mechanics. It helps dictate the complicated patterns formed by the electrons in the atom. The chemical properties of an element are derived from the behaviour of its orbiting electrons. Thus the exclusion principle is one of the pillars of chemistry. Now let us come to the metaphysics of the behaviour of an electron pair in an orbit of an atom. How do the electrons obey this principle? Don't they obey and do they mechanically act? Are they conscious of the principle and do they adhere to it? Some modern philosophers do not recognize the principles or laws of Nature. They consider them as uniformities in Nature. But substitution of one word with another does not solve the basic issue; it only evades it. It is a fact that the laws of Nature are unlike the ones passed in a parliament and codified in legal books. Still they are laws of a different type. Why are there uniformities in Nature? Are they meaningful or meaningless? Is there any necessity for the entities of Nature to act according to some uniformities? Would there be chaos if there are no uniformities in Nature? Let us hypothesize that from today onwards the orbital electrons in atoms violate the Pauli's exclusion principle. If that happens, all chemical reactions in both the living and the non-living world would be in jeopardy. What interests do the electrons have to care for the exclusion principle? Science abhors to answer such questions.

The double-slit experiment shows the importance of the observer in actualizing the micro-universe. When a light-beam passes through a single slit, it produces a distribution on the screen with most particles detected in line with the slit. Next, an experiment may be contrived so that a light-beam may pass through either one of the two slits or both the slits. When one of the two slits is blocked off in turn, we get the usual pattern on the screen for single-slit experiments. When both the slits are open, we do not get the pattern produced by adding up those two patterns. Instead, a pattern for interference by waves is obtained. It is interesting and surprising that a single photon, on its way through one slit, strictly adheres to the statistical laws which are only appropriate if it 'knows' whether the other slit is open or closed.

In 1982, Alain Aspect, J. Dalibard, and G. Roger at the University of Paris-South devised and conducted experiments whose results show that the members of a particle-pair are always in communion and 'know' the status of each other without transmitting any message. The particle-pair, for example, may be an electron and an anti-electron (positron). They are produced from a central source and move in opposite directions to trillions of kilometres apart. Before the appearance of the particle-pair, there was zero manifestation of the spin. After the appearance, the total of the spins of the two partners is also zero, since the spin of one particle is always equal and opposite to that of its antiparticle. We may bring a change in the spin of one member of the particle-pair. The spin of the other member must be simultaneously reflected in a corresponding change irrespective of whether both the members of the pair stay close together or far away at a distance of trillions of light-years. What has been described here is not hypothetical, but experimentally factual. But the experiments do not reveal the mystery. Up-to-date science cannot explain how particles are 'conscious', how they interact, how they communicate with each other, and how they do what should be done.

The examples cited here are only a few. They represent the universe — micro and macro, living and non-living. How can we say that the insentient Nature is sentient? It involves self-contradiction and hence is nonsensical. How can we say that the pluralistic Nature is harmonized and co- ordinated without any central authority to control and co- ordinate? How can unconscious Nature work intelligently? We can't answer all these questions unless we accept what Śaṅkara has said.

No Organism without a Mind

Science and modern psychology generally consider mind as a functional word for the brain which is a structural word. The brain, although a special organ of the body, is made up of matter like other organs some of which are special in some other respects also.

Again, science and modern psychology consider the fertilization of an ovum with a sperm, leading to the formation of a zygote, as the starting time of an individual person, who did not have existence before this said time. According to the concept of science, nothing of a person survives his/her death, except, of course, the elements of which the body is composed. The soul is no longer recognized in natural science and modern psychology. According to the ancient Western concept, mind and soul were identical and hence the old concept of mind has been discarded. To speak in a nutshell, the modern trend in science, psychology, and philosophy is in favour of an identity of mind and brain.

Let us probe deep into the matter and analyse if an identity can be established between mind and brain.

The bacteria *Clostridium tetani* causes the disease tetanus. This micro-organism lives in soil and dust for many years in sporulated condition. The amoeba that causes amoebic dysentery in man is known as *Entamoeba histolytica*. It passes out from the large intestine in the faeces. It leaves outside in sporulated condition for a long period. What are these spores? When the environmental conditions like temperature, humidity, oxygen supply etc. are unconducive to life, some micro-organisms form a protective wall around their cells and they live inside by bringing their basal metabolism to a near standstill state. Whenever a conducive environment is available, the spores germinate to a vegetative state. Bacteria such as Mycobacterium tuberculosis and Mycobacterium leprae are encapsulated. The cell develops a capsule of fatty material around its cell-wall. Polymorphonuclear leucocytes (neutrophils), lymhocytes, and macrophages cannot kill and devour them due to this capsule. Water-soluble drugs cannot enter into their cells. These behaviours and many others that micro-organisms exhibit are self-protective, meaningful and hence may be called 'conscious'. But micro-organisms do not possess brain; neither do they possess nerves. Hence we cannot say that mind and brain are identical.

All species of invertebrate animals have no vertebral column, no spinal cord, and no brain. Still they show ingenious dexterity to protect themselves. Their behaviour is meaningful. They interact with their environment and with their fellow members in an appropriate way. Some species possess a small number of nerve cells. Still they are brainless. Although brainless, they do not behave brainlessly. Thus it would not be correct to identify mind and brain.

Social insects like honey-bee, ants, and termites live in regimental societies. They communicate among themselves. They obey the command of their dictator. They abide by the rules of the society, that enforces division of labour. They behave meaningfully. They act 'intelligently'. Still, anatomically speaking, they are brainless. Their nervous system is composed of supraesophageal ganglia related by connectives to a subpharyngeal ganglion whence originates a ventrally placed, segmentally ganglionated nerve cord. When these brainless tiny creatures work 'intelligently', we cannot justifiably identify mind and brain.

Sir Jagadish Chandra Bose, in 1926, published his book *The Nervous Mechanism of Plants.*[49] The sensitive *Mimosa pudica* was one of the plants he studied. The leaflets of this plant close up and the leaves point downwards at night. During the daytime, the plant responds to mechanical stimulation by closing the leaflets more rapidly. The stimulus causes a wave of electrical depolarization, similar to what occurs in nerves in animals. In case the stimulus is strong, the impulse may spread to other leaves which also fold up. It may be mentioned here that the word 'nerve' for plants has no similarity with that for animals. Another example is the word 'hormone'. The animal hormones have nothing in common with the plant hormones, one example of which is auxin (indolyl-3-acetic acid). If we are not very hard and fast about the details of anatomy, physiology, and biochemistry of plants and animals, and focus our attention on the essential analogy, we would not be wrong to notice 'consciousness' in plants.

Plants are 'conscious' and 'intelligent' in their own way. In this connection, we may quote Richard Gregory: "Plants do have remarkable Potential Intelligence. The humblest plant exhibits photochemical processes that are not yet fully understood by the cleverest human chemists. Their structures for giving strength, accepting light, moisture and so on, are brilliantly clever desings adapted to the problems that the plants have to face. They do not, however, show much ability (compared with animals) in dealing with novel situations. But some plants do have genuine behaviour".[50]

We may consider the tropistic behaviour of plant organs. The inherent response of a plant organ to an environmental influence acting as a stimulus is known as a tropism. The response may be positive or negative. It is positive when the growth of the plant-organ is towards the source of the stimulus. It is negative when the growth of the plant-organ is away from the stimulus. The stimuli may be gravity, light, water, contact, gases, chemicals, etc. We use the term geotropism, phototropism, hydrotropism, chemotropism, thermotropism, galvanotropism, and thigmotropism, depending upon the stimulus — earth's gravitational force, light, sources of moisture, chemicals, heat, electricity, mechanical contact, respectively. Plants exhibit differences in growth rates due to asymmetric distribution of auxins, or growth-regulating hormones. The tropistic reactions are advantageous to the plant. Stems usually are negatively geotropic, i.e., they tend to grow vertically upwards. Roots invariably grow downwards and are thus positively geotropic. Stems and leaves are positively phototropic. They tend to bend towards light, or towards a region of higher light intensity. This response is positively advantageous to the plant since light is necessary for photosynthesis. Roots are negatively phototropic. Roots of plants exhibit positive hydrotropism; they grow towards regions of moisture in the soil. For this reason, desert plants are deep-rooted since the roots penetrate deep into the soil in search of moisture.

The tropistic behaviour of plants is objective and not debatable. The interpretation of this behaviour is, however, debated. Those who are in favour of a mechanistic interpretation say that these characteristics have been evolved in the plants according to the Darwinian principles, and that plants behave as they do purely on mechanical grounds. This mechanical explanation does not recognize anything like consciousness or intelligence in plants. Some others, however, do not accept such a mechanical explanation. The principles of evolution are common to micro-organisms, lower plants, higher plants, animals, and man. When we recognize consciousness and intelligence in man, there is no reason why plants may be considered devoid of consciousness especially when they meaningfully respond to the environmental stimuli with special reference to their own interests, self-protection and self-defence. The tradition of limiting consciousness to human beings only has been deep-rooted in the Western culture due to the fact that soul and mind were considered indentical in the West and that non-human living beings and plants were thought to be soulless. Although this old concept has been discarded, its impact on human thinking is still lingering.

The stalks of some climbing plants twist in one direction only, that is, some are right-handed and some others left-handed. There are, however, a few plants that can twist either way, and change direction as the need arises. Can we say that these plants are conscious since they decide their functions on the basis of needs?

The stalks of runner beans (*Phaseolus multiflorus*) coil only counter-clockwise. They have a sense of gravity. They climb only vertical or near-vertical supports. They avoid to coil around rods, poles, or perches that are horizontal. Their stalks, unlike tendrils, are not touch-sensitive. Can we say that runner bean plants are conscious since they distinguish vertical from horizontal supports?

Droseraceae is a family of plants represented by mostly perennial creeping insectivorous herbs of marshy places with underground stems. The genus Drosera, Dionaea, and Aldrovanda are worth mentioning here for our purpose. Common plants are *Drosera burmanni*, *Drosera indica*, *Aldrovanda vesiculosa*, and *Dionaea muscipula*. Their leaves are metamorphosed for catching insect preys. The upper surface of the leaf lamina of *Drosera* is provided with tentacles which are glandular hairs. The tentacles have peculiar power of movement and curvature. As insects get stuck into the mucilaginous secretions of glands, the tentacles bend down over the body of the imprisoned prey and take a firm grip.

The Venus' fly-trap (*Dionaea muscipula*) is a climbing plant. Its leaves are radical and are arranged in rosettes. Each leaf is a prey-catching trap. This trap has six sensitive hairs. On touch with insects or similar other prey, the hairs are activated, and, as a result, the mobile leaf blades immediately close-up like 'scissor mouse trap', engulfing and killing the victim. But the same fly-trap does not close when a raindrop enters. When the six hairs are touched in fly-walking sequence, then only are they activated and the trap closes. The trap contains glands that secrete digestive enzymes for killing and digesting the fly. Soon after the digestion is over, the trap opens. When the plant has such logic circuits, can't we say that the plant is conscious?

For a discussion on the pitcher plants, here we mention two families, viz., *Sarraceniaceae* and *Nepenthaceae*. The family *Sarraceniaceae* comprises three genera with twelve species. These genera are: *Sarracenia*, *Darlingtonia*, and *Heliamphora*. The family *Nepenthaceae* is monotypic, consisting of single genus *Nepenthes*.

Plants of the *Sarraceniaceae* family are perennial herbs of marshy places with pitcher-like radical leaves meant for catching insect preys. In this family, the leaves are modified into insect-catching traps. The leaf-blade folds itself to form a conical or tubular structure which looks like a pitcher. The upper part of the pitcher is prolonged into a lid or operculum. The operculum is often brightly coloured. It contains nectar-secreting glands. Its upper surface is covered by downwardly curved stiff hairs. The conducting zone to the tube has a velvety smooth slippery surface. Next comes the cupular zone of the pitcher which is beset with glands. The last zone of the pitcher is a small portion covered inside with inwardly directed hairs which prevent the trapped prey from escaping. This zone has no glands and it is absorptive. *Sarracenia psittacina* and *Sarracenia purpurea* are two species belonging to the genus *Sarracenia*. In *Darlingtonia*, the pitcher is very long, about a metre in length sometimes, with a biforked operculum which looks like a fish-tail. Large preys like small snakes, lizards, and frogs are occasionally caught by the pitcher of this genus. The basal interior of the pitcher is filled with fluid containing proteolytic enzymes by which the entrapped prey is digested. Finally, the digested nutrients are absorbed by the plant.

The only one genus *Nepenthes* of the family *Nepenthaceae* contains about sixty species, among which *Nepenthes khasiana*, *Nepenthes pervellei*, *Nepenthes madagascariensis*, and *Nepenthes raja* may be mentioned here. The pitcher, in this family also, functions as an insect-catching trap. The bright colour and honey of the lid of the pitcher attract insects and fleas. Once they sit on the lid, they descend down the slippery part and fall to the bottom of the pitcher. They get drowned in the liquid filling the base of the pitcher, die, and decay. The nutrients released as a result of the digestion of the body of the prey are absorbed by the plant.

Plants of the *Lentibulariaceae* family are insectivorous. The family has genera such as *Pinguicula, Genlisca, Polypompholyx* (terrestrial plants), *Utricularia, Biovularia, Saccolaria* (aquatic plants), and others. In *Utricularia,* the insect-catching apparatus or traps are so-called bladders which are borne on submerged leaves. The mouth of the bladder is fitted with a valve which opens inwards but closes outwards. Sensory hairs are located at the mouth of the bladder. When insects come in contact with these hairs, stimuli are generated, and in response, the bladder closes up by the valve. The insect caught inside cannot come out. Its body is decayed. The nutrients released are absorbed by special glandular hairs lining inside the wall of the bladder.

The leaves of the genus *Pinguicula* are insect-catching traps like *Drosera.* There are glandular hairs on the leaves with adhesive secretion. When an insect sits on a leaf, its margins are infolded for capturing the prey.

What has been written here about the carnivorous plants with reference to their specialized anatomical structures and physiological as well as biochemical functions may be interpreted on the basis of Darwinian evolution and mechanistic actions. Mutation and natural selection are the two pillars on which the edifice of Darwinian evolution stands. We may accept it as a fact. The question is: Is it wrong to infer from the observed data that plants are not devoid of consciousness? If the Venus' fly-trap can distinguish a prey (an insect) from a raindrop, there does not seem to be anything wrong to say that such an action is conscious.

Plants of the family *Passifloraceae* are mostly tendril climbers. A few species of *Passiflora* are cultivated in gardens for beautiful flowers with corona and some are cultivated for edible fruits. The passion-flower belonging to the genus *Passiflora* and family *Passifloraceae* and the white bryony (*Bryonia dioica*) reach out successfully to seek support. Here we may discuss, in more detail, the behaviour of the tendrils of the passion-flower plant, as reported by Richard Gregory.[51] Tendrils of the young plants first grow straight out, then they curve in a fantastically perfect exponential helix for seeking a support to grasp and cling to. After clinging to a support, the later tendrils grow straight outwards initially, but then form tight cylindrical springy coils. After about five turns the spiral reverses in direction, forming a neat loop in the process. This sequence of ten turns and reversal may continue several times, until the tendril finds and clings to a support. The sensitive tip of the tendril recognizes a possible support. The tip transmits information to a posterior region in the tendril, which bends to coil round the support. The tendrils respond to rubbing against objects, but they do not show response to contact by other tendrils and raindrops.

What is the mechanism by which the tip of the tendril transmits information? We do not know. Richard Gregory puts the question: Are these reversals of the spiral initiated by the plant, or are they a geometrical necessity? Gregory argues: If the reversals of the growing spiral occur after the tip is anchored, the number of right and left turns must be equal; but if the reversals occur before the tip has found its anchor point, it must be judged that the reversals must be due to commands from the plant. According to Darwin's observations and report in 1880, the reversals occur only when both ends of the tendril are fixed, one end to the plant, and the other anchored to the support. Gregory's observations are, however, different from Darwin's. The former says that tendrils often grow with reversals before finding anything to cling to. It happens so that many tendrils never find a support on which to anchor. In such situations, they become long spirals with up to five or more reversals. Thus Gregory infers that the reversals of the tendril spiral must be initiated by the plant. The plant decides its own strategy in its behaviour. Because of the springy nature of the tendrils, they do not break when the plant is blown about by the wind, and so the anchoring is sturdy. The reversals in the tendrils may serve the purpose of preventing their twisting up.

We may analyse a difference in the behaviour of two trees in the *Ficus* genus, viz., *Ficus bengalensis* (banyan) and *Ficus religiosa* (*pīpal*). The banyan tree possesses a huge trunk and a large crown. It branches off almost horizontally whereas the branches of the *pīpal* tree go up angularly. This is the major difference that is responsible for the provision of prop roots in the banyan. The huge, almost horizontal branches of the banyan tree cannot be supported unless plank buttresses are formed to provide additional support. The banyan tree behaves as if it knows engineering designs.

Many plants of the old Leguminoseae family 'sleep' during night. This characteristic is very visibly expressed in the Mimosaceae family. In the sensitive plant, *Mimosa pudica*, for example, the leaflets close up and the leaves point downwards at night. In addition to making 'sleep' movements, the leaves of some species move during the daytime in response to the changing position of the sun. The pigeonpea, *Cajanus cajan*, may be taken as an example. Its leaflets, exposed to the intense tropical solar radiation, are oriented approximately parallel to the sun's rays, and thereby expose the minimum surface area to the sun. But the same leaves in the shade orient themselves at right angles to the incident radiation in order to intercept the maximum amount of light. The mechanism lies at the specialized leaf-joints, the pulvini. At night the leaves take up their vertical 'sleep' positions. Thus the pulvini are sensitive to light and gravity and meaningfully respond to environmental stimuli.

Some flowers open and close again daily. Leaves of some plants open during the day and close at night. Patals or leaves open up when specialized cells in the 'hinge' region at their bases become turgid; when these cells lose water due to changes in the permeability of their membranes to inorganic ions, the petals or leaves close. Some 'physiological clocks' operate in some plants, and even if they are placed in an unchanging environment, their movements continue to take place at approximately daily intervals. For what purpose do the plants vary their behaviour so ingeniously? It is said that there cannot be any purpose of insentient objects. Science explains such phenomena by the term 'adaptation' without ascribing to purpose and consciousness. Whether it explains or explains away is a moot point.

Some epiphytic climber plants belonging to the family *Araceae* climb walls or trees. They do so by clinging to the walls or trees by their adventitious roots. *Pothos scandens* (money-plant), *Scindapsus aureus* (old name: *Pothos aureus*), *Scindapsus officinalis*, *Philodendron pertusum*, *Monstera deliciosa*, and *Rhaphidophora decursiva* are some examples that develop adventitious roots from their climbing stems for clinging to the support. These roots appear only on that side of the stem that touches the support, the non-contacting side of the stem being completely free from adventitious roots. These roots pierce into the support and prevent the climber from falling down. Can we ascribe a motive to the climber? Is this activity not a conscious effort of the plant to achieve a certain end, very vitally important for its survival? Science hesitates to say that plants are conscious. We explain away by using some evading terms such as 'adaptation' for this purpose. Sometimes we are satisfied with expressions such as "nature has provided adventitious roots to these climbers so that they cling to their supports". We banished 'God' from science for which there were ample historical justifications. We introduced vague notions such as 'Nature' and assigned the function of providence to it. What is this Nature? Is it a Super-Being? If we answer this question affirmatively, it becomes synonymous with 'God'. If our answer is negative, our use of the word 'Nature' is vague and we unconsciously try to explain away facts in order to escape from our theophobia which is our hallucinatory creation in the mind only.

Next we switch over to embryogenesis of the animal

kingdom. Ordinarily a single sperm fertilizes a single ovum. Both the gametes fuse together to produce a zygote which is also unicellular. The human species has 23 pairs of chromosomes (DNA-strand) in each body (somatic) cell. In the gonads (testes and ovary) reduction division (meiosis) takes place, and, as a result, the number of chromosomes is reduced to a half, i.e., each gamete (sperm or ovum) contains 23 chromosomes only. In the process of fertilization, the original number of chromosomes is restored; the human zygote contains 23 pairs of chromosomes, each partner of each chromosome-pair coming from one of the parents.

The zygote undergoes cleavage division successively. One cell becomes two; two cells become four; and four cells become eight. All these eight cells are indistinguishable. The cleavage divisions of a zygote have been illustrated in *fig.* 10.1. At the eight-cell stage, one of the cells behaves differently. It multiplies by cleavage divisions and a small number of large cells are produced thereby. But this multiplication is suspended in the embryonic life in contrast to the continuation of the proliferation of the somatic cells. These cells, so produced, become recognizable as the primordial sex cells. In the yolk-sac, they stand as large cells in contrast with their neighbours. This happens before any gonad is laid down. The primordial sex cells migrate from the yolk-sac entoderm to their final location in the gonad. They wait there for a number of years until the individual attains puberty. Spermatogenesis in the testis or oogenesis in the ovary takes place from this germ plasm after the onset of puberty only. Thus cells of the germinal epithelium in the gonads do not become differentiated into the primordial sex cells that trace back their origin to one of the daughter cells of the zygote.

Why does one of the third generation cells, produced out of the zygote, offer itself to become the primordial sex cell? Did it offer itself, or did it get 'instruction' to discharge a special duty? Science cannot answer these questions.

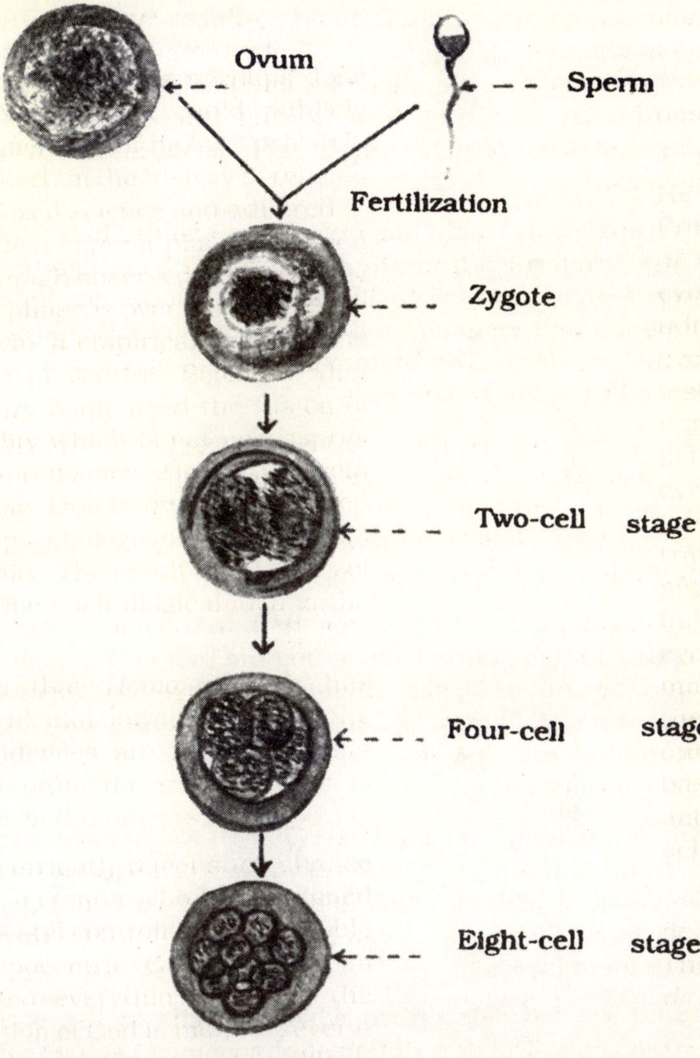

fig. 10.1: The cleavage divisions of a human zygote.

The somatic cells which are produced as a result of the successive cleavage divisions (mitosis) of the zygote are indistinguishable from one another. Even during the early phases of rapid proliferation, the cells thus formed do not remain as an unorganized mass. Almost at once they become definitely arranged. The embryo organizes itself; it first consists of a single, then two, and finally three primary structural layers. Thus, in course of time the cells are arranged in three germ layers, viz., ectoderm, entoderm and mesoderm.

The epidermis, including cutaneous glands, hair, nails and lens are formed from the ectoderm. The epithelium of all sense-organs, nasal cavity, sinuses, mouth (including oral glands and enamel), and anal canal are also formed from the ectoderm. The brain, spinal cord, and nerves are produced from the ectoderm.

The mesoderm is the source of muscles, connective tissue, cartilages, bones, bone marrow, heart, blood, lymphoid tissue, and epithelium of blood vessels, lymphatics, body cavities, kidney, ureter, gonads, genital ducts, suprarenal cortex, and joint cavities.

Organs and tissues that originate from the entoderm are the epithelium of pharynx (including the root of the tongue, the auditory tube), tonsils, thyroid, parathyroids, thymus, larynx, trachea, lungs, gastro-intestinal tube with the associated glands, bladder, vagina, vestibule, and urethra with the associated glands.

Bradley Patten,[52] in his book *Human Embryology*, has given a chart showing derivation of various parts of the body by progressive differentiation and divergent specialization. The origin of all the organs can be traced back to the three primary germ layers.

So far we have described what happens in the early embryogenesis. The description of phenomena is an important activity of science. Now we want to enter into a domain which is forbidden to science. How does differentiation take place in the embryo? Before the origin of the three germ layers, the cells that proliferate consequent on the successive cleavage of the zygote are similar and indistinguishable. How do they form the three germ layers that are distinct in their functions? If the precursor material is the same, how do we get specialized and distinct organs like the brain, heart, lungs, liver, kidneys, bones, muscles, etc.?

Here it is worth quoting the opinion of the embryologist L.B. Arey:

> It was formerly believed that the early germ layers have predetermined capacities and fixed fates, so that they are from the first, rigidly restricted to the kinds of differentiation that they ordinarily show. This concept has not withstood experimental tests. A germ layer, as such, or any part of it is not foreordained to carry out specific programmes of organ building. Rather, the constitutional plan of an organism assigns the various emerging organs and parts to definite spatial positions, and any cells that chance to lie in a particular region at the proper time will be recruited to participate in the specific job of organ construction characteristic of that site. In normal development, therefore, the germ layers serve merely as advantageously located assembly grounds, out of which the constituent parts of an embryo emerge at precise positions and in orderly sequences. Each early germ layer possesses a potential plasticity that would enable it to do many things other than the activities that actually find expression. Sooner or later, nevertheless, this plasticity is lost when a region receives 'instructions' that determine its fate inexorably: but this acquirement of instructions is wholly a secondary matter.[53]

What is a secondary matter in science is a primary matter in metaphysics. The ovum, the sperm, and the zygote are all stupid cells. They are like the wood, nails, and canes for making a chair. Is the wood automatically shaped into a chair? Is there no necessity of an intelligent carpenter for making a chair? The most intelligent scientist has not yet been able to synthesize a cell out of the raw materials necessary for this purpose. How can the zygote or its daughter cells build a heart, a brain, a kidney, or a liver? What or who makes them to differentiate? Who is the architect for designing the body organs? Who is the engineer to execute the plan and design of the body? The molecular biologist may say that the DNA contains the blueprint or programme and has the capacity to execute the programme. We will later take up the DNA which is also a stupid but wonderful molecule.

The brain is formed after the primary differentiation into three germ layers and some subsequent processes of embryogenesis. Much intelligent planning and execution precede the development of the brain in the embryo. The human nervous system is formed after the eighteenth day of conception. During the first eighteen days, the foundation of the embryo has already been laid. Then how can we establish the identity of the brain and mind? Embryogenesis, prior to the development of the brain, is not possible without the divine architect-cum-engineer. The presiding agency in the zygote and the embryo is the individual *jīva*. The *jīva* is the empirical self (*Īśvara* reflected in the individual subtle body or *antaḥkaraṇa*) apparently associated with the subtle body which becomes its limiting adjunct (*upādhi*). Mind or *manas* is an important component of the subtle body. Thus, without the mind, the *jīva* cannot function as the agency that can guide embryogenesis. Whatever may be the interpretation of the materialists, we boldly present this spiritual interpretation which is Vedāntic and scientific. We feel that anything scientific is not necessarily to be antispiritual and materialistic.

The Stationary Magnet and the Moving Coil

Long back Faraday discovered that an electric current can be made to flow through a wire or coil by moving the wire or coil across a magnetic field. By making use of this discovery, electric generators are devised. They convert the motion of a wire or coil into electrical energy. A magnet, a coil, and energy to produce the motion are needed for the production of electricity. It does not matter if the wire or the magnet moves, so long as one moves in relation to the other.

The self (*ātman*) of each individual living being sits in the subtle body as the silent witness. The *antaḥkaraṇa* (inner instrument) of the subtle body which contains the mind (*manas*) is the seat of the self and this seat is as extensive as the entire gross body. The combination of the empirical self and the subtle body is known as the *jīva*. The empirical self is compared with the magnet, and the mind and the body (both subtle and gross) with the moving coil. The self does not act; the mind and the body act; but, without the presiding influence of the empirical self, the mind and the body would be non-functional.

We have many voluntary functions. All the functions which we will are voluntary. I sit; I stand up; I run; I exercise; I meditate. For all such actions, the prerequisite condition is willing.

All the vital functions of the body are, however, involuntary. My heart goes on beating throughout my life. My lungs continue to expand and contract from my birth to my death. My respiratory movements are involuntary. The chemical factory of my liver works all the hours, all the days, and all the years in my life, and it works without my conscious guidance, control, and knowledge. My kidneys contain glomeruli that filter out water and crystalloids from my blood; they reabsorb all useful substances in the uriniferous tubules; and they discard all toxic and harmful substances as urine. I do not consciously control the actions of my kidneys. Many persons and all animals, in possession of kidneys, do not know that they have these two organs. My brain functions in my waking state; it functions when I sleep and dream; and it also functions when I am in dreamless sleep. My brain controls all my organs and tissues. But I do not control my brain. Many persons do not know what the brain is. My brain is sensitive to the glucose (really ATP concentration) concentration in the protoplasm of its cell, and so I feel hungry when the level goes down. I eat rice, bread, vegetables, pulses, etc. All varieties of food are digested and the released nutrients are absorbed into the blood or lymph stream. The digestion takes place even when I sleep. The secretion of the digestive juices is not under my control. The mechanical movements of the stomach and the intestines are not under my control. Many persons do not know that there are many enzymes to hydrolyze carbohydrates, proteins, and lipids. But, even if they don't know, their systems do the necessary work correctly. The nutrients reach the individual cells (the accepted estimate of the number of cells in the human body is about fifty trillion or 50×10^{12}) and are metabolized there. A medical scientist or a biologist takes his/her lifetime to know what happens inside the cell and still the knowledge is incomplete.

The body functions are normally well co-ordinated. There are centres in the medulla oblongata of the brain to co-ordinate the functions of the heart and the lungs. The pituitary gland situated underneath the floor of the brain co-ordinates the functions of all the other endocrine glands to maintain a hormonal balance. It is alert to the age and the need of persons or animals like cows, tigers, lions etc. It starts secreting the gonadotropic hormones to influence the testes and ovaries just before the onset of puberty. It secretes the hormone oxytocin just before parturition in order that the muscles of the gravid uterus contract to expel the foetus. It secretes the hormones necessary for the development of the mammary glands when a woman or a female mammalian animal carries the foetus. It secretes the hormone prolactin for the initiation and maintenance of lactation, and this activity is well-timed with the birth of the offspring. The same pituitary gland remains quiescent, as far as the secretions of these hormones are concerned, when the woman reaches the stage of menopause. Co-ordination and regulation are undoubtedly discernible.

How do we explain the life-processes which we classify under the disciplines of physiology, biochemistry, biophysics, genetics, molecular biology, etc.? Some scientists may say: "We describe what happens in Nature. It is not our duty to transgress the kingdom of empiricism in order to explain life phenomena metaphysically". Some other scientists may interpret all life phenomena mechanistically. But, are they fully successful with their mechanical explanation? Is life as mechanical as they think?

It is a fact that the body is a machine. And the functions of the body are really mechanical. But the body system acts as a single unit, and for the growth, maintenance, preservation, and well-being of this unit, all the body organs, tissues, and cells work for a common end, in harmony and co-ordination. Is there no co-ordinator? Is there no controlling and guiding agency? The materialistic scientist and the materialist philosopher discard the idea of a metaphysical being who controls and guides the body functions. But spiritual science like the *Vedānta* abhors this sort of materialism and asserts that every cell of the body is intelligent by virtue of its being subjected to the presiding influence of the self which is the fundamental Consciousness.

The Conscious, Unconscious, and Superconscious

The idea of the unconscious — the dark side of our mental moon — was initially thought of by some German philosophers such as J.G. Fichte, F.W.J. von Schelling, and the romantic novelist J.P.F. Richter. We may quote here a vital question that was asked by Richter:

> Why should everything come to consciousness that lies in the mind since, for example, that of which it is already aware, the whole great realm of memory, only appears to it illuminated in small areas, while the entire remaining world stays invisible in the shadow? And may there not be a second half-world of our mental moon which never turns toward consciousness?[54]

The word 'unconscious' was first used in Germany in 1776

and in England, by Wordsworth, in 1800. By 1895, this concept took shape in Freud's mind in an embryonic form. He came to realize that consciousness was the least part of the mental processes, and that most of the psychic processes that dominated man's life were concealed from consciousness. Within a few years, he came to the conclusion that the unconscious was the source of all motivation of thought and behaviour. Dreams, insanity, gestures, slips of the tongue, jokes, compulsive actions, obsessional thoughts, artistic creations, and the solution of problems have their origin from the unconscious. Freud theorized that it was the unconcious in which the mental processes took archaic forms, were patterned by infantile and pre-logical experience, and were determined by instinctive and predominatly sexual drives.

We can get some idea about Freud's concept of the unconscious from his emphasis on the role of memory in dreams. According to his view, all dream material must be based on memory traces in the brain, though not necessarily on conscious memories. Very often in dreams is encountered hypermnesia, i.e., the appearance of recollections beyond the reach of conscious memory. This provides a proof for Freud's point that unconscious memory is a major source of dream material, although conscious memory does play a role.

Thus, in Freud's opinion, both conscious and unconscious memories are traces in the brain. He referred to repression, a process by which unpleasant experiences or unbearable feelings are buried in the unconscious.

We do recognize the conscious and the unconscious. We are aware of objects, events, our environment, and ourselves; we are aware of our experiences. All such awareness is attributed to our conscious mind. In contrast, every moment innumerable events happen in our body system, and we are unaware of them. When I am frightened, excited, or anxious, I am aware of my feelings or experiences, but I am unaware of the secretion of adrenaline by my adrenal gland as a co-event of my fear, excitement, tension and anxiety. When some virus enters into my body, my internal system becomes alert and starts manufacturing interferons that block viral replications. It may so happen that my system successfully combats the virus-attack. If the virus becomes over-dominant, I suffer from a disease. I become aware of the suffering, but I am unaware of what had happened inside my body before the symptoms of the disease appeared. Had the virus been killed by my system and had there been no disease, I would have certainly been unaware of the role of my interferon in preventing the multiplication of the virus inside my cells. The bacteria that causes tuberculosis (*Mycobacterium tuberculosis*) gets entrance into my lungs. In a spot of the lung tissue, the bacteria multiplies and attacks the neighbouring cells of my lungs. The reticulo-endothelial system of my body produces special cells that move to the spot. These soldier cells try to cordon off the area and counter-attack the tuberculosis pathogen. Scavenger cells like macrophages are produced in large numbers. They rush to the spot to devour the bacteria. The invasion area is surrounded by a calcified wall through which the bacteria cannot get out. In most probability, I do not get the disease, and I do not become aware of the incidence just narrated here. One of my two kidneys is damaged. The remaining healthy kidney assumes a bigger size by undergoing hypertrophy. This becomes necessary for my living, since one kidney has to do the functions of two. But I am not aware of the compensatory mechanism of my healthy kidney. I get a mild stroke. A small blood vessel in my brain ruptures and so results brain haemorrhage. My system takes emergency action so that the blood clots and haemorrhage stops. In course of time, the blood clot is dissolved and the lesion is repaired. For all this repair activity, my system takes all possible measures without my awareness. I get a simple fracture in my femur bone. The orthopaedist aligns my fractured bones and makes them immobile by a plaster bandage. That's all what he does. My femur bone and my system do too many complicated things to repair the fracture. I am unaware of what my system does to repair the fracture. A good surgeon takes all aseptic measures for an operation in my stomach. His surgical instruments are well sterilized. The operation site is thoroughly sterilized. No micro-organisms are allowed to come in contact with the operation wound. My peptic ulcer is successfully operated. Within a week's time, the operation wound is healed up and a scar is formed. For this healing, my system knows what to do and does exactly the same to bring about a repair of the wounded tissue. But I remain unaware of what my system does.

A few examples have been given in the foregoing paragraph and such events are in legion in the life of every person and every animal too. We are certainly unconscious of such activities although our body-systems are conscious of them and become active participants. The unconscious of Freud is different from this type of unconscious. This unconscious is unconscious-superconscious. My conscious mind is not aware of such events that happen in my system, and so this is unconscious. But some superconscious agent in me presides over my system, and, through that presiding function, my system gains intelligence to do what is exactly necessary. Freud did not touch this aspect of psychology, and he did not recognize the superconscious. The superconscious is the Cosmic Intelligence, the Fundamental Consciousness. We use the pronoun "It" for the Fundamental Consciousness which is non-functional, attributeless, and non-relational. We use the pronoun "He" for the reflection of the same Fundamental Consciousness in *Māyā*, the power of *Brahman*. Here "He" refers to *Īśvara* whose limiting adjunct (*upādhi*) is *Māyā*. The pronoun "he" is used for the reflection of the same Fundamental Consciousness in the subtle body of an individual person, or animal or plant, or non-living object. Here "he" refers to the *ātman* whose limiting adjunct is the individual body. The *ātman* is *jīvātman* or *bhūtātman* in the living body and non-living object, respectively. This *jīvātmā* or *bhūtātmā* is superconscious. There is no trace of insentience or ignorance in the *ātman* which is not different from the Fundamental Consciousness or *Brahman.* It becomes self-contradictory to use the term 'unconscious' for the *Ātman or ātman.*

Ātman (*Paramātman*) or *ātman* (*jīvātman* or *bhūtātman*) cannot be said to be non-functional and attributeless unlike *Brahman.* Nevertheless, they do not have functions and attributes unlike the universe or any person, animal, plant or non-living object. Both *Īśvara* (*Ātman*) and *jīvātmā* (*ātman*) appear to possess attributes and to become functional by virtue of their association with the limiting adjuncts (*upādhi*). It is the *upādhi* that works. But the *upādhi* cannot work unless it is reflected by the light of consciousness of the *Ātman* or the *ātman.*

Irrespective of the subtle difference between *Īśvara* and *jīvātmā* or *Īśvara* and *bhūtātmā*, the self (*ātmā*) in general is superconscious. It is the proximity and pervasiveness of the self that renders the organs, tissues, cells, and macromolecules like DNA super-intelligent to function teleologically without the awareness of the conscious minds. All the systems of the body — circulatory, respiratory, digestive, urinary, reproductive, and others — work in harmony with a common goal of self-protection and self-preservation due to the presiding influence of the superconscious self. Freudian psychology rejects this self and does not accept anything like the superconscious.

Freud says that it is the unconscious mind that creates. Whether it is a scientific discovery, a creative literature, fine art, sculpture, architecture, or music composition, the creative urge comes from the unconscious, as conceived by Freud. In the annals of human history, we have a number of records of the creations or solutions of problems by thinkers and researchers in their dreams. Kekulé (1829-96), the famous chemist, was seized with the problem of determining the molecular structure of benzene. He dreamed of a snake with its tail in its mouth (*fig.* 10.2). This is an age-old symbol depicted in a third century BC Greek manuscript. This dream revealed to him the hexagonal ring structure of

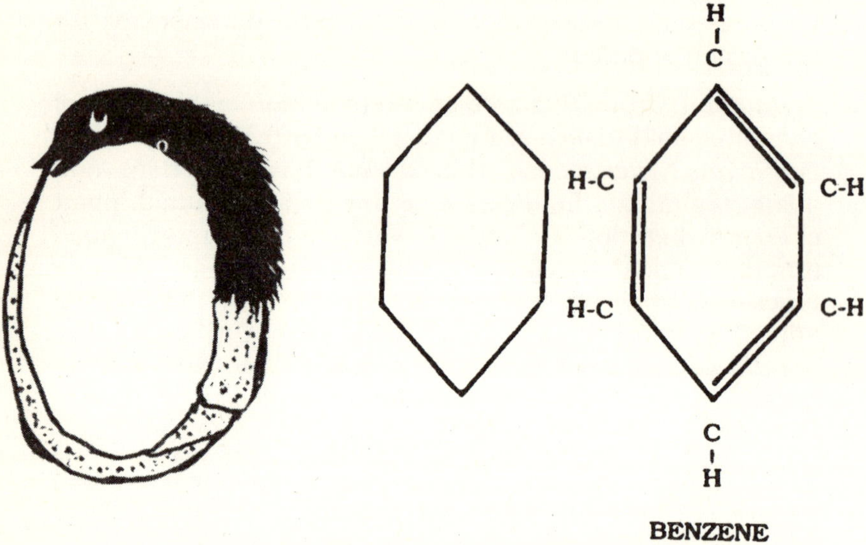

fig. 10.2: The imagery in Kekulé's dream.

benzene.

We do not agree with Freud to the suggestion that the unconscious is the source of creativity. It is rather the superconscious that gives the clue to create or solve.

We have been very much puzzled over trifling, non-creative incidences such as the time-precision of some autosuggestion. Someone, X, gets up daily at 4:00 A.M. He makes an autosuggestion to do so in the beginning. The suggestion may or may not work in the initial stages; and if it works, it may not stick to the exact timing. But, in course of time, its working is precise. Exactly at 4:00 A.M. the person, X, wakes up without fail. This is a commonplace occurrence. Still we do not know its working mechanism. It is decidedly not a Pavlovian conditioned reflex. It does not seem to be any type of reflex, since no stimulus works in the sleeping person to provoke a response. The crux of the problem is how to explain the precise timing at which the sleeping person wakes up. How does he/she see the watch when he/she is asleep? This can be explained only by hypothesizing that the superconscious self knows the time. The *jīva* is a compound entity constituted by the association of the self (*ātmā*) and the subtle-body (*sūkṣma śarīra*) which has mind as an important component. The mind of the sleeping person gets knowledge of the exact time from the self (*ātman*). The brain serves as the instrument of the mind. The mind instructs the brain to rise to wakefulness. In this case, the stimulus comes from the mind, and not from the external environment. Hence this is not a typical reflex action. Neither is it a simple habit. A habit is formed through practice. Through rehearsal, a programme is printed in the brain. This programme is replayed when a person wills to perform the particular work. The concerned organs of the body function in harmony when the work is performed. Whether it is balancing, walking on a rope, cycling, driving, swimming, or any such activity, the work is performed by habit forming. Many reflexes may be operative in such skills. But one thing is important to note here that the person who performs the work is in waking state and he/she wills to perform the task. The sleeping person cannot will and is not in a conscious state.

A sleeping person changes positions dozens of time during the night. Certainly there is no external stimulus to evoke such a response. If there is an internal stimulus, it is hard to be identified. But it is definite that there is a need to change the sides to avoid bed sore. Who commands or instructs the body to change sides? The answer to this question may be sought for in metaphysics that identifies a 'silent witness'.

Several persons sleep in a hall. There is a mother with a baby among them. The baby becomes hungry and cries; this provides an external stimulus. Only the mother wakes up and all others remain sleeping in an undisturbed condition. It seems the mother's brain does not directly respond to the baby's crying sound which could affect the other persons' brains also. It is the 'silent witness' who first responds and brains also. It is the 'silent witness' who first responds and then instructs the mother's brain.

A patient, on the surgical table in an operation theatre, is under anaesthesia. The doctors and nurses hold conversation among themselves. A doctor remarks something favourable or unfavourable about the patient. The unconscious patient's anaesthetized brain retains this remark in its memory and later adversely reacts in case the expert's remarks are unfavourable. Is the brain a photographic plate to record everything it is exposed to? Does some 'silent witness', ever awake and never sleeping, receive all stimuli and pass on some of them to the mind and brain?

Hilgard[55-57] uses the term 'hidden observer' in his experiments on hypnotic subjects. The *Śvetāśvatara Upaniṣad* uses the term "silent and hidden witness" in the verse: "The one Divine Being hidden in all beings, all-pervading, the inner self of all beings, the presiding deity of all deeds, who dwells in all beings, the witness, the knower, the only one (non-dual), devoid of attributes".[58]

The *Vedānta* considers the mind as material (not gross but subtle) and insentient. There can be two components of the mind — conscious and unconscious. But both these components cannot be the source of creativity, since the mind itself is insentient. The source of creativity is the source of knowledge, and the superconscious self is the only source of knowledge.

Through the superconscious self does the mind get extrasensory knowledge. The surgeon transplants a heart. The mind gets knowledge through the superconscious self that the transplanted heart is a foreign body, and that the DNA composition of this foreign body is not compatible with that of its own body. The body produces molecules within the histocompatibility complex (MHC) to evoke very powerful transplantation rejection. Many special cells are produced and deployed. They attack the transplanted heart and destroy it. The process is known as rejection.

Pathogenic microorganisms such as bacteria and viruses enter the body. They multiply there and attack. There is an incubation period during which any symptoms of the disease are not manifested. The would-be patient, during the incubation period, is not conscious of the bacterial or viral invasion. But, the mind gets knowledge about the invasion from the superconscious self, and instructs the body to take immediate measures for a counterattack and defence. The appropriate organs start manufacturing cellular and humoral substances to fight the infection. Hence are produced interferon, antibodies, leucocytes of different types, macrophages, etc. Again, the production of antibodies is not mechanical and foolish. It is a super-intelligent process. Analogous to the lock and key specificity, a specific antibody is produced for a specific antigen, and for such precise activity, a full knowledge of the morphology of the antigen is a prerequisite condition. Antibodies against the typhoid bacteria are different from those against the tuberculosis bacteria. The science of immunology and immunogenetics is wonderful. Super-intelligence is necessary for producing immune bodies. The best drugs in the world cannot protect a person if the immune system fails or is suppressed, and so he is doomed to die in such a situation. It fails in the AIDS disease. It is suppressed when the doctor tries to prevent the rejection of a transplanted organ by corticosteroid therapy. The most intelligent and well-informed doctor will certainly wonder at the super-intelligent dexterity of the immune system of the body. How does the immune system acquire intelligence? It receives instructions from the mind which is illumined by the proximity of the resplendent self (*ātmā*).

The self is superconscious, but not the mind. The mind has a conscious component and an unconscious one. When we speak about the mind, as described in the *Vedānta*, *Sāṅkhya*, and *Yoga*, we refer to a subtle material apparatus which survives death but which is not eternal. It is the apparatus on which our impressions are imprinted and from which the recorded imprints are retrieved. It uses the brain and the gross body in general as its instrument. Freud did not identity this mind. He rejected anything beyond the gross matter and hence could not accept the existence of some subtle-matter which can survive death. He rejected the concept of reincarnation. His 'mind' had a beginning with the formation of the foetal brain and an end in death. He talked about the unconscious and depth psychology. But he did not specify the location in which the unconscious lies. He talked about repression but the location where ideas are repressed or buried was not identified by him.

We come across three terms in the *Vedānta* and *Yoga* with reference to memory, the conscious mind and the unconscious mind. These are *smṛti*, *saṁskāra*, and *vāsanā*. The recollection or retrieval of stored up information, experiences, and feelings is known as *smṛti*. Impressions imprinted in the *citta* or *buddhi* (components of mind) are called *saṁskāra*. All types of *saṁskāra* are stored up in the *citta* in latent form. They are of three types, viz., (1) caused by cognition (*jñānamūla*), (2) caused by the five types of hindrances (*kleśamūla*), (3) caused by meritorious and unmeritorious actions (*dharmādharmamūla*). All *vāsanās* are *saṁskāras*, but all *saṁskāras* are not *vāsanās*. The cognitive dispositions (*jñānaja saṁskāras*) that form the fund of memory are not *vāsanās*. The *vāsanās* are those cognitive, affective, or conative *saṁskāras* that are stored up in the *citta* to assume the form of active tendencies when the time comes for the fruition (*vipāka*). The *vāsanās* are *saṁskāras* that have a determining value on the present or the future life. The five hindrances or afflictions which disturb mental equilibrium are undifferentiated consciousness or ignorance (*avidyā*), ego-sense (*asmitā*), attachment (*rāga*), enmity or hatred (*dveṣa*), and clinging to life or fear of death (*abhiniveśa*).[59] All these five afflictions can generate latent deposits (*āśayāḥ*) in the *citta* (mind-stuff). Merits (*puṇya*) and demerits (*pāpa*) of actions can also generate latent deposits. Thus *vāsanās* can be generated by both *kleśas* and *karma*. *Vāsanās*, as latent deposits, lie in the ground of the mind-stuff (*cittabhūmi*) to incite and stimulate a person's mind that is disturbed from some unconscious bottom to fructify strong propensities. The *vāsanās* create strong urges for the thirst (*tanhā* or *tṛṣṇā*) of senses: they create craving for sensual gratifications; they generate tendencies for passions, infatuation, clinging to life, and acquisition of power and material affluences. This *vāsanāśaya* (store of *vāsanās*) is the unconscious mind, as described in the *Vedānta* and *Yoga*.

Vāsanās are not created in one life only. They are accumulated in the deep layers of the mind through many lives. Man is born and reborn so long as the mind persists to exist and *vāsanās* in the mind are not completely erased. The cumulative *vāsanās* of a person become the antecedent causes of his/her thought and behaviour.

Freud's psychology is deterministic. He believes that nothing mental is accidental. He recognizes repressed urges and trials of psychosexual development as determinants of human goals, wishes, and fantasies. He holds that all thought and behaviour have antecedent causes. So, in Freudian psychology, the unconscious plays a dominant role in shaping one's personality. Freud, however, does not believe in post-death existence, reincarnation, and hence his concept of the unconscious is restricted to this life only. Although *vāsānās* and the unconscious of Freud have many factors in common, there are two major differences that clearly distinguish them. *Vāsanās* have been accumulating since many past lives whereas the unconscious of Freud has a beginning with the birth of the present life. Secondly, the five types of afflictions stated earlier and good as well as bad actions generate *vāsanās*. Freud, however, over-emphasizes the childhood psychosexual development as the prime determinant of the nature of the unconscious.

From the 1970s and afterwards, scientific evidences have been forthcoming to suggest that the unconscious can reach back far beyond birth to earlier incarnations and into the state between lives. Two Californian practising psychiatrists, Dr. Morris Netherton[60] and Dr. Mrs. Edith

Fiore,[61] are past-life therapists through hypnotic regression. They use hypnosis to take their patients back into their former lives in order to uncover the origins of traumas and neuroses afflicting them. Dr. Joel Whitton[62-65] who is a Toronto-based psychiatrist instructs his patients, while in hypnotic trance, to bring traumatic past-life memories into their conscious awareness. There have been several reliable reports on reincarnation. Dr. Raymond Moody[66] first published his book *Life After Life* in 1975. Dr. Ian Stevenson,[67-68] the world's best known investigator of reincarnation, has reported convincing evidences in favour of birth after death. All these findings of recent scientific studies confirm the *Vāsanā* concept of the ancient *Vedānta* and *Yoga* schools of philosophy and psychology.

The *vāsanās* play a deciding role in shaping the personality of an individual. Before we discuss this ancient theory of prsonality development, it may be useful to introduce this topic of modern psychology.

It is hard to define personality. Here we may give a working definition. Personality may be defined as the characteristic patterns of behaviour and modes of thinking that determine a person's adjustment to the environment. When psychologists talk about personality, they focus on individual differences — the characteristics that distinguish one individual from another.

What are the determinants of personality? Heredity and environment determine what the personality would be. Environment is a broad term that includes the physical, cultural, family, social, educational, and moral environment. Nature and nurture interact to shape a personality.

Psychologists have studied personality similarities and differences in fraternal and identical twins. More similarities in personality have been observed in identical twins. The size of the correlations suggests that one's genetic inheritance is an important determinant of personality.

In psychological studies on babies, it has been observed

that they react quite differently to the same situation. In the same family, babies with early individual differences in temperament have been observed. These observations definitely indicate that one is born with some in-built pattern of personality.

But the in-born pattern of personality would be considerably influenced by good training, bad training, and lack of training, and by exposure to conducive or hostile and unfavourable environment.

Individuals can be classified into personality types. The Swiss psychiatrist Carl Jung divided all personalities into introverts and extroverts. Introverts are described as people who share characteristics such as shyness, social withdrawal, and a tendency not to talk much. Extroverts share a tendency to be outgoing, friendly and talkative.

In connection with susceptibility to heart attack, we observe two types of people — type A and type B. Type A persons are hard-driving and competitive. They are too ambitious in life. They hanker after social recognition. They want quick rise. They take on multiple activities with deadlines to meet. They are competent and efficient persons with tight schedule. They are terribly upset when their goal is not fully achieved in time. They live under constant pressure, largely of their own making. They are in tension if everything is not fine. They are likely to become hostile, impatient, anxious, and disorganized. Any interference with their tight schedule violently disturbs their peace and balance of mind.

Type B persons have a behaviour pattern opposite to that of type A. Persons belonging to type B are easygoing, unambitious, non-competitive, placid, and unflappable. They are less sensitive to tension and weather stress easily.

Mental traits are distributed in a normal bell-shaped curve and hence the sharp division of people into types may not be precise. But it is a fact that innate propensities that individuals carry differ from person to person in both quality and quantity. How the *Vedānta* explains the personality differences will be discussed here.

There is a high positive correlation between the latent deposits (*āśayas*) or *vāsanās* in the mental apparatus of the subtle body and the *karma* of a person. God (*Īśvara*) decides the future parentage and the time of rebirth of a *jīva*. This decision is based on the *karma* and is never arbitrary or whimsical. Thus, the galaxy, the solar system, the planet, the country, the family, and the parents of a *jīva* are decided by God in accordance with the *prārabdha karma* (the part of *karma* meant for fruition in the present life) of that particular *jīva*. Secondly, by God's decision of the time of rebirth (the period of inter-life varies from months to thousands or millions of years), the planetary positions from birth to death of an individual are predetermined. By the determination of the parentage by God, the genotype (genetic constitution; DNAs or genes to be inherited from the father and mother) of an individual *jīva* is predetermined. Thus, the heredity and environment of each *jīva* are not left to chance.

The *buddhi* or *citta* is constituted of *sattva*, *rajas*, and *tamas*. Depending upon the qualitative and quantitative nature of *vāsanās* latently deposited in the *citta* (mental apparatus of the material subtle body), one of the three constituents (*sattva, rajas, tamas*) becomes dominant. So are persons *sattva*-dominant, *rajas*-dominant, and *tamas*-dominant. *Sattva* generates goodness, serenity, equanimity, love, kidness, enlightenment, truthfulness, straight-forwardness, righteousness, non-violence, etc. *Rajas* generates activity, motion, vibration, instability, restlessness, possessiveness, desire, lustfulness, power-thirst, wealth-hunger, etc. *Tamas* generates lethargy, sluggishness, inertia, caprice, avarice, sensuality, pride, violence, conceit, hatred, cruelty, envy, malice, etc.

The *vāsanās* that lie deep in the *citta* or *buddhi* and that have accumulated through many lives do not rest in the *cittabhūmi* (bottom of the mind) permanently. Each one of the latent deposits comes to the surface some time or other. And so do the *vāsanās* become determinants of the mental traits and personality. Thus, according to the *Vedānta* and *Yoga*, the latent deposits in the *citta* or *buddhi* constitute the unconscious mind of a person.

It has already been said that the brain serves as an instrument of the mind. Whatever have been said about the brain-physiology in the chapter on "the concept of mind in science" are accepted as facts even if we accept the concept of mind of the *Vedānta* and *Yoga*. The storing up of information in the brain and their retrieval can be accepted by the *Vedānta* and *Yoga* systems. But it may need a mention here that recording in the brain and recording in the mind are done simultaneously through different methods. The brain-recordings are destroyed in the death whereas the mind-recordings survive death.

Some indirect reference has been made to astrology. The time of birth is in consonance with a unique stellar-cum-planetary environment during the whole life-period of a person. This provides a reason for the claim that a horoscope of a person can afford to predict his personality and events surrounding his life. There have been many attempts to establish the validity of astrology. There have also been attempts to refute the claims of astrology. In order to resolve the question unambiguously, Professor Shawn Carlson of the University of California set up a massive and meticulously-planned "double-blind" investigation. He reported his results in the premier international scientific journal "Nature" in 1985. He concluded. "Their predicted connection between the positions of the planets and other astrological objects at the time of birth, and the personalities of the test subjects did not exist. The experiment clearly refutes the astrological hypothesis".[69]

In the investigation of Professor Shawn Carlson, none of the astrologers performed at a level higher than that expected on the basis of pure chance and guesswork. Whether this gave a final deathblow to astrology can hardly be said. The whole subject of astrology is to be properly comprehended in a wider perspective. The environmental factors that are the partial determinants of the personality and events of an individual are too diverse, and the stellar as well as planetary environment is only one out of the many. Secondly the heredity and the *vāsanās* are not less potent in determining the personality and events of an individual. We do not get a comprehensive knowledge on these multivariate factors and their interactions. It is too simplistic to declare that astrology is nonsense. We will not be surprised if future science discoves some sense in it.

Allied to astrology is the discipline of palmistry which is also controversial. Some people think that the palm-lines and palm-prints are artefacts produced in the foetus due to the special posture inside the mother's womb. There is no truth in such hypothesizing, however. The palm-lines, palm-prints, foot-lines, and foot-prints have some relations with the DNA-structure of the body. Thus they represent some type of genetic index of a person. Identical twins have more similarity of this index than fraternal twins. Nevertheless, the palm-indices of a pair of identical twins are not identical. This shows that something other than the genotype such as *vāsanās* partly exert determining influence on the anatomy of the palm-print. For the identity of a person, the criminologist depends upon the thumb-impression and other finger-prints. No two individuals in the world have identical finger-prints. No two individuals in the world, except identical twins, have identical genotypes. These facts strongly suggest that the genotype of a person is somehow reflected on the palm-prints and finger-prints, and that some additional factor(s) exerts some extra influence on these prints. We may refer to the paper of Michael Alan Park[70] who researches in the field of dermatoglyphics. He writes: ". . . it would seem that there is a recognized link within palmistry between various dermatoglyphic pattern types and certain personality traits". "It became apparent during such investigations that pattern types and sizes were under some degree of genetic influence, although the specific details of the genetic mechanism have yet to be determined".

To use the language of Michael Park, "Dermatoglyphics are now added to the growing list of traits whose expressions and frequencies help to distinguish and define the races." Dermatoglyphic data are used in the field of medical genetics. Hence Michael Park writes: "Correlations have been established between dermatoglyphic features and certain human disorders, most of which have a known or suspected genetic basis. Here then is a scientifically testable link between some of the palmist's data and some other features of human biology, some involving behavioural characteristics.

The palmist studies many other features of the hand in addition to the palmar creases. The form of the hand, especially the shape of the palm in relation to the length of the fingers is a clue to personality traits. Various 'types' of hand-shapes are linked with certain professions. The form of the individual fingers, their lengths, their phallanges, and the presence of any curvature in individual fingers have various interpretations. Nail shape and colour, and the mounts on the palms are of importance too. The finger-print patterns are much meaningful.

We may define dermatoglyphics as the study of the patterns of parallel ridges and furrows on the epidermis of the hands and feet. The finger-print traits have three main pattern types, viz., arches, loops, and whorls. There are subtypes of each of these, and also some minor types. Every human finger and toe carries, with few exceptions, one of these types. In addition, some areas of the palm and sole also display these patterns. The pattern size is also used in dermatoglyphics. The number of ridges between the centre of the pattern and the triradius is counted to determine the pattern size.

Arches are associated with crudeness, practicality, and rebelliousness. Loops indicate restraint, lack of originality, and coolness of manner. Whorls are indicative of creativity, restlessness and egocentric behaviour.

An excess of arches is associated with a number of genetic disorders. These include trisomy 18 (possession of three rather than two of the eighteenth chromosome) and Kleinfelter's syndrome (males having XXY instead of XY sex chromosomes) in addition to others. Trisomy leads to infant death. The symptoms that are exhibited in Kleinfelter's syndrome are underdeveloped gonads, sparse body hair, some breast development, usually long legs, and some mental retardation. Too many arches may symbolize certain forms of congenital heart disease, idiopathic mental retardation, epilepsy with mental retardation, and perhaps schizophrenia.

Individuals with an excess of loops are more susceptible to heart disease. Trisomy 21 (possession of three rather than two of the twenty-first chromosome) is correlated with an excess of loops. This disorder is known as Down's syndrome or mongoloid idiocy.

Whorls, in excess of normal frequencies, are associated with Turner' syndrome which is another anomaly of the sex chromosome. Persons with XO chromosome (possessing one X chromosome instead of two) are outwardly physical females. Most XO conceptions end in abortions, but when a live female baby is born, she gets the syndrome. The symptoms include very short stature, broad chest with underdeveloped breasts, webbing appearance of the neck, small uterus, and either no ovaries or very rudimentary ones. Huntington's chorea which is a neurological disorder, resulting eventually in loss of mental faculties is correlated with an excess of whorls. Cardiac disease and perhaps schizophrenia are also associated with an excess of whorls.

Dermatoglyphic specialists have studied flexion creases at the finger joints on their ventral side and correlated with genetically based medical disorders. One anomaly is the presence of single flexion crease, instead of two, on the ventral surface of one or more fingers. Such single digital creases have shown correlations with three disorders. One is trisomy 18, which is fatal. The second one is trisomy 21

(Down's syndrome). The third disorder is known as the oral-facial-digital syndrome, manifested as various deformities of the oral, facial, and digital regions of the body. This syndrome is suspected to be caused by a trisomy of the twenty-first chromosome.

The second flexion crease feature is the simian line or crease (so named due to its presence in some non-human primates). This single line across the palm is found in less than two per cent of humans. This flexion crease shows higher frequencies of a number of genetically based disorders. Some of these disorders are: trisomies 18 and 21, Turner's syndrome, De Lange syndrome (various anomalies of the hands and feet), Ellis-van Creveld syndrome (broad thumb and great toe), idiopathic mental retardation, and two disorders of external origin — thalidomide damage and prenatal rubella.

Palmists report that the simian line indicates a personality with a stronger inner tension. Persons with this line may show creative and artistic talents; or, they may show destructive and criminal tendencies; they may have ritual and religious temperament too.

How do we explain the correlations between the DNA constitution and the palm as well as foot-prints of a person? The DNA constitution or genotype of a person is fixed up at the time of the fertilization of the mother's ovum with one of the father's sperms. The dermatoglyphic features develop between the sixth and twenty-first foetal weeks. Some of what have been coded in the genes are somehow reflected in the dermatoglyphic features. Some physical symptoms of many disorders mentioned in the foregoing paragraphs involve developmental abnormalities of the embryo during the intra-uterine life. Even some such abnormal development may precede the appearance of the dermatoglyphic features. Hence a direct causal relation between the dermatoglyphic features and the abnormal development of organs is ruled out. The genes regulate the embryological developments, and they also regulate the formation of the dermatoglyphic features. The establishment of correlations does not necessarily involve a causal relationship.

The skin and the brain originate from the same embryonic layer, viz., the ectoderm. The skin is, after all, one of the five sense-organs, all of which and the entire nervous system have their origin from the ectoderm. Hence some structural and functional associations seem to be natural. We hypothesize that the finger-prints, palm-prints, and foot-prints reflect two fundamental aspects of each individual life. These two are: the genotype or DNA-constitution, and *vāsānās* or karmic impressions. The involvement of *vāsanās* is responsible for the personality characterization and the behavioural manifestations associated with dermatoglyphics.

We have presented a deterministic psychology and philosophy of the *Vedānta* and *Yoga*. The *karma* of an individual *jīva* determines the present life and the lives to come. Is there no free will? Can't I change the course of my life by willing? What does the "I" do?

Both the *Vedānta* and *Yoga* have provision for the freedom of will. The self can free itself from bondage. Through self-realization (*svānubhūti*) the apparently bound self can be free and become identified with *Brahman*. It will let the *prārabdha* (already initiated) *karma* take its own course in this life. But, in spite of the continuation of the fruition of the *prārabdha karma*, the self can be released from bondage even during the current life. This is the state of the *jīvanmukta* (free even if living). It will prevent the further accumulation of the *kriyamāṇa* or *āgāmī karma* (*karma* which is being or will be deposited). It will burn or erase the stored up (*sañcita*) *karma*. All this is possible if nescience (*avidyā*) is forshaken and knowledge (*vidyā*) is dawned. This can be achieved through immediate realization (*aparokṣānubhūti*).

The unliberated self or the self in *jīva*-hood has the power to will. The free self is apparently embodied; the subtle body (*sūkṣma śarīra*) serves as the apparent limiting adjunct (*upādhi*) of the self; and the association of the two is known as the *jīva*. We refer to this self as the empirical one. The inner instrument (*antaḥkaraṇa*) is the principal component of the subtle body. *Buddhi* (the thinking substance), *ahaṅkāra* (I-sense), and *manas* (mind-stuff) are the constituent parts of the inner instrument. Patañjali uses the term *citta* which is a composite word for all these three components — *buddhi*, *ahaṅkāra*, and *manas*. It is the *ahaṅkāra* that wills. It itself is insentient, and it cannot will unless it gets the light of consciousness from the self (*ātmā*).

The neurophysiologist Sir John Eccles recognizes the role of "will" in our body functions. He writes:

> The neurophysiological hypothesis is that the "will" modifies the spatio-temporal activity of the neuronal network by exerting spatio-temporal "fields of influence" that become effective through this unique detector function of the active cerebral cortex. It will be noted that the 'will' or 'mind influence' has itself some spatio-temporal patterned character in order to allow it this operative effectiveness.[71]

Most modern philosophers and psychologists have discarded this "I" as an entity. They say that the "I" is a linguistic use in the analogy of 'it' standing for the 'chair' or 'book'. Let us probe into the matter if we can afford to do away with this "I".

The "I" makes a lot of difference between the computer and the brain. The computer is I-less, and hence has no volition. It does not desire to do this or that. It does not intend to move this way or that way. It does not wish to write poetry, compose a music, paint a scenery, or make a statue. It cannot plan; cannot make a programme for itself. It cannot love. It cannot do anything which may be called volitional.

A person's gross body contains many organs like the brain, heart, lungs, kidneys, liver, etc. It possesses hands and legs which we call limbs. The body contains different types of tissues. Each type of tissue is made of millions of cells. If we confer sovereignty to each cell, and do not think of a central authority, the body cannot manage to function and live for a moment. A person lives holistically, in harmony, and in co-ordination. Each individual unit or subunit of the body does not go in its own way by ignoring the total interest of the person. All the organs, cells, and subcellular constituents function in perfect harmony under normal circumstances. Each unit of the body does not work randomly and does not work for itself. The units of the body are structurally and functionally separated; but all of them work cooperatively and co-ordinatingly for the good of the whole body which is a single entity. There seems to be a benevolent dictator in each person, each animal, each plant, and each amoeba, bacterium, or virus. The dictator allows individual freedom within limits, but controls and dictates all subjects for the common cause and interest of the whole body as a single entity. This dictator is the *ahaṅkāra* of the mental apparatus (*antaḥkaraṇa*). The common religious notion is different, however. Many think that God (*Paramātmā*) is the dictator. Some others think that the self (*ātmā*) is the dictator. This is, however, not correct. The *Vedas* declare the companionship of the non-functional *Paramātmā* (*Īśvara* or God) and the functional *jīvatmā* (the empirical self) through a nice symbol: "Two birds, companions ever united, cling to the same tree. Of these two, one (*jīvātmā*) eats the sweet fruit and the other looks on without eating."[72] Śaṅkara[73] says that *Īśvara* permits the processes of the world as the witness and thus impels their activities. The individual empirical self, left to itself, does not work, but the *jīvātmā*, the compound entity resulting from the association of the empirical self and the internal organ (*antaḥkaraṇa*) is the agent of actions and the enjoyer as well as the sufferer.

The *ahaṅkāra* of the tripartite mind (*buddhi, ahaṅkāra, manas*) is the dictator and co-ordinator of all the functions of an individual body. This is possible for the insentient *ahaṅkāra* by virtue of its being enlightend by the light of the self (*ātmā*). The self which is consciousness renders the insentient *ahaṅkāra* conscious through the process of reflection. This "I" is cognizant of itself and also cognizant of all other than itself. When a foreign body like a synthetic heart valve, a bacterium, or a virus gets entrance into the body, it is the *ahaṅkāra* that becomes aware of the intruder and takes a defensive role. When a foreign organ or tissue is surgically implanted, it is the *ahaṅkāra* that distinguishes its own DNAs from those of others and takes immediate measures to reject the foreign organ or tissue. The *ahaṅkāra* is the "I".

The principal components of the inner organ, viz., *buddhi*, *ahaṅkāra* and *manas*, function in cooperation. All these three may combinedly be called 'mind' for our purpose here. It is the mind that works for the *jīva* which is made up of the mind and the empirical self. The *jīva* can debase or elevate itself. As the *Bhagavadgītā*[74] says: "The self can elevate itself, and the self can debase itself. It is the self that is its friend or foe". The same *Gītā* asserts that the self is not an agent of any action.[75] In actuality, the *ahaṅkāra* works in association with the *buddhi* and *manas*, with the light of consciousness reflected in it. Thus, the *Vedānta* does have provision for free will in the background of the deterministic doctrine of *karma*.

For a *yogī*, there is nothing involuntary. The whole body is in his full control. All the organs, tissues, cells, and subcellular macro- and micro-molecules obey the dictates of the *yogī*.

Through the practice of *yoga*, one can order one's body to obey one's order. The *saṅkalpa* (resolve) in *yoganidrā* is a command to the whole body, an organ of the body, or a tissue of an organ to change its anatomy and physiology, and to repair its pathological lesions. Through *saṁyama* (*dhyāna, dhāraṇā, samādhi*, done together), one can ask one's hyperactive gastric glands to secrete less hydrochloric acid. If one is a diabetic and one's islet cells in the pancreas are still living, one can practise *saṁyama* on the islet cells to secrete more insulin. If one old man's prostate has been enlarged, he can do *saṁyama* on his prostate gland so that the latter may undergo atrophy. If somebody has eczema or asthma as a result of psychological disturbance (mental allergy), he may do *saṁyama* on his brain to cure the disease. If someone has aplastic anaemia, he may do *saṁyama* on his bone narrow that may be activated to produce red blood corpuscles in normal forms at a normal rate with normal haemoglobin content. If somebody suffers from cancer, he may do *saṁyama* on his DNAs that may speed up the synthesis of immuno-proteins to destroy the cancerous cells. The therapeutic use of *saṁyama* and *yoga-nidrā* are too many; a few specimen examples have been given here to illustrate the important role of a strong will that can be harnessed to evade crisis and correct disasters of the body.

The will is not a constituent part of the brain which belongs to the body. The will is not the functional activity of the brain. Willing or volition is an activity of the *ahaṅkāra* which works in association with *buddhi* and *manas*. By willing alone, by the yogic technique of meditation, the aging process of the brain-cells may be retarded. Hence, the brain, which is an instrument of the mind, is itself one part of the body, and is not outside the influence of mind.

The Holistic Existence

Each individual entity has a holistic existence, and this holism is obviously expressed in the living world. The human body has many organs such as the brain, heart, liver, kidneys, etc. The brain is made up of many specialized components like the cerebral cortex, thalamus, hypothalamus, cerebellum, medulla oblongata, etc. The human brain has about fifteen billion neurons. The human body has about fifty trillion cells. Each cell has many subcellular components such as nucleus, cytoplasm, mitochondria, chromosomes, etc. One basic question may be posed here: Does each organ, tissue, cell or subcellular constituent live for itself alone? The answer is "NO". Every micro-entity in the body exists and functions holistically. The organic whole lives; the component parts **seem** to work individually and automatically, but, in actuality, all of them function as an irreducible whole.

We observe holism through the study of embryology, micro-anatomy, gross anatomy, physiology, molecular biology, immunology, etc. An ovum and a sperm get fused together to produce a zygote which is unicellular. The single cell multiplies; three germinal layers, viz., ectoderm, entoderm, and mesoderm, are formed. Each layer differentiates into specialized tissues and organs. The whole activity of embryogenesis has one basic objective, that is, to live as an organism which would be an irreducible whole.

Why does the heart go on beating from birth to death without a single moment's rest? Why do the lungs labouriously work as bellows to suck oxygen and expell carbon dioxide without taking a nap? Why does the liver work as a chemical factory of a gigantic magnitude without off-hours and holidays? Why do the kidneys filter out the harmful substances from blood and excrete as urine? The heart does not work for itself; neither do the lungs. No organ, no tissue, no cell, or no DNA molecule has any interest to work for itself. In spite of this fact, all of them faithfully and loyally work for the holistic existence of the organism as a whole.

The micro- and macro-structures of each and every component of the body have been designed for a holistic life. They function with the same objective. The intelligently planned and designed structures and functions of the body components are neither automatic nor fortuitous.

The protection of the body as a whole has also been intelligently planned and designed. It is not our purpose here to elaborate the subject of immunology. We would like to cite a few examples of immunology to substantiate the theory of holism.

We live in a potentially hostile world filled with a

bewildering array of infectious agents such as viruses, bacteria, fungi, protozoa, and worms. They attack us and still we live. This is possible due to the provision of innate immunity and acquired immunity in our body system.

The body is built so as to provide potent barriers against infection. Micro-organisms are prevented from gaining access to the body. The intact skin is impermeable to most infectious agents. Most bacteria fail to survive for long on the skin due to the inhibitory effect of sweat and the secretions of the sebaceous glands. Sweat contains lactic acid and fatty acids that are harmful to micro-organisms. Further, these secretions generate low pH (higher acidity) which is unfavourable to micro-organisms. Mucus, secreted by the membranes lining the inner surfaces of the body, is protective against microbial invasion. Microbes are trapped within the adhesive mucus and thus cannot adhere to the epithelial cells. They are mechanically removed from the mucus by stratagems such as ciliary movement, coughing, and sneezing. Some other mechanical factors for protecting the epithelial surfaces are the washing action of tears, saliva, and urine. Lysozyme which is an enzyme is present in tears, nasal secretions and saliva. It is also released through tissue injury. It is a bactericidal substance. Of the soluble bactericidal substances elaborated by the body, lysozyme is perhaps the most abundant and widespread.

The body has two types of innate immunity, viz., cellular and humoral. All the leucocytes or white blood corpuscles defend the body by fighting against the invading micro-organisms. They constitute the military force of the body system. They are of different types, differing structurally and functionally. These micro-soldiers are the polymorphonuclear leucocytes (polymorphs or neutrophils), lymphocytes, monocytes, basophils, and eosinophils. They are the normal cellular constituents of blood in addition to erythrocytes (red blood corpuscles) and platelets. All these cells are produced in the bone marrow from the multipotential haemopoietic stem cell.

In the embryonic life, haemopoiesis originates in the early yolk-sac; later this function is taken over by the foetal liver, and finally by the bone marrow of the developed foetus. Throughout the post-natal life, the bone marrow is the site where the formed elements of blood are produced.

The original multipotential stem cell seeds other organs and renews itself through the creation of further stem cells. The erythrocytes, platelets, and leucocytes are the new stem cells produced in the myeloid system from the original stem cell, whereas the B-cells and T-cells are the new stem cells that are produced in the lymphoid system from the original stem cell. The B-cells are differentiated in the bone marrow and the T-cells in the thymus. Whenever some micro-organisms invade certain organ, the relevant leucocyte(s) is produced in abnormally large number and deployed through the blood stream to the affected area.

Phagocytes are cells that devour and digest the invading micro-organisms. They are of two types, small and large. Both types are produced in the bone marrow. The polymorphonuclear neutrophil which is a short-lived cell with a multi-lobed nucleus is a microphage. It is the smaller type of phagocyte. The polymorphs provide the major defence against pyogenic bacteria.

The macrophages are the larger phagocytes. They derive from bone marrow promonocytes that develop into circulating blood monocytes which eventually become distributed throughout the body and settle in tissues as mature macrophages. Unlike the polymorphs, the macrophages are long-lived cells which are mononuclear. The macrophages which are the large phagocytes combat those bacteria, viruses, and protozoa which are capable of living within the cells of the host.

Phagocytosis is a process in which the phagocyte engulfs and digests the invading micro-organism. The whole process, without becoming passive and mechanical, is quite active, necessitating dexterity, manoeuvres, skill, and intelligence. The micro-organism is attracted towards the phagocyte through chemotaxis, and is adhered to the suface of the latter. The phagocyte's membrane, in contact with the micro-organism, is then activated; it becomes serrated with the formation of a gulf due to the extension of pseudopods around the invader. The micro-organism falls in the gulf and is subsequently completely enclosed in a vacuole called phagosome. Within one minute the cytoplasmic granules appear in the cytoplasm of the phagocyte; they fuse with the phagosome and discharge their contents around the imprisoned micro-organism, that is killed and digested. Finally, the phagosome is opened, the degradation products are released, and the phagocyte resumes its normal cellular structure.

The process of phagocytosis has been designed for combating attack by microorganisms, and not for self-destruction. The phagocytes recognize the cells of the body and distinguish the 'self' from the 'non-self'. For the interest of the self, the phagocytes must identify the foreign micro-organism before they initiate the process of phagocytosis.

There are two types of lymphocytes — small lymphocytes and large granular lymphocytes. The natural killer (NK) cells are large granular lymphocytes. They kill micro-organisms that are extracellular unlike the macrophages that kill intracellularly.

The small, resting lymphocytes produce antibodies which are formed before any antigen is ever seen. The specific antibody is selected for by the specific antigen. The B-lymphocytes (so named because they differentiate in the bone marrow) are made in the bone marrow at a rate of about a million a second. Each B-lymphocyte is programmed to make one, and only one, type of antibody, and it places this antibody on its outer surface to act as a receptor. One B-lymphocyte has on its surface about 10^5 antibody molecules, which can be visualized as little molecular keys sticking out of the lymphocyte cell body. All of the antibodies on a particular B-lymphocyte are identical, although differences do exist from lymphocyte to lymphocyte. Each antibody has an active site called a 'paratope'. We can think of the paratope as notches on a key. Thus each B-lymphocyte has about one hundred thousand 'keys', each one identical, sticking out of it.

Each antigen has another active site called the 'epitope', which functions as a lock. An antigen binds to that receptor with which it makes a good fit. This interaction of an antigen with its corresponding antibody takes place through spatial complementarity. Covalent binding is not involved in this process. The forces of interaction include electrostatic, hydrogen-bonding, hydrophobic, and Van der Waals. Once an antibody's key fits an antigen's lock, the antigen is destroyed.

Once an antibody key finds a lock it fits, it triggers the manufacturing of the antibody-forming plasma cells whose parent cell is the B-lymphocyte. Since each B-lymphocyte is genetically programmed to produce only one type of antibody, the millions of clones associated with the said B-lymphocyte get made each with its set of identical keys, made for the destruction of that particular antigen. This is how the body mobilizes its defence and the size of its army is increased by multiples of millions. This is also the way, in which antigen selects for the antibodies which recognize effectively.

There are lymphocytes called T-cells (so named because they differentiate within the milieu of the thymus gland) which are involved in operating against cells bearing intracellular organisms. Viruses have to replicate inside the host cell and hence are obligate intracellular parasites. Microorganisms like mycobacteria and leishmania can replicate outside the host cell; still they prefer intracellular life because of the protection it affords. Such pathogens are facultative intracellular parasites. It is impossible for humoral antibodies to reach the intracellular parasites that replicate particularly in macrophages. T-cells can recognize antigen only when it is on the surface of a body cell. The surface receptors of T-cells recognize antigen plus a surface marker which belongs to a group of molecules known as the major histocompatibility complex (MHC). This MHC, possessed by each vertebrate species, is controlled by three classes of genes. It was identified originally through its ability to evoke very powerful transplantation rejection, when grafts were exchanged between different members of a species. The T-cells produce lymphokine that helps macrophages to kill intracellular micro-organisms.

Five per cent of the total lymphocytes of the body are replaced daily. Some B-lymphocytes mature to be plasma cells. About five per cent of the total lymphocytes meet their natural death daily. Hence fresh lymphocytes must be produced daily in order that the immune system is effectively maintained.

So far we were dealing with cellular immunity. The body has also mechanism to combat infection with humoral antibodies which are immunoglobulins (abbreviated as Ig). All immunoglobulins are proteins and they are secreted by plasma cells.

The body can make hundreds of thousands, or even millions, of different antibody molecules. There would not be enough room in the body to accomodate too many lymphocytes. To compensate for this, the body makes a device to build up a large clone of plasma cells out of the small lymphocyte. These plasma cells synthesize and secrete immunoglobulins.

Small B-lymphocytes which are triggered by contact with antigen undergo successive waves of proliferation to produce a large clone of plasma cells which will be making immunoglobulins. The antibody of the plasma cells will serve the same purpose for which the parent lymphocyte is programmed.

The proliferation of the clone of plasma cells and the production of immunoglobulins by them are a consequence of antigen exposure. Hence we speak of the acquired immune response. When micro-organisms such as the polio virus or the typhoid bacteria enter the body, plasma cells are formed from small B-lymphocytes and start producing immunoglobulin molecules specific for the type of antigen.

Each immunoglobulin is a four-peptide unit. The molecule is made up of two identical heavy and two identical light chains held together by interchain disulphide bonds. There are perhaps 10^8 or more different Ig molecules in normal serum.

The acquired immunity is specific. Each antibody molecule is able to recognize its corresponding antigen and distinguish it from other antigens. Antibodies which react with the tetanus toxoid do not bind to influenza, mumps, polio, or typhoid antigen.

The antibody made in an individual system recognizes the cells of the system and does not bind to them. In this connection, Roitt remarks: "This ability to recognize one antigen and distinguish it from another goes even further. The individual must also recognize what is foreign, i.e., what is 'non-self'. The failure to discriminate between 'self' and 'non-self' could lead to the synthesis of antibodies directed against components of the subject's own body (autoantibodies) which in principle could prove to be highly embarrassing."[76]

It is surprising that the small lymphocyte acquires memory. We rarely suffer twice from such diseases as measles, mumps, chicken-pox, whooping cough, and so forth. The first contact of the B-lymphocyte with an antigen imprints some information in the former. When the same antigen (micro-organism) attacks a second time some time later, the immune system of the body has already been prepared to effectively repel the later invasion. The earlier attack has imparted some **memory** in the small lymphocyte.

This memory of the small lymphocyte can be transferred from a donor animal to a recipient animal. In an experiment, all the lymphocytes of the recipient animal are destroyed by X-radiation. The donor animal is given a primary injection of tetanus toxoid. By that, the antibody-forming system of this animal is 'tuned up' or 'primed'. A second injection of the tetanus toxoid at a subsequent time would be exhibited by a more rapid and abundant production of antibodies. This secondary antibody response can be demonstrated in a recipient animal by transferring the lymphocytes from the donor animal which has received the primary injection of the toxoid to the recipient animal which is then boosted with the toxoid antigen. This results in a rapid, intense production of antibody characteristic of a secondary response.

Let us terminate our brief sojourn to the kingdom of immunology and divert our attention to metaphysics. Why do the polymorphs, large lymphocytes, small lymphocytes, plasma cells, macrophages, and others labour so hard to protect the body? They must not be getting any pleasure out of their activity. Their labour is not remunerative for them. They do not have any self-interest in the work they do. Why are they so meticulous then in their constant vigilance against external invasion of the body? Under whose command do they work for the defence of the body?

All the organs, tissues, cells and sub-cellular micro-structures work for a common end, and that is for the existence, maintenance and development of the organism as a whole. All exist for a holistic purpose; all function with a holistic object.

All the macro- and micro-structures of the body are apparently conscious and intelligent; all seem to have memory. Some thinkers claim that every cell has a mind. To quote the words of Dr. Deepak Chopra, "Every cell speaks as fluently as we do".[77] Let us examine this concept in some greater detail.

Neurons in the brain transmit signals by electrical impulse through the nerve axon and by special chemicals across the synapse. These special chemicals are neuro-transmitters (communicator molecules). By 1973, acetyl-choline and norepinephrine were known as neurotransmitters. By the mid-1980s, more than fifty neurotransmitters and neuropeptides have been known.

Starting in the early 1980s, receptors for neurotransmitters and neuropeptides have been discovered in monocytes, the precursor cells of macrophages. We may think of monocytes as circulating neurons. Receptors for neurotransmitters and neuropeptides have also been found in organs such as the intestines, stomach, kidneys and heart. These organs can 'think' and receive and transmit messages.

The immune system secretes interleukins, a class of polypeptides that resemble hormones. The production of interleukins by immune cells takes place in many situations such as cuts, bruises, infections, internal tissue damage, allergies, etc. Such production is in tune with the exact dosage, combinations, and timings. Interleukins send signals between leucocytes.

The T-cells are small lymphocytes differentiated in the thymus. The helper T-cells are a class of message-carriers through which the body notifies the rest of the immune system to become activated and start the production of natural killer (NK) cells which are large granular lymphocytes. They recognize structures on high molecular weight glycoproteins which appear on the surface of virally infected cells. This recognition occurs through receptors on the NK cell surface which brings killer and target into close apposition.

Such 'conscious' behaviours of individual cells stimulates Dr. Deepak Chopra to deduce: "The mind is not confined to the brain . . . Mind is projected everywhere in inner space".[78] "Every cell is a little sentient being."[79] He further states: "The physical structure of the body mirrors intelligence and gives it a projected form, but intelligence is not trapped inside this framework of flesh and bones".[80]

A number of examples that have been cited in this chapter establish the fact that the brain and mind are not identical. Here we will cite two more experimental evidences to indicate that the brain is not the mind.

Karl Lashley,[81] a pioneer in neurophysiology, conducted an experiment to locate the seat of memory in the brain. He taught rats to run a maze. This is a skill which is stored in memory and remembered. By steps he removed a small amount of tissue from the cerebral cortex of the experimental rats. Finally, more than ninety per cent of the entire cerebral cortex was removed and only a speck of the cerebral tissue remained. In spite of the almost brainless condition of the rats, they remembered the maze, with a slight fall-off in accuracy and speed. Lashley summed up the results of hundreds of experiments as follows:

> It is not possible to demonstrate the isolated localization of a memory trace anywhere within the nervous system. Limited regions may be essential for learning or retention of a particular activity, but within such regions the parts are functionally equivalent.[82]

B.B. Boycott demonstrated a similar phenomenon in an invertebrate, the octopus. He destroyed various parts of the vertical lobe of the brain of the octopus and still observed the survival of learned habits. Being puzzled over the interpretation of his results, he drew the seemingly paradoxical conclusion that "memory is both everywhere and nowhere in particular."[83]

John Lorber,[84] a British neurologist, was a specialist in examining hydrocephalic patients. This is a congenital pathological condition where the brain cavities are filled with fluid in place of cerebral tissue. This abnormality leads to serious mental impairment. But, to the surprise of Lorber, one of his patients was a gifted college student, majoring in mathematics, with an IQ of 130. The brain scan of the patient revealed that his cerebral cortex was only one millimetre thick, compared to the usual four and a half centimetres. Fluid in this patient's brain had replaced 98 per cent of the neurons needed for thinking, higher mental activity, and remembering. With only two per cent of a normal cerebral cortex, this hydrocephalic man was normal or above average in all respects.

We can interpret the results of these experiments in either of the ways. First, every cell of the brain stores the whole brain while at the same time storing its own specific task. Second, the brain which is the instrument of mind stores information; but this storing is additional, the primary and comprehensive recording being done in mind which is different from the brain. The *Vedānta* and the *Yoga* accept the second interpretation. According to this view, mind is material, but the nature of this materiality is not gross, but subtle. The brain, which is part of the gross body, perishes when a person dies. But the same person's mind survives death. The *saṁskāras* and *vāsanās* imprinted in the mind are the cause of reincarnation.

We have so far discussed the consciousness and intelligence of cells. But, the most intelligent agent that controls and guides the cells of the body and the body as a whole is the DNA molecule. In 1953, James Dewey Watson and Francis H. Crick developed the double-helix model for deoxyribonucleic acid, or DNA, which explains how this giant molecule is capable of transmitting heredity in living organisms. The most significant event about this marco-molecule is that it is capable of replicating itself. It is double-stranded; the two strands separate from one end like a zipper, and each one serves as a template for the reproduction of another strand, with correspondence of A and T, and G and C. These letters stand for the bases adenine, thymine, guanine, and cytosine, respectively. Adenine and guanine are purine bases whereas thymine and cytosine are pyrimidine bases. Three bases in a particular sequence make a genetic code, such as ATC, CTA, CAT, GAC, CGA, CAG, etc. In all, there are $4^3 = 64$ codes. A code stands for an amino acid, and there are usually twenty amino acids in nature. The codes regulate protein synthesis by ordering the amino acid sequence in the biosynthesis of protein molecules. The human body contains more than two million proteins. The synthesis of all these proteins is regulated by twenty-three pairs of DNA molecules in the human body. In addition to the purine and pyrimidine bases already mentioned, the DNA molecule contains the pentose sugar, deoxyribose, and phosphoric acid.

The DNA is always intranuclear. It serves as the template for the biosynthesis of three kinds of ribonucleic acid (RNA), viz., messenger-RNA, transport-RNA, and ribosomal RNA. All these RNAs are synthesized inside the nucleus and subsequently they migrate to the cytophasm where they become instrumental in protein biosynthesis. The RNAs are transcribed inside the nucleus by the DNA; they obey the order of the DNA and translate the order at the ribosomal site in the cytoplasm of the cell.

The elemental composition of the DNA consists of carbon, hydrogen, oxygen, nitrogen, and phosphorus. The molecular composition of this macro-molecule is made by purine and pyrimidine bases, deoxyribose which is a pentose sugar, and phosphoric acid. None of these composite elements and molecules are intelligent. None of them can reproduce themselves. None of them can regulate the synthesis of other molecules. But, when they combine to form the DNA molecule, the product acquires creativity and intelligence. The synthesis of DNA molecule is the most critical event in the history of evolution. No life is conceivable on the earth (other macro-molecules might regulate life processes of extraterrestrial biology) without the DNA molecule.

Barring rare mutations, the DNA molecule maintains its structure unchanged amidst continued changes of individual atoms of its molecules. The old atoms leave and new atoms enter the molecule. The wonder is this that the building stands in an intact condition with continual exit and entry of the constituent bricks.

What is true for the DNA molecule, with reference to the

exit and entry of the constituent atoms, also applies to the whole body in general. Of all the atoms present in a human body today, ninety per cent of them were not there a year ago. One gets a new skeleton every three months. The calcium bound into our bones can take a whole year to replace itself. The skin is new every month. The stomach has a new lining every four days. The cells that actually contact food are renewed every five minutes. A new liver is made every six weeks. Although the brain-cells are not replaced once they die, their constituent elements, viz., carbon, hydrogen, oxygen, nitrogen, phosphorus, sulphur, and so on are totally different today from what they were a year ago. All such exchanges are continual throughout the life of an individual and still the whole blueprint of the body is intact and unaltered in usual conditions. But for the administrative control of the DNA molecule, the blueprint cannot maintain itself.

It is not a fact that the DNA molecule works just from rote memory. It exercises ingenuity and creativity. It can invent new chemicals at will, if and when necessary. The synthesis of a new antibody may be taken as an example. A person may catch a strain of flu he has never been exposed to before. The DNA immediately synthesizes an antibody which can bind with the new antigen. How the DNA accomplishes this job is not exactly known. We can speculate the explanation of such a phenomenon in a number of ways. Moleculer biologists have discovered the spacers that separate different genetic words, or genomes. These spacers may contain codes that are ordinarily latent but become active when need arises. It has also been known that only one per cent of the genetic material in DNA is used, leaving 99 per cent as stand-by for contingent requirements.

This is something very startling. The human species (*Homo sapiens*) uses only one per cent of its genetic material, and 99 per cent are potential and unused. The DNA is keeping a large vocabulary in silent storage. If part of this potentiality is brought into further use, man's creative ability and human quality can be augmented to hitherto unexpected level. Consequent on the discovery of recombinant DNA (pieces of genetic material that can be shuffled in and out of sequence on the DNA strands), the potential vocabulary may be infinitely larger than what it is now. There is much scope for converting the latency into patency through human wisdom.

We do appreciate the marvellous dexterity of the DNA molecule, the programmed blueprint of an individual living being. Nevertheless, we do not accept a wholly mechanistic explanation of life. We do consider that the DNA molecule is the blueprint made by a Divine Designer whose presence alone makes the wheel of evolution move purposefully and intelligently. We see a contrivance; we do not recognize its contriver.

The mechanistic concept in biology has been expressed by T.H. Huxley by the following statements:

> Zoological physiology is the doctrine of the functions or actions of animals. It regards animal bodies as machines impelled by various forces and performing a certain amount of work which can be expressed in terms of the ordinary forces of nature. The final object of physiology is to deduce the facts of morphology on the one hand, and those of ecology on the other, from the laws of the molecular forces of matter.[85]

The molecular biologists are the influential modern advocates of the mechanistic theory. The discovery of the structure of DNA by Watson and Crick, the cracking of the genetic code, and the elucidation of the mechanism of protein synthesis have encouraged molecular biologists to strongly plead for the mechanistic theory. F.H.C. Crick[86] and J. Monod[87] are two famous representatives of the molecular biologists who interpret life processes purely on mechanical basis.

The molecular biologist over-emphasizes the role of DNA as the sole determinant of all life processes. The programmed DNA is recognized while the programmer is ignored. Molecular biologists have compared the non-repeated DNA sequences (those parts believed to be of genetic significance) and found only 1.1 per cent overall difference between the DNA sequence of humans and chimpanzees. A considerable number of human and chimpanzee proteins are identical, and those that are not identical differ only slightly. That there is a genetic resemblance between humans and chimpanzees has been confirmed by amino acid sequencing of the proteins of both these species, and by immunological and electrophoretic studies on them. These studies clearly show that the average human polypeptide is more than 99 per cent identical to its chimpanzee counterpart.[88] Moreover, similar comparisons of the DNA and protein molecules of different species of mice or of the fruit fly (*Drosophila*) have revealed larger differences between these closely related species than between humans and chimpanzees. It is difficult for Crick, Monod, and other molecular biologists to explain the great differences in intelligence and creativity between man and chimpanzee by mere mechanical interpretation. In spite of their genetic resemblance, man is man, and chimpanzee is chimpanzee. The molecular biologists are to go beyond the DNA molecule to search for the so-called 'hidden variable' of the quantum physicists.

The *Vedānta* and the *Yoga* recognize the structures of the material body as component parts of a machine and the functionings of the parts as well as the whole like those of a machine. But something other than the machine is its motive force. This idea has been clearly expressed in the *Bhagavadgītā*. "O Arjuna, God (*Īśvara*) dwells in the heart of all beings, who are seated in the (world) machine made to revolve by His power of *Māyā*."[89]

Unlike classical physics, quantum physics is involved in indeterminism. Einstein's aversion to the probabilistic aspect of the quantum theory was encapsulated in his reply to one of Max Born's letters in 1926 by the following sentences:

> Quantum mechanics is very impressive. But an inner voice tells me that it is not yet the real thing. The theory produces a good deal but hardly brings us closer to the secret of the Old one. I am at all events convinced that He does not play dice.[90]

Einstein's followers, particularly David Bohm, developed the viewpoint of 'hidden variables',[91] according to which there would indeed be some definite reality, but the parameters which precisely define a system would not be directly accessible to us. The views of Einstein and Bohm are in agreement with the *Vedānta* and the *Yoga*, with the single exception that Bohm's 'hidden variable' may be substituted with the term 'hidden constant'. Some philosophers of science in the field of biology borrow this concept from David Bohm and explain life processes by the so-called hidden variables that serve as the motive force. According to this notion, the hidden variables guide the actions of the DNA molecule.

The *Vedānta* speaks of the 'hidden constant' rather than the 'hidden variables'. *Brahman*, the fundamental Consciousness, being attributeless and functionless, is ever unchangeable; it is the only constant (*dhruva*)[92] and nothing else is constant. All things manifested from *Māyā*, the power of *Brahman*, are ever variable. No manifested being can exist and function without the support of the hidden constant.

The DNA molecule has no miraculous power. None of its constituents are sentient. Its first emergence out of inorganic and organic chemical precursors is a miraculous feat in the history of evolution. This event is the dividing line between the non-living and the living world. The evolution of the DNA molecule, according to the *Vedānta*, has been possible, like all processes of evolution, due to the 'presiding influence'[93] of *Īśvara* (God). The whole of scientific evolution can be incorporated in the *Vedānta* without any alteration except this additional concept of divine presidentship as the passive guiding agency, the active agency being *Māyā* or *Prakṛti*.

At the empirical level, we accept the idea that every cell is intelligent and that the DNA molecule is witty. Can we infer from this premise that every cell has a mind?

If we hold that every cell has a mind, we perhaps confuse over the use of the word 'mind'. We agree that the brain is not equivalent to mind. At the same time, we plead that consciousness or intelligence is not the same as mind. Every individual being, whether human being or animal, has one and only one mind which itself is insentient subtle matter. In the Vedāntic and the Yogic terminology, it is called internal instrument (*antaḥkaraṇa*) and *citta*, respectively. Its principal components are *buddhi*, *ahaṅkāra*, and *manas*. With some other constituent parts, the whole thing is known as the subtle body (*sūkṣma śarīra*) which survives death. It serves as the apparent limiting adjunct (*upādhi*) of the empirical self (*ātmā*), the whole complex (*upādhi* + *ātmā*) being known as the *jīva*. The *jīva* is reincarnated again and again until its *saṁkāras* and *vāsanās* which are imprinted in the *buddhi* are not completely erased. This process is analogous to the distilling of muddy water in order to get pure water. The dirty material in water is comparable to the imprinted *saṁskāras* and *vāsanās* (*karmāśaya*) in the subtle body. Without further *karma* deposit in the subtle body, the cause of reincarnation disappears, and, with the attainment of this stage, the self is liberated. This state of the self is called *mokṣa* (liberation) in the *Vedānta*. It is a process of reunion and reidentification. The same state is called *kaivalya* (isolation) in the *Yoga*. It is a process of the separation of the self from *Prakṛti* (the totality of potential matter). Mathematically speaking, the former is addition and the latter subtraction. Although apparently opposite, the two processes are not different in essence.

If we assign one mind to each organ, each cell, and each

macro- and micro-molecule in an individual human being or animal, the doctrine of holistic existence would collapse. In the hypothetical case of pluralistic minds in a single organism, there would be disharmony, in-co-ordination, disorder and chaos. But, empirically we observe holism in the structuring and functioning of each individual organism. The *ahaṅkāra* in each individual is the dictating agent; it functions in a team with the *buddhi* and *manas*. But all these components of the internal instrument are made up of the three strings (*guṇas*), viz., *sattva*, *rajas*, and *tamas*, and all are insentient. The internal instrument in which the light of the self (*ātmā*) is reflected acquires sentience. Thus, the *ātmā* presides, and the *ahaṅkāra* functions. Every organism has one functional agent only, and that agent is the "I". The brain, heart, lungs, kidneys, liver, and other organs enjoy some in-built autonomy; still they obey the order of the dictator "I". The polymorphs, lymphocytes, monocytes, macrophages, plasma cells, and other cellular constituents of the body do exercise freedom; still they work under the command of the "I". The DNA molecule exhibits intelligence, ingenuity, and creativity; but still it works under the direct command of the "I". The observed facts are certainly at variance with the pluralistic functionings of the macro- and micro-constituents of an organism. Of course, a single organism like a human being has plural structures. And each macro- and micro-structure has been assigned specific duties. In this sense, the functionings are pluralistic in the analogy of a nation state headed by a king or a president, under whose control many functionaries work. All these functionaries work individually, but the ultimate aim of all the functions of a nation are meant for the interest of the nation as a whole. So is the pluralism in the body under the presidentship of the self and the executive agency of the "I" (*ahaṅkāra*).

So far we have focused on the holistic existence of the human being as an irreducible individual whole. In principle, everything we have said about the human being holds good for all species of animals, both higher and lower.

And the same principle also applies to plants, fungi, bacteria, and viruses.

We may take the example of regeneration, whereby organisms are able to replace or restore damaged structures. In the animal kingdom, lower animals possess better ability to regenerate themselves. A flatworm, for example, may be cut up into several pieces, and it is seen that each piece can regenerate into a complete worm. Even many vertebrates possess striking powers of regeneration. G. Wolff[94] experimentally demonstrated this in a newt's eye. In normal embryonic development, the lens of the eye is formed from the skin. But regeneration of a lens could take place from the margin of the iris in a newt's eye after Wolff surgically removed the original lens. He deliberately chose this kind of mutilation which could not have occurred accidentally in nature. Without natural occurrence, the Darwinian natural selection for this particular regenerative process could not be conceived of. It was the newt's "I" (*ahaṅkāra*) that made ingenious effort for the regeneration of the eye-lens.

Plants show an amazing range of regenerative abilities. We may take the example of *Ipomoea fistulosa* from whose branches and sub-branches new whole plants can be regenerated. There are many species of plants, whose branches, if planted in moist soil, can regenerate the full plants. When the leaves of *Bryophyllum calycinum* are laid on damp grounds, buds and young plants are produced from the leaf-crenatures. The leaflets of the leaf of a fern plant (*Filicineae*), say *Osmunda cinnamomea*, when fallen on a moist soil, can generate a full plant. The leaflet bears sporangia for the purpose of reproduction. Such examples in the plant kingdom are too many. We may go deep into the matter and analyse the issue. It is not the normal function of a leaf to generate roots, buds, and stems, etc. The stem of a branch does not normally generate roots. Why do they play an unusual role only when their survival is at stake? Why do they crave for a holistic existence? It may seem ludicrous to suggest that each plant does possess an "I" (*ahaṅkāra*) that prompts the regenerative process for the purpose of holistic existence. But that's what the *Vedānta*, the *Sāṅkhya* and the *Yoga* assert. Each plant has a self (*ātmā*) which survives death. And the *Advaita Vedānta* further adds that there is only one Self that is *Brahman* and that the separate empirical selves are different for the empirical world only, they being identical at the absolute (*pāramārthika*) level. Without consciousness, without a holistic existence, and without a central guiding and controlling authority (I), it is not possible to explain how one single leaf, separated from the mother plant, can be able to regenerate a whole plant with the old unaltered blueprint.

Cosmic Link-Up

Advaita Vedānta conceives of reality at two levels — absolute (*pāramārthika*) and empirical (*vyāvahārika*). *Brahman* or Fundamental Consciousness (*Cit*) is absolute. It is non-material, non-dual, non-relational, formless, attributeless, non-functional Existence (*Satya*), which is not dependent on anything else, but on which all empirical existence depends.

Brahman is neuter in gender. Its power (*śakti*) is feminine in gender. This *śakti* is otherwise known as *Māyā* or *Prakṛti*, which functions as the limiting adjunct (*upādhi*) of the reflection of *Brahman* in its power. This reflected Consciousness in *Māyā* or *Prakṛti* is God (*Īśvara*) which is masculine in gender. We come down from absolute attributelessness to states of attributes when we conceive of *Īśvara* and *Prakṛti*, one masculine and the other feminine. Next, we come to the empirical world which is phenomenal only. *Īśvara* is its efficient cause and *Māyā* is the material or substantial cause. We think of Consciousness and Pure Consciousness when we speak of *Brahman*. We speak of reflected Consciousness with reference to *Īśvara*. The empirical universe, however, is the product of *avidyā* or *ajñāna* (nescience). Thus, matter (including energy) which is an epiphenomenon of the power (*śakti*) of Consciousness cannot exist without the background of ignorance. By virtue of the projecting, concealing, and deluding power of *Māyā*, the phenomenal inverted world-tree hangs down, but rooted firmly in *Brahman*.

From *Brahman* we proceed to the world. From non-duality we proceed to multiplicity. The multiple phenomena are likened to the waves, ripples, surfs, and bubbles on the surface of the sea. The substratum of the universe is the Fundamental Consciousness, homogeneous and unbroken whole. The surface is pluralistic, with multiple entities covered with ignorance through which consciousness emerges as light particles.

The empirical world is not the reality, but it is not nothing. We are ourselves parts of the empirical world. The galaxy-clusters, galaxies, stars, planets, molecules, atoms and subatomic particles are component parts of the empirical world. Viruses, bacteria, protozoa, helminths, birds, animals, and human beings belong to the empirical world. All these — both living and non-living — have varying degrees of consciousness. None can exist outside the Fundamental Consciousness which pervades and transcends the manifested beings. And hence everything, both living and non-living, gets consciousnesss reflected in it. This reflected consciousness is *bhūtātmā* in a non-living entity and *jīvātmā*, in a living entity. Whether it is *bhūtātmā* or *jīvātmā*, it has a mental apparatus. Let us call it mind. Thus, there are innumerable minds in the universe. In the world of plurality exist as many minds as the number of entities. But it is to be emphasized here that each entity has a single mind only rather than multiple minds. The development of the mind is in consonance with the simplicity or complexity of the mental apparatus evolved to a certain rung of the long ladder and for certain specific purpose(s).

The world is full of order and disorder. Order rather than disorder is more apparent in the macro-world. Disorder rather than order is more apparent in the micro-world. But the net course of the world (*saṁsāra*, meaning ,'the world moving in harmony') is not chaotic. *Ṛta* (order) prevails in the world. But, how can *ṛta* prevail in the world of multiplicity if the multiple entities are unconnected with one another without any central control? How can there be harmony and co-ordination in a pluralistic world whose basis is matter and where consciousness is an epiphenomenon of matter? Is there any connecting link among the apparently separate objects in Nature? As different computers can be linked up, so can different minds be connected at a deeper and fundamental level. What is that Cosmic Link-Up?

The *Vedas* declare that *Virāḍ* (*Virāṭ*) is the first manifestation out of the Unmanifest. The *Sāṅkhya* says that *Mahat* (*Buddhi*) is the first evolute out of *Prakṛti*. What we call Cosmic Mind or Supermind is this *Virāḍ* or *Mahat*. *Īśvara* uses this Supermind for ruling the universe. The individual minds can be linked up with this Supermind. Through the Supermind, the individual minds can also be linked up with one another. The *Yogī* does this through meditation. When the *Yogī* attains to the state of *samādhi*, his mind merges with the Supermind and can be connected through the Supermind with individual minds. There are special methods in *Yoga*, by practising which supernormal powers such as telepathy, clairvoyance, precognition, etc. can be acquired. The parapsychologists have tried to explain them by various hypotheses, but they have not succeeded. Success is not likely to accrue unless and until the Supermind is not recognized and the concept of Cosmic Link-Up is not accepted.

Carl Gustav Jung developed the concept of the collective unconscious, which is not confined to individual minds, but provides a common substratum shared by all human minds. He writes:

> In addition to our immediate consciousness, which is of a thoroughly personal nature and which we believe to be the only empirical psyche (even if we tack on the personal unconscious as an appendix)

> there exists a second psychic system of a collective, universal, and impersonal nature which is identical in all individuals. This collective unconscious does not develop individually but is inherited. It consists of pre-existent forms, the archetypes, which can only become conscious secondarily and which give definite form to certain psychic contents.[95]

Jung's collective unconscious is the same as the Vedic *Virāḍ* or the *Sāṅkhya-Yoga Mahat.*[96] But he is conceptually wrong when he says that it is inherited. Our knowledge on genetics would prohibit the use of the word 'inherited' for a purpose like this. All created entities — living, and non-living — share *Virāḍ* or *Mahat* on which all events, individual and universal are imprinted. Some gifted persons with inborn ability can link up their individual minds with this Supermind. Yogic training imparts proficiency to an individual mind to link-up with the Cosmic Mind. Once the link-up is established, nothing remains hidden to an individual mind which is otherwise severely limited. An individual mind, linked to the Cosmic Mind, transcends time and space; it no longer is limitedly focused on local space and present time; the totality of universal space is exposed to it; and the past, the present, and the future become extra-transparent.

We float up and down and tussle on a fathomless ocean. We appear as bubbles and again disappear. The bubbles are many with separate existences. The substratum of the ocean, however, is homogeneous and an unbroken whole. That substratum is the Fundamental Consciousness. If the underlying deep water is considered, the bubbles are connected with one another, although apparently separate. Each bubble has to recognize its link with the underlying water-mass. A bubble can realize its link with the other bubbles through the ocean water on which it floats and dances. This link up is the Cosmic Link-Up which has been revealed by the wisdom of the *Vedānta* and the *Yoga* and which awaits discovery by science.

Notes

1. *BU*, III.8.8; IV.4.20
2. *MTU*, VI.15; *ŚU*, VI.5.
3. *BU*, III.8.8.
4. *ṚV*, X.90.5.
5. *SPS*, I.61 (*sattvarajastamasāṁ sāmyāvasthā prakṛtiḥ, prakṛtermahān*).
6. *SDSS*, V.17; V.20; V.78.
7. *SDSS*, V.14.
8. *BS*, II.2.1.
9. Davies, P.C.W., 1988 (1st Publ. 1982), *The Accidental Universe*, p. 1.
10. *Ibid.*, p. 77.
11. Pagels, H.R., 1985, 'A Cozy cosmology', In *The Sciences*, 25(2): 35-38.
12. Davies, P.C.W., 1988 (1st Publ. 1982), *The Accidental Universe*. pp. 77-83.
13. Eddington, A.S., 1931, *Proc. Comp. Phil. Soc.*, 27:15.
14. Eddington, A.S., 1936, *Relativity Theory of Protons Electrons*.
15. Dirac, P.A.M., 1937, *Nature*, 139: 323.
16. Dirac, P.A.M., 1938, *Proc. Roy. Soc.*, 165A: 199.
17. Rees, N.J., Ruffini, R., and Wheeler, J.A., 1974, 'Coincidence or Consequence', In *Block Holes, Gravitational Waves, and Cosmology*.
18. Whitrow, G.J., 1959, *The Structure and Evolution of the Universe*, (See the appendix).
19. Dicke, R.H., 1957, Quoted by Pagels, H.R., 'A Cozy Cosmology', In *The Sciences*, 25(2):35-38. (March/April 1985).
20. Carter, B., 1974, Large number coincidences and the anthropic principle in cosmology, In M.S. Longair (ed.) *Confrontation of Cosmological Theories with Observational Data*, pp. 291-98.
21. Barrow, J.D., and Tipler, F.J., 1986, *The Anthropic Cosmological Principle*.
22. Barrow, J.D., Quoted by P.C.W. Davies, *The Accidental Universe*, p. 121.
23. Silk, J., 1977, Nature, 265: 710. Quoted by P.C.W. Davies, *The Accidental Universe*, p. 121.
24. Wheeler, J., 1980, *Some Strangeness in the Proportion: A Centennial Symposium to Celebrate the Achievements of Albert Einstein*, ed. by H. Woolf.
25. Collins, C.B. and Hawking, S.W., 1973, *Astrophysics Journal*, 180: 317.

26. Carr, B.J. and Rees, M.J., 1979, "The anthropic principle and the structure of the physical world", In *Nature*, 278, 12 April, pp. 605-12.

27. Swinburne, R., 1989, "Argument from the fine-tuning of the universe", In *Physical Cosmology and Philosophy*, ed. by John Leslie, pp. 154-73.

28. Leslie, J., 1982, "Anthropic principle, world ensemble, design", *American Philosophical Quarterly*, 19: 141-51.

29. Leslie, J., 1983, "Cosmology, probability, and the need to explain life", In N. Rescher (ed.) *Scientific Expalantion and Understanding*. pp. 53-81.

30. Pagels, H.R., 1985, "A cozy cosmology", *The Sciences*, 25(2): 35-38, March-April.

31. Gould, S.J., 1985, The *Flamingo's Smile, Reflections in Natural History*, pp. 392-402.

32. Carr, B.J., 1982, "On the origin, evolution and purpose of the physical universe", In *The Irish Astronomical Journal* 15(3): 237-53 (March issue devoted to "Cosmos and Creation").

33. Davies, P.C.W., 1988, (1st publ. 1982) *The Accidental Universe*, p. 122.

34. *ṚV*, X, 129.4; *BS*, I.4.24; II.3.13; *BSŚB*, II.3.13; *CU*, VI.2.3-4; *TU*, II.6.1.

35. *ṚV*, X.81-2, 121; *YV*, XXXI, 19; *BSŚB*, I.1.2; I.1.4-5; I.1.11; 1.2.2; 1.2.9; I.3.30; *ŚBrā*, I.9.3.10, *TBrā*, III, 12.3.1; *BU*, II.6.3; IV.6.3; VI.5.4; *KTU*, II.1.1; *MUU*, I.1.9; III.I.3; *ŚU*, III.4; VI.18; *ŚUŚB*, I.3; *TU*, III. 1.1. *BG*, XIV.3-4; *Mbh*, XII. 160.

36. *BS*, I.2.18; I.3.10-11; I.3.43; *BSŚB*, I.1.2; I.1.4-5; I.1.11; I.2.2; I.2.9; I.2.18; I.3.11; II.3.23; *BU*, III.7.3-23; III.8.7-9; IV.4.22; *BUŚB*, III.8.9; *MAU*, 6; *ŚU*, II.17; III.I-2; III.4; *ŚUŚB*, I.3; *TU*, II.6.1; III.1.1; *BG*. IX 5; XIII.22.

37. *AV*, XI.7.1; *BS*. I.2.9; *BSŚB*, 1.1.2; I.1.4-5; I.1.11; I.2.2; I.2.9; *BU*, I.2.5; *KTU*, I.2.25; *MAU*, 6; *TU*, III.1.1; *Bhā*, IV.7.42; *VPu*, VI.4.39.

38 *ŚU*, II.17; IV.11; V.2; VI.11; *TU*, II.6.1; *BSŚB*, II.3.17; *BU*, 1.4.7; *CU*. VI.3.2.

39 *ṚV*, VI.47.18; *KTU*, II.2.9-10.

40. *BS*, I.2.18; *BSŚB*, II.2.3; *BU*, III.7.3-23.

41. *BS*, I.3.10-11; I.3.43; *BSŚB*, I.3.11; II.3.23; *BU*, III.7.3-23; III.8.7-9; IV 4.22; *MAU*, 6; *ŚU*, II.17; III.I, 2, 4, 17, 18; VI.12, 17; *TU*, II.8.1; *KTU*, II:2.12; *BG*, IV.6; VIII.9; X.3.

42. *ṚV*, X.129.7; *ŚU*, VI.11; *TUŚB*, II.8.9; *BGŚB*. IX.10.

43. *ŚUŚB*. VI.12; *BGŚB*, XIII.29.

44. *BG*, IX.10.

45. *ṚV*, X.190.1.

46. *BUŚB*, III.8.9.

47. *BSŚB*, I.3.11 (*nācetanasya pradhānasya praśāsanaṁ bhavati. na hyacetanānāṁ ghaṭādikāraṇānāṁ mṛdādīnāṁ ghaṭādiviṣayaṁ praśāsanamasti*).

48. *BSŚB*, I.3.11 (*paraśāsanañca pārameśvaraṁ karma*); I.3.30.

49. Bose, J.C., 1926, *The Nervous Mechanism of Plants.*

50. Gregory, R.L., 1984, (1st publ. 1981) *Mind in Science*, pp. 317-18.

51. *Ibid.*, p. 318.

52. Patten, B.M., 1968, *Human Embryology*, 3rd edn. p. 59.

53. Arey, L.B., 1954, *Developmental Anatomy*, 6th edn., p. 83.

54. Richter, J.P.F. Quoted by MacKenzie, N., In *Dreams and Dreaming*, 1989 (1st publ. 1965). p. 90.

55. Hilgard, E.R., 1973a. "A neodissociation interpretation of pain reduction in hypnosis", In *Psychological Review*, 80; 396-411.

56. Hilgard, E.R., and Hilgard, J.R., 1975, *Hypnosis in the Relief of Pain.*

57. Hilgard, E.R., 1977: *Divided Consciousness: Multiple Controls in Human Thought and Action.*

58. *ŚU*, VI.11 (*eko devas sarvabhūteṣu gūḍhas, sarvavyāpī sarvabhūtāntarātmā; karmādhyakṣas sarvabhūtādhi sākṣī cetā kevalo nirguṇaśca).*

59. *PYD*, II.3.

60. Netherton, M. and Schiffrin, N., 1978, *Past Lives Therapy.*

61. Fiore, E., 1978, *You Have Been Here Before.*

62. Whitton, J.L., 1976, "Hypnotic time regression and reincarnation memories", In *New Horizons*, June.

63. Whitton, J.L., 1978, "Karma in reincarnation memories", In *The Rosicrucian Digest*, October.

64. Whitton, J.L., 1978, "Xenoglossia: A subject with two possible instances", In *New Horizons*, September.

65. Whitton, J.L., and Fisher, J., 1990 (1st publ. 1986) *Life Between Life.*

66. Moody, R.A. Jr., 1981 (1st publ. 1975), *Life After Life.*

67. Stevenson, I., 1977, "Research into man's survival after death", In *Journal of Nervous and Mental Disease*, 165: 152-70.

68. Stevenson, I., 1983, "American children who claim to remember past lives", In *Journal of Nervous and Mental Disease*, 171: 742-48.

69. Carlson, S., 1985, Quoted by Dixon, B., 1989, In *The Science of Science*, p. 124.

70. Park, M.A., 1982-83, "Palmistry: Science or hand-jive?", In The *Skeptical Inquirer*, Vol. VII, No. 2, Winter. Reprinted in *Science, Non-Science and the Paranormal*, 1987, Narasimhaih (chief ed.).

71. Eccles, J.C., 1953, *The Neurophysiological Basis of Mind.*

72. *ṚV,* I.164.20, *MUU,* III.1.1; *KTU,* I.3.1; *ŚU,* IV.6.

73. *MUUŚB,* III.1.1 (*paśyatyeva kevalaṁ, darśanamātreṇa hi tasya prerayitṛtvam rājavat*).

74. *BG,* VI.5.

75. *BG,* V.14; XIII.29.

76. Roitt, I.M., 1988 (1st publ. 1971) *Essential Immunology,* 6th edn. p. 23.

77. Chopra, D., 1989, *Quantum Healing,* p. 70.

78. *Ibid.,* p. 70.

79. *Ibid.,* p. 146.

80. *Ibid.,* p. 147.

81. Lashley, K.S., 1929, *Brain Mechanisms and Intelligence.*

82. Lashley, K.S., 1950, "In search of the engram", In *Symposia of the Society for Experimental Biology,* 4:454-82.

83. Lorber, J. Quoted by Dr. Deepak Chopra 1989, In *Quantum Healing.* pp. 147-48.

84. Boycott, B.B., 1965, "Learning in the octopus", In *Scientific American.* 212(3): 42-50.

85. Huxley, T.H., 1867, *Hardwicke's Science Gossip,* 3: 74.

86. Crick, F.H.C., 1967, *Of Molecules and Men.*

87. Monod, J., 1972, *Chance and Necessity.*

88. King, M.C. and Wilson, A.C., 1975, "Evolution at two levels in humans and chimpanzees", In *Science* 188: 107-16.

89. *BG,* XVIII.61 (*īśvaraḥ sarvabhūtānāṁ hṛddeśe'rjuna tiṣṭhati, bhrāmayan sarvabhūtāni yantrārūḍhāni māyayā*).

90. Pais, A., 1982, *Subtle is the Lord. The Science and the Life of Albert Einstein,* p. 443.

91. Bohm, D., 1952, "A suggested interpretation of the quantum theory in terms of 'hidden variables', I and II", In *Quantum Theory and Measurement* (ed., J.A. Wheeler and W.H. Zurek), originally in *Physical Review,* 85: 166-93.

92. *BU,* IV.4.20; *KTU,* I.3.15; *MTU,* VI.38; VII.3; *BG,* XII.3.

93. *BG,* IX.10 (*mayādhyakṣeṇa prakṛtiḥ sūyate sacarācaram; hetunānena kaunteya jagadviparivartate*).

94. Wolff, G., 1902, *Mechanisms and Vitalisms.* Quoted by Needham, J., 1942, In *Biochemistry and Morphogensis.*

95. Jung, C.G., 1959, *The Archetypes and the Collective Unconscious.* p. 43.

96. *PYD,* II.22 (*kṛtārthaṁ pratinaṣṭamapyanaṣṭaṁ tadanyasādhāraṇatvāt*).

Glossary

abāhya: Without exterior.

ābhāsavāda: The doctrine of appearance.

abhāva: Non-existence.

abhayamudrā: The gesture for dispelling fear.

abhimāna: Self-sense or self-conceit.

abhiniveśa: Clinging to life; fear of death; the will to live.

ābhoga: Enjoyment; satiety.

abhyāsa: Practice; repetition.

acala: Motionless.

acintya: Inconceivable; unthinkable.

acit: Insentient.

adharma: Unmeritorious action; wrong living; demerit; vice.

ādhibhautika: Proceeding from natural objects.

ādhidaivika: Proceeding from gods.

adhiṣṭhāna: Substratum.

adhiṣṭhāna śarīra: Vehicular body.

adhyakṣa: President; the presiding deity.

adhyāsa: Superimposition (When a rope appears as a snake, the snake-appearance is superimposed on the rope).

ādhyātmika: Proceeding from the self.

adhyavasāya: Ascertainment.

advaita: Non-dual.

advaya: Non-dual.

Āgama: The original scriptures of the *Tantra*.

āgāmī karma: *Karma* which is being or will be deposited for fruition in future lives.

āgneyāstra: A fire-weapon.

agni: Fire; heat; light; energy; the subtle element of fire; the god presiding the subtle element of fire.

agnisāra kriyā: Otherwise known as *vahnisāra dhauti*; a yogic practice of *antardhauti* (inner cleansing) in which the abdomen is drawn in and out.

aham: I; first person singular.

ahamasmi: I am.

ahaṅkāra: The self-sense; the egoity; the I-sense; one of the components of the *antaḥkaraṇa* or the inner instrument, responsible for the individuation; sense of individuality.

ahiṁsā: Non-violence.

aikāgrya: Singleness of intent.

airāvata: The heavenly elephant of god *Indra*.

aiśvarya: Power.

aiśvaryapriya: Fond of power.

aja: Unborn.

ajapā japa: The spontaneous repetition of the *mantra* "*so'haṁ*".

ājñā: It is the sixth and final *cakra* in the subtle body in the ascending order. It is located behind the spot between the two eye-brows.

ajñāna: Ignorance; nescience.

akala: Partless.

akāla: Timeless.

akartā: Non-doer.

ākāśa: Space; the subtle element of space.

ākāśa-bīja: The seed of the subtle element of *ākāśa* or space.

akāya: Devoid of structures and substructures; bodiless.

akhaṇḍa: The unbroken whole.

akliṣṭa: Non-painful.

akṛṣṇa: Not-black.

akṣaranyāsa: *Nyāsa* on mystic syllables.

akuśala: Bad.

alakṣaṇam: Devoid of distinguishing characteristics.

ālambana: A support to rest upon; supporter; manifester.

alambuṣā: It is a supersensible psychic channel in the subtle body for the flow of *prāṇa*.

ālaya: Repository; carrier; a place for storage.

ālayavijñāna: A modified state of consciousness which is the repository of all *vāsanās*; this is a term used by the Buddhist school of *Vijñānavāda* for the abode of *vāsanās*.

aliṅga: Unresoluble-primary-matter; same as *Prakṛti*; devoid of distinguishing characteristics.

amanāḥ (*amanas*): Devoid of mind.

amara: Deathless; immortal.

amātra: Dimensionless.

amṛta: Ambrosia or nectar.

amṛta-pāna: The act of drinking ambrosia.

amūrta: Formless.

anādi: Beginningless.

anādikāraṇa: Beginningless cause.

anāditva: No beginning.

anāhata: It is the fourth *cakra* in the subtle body. It is located behind the base of the heart, at the level of the depression in the sternum. This level corresponds to that of the cardiac plexus of nerves.

anaiśvarya: Powerlessness.

anākāśa: Spaceless.

ānanda: Bliss; a state devoid of joyfulness and sorrowfulness.

ānandabhuk: That which experiences bliss.

ānandamaya: Full of bliss.

ānadamaya kośa: The blissful sheath.

ananta: Endless; without terminations; without boundaries; one whose terminations, extensions, dimensions, and quantifications are not subject to human intellection; the name of the Divine Serpent on whose hood Lord *Nārāyaṇa* reposes.

anantara: Without interior.

anantarya: Immediate sequence.

anapara: Without a consequent state.

anātman: Not-self.

anātmavāda: The doctrine of no-self.

anattāvāda: The doctrine of no-self.

aṅgamajayatva: Unsteadiness of the body.

anirukta: Indefinable.

anirvacanīyā: Indescribable.

aṅkuśa: A goad.

anna: Matter.

annamaya kośa: The material sheath; it is the gross body which is sense-perceptible.

anṛta: Disorder; entropy.

antaḥkaraṇa: Inner instrument; it is the principal component of the subtle body; it is made up of nineteen components, viz., the five subtle sensory potentialities, the five subtle motor potentialities, *buddhi, ahaṅkāra, manas, citta*, and the five *prāṇas*.

antaḥprajña: That which cognizes internal objects.

antarāya: Obstacle.

antardhauti: Internal cleansing technique adopted in *yoga* practice.

antaryāmī: The inner controller.

anubhava: Experience.

anubhavaja: Produced from experience.

anuloma-viloma prāṇāyāma: A type of *prāṇāyāma* in which inhalation is done through the left nostril for x seconds, the breath is retained for 4x seconds, and exhalation through the right nostril is done for 2x seconds. This is followed by inhalation through the right nostril for x seconds, retention of the breath for 4x seconds, and exhalation through the left nostril for 2x seconds. This completes one cycle. The cycles are repeated in the sequence described.

anumāna: Inference.

anusandhāna: Search; investigation.

anuttama: Superlative.

āpaḥ: Water; the primeval waters; the subtle element of water; liquid matter.

apāna: One of the five *prāṇas*, operating below the navel; it is expulsive in activity.

apāna vāyu: The prāṇic force that expels or excretes.

aparigraha: Non-acceptance or non-accumulation.

apariṇāmī: Immutable.

aparokṣānubhūti: Experience without mediation; immediate experience.

aparokṣasaṁvedana: Direct or immediate presentation.

aprajña: Non-cognitive.

aprameya: Immeasurable.

aprāṇa: Devoid of life principle.

apuṇya: Demeritorious.

āpūra: Filling in.

apūrva: Without a precedent state.

ardhanārīśvara: The androgynous divinity in the *viśuddha cakra*— half Śiva and half Śakti; the androgynous god (Sadāśiva in the right, fused with Sadāgaurī in the left) who dwells in the *viśuddhi*.

arka: The primeval cosmic waters; the essence of all materiality; *āpaḥ*.

artha: Intended object; meaning.

arthitva: Need.

arūpa: Formless.

aśabda: That which cannot be described by language; that to which words cannot be applied.

aśakti: Weakness.

asambandhī: Non-relational.

asamprajñāta: Not conscious of objects.

asampramoṣa: Non-obscuration.

āsana: Yogic pose or posture.

asaṅga: Unattached.

asat: Non-existence.

āśaya: Latent deposit; reservoir; receptable; a storing place; latent impression.

asi: Are (Be verb for second person singular).

aśiṣa: Desire.

asmi: Am (Be verb for first person singular).

asmitā: The feeling of personality; one of the five *kleśas* (hindrances).

āśraya: Supportor; substrate; that which provides a shelter.

āśrita: One that is supported.

aṣṭāṅga yoga: The eight limbs of *yoga*; the eight aids to *yoga*.

asteya: Non-stealing.

asti: Is, exists; be verb for the third person singular.

astīti: That it exists.

aśukla: Non-white.

aśvinī mudrā: The yogic practice of contracting the anal sphincter, simulating the movement of a horse's anus.

atarkya: Logically inderivable.

atha: Used for starting a discourse.

atīndriya: What cannot be grasped by senses; not sense-perceptible.

atīndriyatvena: Since it is transcendental to the apparatus of cognition.

atiśaya: Excess.

ātmā (*ātman*, *Ātmā*, *Ātman*): Self; *Brahman* Itself; written as *ātmā* or *ātman* when the limiting adjunct of *Brahman* is the individual body; written as *Ātmā* or *Ātman* to refer to *Brahman* Itself.

ātma-darśana-yogyatva: The fitness for the sight of the self.

Auṁ (*Oṁ*): The mystic monosyllable which is the symbol for *Brahman*.

auṣadhi: Drug.

avacchedavāda: The doctrine of limitation.

avairāgya: Passionlessness.

āvaraṇa: Concealment; cover.

avastu: Not an object.

avidyā: Nescience; ignorance; undifferentiated consciousness.

avikalpa: Devoid of predicate relations.

avikārya: Changeless; unmodifiable.

aviṣaya: Not an object.

aviṣayatvāt: Because it is not an object.

aviveka: Non-discrimination.

avivekāt: Due to the lack of discrimination.

avyakta: Unmanifested.

avyavahāryam: Unusable.

ayam: This (used for masculine gender).

āyu: Length of life.

bādhate: Inhibits.

bahiṣprajña: That which cognizes external objects.

bala: Strength.

Bāla-Brahmā: The name of the god in the *mūlādhāra cakra*. The word *bāla* means 'infant'; *Brahmā* is the creator god.

Bāṇa liṅga: The phallic form inside the *anāhata cakra*.

bandha: Binding; bond; yogic postures in which organs and muscles are contracted and controlled.

bandhuka: The name of a tree.

bhadrāsana: The yogic 'gracious pose' which is a sitting posture.

bhāgyavāda: The doctrine of fatalism.

bhairava: Lord Śiva; a male *tāntrik*.

bhairavī: The consort of Lord Śiva; a female *tāntrik*.

bhakti: Devotion.

bhaktivāda: The doctrine of devotion.

bhakti-yoga: The method of union with God through devotion.

bhautika sarga: The manifest world.

bhāva: Disposition; being.

bhāvika: Prophetic in character.

bhaya: Fear.

bhoga: Kind of experience.

bhoktā: Experiencer; enjoyer.

bhramarī prāṇāyāma: A type of yogic breath-control in which a soft humming sound is produced during exhalation like the murmuring of a bee.

bhujaṅgāsana: The yogic cobra pose (*bujaṅga* means 'snake').

bhūmi: Ground.

bhūrloka: The terrestrial plane of existence; the name of the world corresponding to the *mūlādhāra cakra*; the first division of the universe in the higher realm.

bhūta: Created thing; subtle element.

bhūtātmā (*bhūtātman*): *Brahman* reflected on a non-living body that serves as the limiting adjunct.

bhuvarloka: The name of the world corresponding to the *svādhiṣṭhāna cakra*; the intermediate realm between the earth and heaven; the astral plane of existence; the second division of the universe in the higher realm.

bīja: Seed.

bīja mantra: Seed *mantra*; mystic vibration which has its origin in transcendental consciousness.

bījāṅkura: Seed and sprout.

bīja-śakti: Seminal power.

bindu: Point.

bindu-visarga: It is a psychic centre in the subtle body, located at the top of the back of the head. It is briefly known as the *bindu* which literally means a point.

bodha: Consciousness.

Brahmā: The one and the only one God, described with reference to His creative functions.

brahmacarya: Continence.

brahmadvāra: The starting orifice of the *brahmanāḍī* at the bulb of the *mūlādhāra*.

Brahmagranthi: The knot made by the *suṣumṇā*, the *iḍā*, and the *piṅgalā* at the *mūlādhāra*.

Brahman: The primary or fundamental Consciousness; the non-dual Being which is Existence, Consciousness, and Bliss, and which is attributeless, actionless, formless, non-relational, immutable, homogeneous, unbroken whole; that which is great or big; the Supreme Being.

brāhmaṇa: The priestly class among the Hindus; one who knows *Brahman*; one who practises principles and rituals prescribed in the *Vedas*; one who lives a sanctified life and dedicates himself to the welfare of the universe.

Brahmanāḍī: It is the central psychic core channel inside the *citrā*. Its starting orifice at the bulb of the *mūlādhāra* is known as the *brahmadvāra*. Its terminal orifice at the *sahasrāra* in the head is called the *brahmarandhra*.

Brahmāṇḍa: Macrocosm; the entire cosmos.

Brahma-Nirvāṇa: Complete re-union and re-indentification with *Brahman*.

Brahmarandhra: The terminal orifice of the *Brahmanāḍī* at the *sahasrāra* in the head.

Brahmavid: One who has known *Brahman*; one who has realized the identity of the *ātman* with the *Brahman*.

Buddhi: Same as *Mahat* in the *Sāṅkhya*; it is the first manifested entity evolved from the primordial matter or *Prakṛti*.

buddhi: The intellect; the thinking substance; one of the components of the *antaḥkaraṇa*, the internal instrument.

buddhīndriya: The subtle sensory organs for cognition.

buddhisaṁvit: The consciousness of the thinking substance.

ca: And.

caitanya: Consciousness.

caitanyādhyāsa: The phenomenon of the reflection of the consciousness of the *puruṣa* on the *buddhi* which consequently gains empirical consciousness.

cakra: A discus; a wheel; a vortex; a major psychic centre in the subtle body, responsible for specific physiological and psychic functions.

cakra-pūjā: *Cakra* means 'circle' and *pūjā* means 'worship'. *Cakra-pūjā* is an esoteric ritualism of the *tāntriks*.

cakrāsana: The 'wheel pose' in yogic practice.

candramaṇḍala: A round diagram resembling the lunar halo.

candranāḍī: The lunar channel or *iḍā* that is a supersensible psychic channel, flowing in the left side of the central channel *suṣumṇā*.

Candraśekhara: The presiding god in the *ājñā cakra*; Lord *Śiva* who carries the moon in his forehead.

Cārvāka: A materialistic school of philosophy of ancient India; it is the most ancient materialistic philosophy of the world.

caṣaka: A drinking cup.

catuṣpāt: Quadripartite.

cetomukha: One whose all doors are consciousness only.

cidāveśa: The phenomenon of the reflection of the consciousness of the *puruṣa* on the *buddhi* which consequently gains empirical consciousness.

cinmudrā: An attitude of consciousness, in which the index finger is kept at the root of the thumb, the middle, the ring and the little finger are separated.

Cit: Consciousness that is fundamental; *Brahman* that is pure Consciousness.

cit: Individual consciousness; awareness.

citcchāyāpatti: The phenomenon of the reflection of the consciousness of the *puruṣa* on the *buddhi* which consequently gains empirical consciousness.

Citi: The consciousness of the *puruṣa*.

citiśakti: The Energy of Consciousness; the *puruṣa*'s Energy of Thought.

citrā: Otherwise known as *citriṇī*. It is a psychic channel that flows inside the *Vajrā* which is broader in diameter than the former.

citriṇī: Otherwise known as *citrā*.

citta: Mind-stuff; the thinking organ; this word is used in *Pātañjala Yoga* for the totality of the mental apparatus. The *Vedānta* uses this word for the discriminating mind.

cittabhūmi: The ground of the mind-stuff; the bottom of the mind.

cittadharmā: One that exhibits the properties of the mind-stuff.

cittanadī: The river of the mind-stuff.

cittanivṛtti: The obliteration of the mind-stuff.

cittaśuddhi: The purification of the mind-stuff.

cittavṛtti: The modifications or fluctuations of the mind-stuff.

dāḍima: Pomegranate.

dahana: Fire.

Ḍākinī: The name of the goddess in the *mūlādhāra cakra.*

dakṣiṇācārī: The right-follower *tāntriks* who reject the use of 5-m's.

dama: The restraint of the external functions of the organs.

ḍamaru: A hand-drum.

daṇḍa: Staff.

darśana: Philosophy; the act of seeing.

darśana-śakti: The power by which one sees.

darśanendriya: The supersensible visual sensory organ.

daurmanasya: Despondency.

devatā: The presiding deity in the *cakra*; deity.

Devī: Goddess; goddess; the Divine Mother in the *Tantra.*

dhanurāsana: The 'bow-pose', one yogic posture of backward bending.

dharā-bīja: The seed of the subtle element of earth.

dhāraṇā: The focusing of attention on a spot; one-pointed attention; fixed attention.

dharma: Property; actions and properties; meritorious actions; virtue; right living.

dharmādharmamūla: Caused by meritorious and unmeritorious actions.

dharmamegha dhyāna: A stage of the highest attainment in *Yoga*, in which the *puruṣa* (self) is isolated from the *sattva* (strand of serenity).

dharmamegha-samādhi: All-time discriminative discernment of the *sattva* and the *puruṣa*; it is so-called, because, by its light it rains; or in other words, it pours down all kinds of knowable things, and hence knowledge becomes endless.

dharmī (*dharmin*): The prossessor of a property.

dhauti: Yogic techniques for cleaning the eyes, ears, tongue, forehead, esophagus, stomach, rectum, and anus.

dhruva: Absolutely constant; what is *bindu-visarga* in the *Tantra* system is the *dhruva* or the *prātibha* in the *Yoga* system.

dhūmra liṅga: Phallus of smoky colour; the *Svayambhū liṅga* in the *mūlādhāra* is ill-defined and hence is known as *dhūmra liṅga*.

dhyāna: The continuous flow of a single concept in the mind without interruption and without admixture of any other concept; contemplation.

diṅnyāsa: *Nyāsa* on the different directions.

divya cakṣu: Divine eye.

divya-gandha-saṁvit: The consciousness of supernormal odour.

divya-rasa-saṁvit: The consciousness of supernormal taste.

divya-rūpa-saṁvit: The consciousness of supernormal colour.

divya-śabda-saṁvit: The consciousness of supernormal sound.

divya-sparśa-saṁvit: The consciousness of supernormal touch.

doṣaja: Caused by some defect or deficiency; caused by some pathological disorder.

draṣṭā: Seer; knower.

dravya: Material; thing; substance; object.

dṛḍhabhūmi: Confirmed; with ground reinforced.

dṛkśakti: The power of seeing.

duḥkha: Pain; painfulness; suffering.

duḥkhasaṁskārāśaya: Store of subliminal impressions due to the experience of pain.

duḥkha-srota: The stream of pain.

durātmā: Villain.

dvaita: Dual.

dvandva: Contradiction.

dvaya-śūnyatā: Devoid of the duality of subject and object.

dveṣa: Enmity; hatered; aversion.

dveṣaja: Generated by aversion.

ekāgra: One-pointed attention; single in intent.

ekāgratā: Singleness of intent.

ekakārya: Having identical functions.

ekaliṅga: The constant flow of the one idea only, the idea of Being.

ekarūpatva: Homogeneously the same for all.

ekatattva: A single entity.

ekībhūta: A unitary state devoid of diversity.

eva: Only.

evam: Like this.

gadā: A mace.

gandha: Smell; odour.

gandha-pravṛtti: Sense-activity with odour as object.

gāndhārī: A supersensible psychic channel in the subtle body for the flow of *prāṇa*.

gandharva: A celestial musician; a class of demi-gods regarded as the musicians of gods.

gardhaḥ: Greed.

garuḍa: The bird-vehicle of Lord Viṣṇu.

Gaurī: The goddess in the *viśuddha cakra*.

ghaṇṭa: Bell.

ghaṭa: Pot.

ghaṭākāśa: Space limited in a pot.

ghrāṇendriya: The supersensible olfactory sensory organ.

Girijā: The goddess in the *viśuddha cakra*; the goddess born of the *Himālaya* mountains.

grahaṇa: The process of knowing.

grahītā: Knower.

grāhya: Object known; intended object.

granthi: Knot.

guṇa: Quality; attribute; string or strand; constituent; secondary without being primary.

guṇādhikāra: The authority of the strings.

guru: Preceptor.

Hākinī: The name of the goddess in the *ājñā cakra*.

harṣa: Joyfulness.

hastendriya: The supersensible prehensive motor organ.

hastijihvikā: A supersensible psychic channel in the subtle body for the flow of *prāṇa*.

haṭha-yoga: A system of Yoga specially dealing with rigorous practices for the invigoration and the purification of the body, and consequently of the mind.

hetu: Cause.

hetuprabhava: What springs from a cause.

hiṁsākṛta: Caused by violence.

hita: Good; benefit; welfare.

hlāda: Joy.

hṛdaya: Heart; the heart-lotus recognized as a psychic centre in the *Yoga* system; equivalent to the *anāhata* of the *Tantra* system.

hṛdayādinyāsa: *Nyāsa* on parts of the body such as the heart, etc.

hṛdayapuṇḍarīkam: Literally means the 'heart lotus'; situated inside the chest below the throat-pit; otherwise known as the *kūrmanāḍī*.

icchā: Desire.

iḍā: It is a supersensible psychic channel in the subtle body, otherwise known as the *candranāḍī*. It flows on the left side of the central channel, *suṣumṇā*.

idam: This (used for neuter gender).

indriya: Supersensible cognitive and motor organs as component parts of the mind.

indriyajaya: Subjugation of the senses.

Īśa: The god in the *anāhata cakra*.

Īśvara: God; conditioned *Brahman*; *Brahman* with *Māyā* as the limiting adjunct; *Brahman* with attributes and functions.

Īśvara-praṇidhāna: Devotion to God.

Itara liṅga: The phallic form inside the triangle of the *ājñā cakra*.

jaḍa: Insentient.

jagat: The empirical universe; the one which is in motion; the one which constantly changes.

jālandhara bandha: Throat-lock in which the chin is pressed against the upper sternum, arresting the flow of breath through the throat.

jala neti: Nasal cleansing with saline water through each nostril alternately.

jananendriya: The reproductive motor organ.

janarloka: The name of the world corresponding to the *viśuddha cakra*; the fifth division of the universe in the higher realm.

japa: The continuous repetition of a *mantra*, or of the name of God.

jātasmara: A person who can recollect some incidences of his previous lives.

jāti: Birth.

jatru: Clavicle; collar bone.

jijīviṣā: Craving for life.

jīva: Empirical self (*Brahman* reflected on the individual subtle body which serves as the limiting adjunct); a compound entity constituted by the apparent association of the self and the subtle body, especially the blissful sheath of the subtle body.

jīvanmukta: Free even if living; liberated soul while in life; released even while yet alive.

jīvanmukti: The phenomenon of being a *jīvanmukta*.

jīvātmā (*jīvātman*): See *jīva*.

jñāna: Knowledge; consciousness; cognition; idea.

jñāna-cakṣu: The eye of intuition.

jñānaja: Produced from knowledge; produced from cognition.

jñāna saṁskāra: Cognitive dispositions that form the fund of memory.

jñāna-mūla: Caused by cognition; rooted in knowledge.

jñāna-netra: The eye of intuition.

jñānāntara: Another kind of knowledge.

jñāna-śakti: The cognizing power.

jñānendriya: Subtle sensory potentialities located in the mind.

Jyotirliṅga: Luminous phallus; the luminous *Sivaliṅga* in the *sahasrāra*.

kaḥ (*ka*): The primeval cosmic waters or *āpaḥ*; Lord *Brahmā*, the *Prajāpati*.

kaivalya: Isolation; this term is used in *Sāṅkhya* and *Yoga* for the process of the separation of the self from the *Prakṛti* (the totality of the potential matter); the Yogic freedom of the self from its apparent bondage; liberation in *Sāṅkhya* and *Yoga*.

Kākinī: The name of the goddess in the *anāhata cakra*.

kalā: Part.

kāla: Time.

kalpa: World period.

kalpataru: A wish-fulfilling tree.

kalpavṛkṣa: A wish-fulfilling tree.

kalpita: Something creatively imagined.

kāma: Desire.

kāmabīja: The seed of passion inside the triangle in the *mūlādhāra*.

kāmanā: Desire.

kamaṇḍalu: Gourd.

kāmarūpa: The inverted triangle in the pericarp of the *mūlādhāra cakra*.

kanda: Bulb; the bulbous structure in the *mūlādhāra cakra*.

Kandarpa: The deity of love and passion, seated in the triangle of the *mūlādhāra cakra*.

kaṇṭhakūpa: Throat-pit; this term is used in the *Yoga* system and is equivalent to the *viśuddhi* of the *Tantra* system.

kāraṇa: Cause.

kāraṇa śarīra: The causal body; it is the combined entity of the embodied self and the blissful sheath, the former being encased in the latter.

karanyāsa: *Nyāsa* on the fingers and the palms of hands.

karma: The totality of the *vāsanā* traces imprinted in the mind of an individual and caused by his/her actions in all incarnations.

karma-saṁskāras: Karmic impressions of merits and demerits in the *buddhi* of the mind.

karmāśaya: The reservoir of *karmas*; the locality in the subtle body where *saṁskāras* and *vāsanās* are imprinted and stored; the reservoir of karmic impressions; the abode of impressions, being a component of the inner instrument (*antaḥkaraṇa*).

karmavāda: The doctrine of *karma*.

karma-vipāka: The fruition of *karma*.

karmavipāka-karmāśaya: Formation of karmic store consequent on the fruition of *karma* and the concomitant experience of pleasure and pain.

karmendriya: Subtle motor potentialities, located in the mind (not in the gross body).

karṇikā: Pericarp; the pericarp of a psychic lotus or *cakra*.

kartā: Agent; doer.

karuṇā: Compassion.

kaustubha: The name of a celebrated gem obtained with thirteen other jewels when the ocean was churned by the gods and the demons (Hindu mythology); Lord Viṣṇu wears this gem on His breast.

keśara: Filament.

kevala: Solitary; isolated.

kha: *Ākāśa* or space; the fourth sequential evolute from the Primeval Matter (*Prakṛti*) according to the *Vedānta* (*Prakṛti* → *Virāḍ* or *Mahat* → *Āpaḥ* → *Prāṇa* → *Kha* or *Ākāśa*).

khaḍga: A sword.

khalu: Verily.

khandha: Group of elements; the Pāli equivalent of the Sanskrit word *skandha*.

khatvāṅga: A staff with a human skull on top.

khecarī mudrā: *Khecarī* literally means 'roaming through space'. This is a *mudrā* in which the tongue is turned up and back so as to touch the palate, till at length it reaches the holes of the nostrils opening into the mouth.

khyāti: Discernment.

kleśa: Hindrance; affliction.

kleśaja: Caused by hindrances (afflictions); affective.

kleśakarmanivṛtti: Freedom from hindrances and *karma*.

kleśakṣaya: The dwindling of the hindrances.

kleśamūla: Rooted in (caused by) hindrances or afflictions.

kliṣṭa: Painful.

kośa: Sheath.

kriyā: Action; function; activity.

kriyāja: Produced from actions; conative.

kriyamāṇa karma: *Karma* which is being or will be deposited for fruition in future lives.

kriyā-yoga: Special practices of *Kuṇḍalinī Yoga*; the *Yoga* of action; all the three aspects of *tapas, svādhyāya* and *Īśvara-praṇidhāna* in *Pātañjala Yoga*.

krodha: Anger, wrath.

kṛpāṇa: A sword.

kṛṣṇa: Black.

kṛṣṇasāra: A black antelope.

kṛtsna: The whole.

kṣaṇa: Moment.

kṣaṇika: Momentary.

kṣaṇikavāda: The doctrine of momentariness.

kṣetra: Field.

kṣīṇavṛtti: Fluctuations having dwindled away.

kṣiti: Earth, solid matter.

kṣīyamāṇabīja: Seeds in the process of dwindling.

kṣobha: Agitation.

kuhū: A supersensible, psychic channel in the subtle body for the flow of *prāṇa*.

Kuṇḍalinī: Coiled up Power, dormantly lying at the base lotus, the *mūlādhāra cakra*, in normal circumstances; she is the goddess who coils, like a sleeping serpent, three and a half times round the *Svayambhū-liṅga*.

kūrmanāḍī: A psychic centre shaped as a tortoise, situated inside the chest below the throat-pit. Patañjali refers to it in his *Yoga* system. This *nāḍī* is otherwise known as the *hṛdayapuṇḍarīkam.*

kuśala: Good.

kūṭastha: Immutable.

kūṭasthanityatā: One type of eternality in which there is no change, no modification, and no transformation whatsoever.

Lākinī: The name of the goddess in the *maṇipūra cakra.*

lakṣaṇa: Distinguishing feature; symptom.

lakṣyate: Can be indicated; can be pointed out; can be shown.

lalana cakra: A small psychic centre situated in the back of the nasopharynx between the *bindu* and the *viśuddhi.*

liṅga: Phallus; the Divine Father worshipped as a phallic symbol; subtle; subtle body; a suggestive sign.

liṅgamātra: Resoluble-primary-matter-as-such; same as *Buddhi* or *Mahat.*

liṅga śarīra: The subtle body which is material, albeit sense-imperceptible.

lobha: Greed; covetousness.

lobhakṛta: Caused by greed.

loka: World; one of the fourteen divisions of the universe.

mada: Pride; arrogance; conceit.

Mādhyamika: A Buddhist philosophical school of nihilism that denies the existence of everything.

madya: Alcoholic drink.

mahābhūta: Great material substance — solid, liquid, gas, energy, space.

mahākāśa: All-pervasive, great space.

Mahākuṇḍalinī: Mother Goddess in the macrocosm whereas *Kuṇḍalinī* is Mother Goddess in the individual microcosm.

maharloka: The name of the world corresponding to the *anāhata cakra*; the fourth division of the universe in the higher realm.

Mahāśakti: The Great Power; Mother Goddess.

Mahat: The Cosmic Mind; the Cosmic Memory; the Collective Unconscious; the first product evolved from the primeval Nature (*mūlaprakṛti*); this is a word of the *Sāṅkhya* system, equivalent to the Vedic word *Virāḍ*; *Mahat* and *Buddhi* are synonymous.

mahāvrata: Great observance, unaffected by conditions.

Mahāyāna: The word *Mahāyāna* literally means 'great vehicle'. It is one of the two main schools within Buddhism, the other being the *Hīnayāna*.

Maheśvara: The Great Lord; the Great Controller.

maithuna: Coitus.

maitrī: Friendliness.

makara: Allegator; *Varuṇa's* animal-vehicle in the shape of an allegator.

māṁsa: Meat.

manas: Mind; the mental substance.

maṇḍala: A kind of mystical diagram used in invoking a deity.

maṇipūra: The third *cakra* in the subtle body in the ascending order; located exactly at the level of the navel which corresponds to that of the solar plexus of nerves.

manomātraprabhava: Pure creation of the mind.

manomaya kośa: The mental sheath working at the conscious level.

manovijñāna: A modified state of consciousness which is the actualized process of intellection.

mantra: Incantation; spell; that by which the mind thinks of and by that thinking something or somebody is influenced; that by which the mind is capable of communicating with a deity.

maraṇatrāsa: Fear of death.

mārjāri-āsana: The cat-pose, a yogic *āsana*.

marut: Gases; the airy matter.

mātsarya: Envy; jealousy.

matsya: Fish.

matsyāsana: The fish-pose, a yogic *āsana*.

Māyā: The Power of *Brahman*; it is co-eternal with *Brahman*, always dependent on the latter without being a separate entity; it has concealing, deluding, and projecting power; it is the precuror material of the universe; *Brahman* reflected on it is *Īśvara* or God.

māyāmātram: Mere illusion.

māyopahita: With *Māyā* as the limiting adjunct.

meru: The vertical axis.

meṣa: Ram; *Agni*'s (the fire-god's) animal-vehicle.

moha: Delusion; infatuation.

mohakṛta: Caused by infatuation.

mokṣa: Liberation; the liberation of the self from the bondage of ignorance; re-identification of the self with *Brahman*.

mudita: Joy.

mudrā: Gesture; sealing postures; yogic postures through which physical, mental, and psychic attitudes are expressed and cosmic energy is channelized within the body and the mind; parched grain or fried rice.

mūla: Root.

mūlabandha: A posture by which the body, from the anus to the navel, is contracted and lifted towards the spine.

mūlādhāra: The base or root foundation; the basal psychic centre located at the base of the spine in between the genital and the anus; its level corresponds to that of the coccygeal plexus of nerves; here dwells the *Kuṇḍalinī*.

mūlaprakṛti: Primeval Nature; Primordial Nature; the totality of the unmanifest material potentiality.

mumukṣutva: The yearning for the freedom from ignorance; the desire for liberation.

Murāri: The enemy of a demon known as *Mura*; this demon was slain by Kṛṣṇa who bears this epithet.

mūrcchā prāṇāyāma: A type of *prāṇāyāma* where breath is held almost to the swooning or fainting (*mūrcchā*).

mūrdhajyotis: It literally means the "light in the crown of the head". This term is used in the *Yoga* system and is equivalent to the *sahasrāra* of the *Tantra* system.

muṣka: Scrotum.

na: Not.

nābhicakra: The umbilical psychic centre; this term is used in the *Yoga* system and is equivalent to the *maṇipūra* of the *Tantra* system.

nāda: Vibration; an inner mystical sound.

nāda yoga: A special branch of *Kuṇḍalinī Yoga* that deals with sound vibrations originated mainly from the *mūlādhāra* and the *viśuddhi*.

nāḍī: Psychic channels in the subtle body for the circulation of *prāṇa*.

nāgendra: Snake-king.

nāhamasmi: I am not.

nairātmya: Soul-less; egoless.

naivam: Not like this.

nāmarūpa: Name and form.

nāra: The primeval cosmic waters or the *āpaḥ*.

Nārāyaṇa: Lord Viṣṇu, the sustainer and controller of the universe.

nāsikāgra-dṛṣṭi: Nose-tip-gazing.

nāsti: Is not,

nauli kriyā: A Yogic practice of abdominal massage in which the rectus abdomini muscles are contracted and isolated vertically.

nava: New.

neti: Not this; a Yogic practice of nasal cleansing.

nibandha: Context; the fixing of the mind in a certain spot.

nidāna: Cause.

nidrā: Sleep.

niḥsaṅga: Unassociated with anything; unattached.

nirākāra: Formless.

nirālambana: Without supporting object.

nirātmakatā: The negation of the "I".

niravayava: Devoid of structures and substructures; bodiless.

nirbhāsa: shining forth in consciousness.

nirbīja samādhi: Seedless concentration.

nirguṇa: Attributeless; devoid of qualities.

nirodha: Restriction.

nirupabhoga: Devoid of ordinary experience.

nirupādhikam: Unconditioned; devoid of limiting adjunct.

Nirvāṇa: The state of being extinguished; the only positive entity which cannot be predicated and which can be immediately and directly realized.

nirvicāra: Super-reflective.

nirvicāra samādhi: Super-reflective balanced-state.

nirvikalpa (*nirvikalpaka*): Seedless; devoid of alternatives and determinations, without the sense of A and B and A and not-A.

nirviśeṣa: Undifferentiated and homogeneous.

nirvitarka: Super-deliberative.

niṣkala: Partless.

niṣkriya: Actionless; functionless.

nistaranga śāgara: Waveless sea.

nivṛtti: Abstinence and control of senses.

niyama: Observances — cleanliness, contentment, self-castigation, study of scriptures, devotion to God.

niyantraṇa: Control.

nyāsa: Placing; the shifting of consciousness to different points of the body.

Nyāya Darśana: A system of Indian philosophy founded by the sage Gautama; the science of logical philosophy.

Oṁ (*Auṁ*): The mystic monosyllable which is the symbol (*vācaka*) for *Brahman*.

pādendriya: The supersensible locomotor motor organ.

padma: Lotus.

padmāsana: 'Lotus pose'; a classical meditative posture with the right foot on the left thigh and the left foot on the right thigh.

pañca: Five.

pañcamakāra: The five m's used in Tāntric ritual, viz., *māṁsa* (meat), *matsya* (fish), *mudrā* (fried rice), *madya* (alcohol), and *maithuna* (sexual union).

pāpa: Demerits.

para: The cosmic period between the manifestation and the dissolution of the universe (from t_o to t_m).

parama: Supreme.

pāramārthika: Absolute.

Paramaśiva: The Lord of the universe; the Supreme Being.

Paramātmā (*Paramātman*): God; the Great Self; *Brahman* reflected on its own power, *Māyā*.

Parameśvara: Supreme Controller.

parārdha: One-half of the cosmic period (*para*), from t_o to $t_{1/2}$ or $t_{1/2}$ to t_m.

parigraha: Ownership.

pariṇāma: Mutation; transformation.

pariṇāminityatā: One type of eternality, in which there are mutations without annihilation of the essence or substance.

parispandamāna: Shaking.

paryāya: Mode.

pāśa: A noose.

paścimottānāsana: Back-stretching pose in which one bends forward and clasps the toes of the outstretched legs.

pavanamuktāsana: A Yogic pose for the expulsion of air from the stomach and the intestines.

payasvanī: A supersensible psychic channel in the subtle body for the flow of *prāṇa*.

pāyuvindriya: The supersensible excretory motor organ.

phala: Result; fruit; effect.

Pinākī: The presiding god in the *anāhata cakra*.

piṇḍa: Microcosm; the individual body as the microcosm.

piṅgalā: It is a supersensible psychic channel in the subtle body, otherwise known as the *sūryanāḍī*. It flows on the right side of the central channel, the *suṣumṇā*.

Pradhāna: A term used in the *Sāṅkhya* philosophy for the primordial matter or *Prakṛti*; insentient Nature.

prajña: Cognitive.

prajñā: Insight.

prājña: The state of dreamless sleep; the third quarter of *Brahman*.

prajñākṛta: Caused by insight.

prajñāna: Pure Consciousness.

prajñānaghana: A mass of consciousness.

prakhyā: Vividness.

Prakṛti: The primordial matter; the unmanifested, supersensible, subtle matter made up of the three strands — *sattva*, *rajas*, and *tamas*.

prakṣīṇamohāvaraṇa: The dwindling away of the infatuation-cover.

pralaya: Dissolution.

pramāṇa: Source of valid ideas; evidence.

pramāṇābhāva: The negation of the source of valid ideas.

Prāṇa: Life principle; vitalizing force; the precursor of the four fundamental forces and all types of energy; the prime, moving force of all created entities, both living and non-living.

prāṇa: One of the five *prāṇas* operating in the area above the diaphragm and below the throat; it has respiratory and absorptive functions.

prāṇamaya kośa: The vital sheath.

prāṇāyāma: An Indian Yogic and Tāntric practice in which inhalations and exhalations are regulated for the collection, storage, and utilization of the vitalizing force; breath-control.

prāṇic: Pertaining to the *prāṇa*, the vitalizing force.

praṇidhāna: Attention.

prapañcopaśama: The one into which the phenomenal universe dissolves.

prāpti: Attainment.

prārabdha: The part of *karma* for fruition in the present life; *karma* that has already initiated in the present life.

prārthita: One with fulfilled desires.

prasaṅkhyāna: The *Yoga* technique of elevation.

praśāntavāhitā: Flows on in undisturbed calm.

praśāsaka: Executor and ruler.

praśāsana: Execution; control; ruling; administration.

praśāsitā: Ruler.

prasavabhūmi: Propagative soil.

praśvāsa: Expiration.

prātibha: The *prātibha* or the *dhruva* of the *Yoga* system is equivalent to the *bindu-visarga* of the *Tantra* system. This word literally means divination, genius, vivid intellection.

prātibhāsika: phenomenal.

pratibimbavāda: The doctrine of reflection.

pratimā: Icon; idol.

pratiprasava: Inverse generation.

pratītyasamutpāda: The Buddhist doctrine of flux and dependent origination; the Buddhist doctrine of the dynamic state of flux.

pratyabhijñāna: Recognition.

pratyagātman: The directly perceived Being.

pratyāhāra: The withdrawal of the senses.

pratyakṣa: Direct perception without mediation; perceptual knowledge through the mediation of senses.

pratyaya: Presented-idea.

pratyaya-nivṛtti: Cessation of presented-ideas.

pravṛtti: Mental tendency for activity and enjoyment; indulgence in activity; sense-activity.

pravṛttimārga: The path of sense-gratification.

pravṛtti-vijñāna: A modified state of conciousness which gives the six kinds of objectivity.

prāyaścitta: Expiatory rites.

prayatna: Struggle.

preya: Pleasurable.

Pṛthivī: Earth; solidity; the subtle element of earth.

pūjā: Worshipping.

punarjanma: Reincarnation; rebirth.

puṇḍit: A learned person well-versed in scriptures, especially Sanksrit scriptures.

puṇya: Merits; meritorious actions.

purāṇa: Ancient mythological scriptures of the Hindus.

pūrṇa: Full.

Puruṣa: The Cosmic Person; the Cosmic Self; God; the primordial matter or *Prakṛti* or *Māyā*; the individual self according to the *Sāṅkhya*.

puruṣatantra: Subjective.

pūṣā: A supersensible psychic channel in the subtle body for the flow of *prāṇa*.

racanā: Design.

rāga: Attachment; passion; affection.

rāgaja: Generated by passion.

rajas: The strand or string of activity.

rājasic: Pertaining to the strand of *rajas.*

rājasika: Of the nature of *rajas.*

Rākiṇī: The name of the goddess in the *svādhiṣṭhāna cakra.*

rasa: Taste.

rasanendriya: The supersensible gustatory or taste sensory organ.

ripu: Enemy.

ṛṣi: Seer; saint.

ṛṣyādinyāsa: *Nyāsa* on the seers, etc.

ṛta: Order.

ṛtambharā: Order-bearing.

Rudra: The one and the only one God, described with reference to the annihilative functions. This word literally means "the roaring or terrible one".

Rudragranthi: The knot made at the *ājñā* by the *suṣumṇā*, the *iḍā*, and the *piṅgalā.*

Rudrākṣa: A rosary made of the berries of the *Rudrākṣa* tree.

rūpa: Sight; vision; form; the corporeal group of *skandhas.*

śabda: Sound; word.

śabda-brahma: *Māyā*; *Prakṛti*; the seminal principle for which language (words) can be used.

sabīja samādhi: Concentration with seed.

Sadāgaurī: The goddess in the *viśuddha cakra.*

ṣaḍaram: Six-spoked.

Sadāśiva: The god in the *viśuddha cakra.*

ṣaḍāyatana: The six organs.

sadbhāva: Existence.

sādhanā: Spiritual practice; practice with sustained effort and perseverance for attaining a certain goal.

sādhanapāda: The chapter on the means of attainment.

sādṛśya: Similarity.

saguṇa: With attributes.

sahajoli mudrā: The practice of *vajroli* by a woman, involving the contraction of the lower urinary muscles.

sahasrāra: The thousand-petalled lotus located in the crown of the head. It is a subtle structure where dwells *Paramaśiva* (the Supreme Being). It is above the *bindu* and occupies the peak position in the subtle body of a person.

Śākinī: The name of the goddess in the *viśuddha cakra*.

sākṣātkaraṇa: Direct or immediate perception.

sākṣī: Witness.

Sākṣī Ātmā: The witnessing Self.

śākta: A devotee of Śakti or Mother Goddess.

Śakti: The feminine aspect of the Śiva-Śakti bipolarity, the masculine aspect being Śiva; the same as Mother Goddess, *Māyā*, or *Prakṛti*.

śakti: A type of fireweapon; that which has the ability to do work.

śaktipāta: Descent of power.

sālambana: With an object to rest upon.

śama: Abandonment of all desires at all times.

samādhāna: Deep concentration of the mind on *Brahman* alone.

samādhi: Deep concentration; meditative trance.

samādhiprajñā: Concentrated insight.

samāna: One of the five *prāṇas* operating in the area above the navel and below the diaphragm; it has digestive, assimilative, and metabolic functions.

samāpanna: To be in a balanced state.

samāpatti: Balanced state.

samavāya: Harmony.

sambandha: Relation.

śāmbhavī mudrā: A Yogic gesture in which one gazes at the mid-eyebrow centre.

Śambhu: Lord Śiva; the presiding god of the *ājñā cakra*.

saṁjñā: The perception of physical objects within the human psyche.

samprajñāta: Conscious of objects.

sampramoṣa: Obscuration.

saṁsāra: The universe with order, co-ordination, and harmony; metempsychosis; the world moving and functioning in harmony; the whirlpool of existence; transmigratory existence.

saṁsāra-cakra: The wheel of the round of rebirths.

saṁskāra: Impressions imprinted in the mind; dispositional impressions; dispositions; subliminal impressions.

saṁskāra-piṇḍa: Dispositional masses.

samyagjñāna: Full knowledge.

saṁyama: A *Yoga* technique by whch *dhāraṇā*, *dhyāna*, and *samādhi* are simultaneously done; constraint.

sāmyāvasthā: Equipoised condition.

sañcita karma: The stored up *karma*; *karma* that has already been accumulated, but has not started functioning.

sanghāta: Combination.

saṅkalpa: Resolve; deliberation; will.

śaṅkha: Conch-shell.

Saṅkhāra: A Pāli word for mental impressions or formations, equivalent to the Sanskrit word *saṁskāra*.

śaṅkhinī: It is a supersensible psychic channel in the subtle body for the flow of *prāṇa*.

Sāṅkhya: An Indian school of philosophy, founded before 1,000 BC by Kapila; atheistic and dualistic; the insentient, primordial Nature (*Pradhāna* or *Prakṛti*) is one category of existence, and the innumerable, sentient selves (*puruṣas*) belong to the second category; it is the first philosophical school in the world to advocate the doctrine of evolution.

sanmūla: Rooted in something which is real; all phenomenal existences rooted in the real existence.

sannyāsī: Mendicant — saint.

śāntam: Serene.

santāna: Unbroken series.

santoṣa: Contentment.

sarasvatī: A supersensible, psychic channel in the subtle body for the flow of *prāṇa*.

śarīra: Body.

śarīropahita: With the body as the limiting adjunct.

sarva: All.

sarvajña: Omniscient.

sarvāṅgāsana: The Yogic 'shoulder-stand' pose.

sarvaśaktimān: Omnipotent.

sarvāstivāda: A school of Buddhist philosophy which rejects anti-substantialism and which upholds the notion of the existence of everything.

sarvāstivādin: One who is a supporter of *sarvāstivāda*.

sarvaśūnyavādin: The Buddhist nihilist who denies the existence of everything.

sarvavyāpī: All-pervading.

sarveśvara: The Lord of all.

śaśāṅka-bhujaṅgāsana: A variant of the 'cobra pose' practised in *Yoga*.

śaśāṅkāsana: The 'moon pose', a Yogic *āsana*.

śāstra: Scripture.

śāstra-pramāṇa: Scriptural evidence.

śāśvata: Permanent; eternal.

sat: Existence.

ṣaṭsampatti: The six valuable qualities (properties).

sattā: Existence; Being.

sattva: The strand or string of serenity; substance or essence.

sāttvic: Pertaining to the strand of *sattva*.

sāttvika: Of the nature of *sattva*.

satya: Existence; whatever exists; that which exists; truthfulness.

śauca: Cleanliness — physical, mental, and vocal.

saumanasya: Gentleness.

Sautrāntika: A school of Buddhist philosophy believing in the doctrine of momentariness.

savicāra: Reflective.

savikalpa (*savikalpaka*): With seed.

savitarka: Deliberative.

śayana: Sleep.

Śeṣa: The name of the Divine Serpent (otherwise known as *Ananta*) on whose hood Lord *Nārāyaṇa* reposes.

siddhāsana: The perfect pose; the adept's pose; a Yogic *āsana* practised by the perfected sages for meditation.

siddha-yoni āsana: A Yogic posture for women as a substitute for the accomplished pose (*siddhāsana*) for men.

siddhi: Yogic attainment.

śīla: Conduct.

śīrṣāsana: The headstand pose in which the body is inverted and balanced on the crown of the head.

Śiva: The masculine aspect of the Śiva-Śakti bipolarity.

śiva: Benign; auspicious.

Śiva-Śakti: The bipolar Reality; the Being with two poles — the masculine pole is Śiva and the feminine pole is Śakti.

skandha: Group of elements.

Smṛti: Epic and Purāṇic (mythological) scriptures of the Hindus.

smṛti: Memory; the recollection or retrieval of stored up information, experiences, and feelings.

smṛtirūpa: A form of memory.

śoka: Sorrowfulness.

soma: The juice of a specific plant used by the Vedic Āryans as an invigorating (not intoxicant) drink, and also for offering to God in fire-sacrifices (*yajñas*); moon; something that has cooling and smoothing effect.

sopādhika: With limiting adjunct(s).

sparśa: Touch.

sparśendriya: The supersensible, tactile, sensory organ.

śraddhā: Unwavering sincerity and liking; faith.

śravaṇendriya: The supersensible, auditory, sensory organ.

śreya: Useful; good.

śrīvatsa: A mark on the breast of Lord *Viṣṇu*.

sṛṣṭi: Creation; manifestation; emanation.

śruti: Revealed scripture; the *Vedas*.

sthiti: Inertia; tendency not to move, act and change; stability.

sthitipada: Stable state.

sthitiśīlatā: Inertia.

sthūla: Gross.

sthūlabhuk: That which enjoys or experiences gross objects.

sthūla śarīra: The gross body.

sūcaka: Omen; indicator.

śuddha: Pure.

sukha: Pleasure; happiness.

sukhasaṁskārāśaya: Store of subliminal impressions due to the experience of pleasure.

śukla: White.

śuklakṛṣṇa: White and black.

sūkṣma: Subtle; not perceptible to senses.

sūkṣma śarīra: Subtle body which is material, albeit sense-imperceptible.

Sūkta: The Vedic hymn.

śūla: Spear.

śūnya: Void; nihil.

śūnyatā: The state of void.

śūnyavāda: The doctrine of nihilism.

supta vajrāsana: The supine thunderbolt pose — a Yogic *āsana*.

sūryanāḍī: The solar channel or *piṅgalā* that is a supersensible psychic channel, flowing on the right side of the central channel — the *suṣumṇā*.

suṣumṇā: The supersensible, central psychic channel in the subtle body, flowing vertically in the middle of the spine.

suṣupti: Deep sleep; dreamless sleep.

sūtra neti: Nasal cleansing with a narrow strip of long cloth.

svabhāva: Own nature.

svādhiṣṭhāna: The second *cakra* (psychic centre) in the subtle body in the ascending order, located at the point where the spinal cord terminates; its level corresponds to that of the sacral plexus of nerves.

svādhyāya: The study of books on liberation; the study of sacred scriptures; the repetition of the mystic syllable "OṀ".

svakāraṇa: Own cause.

svānubhava: Self-realization.

svapna: Dream.

svara: The flow of exhaled air in one or both nostrils; sound or tone.

svara yoga: The Tāntric science of breath.

svarloka: The third division of the universe in the upper realm; the world corresponding to the *maṇipūra cakra*.

svarūpa: Own essence.

svarūpa-pralaya: The merger of the organ.

śvāsa: Inspiration.

svastika: A kind of mystical mark denoting good luck; a *maṇḍala* of the Hindus and the Jainas; a symbol of creativity and auspiciousness.

svastikāsana: 'Auspicious pose'; a meditative posture, somewhat similar to *siddhāsana*.

svataḥsiddha: Self-evident.

svatantra: Independent.

Svayambhū-liṅga: The phallic form in the *mūlādhāra cakra*.

svayaṁjyotiḥ: The light which expresses itself.

śyāma (*śyāmā*): Deep blue; blue-green.

taijasa: The second quarter of *Brahman* in the dream state.

tālu: Palate.

tamas: The strand or string of inertia.

tāmasic: Pertaining to the strand of *tamas*.

tāmasika: Of the nature of *tamas*.

tanhā: The Pāli word for thirst, derived from the Sanskrit word *tṛṣṇā*.

ṭaṅka: A sharp battle-axe.

tanmātra: Subtle element; subtle states of matter; literally means 'only that'.

tanmaya: One who remains engrossed with something.

Tantra: An Indian system of philosophical theory and ritual practices, in which Mother Goddess is worshipped.

Tāntric: Pertaining to *Tantra*.

Tāntrika: A person adept in the theory and practices of the *Tantra*.

tapa: Anxiousness.

tapaduḥkhatā: The painfulness of anxiousness.

tapaḥ: Self-castigation; austerity.

tapas: Austerities; suffering for some good cause without grudging; self-castigation.

tapasyā: Austerities.

tapoloka: The sixth division of the universe in the upper realm; the name of the world corresponding to the *ājñā cakra*.

tat: That; thatness permanently existing as such without modifications.

tathatā: Suchness.

tātparyaviṣayatvam: Meaningful.

tattva: Thatness; subtle element (five in number).

tattvamasi: That thou art.

tattva-pralaya: The merger of the organ.

tejaḥ (*tejas*): Energy; fire; heat; light; the subtle element of fire.

Theravādin: A Buddhist belonging to the philosophical school of *Theravāda* which is the oldest of the main schools of *Hīnayāna* Buddhism, the other two being *Sarvāstivāda* and *Sautrāntika*. The Pāli canon is the product of *Theravāda*.

titikṣā: Patient endurance of all sorrow or pain.

Traipura: The inverted triangle in the pericarp of the *mūlādhāra*.

trāṭaka: Fixed gazing at one point.

trayodaśa karaṇa: The thirteen-fold instrument.

triveṇī: The conflux of the three channels — the *suṣumṇā*, the *iḍā* and the *piṅgalā* — at the *ājñā cakra*.

tṛṣṇā: Thirst; intense desire; craving.

tu: But.

Turīya: The transcendental fourth state; the fourth quarter of *Brahman*.

tvam: You; second person singular.

ucyate: Can be described or spoken of.

udāna: One of the five *prāṇas*, operating in the head area above the throat; it pushes upwards and exerts levitating effect.

udāsīna: Indifferent.

udbodha: Awakening.

udbodhaka: Awakener; excitant.

uḍḍīyāna bandha: A Yogic practice of abdominal retraction lock; in this *bandha*, air is exhaled from the lungs and the abdomen and the stomach are drawn in towards the backbone.

ujjayī prāṇāyāma: A type of Yogic *prāṇāyāma* performed by contracting the epiglottis, in which a light sonorous sound is produced.

upacāra: False superimposition.

upādāna: Clinging; material; substance.

upādāna kāraṇa: Material or substantial cause.

upādhi: Limiting adjunct.

uparāga: Tinging.

uparati: Turning away completely from all sense-objects.

upaśānta: Silence; quietude.

upāśraya: An adjacent shelter.

upasthendriya: The supersensible, generative, motor organ.

upekṣā: Indifference.

uṣṭrāsana: A Yogic *āsana* known as the 'camel posture'.

vāda: Doctrine.

vāgindriya: The supersensible, vocal (speech), motor organ.

vāhana: Animal or bird vehicle.

vahni-bīja: The seed of the subtle element of fire.

Vaibhāsika: One of the four cheif philosophical schools of Buddhism; it belongs to *Hīnayāna* Buddhism and stands for the epistemology of direct realism.

vairāgya: Dispassion; detachment.

Vaiśeṣika: Particularity; one of the six systems of Indian philosophy; it is the Indian school of atomism, founded by Kaṇāda.

Vaiśvānara: The first quarter of *Brahman* whose sphere of activity is the waking state.

vajra: Thunderbolt.

vajrā: Otherwise known as *vajriṇī*; it is a psychic channel that flows inside the *suṣumṇā*.

vajriṇī: Otherwise known as *vajrā*; it is a psychic channel that flows inside the *suṣumṇā*.

vajroli mudrā: 'Thunderbolt seal' in which the muscles of the male sexual organ and lower urinary tract are contracted.

vāmācārī: The left-follower *Tāntriks* who participate in the 'Circle' and use 5-m's.

vāṁ: The subtle speech organ in the internal instrument (*antaḥkaraṇa*).

vanamālā: A garland made of forest flowers.

varadā mudrā: The gesture of granting boons.

Varuṇa: The divinity presiding the firmament or the oceans, with a noose in hand; the god presiding the subtle element of water.

Varuṇa-bīja: The seed of the subtle element of water.

vāruṇī: A supersensible psychic channel in the subtle body for the flow of *prāṇa*.

vāsanā: Subconscious impressions deeply buried in the *buddhi*; traces; the cognitive, affective, or conative *saṁskāras* (latent deposits) that are stored up in the mind to assume the form of active tendencies when the time comes for fruition; *vāsanās* are those *saṁskāras* that have a determining value on the present or the future life; all *vāsanās* are *saṁskāras* although all *saṁskāras* are not *vāsanās*.

vāsanāśaya: The store of latent deposits (*vāsanās*) laid in the ground of the subtle body; the individual unconscious.

vastu: Object; thing.

vastutantra: Objective.

vāyu: Air; gaseous matter; the subtle element of air.

vāyu-bīja: The seed of the subtle element of air.

vedanā: The feeling group of *skandhas*; sensation.

Vedānta: Literally the end (*anta*) of knowledge (*Veda*); one of the six philosophical systems of India, arising after the period of the *Vedas*, and in response to the heterodox system.

vicāra: Reflection.

videhamukti: Disembodied liberation.

vidyā: Knowledge.

vihanyate: Annihilated.

vijñāna: Consciousness; undistinguished mass of consciousness; subjective consciousness in Buddhist philosophy.

vijñānamaya kośa: The unconscious sheath; the intellectual sheath.

Vijñānavāda: A school of Buddhist philosophy that supports subjective idealism; both matter and mind are not real for it, but mind is the formative factor for the existence of the world.

Vijñānavādin: One who upholds *Vijñānavāda*.

vijñeya: To be known; should be known.

vikalpa: Imaginary thought without factual evidence; predicate-relations; knowledge arising from predicate relations without corresponding object.

vikalpanāḥ: Alternate propositions.

vikṣepa: Distraction; projection.

vikṣepa śakti: The projecting power.

vipāka: Fruition; maturation.

viparīta: Opposite.

viparīta karaṇī: A type of *mudrā* (sealing posture) in which a person lies on the ground with face upwards, raises both the legs, and supports the buttocks with the hands while the elbows rest on the ground.

viparyaya: Misconception; erroneous thinking; erroneous perception.

Virāḍ: The first evolute from the primordial matter (*Prakṛti* or *Māyā*); it is the Vedic term equivalent to the *Mahat* or *Buddhi* of the *Sāṅkhya*.

Virāj: The same as *Virāḍ*.

Virāṭ: The same as *Virāḍ*.

virodha: Antagonism.

viṣāda: Sorrowfulness.

visarga: Dripping down; separation.

viṣaya: Object.

viṣayapriya: Fond of object-of-sense.

viṣayasukha: Pleasure in an object-of-sense.

viṣaya-vijñāna: The same as *pravṛtti-vijñāna*.

viśiṣṭa: Particular.

Viśiṣṭādvaita: A type of non-dualistic *Vedānta* in which the particulars are recognized as parts of the one non-dual fundamental Being.

Viṣṇu: One who pervades; the one and the only one God, described with reference to His sustaining or supporting activity.

Viṣṇugranthi: The knot formed at the *anāhata cakra* by the *suṣumṇā*, the *iḍā* and the *piṅgalā*.

viśuddha: Pure; the psychic centre at the throat-pit.

viśuddhi: The fifth psychic centre (*cakra*) in the subtle body in the ascending order; located at the level of the throat-pit; this level corresponds to that of the cervical plexus of nerves.

viśva: All; the universe; the waking state which is the first quarter of *Brahman*.

viśvodarī: A supersensible psychic channel in the subtle body for the flow of *prāṇa*.

vitarka: Deliberation.

viveka: Discrimination between right and wrong, good and bad.

viyoga: Separation; subtraction.

vṛtti: Modes, modifications, or fluctuations of the mind-stuff.

vṛttibheda: Functional difference.

vṛttijñāna: Mental cognition.

vṛttipralaya: Cessation of functions.

vyāna: One of the five *prāṇas*, operating throughout the body.

vyañjaka: Manifester; expresser; stimulus; condition which phenomenalizes.

vyañjana: Expression; manifestation; phenomenalization.

vyavadhāna: Concealment.

vyāvahārika: Empirical.

vyoma: Space.

vyutthāna: Emergent.

yama: Abstentions; they are five in number, viz., non-violence, truthfulness, non-stealing, continence, and non-accumulation.

yantra: A geometrical diagram inside a *cakra* or a psychic centre; a kind of mystical diagram used for invoking a divinity; synonymous with *maṇḍala* for this purpose.

yasasvinī: A supersensible psychic channel in the subtle body for the flow of *prāṇa*.

yat: Whatever.

Yoga: An Indian school of philosophy founded by Patañjali in the pre-Christian era; it specifically prescribes physical and mental practices for the well-being of the body and the mind and for spiritual attainment.

Yogācāra: A Buddhist school of philosophy of subjective idealism, which denies the reality of both matter and mind, and which regards the world as a mental construct.

yoga-mudrā: A Yogic sealing posture which is practised in *padmāsana* and in which the forehead touches the ground.

yoga-nidrā: 'Psychic sleep' in which the conscious mind is asleep but awareness remains intact.

yogī: One who knows the theories of *Yoga* and one who practises *Yoga*.

Yogic: Pertaining to *Yoga*.

yoni: Source; the female genital organ; the female generative organ used as a symbol for worshipping Mother Goddess; the symbol is represented by an inverted triangle.

yoni-mudrā: A sealing gesture in which all the seven gates of perceptions in the head are closed with the fingers of both the hands.

Bibliography

(This Bibliography includes some selected books. References to journals have been given in the notes at the end of the chapters).

Indology, Indian Philosophy and Related Books

A Dictionary for Believers and Non-Believers, 1989 : (1st Publ. in Russian in 1985). Moscow: Progress Publishers.

Agrawala, P.K., 1984 : *Goddesses in Ancient India*. New Delhi: Abhinav Publications.

Aitareya Brahmanam, Vols. 1-3. Reprinted by Nag Publishers, Delhi, 1991.

Aiyer, C.V.R. (tr. & ed.), 1988 : *Śrī Śaṅkara's Gītā Bhāṣya*. Bombay: Bharatiya Vidya Bhavan.

Bahadur, K.P., 1988 : *The Wisdom of Sāṅkhya*. New Delhi: Sterling Publishers.

Banerji, P., 1985 : *Naṭarāja: The Dancing God*. New Delhi: Cosmo Publications.

Banerji, S.C., 1988 : *A Brief History of Tantra Literature*. Calcutta: Naya Prakash.

Bernard, T., 1977 : *Haṭha Yoga*. New Delhi: B.I. Publications. (Originally published by Rider & Co., London).

Bharati, A., 1976 : (1st Publ. 1965 by Rider & Co., London). *The Tantric Tradition*. New Delhi: B.I. Publications.

Bhatacharya, N.N., 1982 : *History of the Tantric Religion.* New Delhi: Manohar Publications.

Bhattacharya, V. (tr. & ed.), 1989 (1st publ. 1943) : *The Āgamaśāstra of Gauḍapāda.* Delhi: Motilal Banarsidass.

Bose, D.N. and Haldar, H., 1956 : *Tantras : Their Philosophy and Occult Secrets,* 3rd edn. Calcutta: Oriental Publishing Co.

Chand, D., 1980/1988 : *The Yajurveda.* New Delhi: Munshiram Manoharlal Publishers.

Chand, D., 1980/1990 : *The Sāmaveda.* New Delhi: Munshiram Manoharlal Publishers.

Chand, D., 1982/1990 : *The Aharvaveda.* New Delhi: Munshiram Manoharlal Publishers.

Chattopadhyaya, D., 1981 (1st publ. 1959) : *Lokāyata: A Study in Ancient Indian Materialism,* 5th edn. New Delhi: People's Publishing House.

Chennakesavan, S., 1980 (1st publ. 1960) : *Concept of Mind in Indian Philosophy.* Delhi: Motilal Banarsidass.

Conze, E., 1983 (1st publ. 1962) : *Buddhist Thought in India.* London : George Allen and Unwin.

Cozort, D., 1986 : *Highest Yoga Tantra: An Introduction to the Esoteric Buddhism of Tibet.* Ithaca, New York: Snow Lion Publications.

Danielou, A., 1973 (1st publ. 1949) : *Yoga.* London: Johnson Publicaions.

Darling, G.J., 1987 : *An Evaluation of the Vedāntic Critique of Buddhism.* Delhi: Motilal Banarsidass.

Dasgupta, S.N., 1979 (1st publ. 1930) : *Yoga Philosophy in Relation to Other Systems of Indian Thought.* Delhi: Motilal Banarsidass.

David-Neel, A., 1978 (1st publ. 1939) : *Buddhism: Its Doctrines and Its Methods.* London: Mandala Books, Unwin Paperbacks.

Desai, M. (tr. & ed.) 1946 : *The Gita according to Gandhi.*

Ahmedabad: Navajivan Publishing House.

Deshpande, N.A. (tr. & ed.) 1988-92 : *Ancient Indian Tradition & Mythology: The Padma Purana*, Vols. 1-10. (Gen. ed. Bhatt, G.P.). Delhi: Motilal Banarsidass.

Deussen, P., 1983 (tr. Johnston, C.) : *The System of the Vedānta*. New Delhi: Puja Publications.

Devī-Bhāgavatam. Gorakhpur, U.P.: Gita Press.

Dhiravamsa, 1982 : *The Dynamic Way of Meditation*. Wellingborough, Northamptshire: Turnstone Press.

Donat, L.K., 1976 (1st publ. 1974) : *Unisex Yoga*. London: Marshall Cavendish Publications.

Dutt, N., 1981 (1st publ. 1960) : *Early Monastic Buddhism*. Calcutta: Firma KLM.

Dutt, N., 1977 (1st publ. 1970) : *Buddhist Sects in India*. Calcutta: Firma KLM.

Dutt, N., 1976 (1st publ. 1973) : *Mahāyāna Buddhism*. Calcutta: Firma KLM.

Gautam, C. (ed. & comm.), 1980 : *Manusmṛti*, 3rd edn. Bareilly, U.P.: Samskrit Samsthan.

Gopi Krishna: *Kuṇḍalinī: The Secret of Yoga*. New Delhi: UBS Publishers' Distributors. (First publ. by F.I.N.D. Research Trust, Ontario, Canada).

Gopi Krishna, 1971 (1st publ. 1967) : *Kuṇḍalinī — The Evolutionary Energy in Man*. Boulder, Colorado/ London: Shambhala.

Gough, A.E. (tr.), 1975 (1st publ. 1873) : *The Vaiśeṣika Aphorisms of Kaṇāda*. New Delhi: Oriental Books Reprint Corporation.

Griffith, R.T.H., 1985 (1st publ. 1895-96) : *Hymns of the Atharvaveda*, Vols. 1-2. New Delhi: Munshiram Manoharlal Publishers.

———, 1986 (1st publ. 1895-96) : *Hymns of the Sāmaveda*. New Delhi: Munshiram Manoharlal Publishers.

———, 1987 (1st publ. 1889). *Hymns of the Ṛgveda*, Vols. 1-2. New Delhi: Munshiram Manoharlal Publishers.

———, 1987 (1st publ. 1899) : *The Texts of the White Yajurveda (Vājasaneyā Saṁhitā)*. New Delhi: Munshiram Manoharlal Publishers.

Gupta, M. (tr.), 1990 : *Viṣṇu Purāṇa*. Gorakhpur: Gita Press.

Harikrishnasharma (ed.), 1984 : *Śrī-Durgā-Saptaśatī*. Delhi: Butala & Co.

Hewitt, J., 1978 (1st publ. in 1974 by Barrie and Jenkins, London) : *Yoga and Meditation*. New Delhi: Vikas Publishing House (Bell Books).

Humphreys, C., 1983 : *Karma and Rebirth*. London: Curzon Press/USA: The Theosophical Publishing House.

Iengar, B.K.S., 1965 : *Light on Yoga — Yoga Dīpikā*. London: George Allen & Unwin. Also publ. in 1966 by Schocken Books, New York.

———, 1981 : *Light on Prāṇāyāma (Prāṇāyāma Dīpikā)*. London: George Allen and Unwin.

———, 1993 : *Light on the Yoga Sūtras of Patañjali*. London: The Aquarian Press.

Iengar, G.S., 1983 : *Yoga: A Gem for Women*. New Delhi: Allied Publishers.

Jennings, J.G., 1948 : *The Vedāntic Buddhism of the Buddha*. London: Oxford University Press.

Jnanadeva, 1991 : *Bhāvārtha-Dīpikā*. (Tr. from Marathi by M.R. Yardi). Pune: Bharatiya Vidya Bhavan.

Joshi, K.L. (ed.), 1981 : *The Brahmasūtra Śāṅkara Bhāṣyam*, Vols. 1-2. Delhi: Parimal Publications.

Joshi, K.S., 1983 : *Yogic Prāṇāyāma — Breathing for Long Life and Good Health*. Delhi: Vision Books.

Kalupahana, D.J. (ed. & tr.), 1991 (1st publ. 1986 by State University of New York) : *Mūla-Mādhyamikakārikā of Nāgārjuna*. Delhi: Motilal Banarsidass.

Karanjia, R.K., 1977 : *Kuṇḍalinī Yoga*. New Delhi: Arnold-Heinemann Publishers (India).

Kashyap, B.J., 1982 : *The Abhidhamma Philosophy*. Delhi: Bharatiya Vidya Prakashan.

Katz, N. (ed.), 1981 : *Buddhist and Western Philosophy*. New Delhi: Sterling Publishers.

King, W.L., 1964 : *In the Hope of Nibbana*. LaSalle, Ill.: Open Court.

Kirthisinghe, B.P. (ed.), 1984 : *Buddhism and Science*. Delhi: Motilal Banarsidass.

Krishna Warrier, A.G. (tr.), 1983 : *Śrīmad Bhagavad Gītā Bhāṣya of Śrī Śaṅkarācārya*. Mylapore, Madras: Sri Ramakrishna Math.

Ku Shoukang, L.J., 1986 (1st publ. in 1985 by the Commercial Press, Hongkong). *The Realm of Tibetan Buddhism*. New Delhi: UBS Publishers' Distributors.

Lidell, L., Naryani and Rabinovitch, G., 1983 : *The Book of Yoga*. London: Ebury Press.

Lysebeth, A., 1988 (1st publ. 1979) : *Prāṇāyāma: The Yoga of Breathing*. London: Unwin Paperbacks.

Mahabodhisattva, P.J., 1976 : *Zen-Yoga*. Delhi: Motilal Banarsidass.

Mehta, R., 1981 (1st publ. 1978) : *The Science of Meditation*. Delhi: Motilal Banarsidass.

Mishra, N. (ed.), 1971 : *Pātañjala Yoga Darśanam*. Varanasi: Bharatiya Vidya Prakashan.

Mookerjee, A., 1982 : *Kundalini — The Arousal of the Inner Energy*. Delhi: Clarion Books/London: Thames and Hudson.

Mukhopadhyay, S., 1984 : *Caṇḍī in Art and Iconography*. Delhi: Agam Kala Prakashan.

Nyāya-Tarkatīrtha, T. and Tarkatīrtha, A. (eds.), 1985 : (First publ. 1936-44 by Metropolitan Printing and Publishing House, Calcutta). *Nyāya-Darśanam*, 2nd edn. New Delhi: Munshiram Manoharlal Publishers.

Odier, D. (tr. by John Maboney), 1974 : *Nirvana Tao*. London: East West Publications.

O'flaherty, W.D. (ed.), 1980 : *Karma and Rebirth in Classical*

Indian Traditions. Berkeley/Los Angeles: University of California Press.

Pandeya, R.N.D.S. (tr.) : *Harivaṁśa Purāṇa*. Gorakhpur: Gita Press.

Pathak, P.V., 1984 : *The Heyapaksha of Yoga: Towards a Constructive Synthesis of Psychological Material in Indian Philosophy*. New Delhi: Asian Publication Services.

Pradhan, A.P., 1986 : *The Buddha's System of Meditation*. Vols. 1-5. New Delhi: Sterling Publishers.

Radhakrishnan, S., 1966 (1st publ. 1923). *Indian Philosophy*, Vols. 1-2. London: George Allen and Unwin.

———, (tr. & ed.), 1953 : *The Principal Upaniṣads*, London: George Allen and Unwin.

———, (tr. & ed.), 1960 : *The Brahma-Sūtra*. London: George Allen and Unwin.

———, (tr. & ed.), 1967 (1st publ. 1948) : *The Bhagavadgītā*. London: George Allen and Unwin.

——— (tr. & comm.), 1980 (1st publ. 1950) : *The Dhammapada*. Madras : Oxford University Press.

———, and others (eds.), 1967 (1st publ. 1952-53) : *History of Philosophy Eastern and Western*, Vols. 1-2. London: George Allen & Unwin.

Rawson, P., 1973/1978 : *The Art of Tantra*. London: Thames and Hudson.

Sachdeva, I.P., 1978 : *Yoga and Depth Psychology*. Delhi: Motilal Banarsidass.

Sanella, L., 1976 : *Kuṇḍalinī— Psychosis or Transcendence*. San Francisco: Dakin.

Śaṅkara, 1992 (1st publ. 1964) : *Īśādidaśopaniṣadaḥ* (with Śāṅkarabhāṣya). Delhi: Motilal Banarsidass.

Śaṅkaranārāyaṇan (tr.), 1988 : *Vivekacūḍāmaṇi*. Bombay: Bharatiya Vidya Bhavan.

Sarasvati, S.S.P. and Vidyalankar, S., 1977-87 : *Ṛgveda*

Saṁhitā, Vols. 1-13. New Delhi: Veda Pratisthana.

Sastri, A.M. and Rangacharya, K. (eds.), 1986 (1st publ. 1894-98) : *The Taittirīya Saṁhitā of Black Yajurveda* (with the commentary of Bhatta Bhaskar Mishra), Vols. 1-10. Delhi: Motilal Banarsidass.

Sastri, G.D. (ed.), 1990 (reprint) : *Sāṅkhya-Yoga-Darśanam or Yoga-Darśanam of Patañjali*. Varanasi : Chaukhamba Sanskrit Sansthan.

Sastry, A.M. (tr. & ed.), 1977 (1st publ. 1897) : *The Bhagavadgītā* with the Commentary of Śrī Śaṅkarācārya. Madras: Samata Books.

Śatapatha-Brāhmaṇa, Vols. 1-5, Reprinted in 1990 by Nag Publishers, Delhi.

Satavalekar, D. (tr. & ed.), 1980 : *The Mahābhārata of Vyāsa*. Paradi, Gujarat: Vasant Sripad Satavalekar.

Scott, M., 1983 : *Kundalini in the Physical World*. London: Routledge and Kegan Paul.

Shah, P.R., 1987 : *Tantra: Its Therapeutic Aspect*. Calcutta: Punthi Pustak.

Sharma, P.S. and Sharma, K.N., 1973 : *Yoga and Sex*. London: George G. Harrap & Co.

———, 1977 : *Instant Yoga for Over-Busy People*. New Delhi: Arnold-Heinemann.

Shastri, J.L. (Gen. ed.), 1978-80 : *Ancient Indian Tradition & Mythology: The Garuḍa Purāṇa*, Vols. 1-3. Delhi: Motilal Banarsidass.

——— (Gen. ed.) and Bhatt, G.P. (ed.), 1985-86 : Ancient Indian Tradition & Mythology: The Brahma Purāṇa, Vols. 1-4. Delhi: Motilal Banarsidass.

Singh, J. (tr.), 1979 : *Śiva-Sūtras* by Vasu Gupta. Delhi: Motilal Banarsidass.

Sinha, J., 1986 (1st publ. in 1938 by Routledge and Kegan Paul, London) : *Indian Realism*. Delhi: Motilal Banarsidass.

———, 1986 (1st publ. 1958) : *Indian Psychology*, Vols. 1-3.

Delhi: Motilal Banarsidass.

Sinha, N. (tr.), 1979 (1st publ. in 1915 by Panini Office, Allahabad) : *The Sāṅkhya Philosophy* (*Sāṅkhya-Pravacan-Sūtram*). New Delhi: Oriental Books Reprint Corpn. (Distributed by Munshiram Manoharlal Publishers, New Delhi).

Śrīmad-Bhāgavata-Mahāpurāṇam, Gorakhpur, U.P.: Gita Press.

Srivastava, L.K.L., 1990 : *Advaitic Concept of Jīvanmukti*. Delhi: Bharatiya Vidya Prakashan.

Srivastava, M.C.P., 1979 : *Mother Goddess in Indian Archaeology and Literature*. Delhi: Agam Kala Prakashan.

Stcherbatsky, T., 1989 (1st publ. 1968) : *The Conception of Buddhist Nirvāṇa*. Delhi: Motilal Banarsidass.

Subramanian, V.K. (tr. & ed.), 1990 (1st publ. 1977) : *Saundaryalaharī of Śaṅkarācārya*. Delhi: Motilal Banarsidass.

Śukla-Yajurveda-Saṁhitā (with commentary by Uvaṭa and Mahīdhara), 1971/1987 : Delhi: Motilal Banarsidass.

Suzuki, B.L., 1981 (1st publ. 1938) : *Mahāyāna Buddhism*, 4th edn. London: George Allen and Unwin.

Swami Chidbhavananda, 1971 : *The Bhagvadgītā*. Tiruchirapalli, Tamilnadu: Sri Ramakrishna Tapovanam.

Swami Chinmayananda (comm.), 1977 : (tr. into Hindi by Viśvanath Miśra). *Śaṅkara's Bhaja-Govindam Moha-Mudgara*. Bombay: Central Chinmay Mission Trust.

———, (tr. & comm.) : *The Holy Geeta*. Bombay: Central Chinmay Mission Trust.

Swami Gambhirananda (ed.), 1977 : *Brahma-Sūtra-Bhāṣya of Śrī Śaṅkarācārya*. Calcutta: Advaita Ashram.

Swami Jitatmananda, 1991 : *Holistic Science and Vedānta*. Bombay: Bharatiya Vidya Bhavan.

Swami Madhavananda (tr. & ed.), 1972 : *Vedānta Paribhāṣā of Dharmarāja Adhvarīndra*. Belur Math, Howrah: The Ramakrishna Mission Saradapith.

Swami Nikhilananda (tr. & ed.), 1974 : *Vedāntasāra of Sadānanda*. Calcutta: Advaita Ashram.

Swami Omananda Tirtha. *Pātañjala-Yoga-Pradīpa*. Gorakhpur, U.P.: Gita Press.

Swami, R., Ballentine, R. (M.D.) and Hymes, A. (M.D.), 1981 (1st publ. 1979) : *Science of Breath: A Practical Guide*. Honesdale, Pennsylvania: The Himalayan International Institute of Yoga Science and Philosophy.

Swami Satyananda Sarasvati, 1975 (1st publ. 1974) : *Meditations from the Tantras*. Munger, Bihar: Bihar School of Yoga.

———, 1983 (1st publ. 1969) : *Āsana, Prāṇāyāma, Mudrā, Bandha*. Munger, Bihar: Bihar School of Yoga.

———, 1984 (1st publ. 1976) : *Yoga Nidrā*, 5th edn. Munger, Bihar: Bihar School of Yoga.

———, 1984 : *Kuṇḍalinī Tantra*. Munger, Bihar: Bihar School of Yoga.

——— (with commentary by Swami Muktibodhananda Saraswati), 1985 : *Haṭhayoga Pradīpikā*. Munger, Bihar: Bihar School of Yoga.

Swami Sivananda, 1971 (1st publ. 1935) : *Kuṇḍalinī Yoga*, 6th edn. Sivanandanagar, U.P., India: The Divine Life Society.

Swami Sivananda Radha, 1992 (1st publ. 1978) : *Kuṇḍalinī Yoga*. Delhi: Motilal Banarsidass.

Swami Vimuktananda (ed.), 1973 : *Aparokṣānubhūti of Śaṅkara*. Calcutta: Advaita Ashram.

Swami Vishnudevananda, 1959 : *The Complete Illustrated Book of Yoga*. New York: Souvenir Press (Originally published by the Julian Press).

Tagare, G.V. (tr. & ed.), 1976-78 : *Ancient Indian Tradition & Mythology : The Bhāgavata Purāṇa*, Vols. 1-5, (Gen. ed. Shastri, J.L.). Delhi: Motilal Banarsidass.

———, 1981-82 : *Ancient Indian Tradition & Mythology: The Kūrma Purāṇa,* Vols. 1-2, (Gen. ed. Shastri, J.L.). Delhi: Motilal Banarsidass.

———, 1983-84 : *Ancient Indian Tradition & Mythology: The BrahmāṇḍaPurāṇa,* Vols. 1-5, (Gen. ed. Shastri, J.L.). Delhi: Motilal Banarsidass.

———, 1987-88 : *Ancient Indian Tradition & Mythology: The Vāyu Purāṇa,* Vols. 1-2, (Gen. ed. Bhatt, G.P.). Delhi: Motilal Banarsidass.

Taittirīya Brāhmaṇa. Delhi: Motilal Banarsidass.

Tilak, B.G. (ed.) 1971 : *Śrīmad Bhagavad Gītā Rahasya,* 3rd edn. (tr. into English by Sukthankar, B.S.). Poona: Tilak Brothers.

Udupa, K.N. (ed. by Prasad, R.C.), 1985 (1st publ. 1978) : *Stress and Its Management by Yoga,* 2nd edn. Delhi: Motilal Banarsidass.

Upaniṣatsaṅgrahaḥ, 1984 (1st publ. 1970). Delhi: Motilal Banarsidass.

Vandana, S., 1984 : *Nāma Japa.* Bombay: Bharatiya Vidya Bhavan.

Vasu, R.B.S.C., 1990 (1st publ. 1914-15 by Pāṇini Office, Allahabad) : *The Śiva Saṁhitā,* 4th edn. New Delhi: Munshiram Manoharlal Publishers.

Vedantavagisha, A.C. (ed.), 1989 : *Tāṇḍya-mahābrāhmaṇa,* Vols. 1-2. Delhi: Chaukhamba Sanksrit Pratisthana.

Vidyaratna, T. 1987 (1st publ. 1941) : *Ṣaṭcakra Nirūpaṇa and Pādukā-Pañcaka.* New Delhi: Aditya Prakashan.

Watson, D., 1991 : *A Dictionary of Mind and Spirit.* Calcutta: Rupa (1st publ. in London in 1991 by Andre Deutsch).

Woodroffe, S.J., 1975 (1st publ. 1918) : *Śakti and Śākta,* 8th edn. Madras: Ganesh & Co.

———, 1981 (1st publ. 1922) : *The Serpent Power.* Madras: Ganesh & Co.

Woods, J.H. (tr.), 1983 (1st publ. in 1914 by Harvard

University) : *The Yoga System of Patañjali.* Delhi: Motilal Banarsidass.

Yogi Pranavananda (tr. & comm.), Rodriguez, T. and Ram, K. (eds.), 1992 : *Pure Yoga (Gheraṇḍa Saṁhitā).* Delhi: Motilal Banarsidass.

Zimmer, H., 1984 : *Artistic Form and Yoga in the Sacred Images of India.* Princeton, N.J.: Princeton University Press/Delhi: Oxford University Press. (Tr. from *Kunstform und Yoga im Indischen Kultbild,* Frankfurter Verlags Anstalt AG, Berlin, 1926).

Western Philosophy and Religions

Aaron, R.I., 1955 : *John Locke.* Oxford: Oxford University Press.

Abelson, R., 1977 : *Persons — A Study in Philosophical Psychology.* New York: Macmillan Press.

Ackrill, J.L., 1981 : *Aristotle the Philosopher.* Oxford: Oxford University Press.

Afanasyev, V.G., 1980 (1st publ. 1963) : *Marxist Philosophy,* 4th edn. Moscow: Progress Publishers.

Anderson, A.R. (ed.), 1964 : *Minds and Machines.* Englewood Cliffs, N.J.: Prentice-Hall.

Annas, J., 1981 : *An Introduction to Plato's Republic.* Oxford: Clarendon Press.

Anscombe, E. and Geach, P.T. (tr. & ed.), 1954 : *Descartes: Philosophical Writings.* London: Nelson.

Aune, B., 1967: *Knowledge, Mind and Existence.* New York: Random House.

Ayer, A.J., 1946 (1st publ. 1936) : *Language, Truth and Logic.* London: Gollancz.

———, 1969 (1st publ. 1940) : *The Foundations of Empirical Knowledge.* London: Macmillan.

———, 1956 : *The Problem of Knowledge.* London: Penguin Books.

———, 1959 : *Logical Positivism.* London: George Allen and Unwin.

———, 1963 : *The Concept of a Person and Other Essays.* London: Macmillan.

———, 1982 : *Philosophy in the Twentieth Century.* London: Unwin Paperbacks.

———, 1982 : *The Central Questions of Philosophy.* London: Penguin.

Barnes, J., 1982 : *Aristotle.* Oxford: Oxford University Press.

———, Schofield, M. and Sorabji, R. (eds.), 1979 : *Articles on Aristotle,* 4 Vols. London: Duckworth.

Barrett, C. (ed.), 1966 : *Lectures and Conversations on Aeshetics, Psychology and Religious Belief.* Oxford: Basil Blackwell.

Beaver, R.P. and Others (eds.), 1984 (1st publ. 1982) : *The World's Religions.* England: Lion Publishing.

Beck, L.W., 1960 : *A Commentary on Kant's Critique of Practical Reason.* Chicago: University of Chicago Press.

Berkeley, G., 1975 : *Philosophical Works.* London: Everyman/Dent.

Block, N. (ed.), 1980 : *Readings in the Philosophy of Psychology.* London: Methuen.

Bullock, A., Stallybrass, O., Trombley, S. and Eadie, B. (eds.), 1990 (1st publ. 1977) : *The Fontana Dictionary of Modern Thought.* London: Fontana Paperbacks.

Cahn, S.M., Kitcher, P., Sher, G. and Fogelin, R.J., 1984 : *Reason at Work: The Introductory Readings in Philosophy.* New York: Harcourt Brace Jovanovich.

Campbell, K., 1980 : *Body and Mind.* Notre Dame, Indiana: Notre Dame Press.

Carnap, R., 1935 : *Philosophy and Logical Syntax.* London: Routledge and Kegan Paul.

Charlesworth, M.J. (tr.), 1965 : *Anselm's Proslogion.* Oxford: Clarendon Press.

Copleston, F.C., 1955 : *Aquinas.* Harmondsworth: Penguin Books.

Cornman, J.W. and Others (eds.), 1982 : *Philosophical Problems and Arguments: An Introduction.* New York: Macmillan.

Cottingham, J., 1986 : *Descartes.* Oxford: Basil Blackwell.

Cottingham, J., Stoothoff, R. and Murdoch, D. (trs. & eds.), 1984-85 : *Philosophical Writings of Descartes*, 2 vols. Cambridge: Cambridge University Press.

Coval, S., 1966: *Scepticism and the First Person.* London: Methuen.

Curley, E., 1985 : *The Collected Works of Spinoza.* Princeton: Princeton University Press.

Daglish, R. (tr.), 1974 : *The Fundamentals of Marxist-Leninist Philosophy.* Moscow: Progress Publishers.

Delahunty, R.J., 1985 : *Spinoza.* London: Routledge and Kegan Paul.

Dennett, D. and Hofstadter, D., 1978 : The *Mind's I.* Harmondsworth: Penguin Books.

Descartes, R. : *Meditations.* Reprinted by Bobbs-Merrill Co., New York, 1960.

———, *Essential Works of Descartes.* Reprinted by Bantam, New York, 1961.

Edel, A., 1982 : *Aristotle and His Philosophy.* London: Croom Helm.

Edwards, P. (ed.), 1967 : *The Encyclopedia of Philosophy.* London: Collier-Macmillan.

Engels, F., 1974 (1st publ. 1934) : *Dialectics of Nature.* Moscow: Progress Publishers.

———, 1975 : *Anti-Dühring.* Moscow: Progress Publishers.

Evans, C.O., 1970 : *The Subject of Consciousness.* London: George Allen and Unwin.

Feaver, J.C. and Horosz, W. (eds.), 1971 (1st publ. 1967) : *Religion in Philosophical and Cultural Perspective.* New York : Van Nostrand Reinhold/New Delhi: Affiliated East-West Press.

Feigl, H., 1967 : *The 'Mental' and the 'Physical': The Essay and the Postscript*. London: Oxford University Press.

Fodor, J., 1981 : *Representations*. Hassocks: Harvester.

Fogelin, R.J. and Others (eds.), 1984 : *Reason at Work*. New York: Harcourt Brace Jovanovich.

Gallop, D. (tr.), 1975 : *Plato: Phaedo*. Oxford: Clarendon Press.

Geach, P.T., 1969: *God and the Soul*. London: Routledge and Kegan Paul.

Ghose, R., 1990 : *The Idea of a Person*. Calcutta: Punthi Pustak.

Glover, J. (ed.), 1976 : *The Philosophy of Mind*. Oxford: Oxford University Press.

Gosling, J.C.B., 1973 : *Plato*. London: Routledge and Kegan Paul.

Gunderson, K., 1985 : *Mentality and Machines*, 2nd edn. Minneapolis: University of Minnesota Press.

Gustafson, D.F. (ed.), 1967 : *Essays in Philosophical Psychology*. London: Macmillan.

Hackforth, R. (tr.), 1952 : *Plato's Phaedrus*. New York: Bobbs-Merrill.

Hamilton, E. and Cairns, H. (eds.), 1961 : *Plato : The Collected Dialogues*. Bollinger Series, LXXI. New York: Pantheon Books.

Hamlyn, D.W. (tr. & ed.), 1968 : *Aristotle De Anima Books* II and III. Oxford: Clarendon Press.

Hamlyn, D.W., 1983 : *Perception, Learning and the Self*. London: Routledge and Kegan Paul.

Hampshire, S., 1951 : *Spinoza*. Harmondsworth: Penguin Books.

———, 1966 : *Philosophy of Mind*. New York: Harper and Row.

Hick, J.H., 1990 : *Philosophy of Religion*, 4th edn. Englewood Cliffs, N.J.: Prentice-Hall.

Hobbes, T., 1651 : *Leviathan*. Edited by M. Oakeshott and reprinted in 1960 by Basil Blackwell, Oxford.

Hook, S. (ed.), 1961 : *Dimensions of Mind.* London: Collier-Macmillan.

Hookway, C. (ed.), 1985 : *Minds, Machines and Evolutions.* Cambridge: Cambridge University Press.

Hume, D., 1739-40 : *A Treatise on Human Nature.* Edited by L.A. Selby-Bigge in 1975 and reprinted by Oxford University Press, Oxford. (Also reprinted in 1962 by Collins, London).

———, 1740 : *An Enquiry Concerning Human Understanding,* Edited by L.A. Selby-Bigge and reprinted in 1975 by Oxford University Press, Oxford.

Huxley, J., 1931 : *Science and Religion.* London: Gerald Howe.

Ilitskaya, L. (tr.), 1978 (1st publ. 1975) : *ABC of Dialectical and Historical Materialism.* Moscow: Progress Publishers.

Institute of Social Sciences, 1985 : *Fundamentals of Marxists-Leninist Philosophy.* Moscow: Progress Publishers.

James, W., 1902 : *The Varieies of Religious Experience.* New York: Longmans, Green/Crowell-Collier (1961 reprint) London: Fontana (1972 reprint).

Kant, I., 1790 : *The Critique of Judgement,* trans. by J.C. Meredith, 1928. Oxford: Oxford University Press.

———, 1959 : *The Critique of Practical Reason,* trans. by T.K. Abbott. London: Longmans, Green. (This Engl. edn. 1st publ. 1873; the original German edn. 1st publ. 1788).

———, 1970 (1st publ. 1929) : *The Critique of Pure Reason,* trans. by Norman Kemp Smith. London: Macmillan/New York: Random House (1958 edn.). (Original German edn. 1st publ. 1781).

——— : *The Moral Law.* Tr. by H.J. Paton, 1948. London: Hutchinson.

Karl Marx and Frederick Engels: Selected Works. Moscow: Progress Publishers, 1968.

Katz, S., 1978 : *Mysticism and Philosophy*. New York: Oxford University Press.

Kenny, A., 1968 : *Descartes*. New York: Random House.

———, 1973 : *Wittgenstein*. Harmondsworth: Penguin Books.

———, 1979 : *Aristotle's Theory of the Will*. London: Duckworh.

———, 1980 : *Aquinas*. Oxford: Oxford University Press.

Lacey, A.R., 1982 : *Modern Philosophy: An Introduction*. London: Routledge and Kegan Paul.

Lee, H.D.P. (tr.), 1986 (1st publ. 1955) : *Plato, The Republic*, 2nd edn. Harmondsworth, Middlesex: Penguin Books.

Lenin, V.I., *Collected Works*, Vol. 14. Moscow: Progress Publishers.

———, 1973 (Ist publ. 1947) : *Materialism and Empirio-Criticism: Critical Comments on a Reactionary Philosophy*, 4th edn. Moscow: Progress Publishers.

Lewis, H.D., 1965 : *Philosophy of Religion*. London: The English University Press.

Locke, D., 1968 : *Myself and Ohers: A Study in our Knowledge of Minds*. Oxford: Oxford University Press.

———, 1971 : *Memory*. London: Macmillan.

Locke, J., 1690. *An Essay Concerning Human Understanding*. Ed. P. Nidditch 1975. Oxford: Clarendon Press.

Lucas, P.G. and Grint, L. (trs.), 1955 : *Discourse on Metaphysics*. (Written by G.W. Leibniz 1685-86; Ist publ. 1846). Manchester: Manchester University Press.

MacKay, D.M., 1974 : *The Clockwork Image*. London: Inter-Varsity Press.

MacNabb, D.C.G., 1966 : *David Hume*. Oxford: Basil Blackwell.

Madell, G., 1981 : *The Identity of the Self*. Edinburgh: Edinburgh University Press.

Magee, B., 1978 : *Men of Ideas: Some Creators of Modern Philosophy.* London: British Broadcasting Corporation.

Malcolm, N., 1967 : "Anselm's Ontological Argument", In Phillips, D.Z. 1967 (Ist publ. 1966) *Religion and Understanding,* Oxford: Basil Blackwell.

Margolis, J., 1978 : *Persons and Minds: The Prospect of Nonreductive Materialism.* Holland: D. Reidel Publ. Co.

Maritain, J., 1953 : *The Range of Reason.* London: Geoffrey Bles/New York: Scribner's Sons.

Martin, C.B., and Armstrong, D.M. 1968 : *Locke and Berkeley.* London: Macmillan.

Marx, K. and Engels, F., 1976 : (Ist publ. 1964). *The German Ideology.* Moscow: Progress Publishers.

Marx, K., Engels, F. and Lenin, V.I., 1977 : *On Dialectical Materialism.* Moscow: Progress Publishers.

May, W. and Brown, S.C. (eds.), 1972 : *Linguistic Analysis and Phenomenology.* London: Macmillan.

McGinn, C., 1982 : *The Character of Mind.* Oxford: Oxford University Press.

———, 1983 : *The Subjective View.* Oxford: Oxford University Press.

McKeon, R. (ed.), 1941 : *Aristotle: Basic Works.* London: Random House.

Medawar, P., 1984 : *Plato's Republic.* New York: Oxford University Press.

Mitchell, B. (ed.), 1971 : *The Philosophy of Religion.* London: Oxford University Press.

Morris, M. and Parkinson, G.H.R. (tr.), 1973 : *Leibniz: Philosophical Writings.* London: Dent. (*The Monadology* was written by G.W. Leibniz; Ist publ. 1714).

Munitz, M. K. (ed.), 1971. *Identity and Individuation.* New York: New York University Press.

Nagel, T., 1971 : *Mortal Quesions.* Cambridge: Cambridge University Press.

Nozick, R., 1981 : *Philosophical Explanations.* Cambridge, Mass: Harvard University Press.

O'Connor, J. (ed.), 1969 : *Modern Materialism: Readings in Mind-Body Identity.* New York: Harcourt/Brace and World.

O'Hear, A., 1984 : *Experience, Explanation and Faith: An Introduction to the Philosophy of Religion.* London: Routledge and Kegan Paul.

Parfit, D., 1984 : *Reasons and Persons.* Oxford: Oxford University Press.

Parkinson, G.H.R. and Others (eds.), 1988 : *An Encyclopaedia of Philosophy.* London: Routledge and Kegan Paul.

Penelhum, T., 1974 : *Survival and Disembodied Existence.* London: Routledge and Kegan Paul.

Perry, J. (ed.), 1975 : *Personal Identity.* Berkeley: University of California Press.

Pitcher, G., 1964 : *The Philosophy of Wittgenstein.* Englewood Cliffs: Prentice-Hall.

Plant, R., 1973 : *Hegel.* London: George Allen and Unwin.

Plato, 1952 : *Symposium.* (Trans. by Walter Hamilton). Harmondsworth: Penguin Books.

———, 1954 : *Phaedo.* (Trans. by Hugh Tredennick). Harmondsworth: Penguin Books.

———, 1973 : *Phaedrus.* (Trans. by Walter Hamilton). Harmondsworth: Penguin Books.

Popper, K.R., 1979 (Ist publ. 1972) : *Objecive Knowledge.* Oxford: Oxford University Press.

Robinson, H., 1982 : *Matter and Sense.* Cambridge: Cambridge University Press.

Rorty, A.O. (ed.), 1976 : *The Identities of Persons.* Los Angeles: University of California Press.

———, 1986 : *Essays on Aristotle's Ethics.* Los Angeles:

University of California Press.

Rorty, R., 1979 : *Philosophy and the Mirror of Nature.* Princeton, N.J.: Princeton University Press/Oxford: Basil Blackwell, 1980 edn.

Rucker, R., 1982 : *Infinity and the Mind.* Hossocks, Sussex: Harvester Press.

Russell, B., 1929 (Ist publ. 1917) : *Mysticism and Logic.* London: George Allen and Unwin

———, 1921 : *The Analysis of Mind.* London: George Allen and Unwin.

———, 1975 : (Ist publ. 1946). *History of Western Philosophy.* London: George Allen and Unwin.

———, 1989 : (Ist publ. 1959). *Wisdom of the West.* London: Bloomsbury Books.

Ryle, G., 1949 : *The Concept of Mind.* Harmondsworth: Penguin Books/London: Hutchinson.

Saw, R.L., 1954 : *Leibniz.* Harmondsworth: Penguin Books.

Schaffer, J.A., 1991 : *Philosophy of Mind.* Englewood Cliffs, N.J.: Prentice-Hall.

Schilpp, P.A. (ed.), 1949 : *Albert Einstein: Philosopher-Scientist.* La Salle, Ill.: Open Court.

———, 1974 : *The Philosophy of Karl Popper*, 2 Vols. La Salle, Ill: Open Court.

Sharma, K.K., 1989 : *A Commentary on Kant's Critique of Practical Reason.* New Delhi: Indus Publishing Co.

Shoemaker, S., 1971 : *Self-Knowledge and Self-Identity.* New Delhi: Allied Publishers.

———, 1984 : *Identity, Cause and Mind.* Cambridge: Cambridge University Press.

Shoemaker, S., and Swinburne, R., 1984 : *Personal Identity.* Oxford: Basil Blackwell.

Smith, N.K., 1952 : *New Studies in the Philosophy of Descartes.* London: Macmillan.

Smythies, J.R. (ed.), 1968 : *Brain and Mind.* London: Routledge and Kegan Paul.

Spicker, S.F. (ed.), 1970 : *The Philosophy of the Body*. Chicago: Chicago University Press.

Sprague, E., 1978 : *Metaphysical Thinking*. New York: Oxford University Press.

Stanesby, D., 1988 : (Ist publ. 1985 by Croom Helm). *Science, Reason and Religion*. London: Routledge.

St. Augustine, 1961 : *Confessions*. Harmondsworth: Penguin Books.

Stich, S., 1983 : *From Folk Psychology to Cognitive Science*. Cambridge, Mass.: MIT Press.

Stranten, Z.V. (ed.), 1983 : *Philosophical Subjects*. Oxford: Oxford University Press.

Strawson, P.F., 1959/1977 : *Individuals: An Essay in Descriptive Metaphysics*. London: Methuen.

———, 1974 : *Freedom and Resentment and Other Essays*. London: Methuen.

Stroll, A. (ed.), 1967 : *Epistemology* (See "P predicates" by T. Forrest). London: Harper and Row.

Stroud, B., 1977 : *Hume*. London: Routledge.

Swinburne, R., 1977 : *The Coherence of Theism*. Oxford: Clarendon Press.

Taylor, C., 1975 : *Hegel*. Cambridge: Cambridge University Press.

The Fundamentals of Marxist-Leninist Philosophy, 1974. Moscow: Progress Publishers.

The Holy Bible. New York: The World Publishing Company.

The Holy Qur'ān. Qadian: M.W. Ahmad.

Thorpe, W.H., 1978 : *Purpose in a World of Chance*. Oxford: Oxford University Press.

Tiwari, K.N., 1986 : *The Logic of Religious Belief*. New Delhi: Classical Publishing Co.

Urmson, J.O., 1982 : *Berkeley*. Oxford: Oxford University Press.

Vesey, G.N.A. (ed.), 1964 : *Body and Mind*, Ch. 30. London:

George Allen and Unwin.

———, 1974 : *Personal Identity*, London: Macmillan.

Walker, R., 1978 : *Kant*. London: Routledge.

Warnock, G.J., 1953 : *Berkeley*. Harmondsworth: Penguin Books.

White, A.R., 1987 : *Methods of Metaphysics*. New York: Croom Helm.

Wiggins, D., 1967 : *Identity and Spatio-Temporal Continuity*. Oxford: Basil Blackwell.

———, 1980 : *Sameness and Substance*. Harvard: Harvard University Press.

Williams, B., 1973 : *Problems of the Self*. Cambridge: Cambridge University Press.

———, 1978 : *Descartes: The Project of Pure Inquiry*. Harmondsworth: Penguin Books.

Williams, H.A., 1972 : *The Resurrection*. London: Mitchell Beazley.

Wisdom, J., 1953 : 'Gods' in *Philosophy and Psycho-analysis*. Oxford: Basil Blackwell.

Wisdom, J., 1965 : *Other Minds*. Oxford: Basil Blackwell.

Wittgenstein, L., 1914-16 : *Notebooks*. (Ed. by G.H. von Wright and G.E.M. Anscombe, with an English translation by G.E.M. Anscombe, 1961). Oxford: Basil Blackwell.

Wittgensein, L., 1961 (1st publ. 1921) : *Tractatus Logico-Philosophicus*. London: Routledge and Kegan Paul.

———, 1988 (1st publ. 1953) : *Philosophical Investigations* (tr. by G.E.M. Anscombe). Oxfod: Basil Blackwell.

———, 1958 : *The Blue and Brown Books*. Oxford: Basil Blackwell.

Woodfield, A, 1976 : *Teleology*. Cambridge: Cambridge University Press.

Psychology

Adler, A., 1907 : *A Study of Organic Inferiority and its Psychical Compensation.* Berlin: Urban and Schwarzenberg.

Alexander, F., 1950 : *Psychosomatic Medicine.* New York: Norton.

Allport, G.W., 1937 : *Personality: A Psychological Interpretation.* New York: Holt.

Angell, J.R., 1904 : *Psychology.* New York: Holt.

Ansbacher, H.L. and Ansbacher, R.R. (eds.), 1956 : *The Individual Psychology of Alfred Adler.* New York: Basic Books.

Arendt, H., 1977-78 : *The Life of the Mind,* Vol. I: *Thinking.* New York: Harcourt Brace Jovanovich.

Arkin, A.M., Antrobus, J.S. and Ellman, S.J., (eds.), 1978 : *The Mind in Sleep: Psychology and Psychophysiology.* New York: John Wiley and Sons.

Armstrong, D.M., 1968 : *A Materialist Theory of the Mind.* London: Routledge and Kegan Paul.

Aronson, L.P., Tobach, E., Lehrman, D.S. and Rosenblatt, J.S. (eds.), 1970 : *Development and Evolution of Behaviour.* San Francisco: Freeman.

Bailey, P., 1965 : *Sigmund the Unserene.* Springfield, Ill: Thomas.

Bain, A., 1964 : *The Senses and the Intellect,* rev. edn. London: Parker.

Bekhterev, V.M., 1913 : *Objective Psychologie.* Leipzig: Tuebner.

Beloff, J., 1962 : *The Existence of Mind.* London: MacGibbon and Kee.

Bergson, H., 1911-16 : *Matter and Memory.* London: George Allen and Unwin.

Blackemore, C., 1988 : *The Mind Machine.* Oxford: Basil Blackwell.

Boring, E.G., 1950 : *A History of Experimenal Psychology.*

New York: Appleton-Century-Crofts.

Brigmann, W.G. and Tweney, R.D. (eds.), 1980 : *Wundt Studies.* Toronto: C.J. Hogrefe.

Broadbent, D.E., 1961 : *Behaviour.* London: Eyre and Spottiswoode.

Brome, V., 1978 : *Jung.* New York: Atheneum.

Brower, G.H. and Hilgard, E.R., 1981 : *Theories of Learning.* Englewood Cliffs: Prentice-Hall International.

Brown, J.L., 1975 : *The Evolution of Behaviour.* New York: Norton.

Cannon, W., 1915 : *Bodily Changes in Pain, Hunger, Fear and Rage.* New York: Appleton.

Chomsky, N., 1972 : *Language and Mind.* New York: Harcourt Brace Jovanovich.

Clarke, A., 1980 : *Phychological Models and Neural Mechanisms.* Oxford: Clarendon Press.

Cohen, D., 1979 : *J.W. Watson: The Founder of Behaviourism.* London: Routledge and Kegan Paul.

Coleman, J.C., 1982 : *Abnormal Psychology and Modern Life.* Bombay: D.B. Taraporevala Sons & Co. (1st publ. 1964 by Scott Foresman & Co., U.S.A.).

Curtiss, S., 1977 : *Genie: A Psycholinguistic Study of Modern-Day* 'Wild Child'. New York: Academic Press.

Darwin, C., 1872 : *The Expressions of the Emotions in Man and Animals.* London: Murray/New York: Philosophical Library.

Davidson, J. and Davidson, R. (eds.), 1980 : *The Psychology of Consciousness.* New York: Plenum Press.

Dennis, W. and Others (eds.), 1972 : *Current Trends in Psychological Theory.* Pittsburg: University of Pittsburg Press.

Descartes, R.: *Discourse on Method* (ed. & tr. L. Fafleur, 1960). New York: Library of Liberal Arts.

De Vore, I. (ed.), 1965 : *Primate Behaviour.* New York: Holt, Rinehart and Winston.

Dewey, J., 1886 : *Psychology.* New York: Harper.

Dreyfus, H.L. and Dreyfus, S.E., 1986/88 : *Mind Over Machine.* London: The Free Press/New York: Macmillan.

Driesch, H., 1927 : *Mind and Body.* London: Methuen.

Ebbinghaus, H., 1885 : *Über das Gedächtnis.* Leipzig: Dunker and Humblot.

Ebbinghaus, H., 1902-11 : *Grundzüge der Psychologie,* 2 vols. Leipzig: Veit.

Eccles, J.C., 1953 : *The Neurophysiological Basis of Mind.* Oxford: Oxford University Press.

———, 1961 : "The Effects of Use and Disuse on Synaptic Function", In J.F. Delafresnaye *et al.* (eds.), *Brain Mechanisms and Learning.* Oxford: Blackwell Scientific.

Ellenberger, H.F., 1970 : *The Discovery of the Unconscious.* New York: Basic Books.

Faraday, A., 1972 : *Dream Power.* New York: Coward, McCann and Geoghegan.

———, 1974 : *The Dream Game.* New York: Harper and Row.

Fearing, F., 1930 : *Reflex Action: A Study in the History of Physiological Psychology.* Baltimore: Williams and Wilkins.

Fechner, G.T., 1860 : *Elemente der Psychophysik.* Leipzig: Breitkopf and Härtel.

Federn, P., 1952 : *Ego Psychology and the Psychoses.* New York: Basic Books.

Feist, J., 1985 : *Theories of Personality.* New York: Holt, Rinehart and Winston.

Ferster, C.B. and Skinner, B.F., 1957 : *Schedules of Reinforcement.* New York: Appleon-Century-Crofts.

Fodor, A., 1968 : *Psychological Explanation.* New York: Random House.

Freedman, A., Kaplan, H. and Sadock, B. (eds.), 1980 : *Comprehensive Text Book of Psychiatry,* 3 vols.

Baltimore: Williams and Wilkins.

Freud, A., 1967 : *The Ego and the Mechanisms of Defense*, rev. edn. New York: International Universities Press.

Freud, S., 1887-1902 : *The Origins of Psychoanalysis — Letters to William Fliess.* Standard Edition (abbr. as SE), Vol. 1, 1966.

———, 1895 : *Project for a Scientific Psychology.* SE, Vol. 1, 1966.

———, 1896 : *Further Remarks on the Neuropsychoses of Defence.* SE, Vol. 3, 1962.

———, 1900 : *The Interpretation of Dreams.* SE, Vols. 4-5, 1953.

———, 1901 : *The Psychopathology of Everyday Life.* SE, Vol. 6, 1960.

———, 1901a : *Autobiographical Note.* SE, Vol. 3, 1962.

———, 1905 : *Three Essays on the Theory of Sexuality.* SE, Vol. 7, 1953.

———, 1905a : *Jokes and Their Relation to the Unconscious.* SE, Vol. 8, 1960.

———, 1910 : *The Origin and Development of Psychoanalysis.* SE, Vol. 11, 1957.

———, 1913 : *Totem and Taboo.* SE, Vol. 13, 1955.

———, 1914 : *On the History of the Psychoanalytic Movement.* SE, Vol. 14, 1957.

———, 1914a : *On Narcissism: An Introduction.* SE, Vol. 14, 1957.

———, 1915 : *Instincts and Their Vicissitudes.* SE, Vol. 14, 1957.

———, 1921 : *Group Psychology and the Analysis of the Ego.* SE, Vol. 18, 1955.

———, 1923 : *The Ego and the Id.* SE, Vol. 19, 1961.

———, 1925 : *An Autobiographical Study.* SE, Vol. 20, 1959.

———, 1926 : *Inhibitions, Symptoms and Anxiety.* SE, Vol. 20, 1959.

———, 1927 : *The Future of an Illusion.* SE, Vol. 21, 1961.

———, 1930 : *Civilization and Its Discontents.* SE, Vol. 21, 1961.

———, 1935 : *Postscript to an Autobiographical Study.* SE, Vol. 20, 1959.

Fuller, J.L. and Thompson, W.R., 1960 : *Behaviour Genetics.* New York: Wiley.

Galton, F., 1869 : *Hereditary Genius.* London: Macmillan.

———, 1883 : *Inquiries into Human Faculty and Its Development.* London: Macmillan.

Gazzaniga, M.S. and Ledoux, J., 1978 : *The Integrated Mind.* New York: Plenum Press.

Geis, G.L., Stebbins, W.C. and Lundin, R.W., 1965 : *Reflexes and Conditioned Reflexes: A Basic Systems Program.* New York: Appleton-Century-Crofts.

Gibson, J.J., 1966 : *The Senses Considered as Perceptual Systems.* Boston: Houghton Mifflin.

Globus, G.G. *et al.* (eds.), 1977 : *Consciousness and the Brain.* New York: Plenum.

Grof, S., 1975 : *Realms of the Human Unconscious.* New York: Viking.

Grossman, S.P., 1967 : *A Textbook of Physiological Psychology.* New York: Wiley.

Hadamard, J., 1945 : *The Psychology of Invention in the Mathematical Field.* Princeton: Princeton University Press.

Hall, C.S. and Lindzey, G., 1978 : *Theories of Personality.* New York: John Wiley and Sons.

Hall, C.S., Lindzey, G., Loehlin, J.C. and Manosevitz, M., 1985 : *Introduction to Theories of Personality.* New York: John Wiley and Sons.

Hamilton, W., 1859-60 : *Lectures on Metaphysics.* London: Blackwood.

Hanfling, O., 1980 : *Body and Mind.* Milton Keynes: Open University.

Harris, C.S. (ed.), 1977 : *Visual Coding and Adaptability.* Hillsdale, N.J.: Eribaum.

Hartmann, G.W., 1935 : *Gestalt Psychology.* New York: Ronald Press.

Heidbreder, E., 1961 : *Seven Psychologies.* New York: Appleton-Century-Crofts.

Heil, J., 1983 : *Perception and Cognition.* Berkeley & Los Angeles: University of California Press.

Herrnstein, R.J. and Boring, E.G. (eds.), 1965 : *A Source Book in the History of Psychology.* Cambridge, Mass.: Harvard University Press.

Hilgard, E.R., 1977 : *Divided Consciousness: Multiple Controls in Human Thought and Action.* New York: Wiley Interscience.

Hilgard, E.R. and Atkinson, R.L. and Atkinson, R.C., 1979 : *Introduction to Psychology.* New York: Harcourt Brace Jovanovich.

Hilgard, E.R. and Bower, G.H., 1975 : *Theories of Learning.* Englewood Cliffs, N.J.: Prentice-Hall.

Hilgard, E.R. and Hilgard, J.R., 1975 : *Hypnosis in the Relief of Pain.* Los Altos, California: William Kaufmann.

Hilgard, E.R. and Marquis, D.G., 1940 : *Conditioning and Learning.* New York: Appleton-Century.

Hill, W.F., 1980 : *Learning.* London: Methuen.

Hinde, R.A., 1970 (1st edn. publ. 1966) : *Animal Behaviour: A Synthesis of Ethology and Comparative Psychology,* 2nd edn. New York: McGraw-Hill.

Hingston, R.W.G., 1928 : *Problems of Instinct and Intelligence.* London: Arnold.

Hjelle, L.A. and Ziegler, D.J., 1981 : *Personality Theories.* Tokyo: McGraw-Hill International Book Company.

Hobhouse, L.T., 1901 : *Mind in Evolution.* London: Macmillan.

Hollingworth, H.L., 1926 : *The Psychology of Thought.* New York: Appleton.

Holt, E.B., 1914 : *The Concept of Consciousness.* New York: Macmillan.

———, 1915 : *The Freudian Wish and Its Place in Ethics.* New York: Holt.

Holtzman, W., Thorpe, J., Swartz., J. and Herron, E., 1961 : *Ink-Blot Perception and Personality.* Austin: University of Texas Press.

Honing, W.K. (ed.), 1966 : *Operant Behaviour: Areas of Research and Application.* New York: Appleton-Century-Crofts.

Horowitz, M.J., 1970 : *Image Formation and Cognition.* New York: Appleton-Century-Crofts.

Houston, J.P., 1976 : *Fundamenals of Learnings.* New York: Academic Press.

James, W., 1890 : *Principles of Psychology,* 2 Vols., New York: Henry Holt/Dover (1950 reprint).

———, 1897 : *The Will to Believe.* New York: Longmans, Green.

———, 1898 : *Human Immortality.* Boston: Houghton Mifflin.

———, 1907 : *Pragmatism.* New York: Longmans, Green.

———, 1909 : *The Meaning of Truth.* New York: Longmans, Green.

———, 1909a : *A Pluralistic Universe.* New York: Longmans, Green.

Jones, E., 1953-57 : *The Life and Work of Sigmund Freud,* 1856-1900, 3 Vols., New York : Basic Books.

Jung, C.G., 1907 : *The Psychology of Dementia Praecox.* Halle: Marhold.

———, 1931 : *Modern Man in Search of a Soul.* Zurich: Rascher.

———, 1953 : *The Psychology of Unconscious,* In *Collected Works,* Vol. 7. Princeton: Princeton University Press.

———, 1958 : *Psychology of Religion: West and East.* London: Routledge and Kegan Paul.

———, 1959 : *The Archetypes and the Collective*

Unconscious. London: Routledge and Kegan Paul.

———, 1960 : *The Structure and Dynamics of the Psyche*. London: Routledge and Kegan Paul.

———, 1963 : *Memories, Dreams, Reflections*. New York: Vintage/London: Collins/Routledge and Kegan Paul. (Also published in 1983 by Flamingo, Fontana Paperbacks, London).

———, 1968 (1st publ. 1928) : *Analytical Psychology: Its Theory and Practice*. New York: Pantheon.

Kenny, A., 1963 : *Action, Emotion and Will*. London: Routledge.

Koestler, A., 1967 : *The Ghost in the Machine*. London: Hutchinson.

Koffka, K., 1935 : *The Principles of Gestalt Psychology*. New York: Harcourt Brace Jovanovich.

Kramer, M. (ed.), 1969 : *Dream Psychology and the New Biology of Dreaming*. Springfield, Ill.: Charles C. Thomas.

Lamarck, J.B., 1809 : *Philosophie Zoologique*, 2 Vols. Paris: Bailliere.

La Mettrie, J.-O. de 1748 : *L'Homme Machine* (*Man as Machine*). Leyden: Luzac.

Leahey, T.A., 1980 : *A History of Psychology*. Englewood Cliffs, N.J.: Prentice-Hall.

Lefrancois, G.R., 1983 : *Psychology*. California: Wadsworth Publishing Co.

Lenneberg, E.H., 1967 : *Biological Foundaions of Language*. New York: Wiley.

Lotze, R.H., 1882 : *Grundzüge der Psychologie*. Leipzig: Hirzel.

Mach, E., 1886 : *Die Analyse der Empfindungen und das Verhältnis des Psychischen zum Physischen*. Jena: Fischer.

Maier, N.R.F. and Schneirla, T.C., 1935 : *Principles of Animal Psychology*. New York: McGraw-Hill.

Malcolm, N., 1972 : *Problems of Mind — Descartes to Wittgenstein.* London: George Allen and Unwin.

Marler, P. and Hamilton, W.J., 1966 : *Mechanisms of Animal Behaviour.* New York: Wiley.

Marx, M.H. (ed.), 1969 : *Learning Processes.* New York: Macmillan.

Marx, M.H. and Cronan-Hillix, W.A., 1987 : *Systems and Theories of Psychology.* New York: McGraw-Hill Book Co.

Maslow, A.H., 1954/1970 : *Motivation and Personality.* New York: Harper and Bros.

———, 1966 : *The Psychology of Scienc.* New York: Harper and Row.

Maudsley, H., 1867 : *Physiology and Pathology of Mind.* London: Macmillan.

———, 1884 : *Body and Will.* New York: Appleton.

McDougall, W., 1905 : *Physiological Psychology.* London: Dent/New York: Macmillan.

———, 1908 : *Social Psychology.* New York: G.P. Putnam's Sons.

———, 1920 : *The Group Mind.* New York: Putnam.

McGurie, W. (ed.), 1974 : *The Freud/Jung Letters: The Correspondence between Sigmund Freud and C.G. Jung*, Princeton, N.J. : Princeton University Press.

McKenzie, N., 1989 (1st publ. 1965) : *Dreams and Dreaming.* London: Bloomsbury Books.

Mesmer, F.A., 1766 : *The Planetarum Influxu.* Vienna: Ghelen.

Mill, J., 1829 : *Analysis of the Phenomena of the Human Mind.* London: Longmans and Dyer.

Montague, W.P., 1908 : "Consciousness, a Form of Energy", In (Colleagues of Columbia University). *Essays Philosophical and Psychological in Honour of William James.* New York: Longmans, Green.

Morgan, C.L., 1890-91 : *Animal Life and Intelligence.* London: Arnold.

———, 1894 : *An Introduction to Comparative Psychology.* London: Scott.

Morgan, C.T., King, R.A., Weisz, J.R. and Schopler, J., 1986 (1st publ. 1956) : *Introduction to Psychology*, 7th edn. New York: McGraw-Hill.

Murphy, G., 1966 : *Personality.* New York: Basic Books. (Originally publ. in 1947 by Harper, New York).

Murphy, G., and Kovach, J.K. (edited by Ogden, C.K.), 1992 : *Historical Introduction to Modern Psychology.* London: Routledge and Kegan Paul.

Neumann, E., 1954 : *The Origins and History of Consciousness.* New York: Pantheon Books.

Osler, S. and Cooke, R. (eds.), 1965 : *The Bio-Social Basis of Mental Retardation.* Baltimore: John Hopkins University Press.

Pavlov, I.P., 1897 : *Lectures on the Work of the Principal Digestive Glands.* St. Petersburg: Kushnereff.

Pribram, K.H. (ed.), 1969 : *On the Biology of Learning.* New York: Harcourt Brace Jovanovich.

Pribram, K.H. and Broadbent, D.E. (eds.), 1970 : *Biology of Memory.* New York: Academic Press.

Prince, M., 1885 : *Nature of Mind and Human Automatism.* Philadelphia : Lippincott.

Randhawa, B.S. and Coffman, W.E. (eds.), 1978 : *Visual Learning, Thinking and Communication.* New York: Academic Press.

Razran, G., 1971 : *Mind in Evolution: An East-West Synthesis of Learned Behaviour and Cognition.* Boston: Houghton Mifflin.

Reber, A.S., 1985 : *The Penguin Dictionary of Psychology.* Harmondsworth, Middlesex: Penguin Books.

Reese, W.L., 1980 : *Dictionary of Philosophy and Religion: Eastern and Western Thought.* Atlantic Highlands, N.J.: Humanities Press/Hassocks, Sussex: The Harvester Press.

Richards, A. (ed.), trans. by Starchey, J., 1985 (1st publ. in Pelican Books 1984) : *On Metapsychology: The Theory of Psychoanalysis.* Harmondsworth, Middlesex: Penguin Books.

Romanes, G.J., 1883 : *Animal Intelligence.* New York: Appleton.

———, 1884 : *Mental Evolution in Animals.* London: Kegan, Paul, Trench.

Sartre, J., 1957 : *The Transcendence of the Ego : An Existentialist Theory of Consciousness.* (Trans. by F. Williams and B. Kirkpatrick). New York: Noonday Press.

Schafer, R., 1978 : *Language and Insight.* New Haven: Yale University Press.

Schmitt, F.O. and Worden, F.G. (eds.), 1974 : *The Neuro-Sciences: Third Study Program.* Cambridge, Mass: MIT Press.

Senden, M.V., 1960 : *Space and Sight.* (Trans. by P. Heath). New York: Free Press.

Sharpe, E.F., 1961 : *Dream Analysis.* London: The Hogarth Press.

Sheehan, P.W. (ed.), 1972 : *The Function and Nature of Imagery.* New York: Academic Press.

Sheikh, A.A. (ed.), 1982 : *Imagery: Current Theory, Research and Application.* New York: John Wiley.

Shikhirev, P. (ed.), 1987 (1st publ. in Russian in 1985) : *A Concise Psychological Dictionary.* Moscow: Progress Publishers.

Singer, J.L., 1975 : *The Inner World of Daydreaming.* New York: Harper and Row.

Singh, A.K., 1991 : *The Comprehensive History of Psychology.* Delhi: Motilal Banarsidass.

Skinner, B.F., 1938 : *The Behaviour of Organisms: An Experimental Analysis.* New York: Appleton-Century-Crofts.

———, 1948 : *Walden Two*. New York: Macmillan.

———, 1953 : *Science and Human Behaviour*. London/New York: Macmillan.

———, 1957 : *Verbal Behaviour*. New York: Appleton-Century-Crofts.

———, 1971 : *Freedom and Dignity*. Harmondsworth: Penguin Books.

———, 1973 : *Beyond Freedom and Dignity*. Harmondsworth: Penguin Books. (1st publ. in 1971 by Alfred A. Knopf, New York).

Smith, S. and Guthrie, E.R., 1921 : *General Psychology in Terms of Behaviour*. New York: Appleton.

Spence, K.W., 1956 : *Behaviour Theory and Conditioning*. New Haven: Yale University Press.

Spencer, H., 1855 : *The Principles of Psychology*, 8 Vols. London: Williams Norgate.

Starbuck, E.D., 1899 : *The Psychology of Religion*. New York: Scribner.

Starchey, J. (ed.), 1955 : *The Standard Edition of the Complete Work of Sigmund Freud*. London: Hogarth Press.

Stellar, E. and Sprague, J.M. (eds.) 1966 : *Progress in Physiological Psychology*, Vol. I. New York: Academic Press.

Stevens, S.S. (ed.), 1951 : *Handbook of Experimental Psychology*. New York: Wiley.

Thorndike, E.L., *Educational Psychology*, Vol. 1 (1903), Vol. 2 (1913), Vol. 3 (1914). New York: Lemcke and Buechner (Vol. 1)/Teachers College, Columbia University (Vols. 2 & 3).

———, 1905 : *The Elements of Psychology*. New York: Seiler.

———, 1905 : *The Measurement of Twins*. New York: Science Press.

———, 1932 : *The Fundamentals of Learning*. New York: Teachers College, Columbia University.

———, 1949 : *Selected Writings from a Connectionist's Psychology.* New York: Appleton-Century-Crofts.

Thorpe, W.H., 1963 : *Learning and Instinct in Animals*, 2nd edn. London: Methuen.

———, 1974 : *Animal Nature and Human Nature.* London: Methuen.

Tinbergen, N., 1951 : *The Study of Instinct.* Oxford: Oxford University Press.

Titchener, E.B., 1901-5 : *Experimental Psychology*, 4 Vols. New York: Macmillan.

———, 1908 : *The Elementary Psychology of Feeling and Attention.* New York: Macmillan.

———, 1909 : *Lectures on the Experimental Psychology of the Thought Processes.* New York: Macmillan.

———, 1909-10 : *A Text-Book of Psychology.* New York: Macmillan.

———, 1929 : *Systematic Psychology: Prolegomena.* New York: Macmillan.

Tolman, E.C., 1932 : *Purposive Behaviour in Animals and Men.* New York: Appleton-Century.

Tulving, E. and Donaldson, W. (eds.), 1962 : *Organization of Memory.* New York: Academic Press.

Vernon, J.A., 1963 : *Inside the Black Room.* New York: Clarkson N. Potter.

Washburn, M.F., 1908 : *The Animal Mind.* New York: Macmillan.

Watson, J.B., 1914 : *Behaviour: An Introduction to Comparative Psychology.* New York: Holt.

———, 1919 : *Psychology from the Standpoint of a Behaviourist.* Philadelphia : Lippincott. (2nd edn. 1924).

———, 1924 : *Behaviourism.* Chicago : University of Chicago Press. (Rev. edn. publ. in 1930 by Norton, New York).

Watson, R.I., 1978 : *The Great Psychologists.* Philadelphia: J.B. Lippincott.

Weiss, A.P., 1925 : *A Theoretical Basis of Human Behaviour.* Columbus, Ohio: Adams.

Whorf, B.L., 1956 : *Language, Thought and Reality.* Cambridge, Mass.: MIT Press.

Wollheim, R. (ed.), 1974 : *Freud.* New York: Doubleday.

Wolman, B.B., 1960/1979 : *Contemporary Theories and Systems in Psychology.* New York: Harper and Row.

Wood, O.P. and Pitcher, G. (eds.), 1970 : *Ryle.* London: Macmillan.

Wundt, W.M., 1873-74 : *Grundzüge der Physiologischen Psychologie.* Leipzig: Engelmann.

Yalcom, I., 1980 : *Existential Psychotherapy.* New York: Basic Books.

Parapsychology

Abell, G.O. and Singer, B. (eds.), 1981 : *Science and the Paranormal.* New York: Charles Scribner & Sons.

Allen, T.G. (tr.), 1974 : *The Book of the Dead.* Chicago: University of Chicago Press.

Allison, R. (M.D.) and Schwarz, T. (eds.), 1980 : *Minds in Many Pieces.* USA: Library of Congress.

Ashby, R.H., 1972 : *The Guidebook for the Study of Psychical Research.* London: Rider.

Ayala, F.J. and Dobzhansky, T. (eds.), 1974 : *Studies in the Philosophy of Biology.* London: Macmillan.

Baker, R., 1980 : *The Mystery of Migration.* London: Macdonald Futura Books.

Bancroft, A., 1982 : *The Luminous Vision.* London: George Allen and Unwin/USA: Allen and Unwin.

Barrett, S.W., 1986 (1st publ. 1926) : *Death-Bed Visions.* Northampshire: The Aquarian Press.

Beauchamp, T.L. and Rosenberg, A., 1981 : *Hume and the Problem of Causation.* Oxford: Oxford University Press.

Becker, E., 1973 : *The Denial of Death.* New York: The Free Press.

Beloff, J., 1977a : "Backward Causation", In Shapin and Coly (eds.) : *The Philosophy of Parapsychology.* New York: Parapsychology Foundation.

———, 1977b : "Historical Overview", In B.B. Wolman (ed.). *Handbook of Parapsychology.* New York: Van Nostrand Reinhold.

Bender, H., 1975 : "Modern Poltergeist Research", In J. Beloff (ed.) *New Directions in Parapsychology.* Metuchen, N.J.: Scarecrow Press.

Bernard, R., 1980 : *Messages from the Celestial Sanctum.* San Jose: Rosicrucian Press.

Bird, C., 1979 : *The Divining Hand.* New York: E.P. Dutton.

Blackmore, S.J., 1983 : *Beyond the Body.* London: Granada Publishing.

Blakeslee, T.R., 1980 : *The Right Brain.* London: Macmillan Press.

Brandon, R., 1983 : *The Spiritualists.* New York: Alfred A. Knopf.

Braude, S.E., 1979 : *ESP and Psychokinesis : A Philosophical Examination.* Philadelphia: Temple University Press.

———, 1986 : *The Limits of Influence.* London: Routledge and Kegan Paul.

Brier, B., 1974 : *Precognition and the Philosophy of Science.* New York: Humanities Press.

Briggs, J. and Peat, F.D., 1984 : *Looking Glass Universe.* New York: Simon and Schuster.

Broad, C.D., 1953 : *Religion, Philosophy and Psychical Research.* London: Routledge and Kegan Paul.

———, 1962/1966 : *Lectures on Psychical Research.* London: Routledge and Kegan Paul/New York: The Humanities Press.

———, 1976 : *The Mind and Its Place in Nature.* New York: Humanities Press. (1st publ. in 1925 by Routledge and Kegan Paul, London).

Brown, M.H., 1976 : PK, *A Report on the Power of Psychokinesis.* Blauvelt, New York: Steinerbooks.

Buchanan, J.R. (M.D.), 1885 : *Manual of Psychometry: The Dawn of a New Civilization.* Boston: Holman Brothers.

Bucke, R.M. (M.D.), 1967 : *Cosmic Consciousness.* New York: E.P. Dutton. (Also publ. by University Books, New York, 1961).

Burr, H.S., 1972 : *Blueprint for Immortality.* London: Neville Spearman.

Bursen, H.A., 1978 : *Dismantling the Memory Machine.* Dordrecht, Boston/London: D. Reidel.

Carington, W., 1945 : *Telepathy.* London: Methuen.

Carlson, R.J., 1975 : *The Frontiers of Science and Medicine.* London: Wildwood House.

Cartwright, N., 1983 : *How the Laws of Physics Lie.* Oxford/New York: Oxford University Press.

Cheney, S., 1968 : *Men Who Have Walked with God.* New York: Alfred A. Knopf.

Christie-Murray, D., 1981 : *Reincarnation : Ancient Beliefs and Modern Evidence.* Newton Abbot, Devon: David and Charles.

Connelly, D.M., 1977 : *Traditional Acupuncture: The Law of the Five Elements.* Columbia, Md. : Centre for Traditional Acupuncture.

Corlish, W.R., 1982 : *The Unfathomed Mind: A Handbook of Unusual Mental Phenomena.* Glen. Arm., USA: The Sourcebook Project.

Cracknell, R., 1981 : *Clues to the Unknown.* Middlesex: Hamlyn Paperbacks.

Crookall, R., 1960 : *The Study and Practice of Astral Projection.* New Hyde Park, NY: University Books. (publ. in 1961 by Aquarian Press, London).

———, 1965 : *Intimations of Immortality.* London: James Clarke.

———, 1968 : *The Mechanisms of Astral Projection.* India: Darshana International.

Currie, I., 1978 : *You Cannot Die.* Toronto: Methuen Publications.

Davies, P., 1987 : *The Cosmic Blueprint.* London: William Heinemann.

Dean, S.R. (ed.), 1979 : *Psychiatry and Mysticism.* Chicago: Nelson Hall.

Denton, W., 1988 (1st publ. 1863) : *The Soul of Things.* Northampshire: The Aquarian Press/Thorsons: Wellingborough.

Dethlefsen, T., 1977 : *Voices from Other Lives.* New York: M. Evans.

Duncan, R. and Weston-Smith, M. (eds.), 1977 : *Encyclopedia of Ignorance.* Oxford: Pergamon Press.

Dunne, B.J., Jahn, R.G. and Nelson, R.D., 1983 : *Precognitive Remote Perception.* Princeton: Princeton University School of Engineering/Applied Science.

Ebon, M., 1974 : *Exorcism : Fact Not Fiction.* New York: New American Library.

Edge, H.L., Morris, R.L., Rushand, J.H. and Palmer, J., 1986 : *Foundations of Parapsychology.* London: Routledge and Kegan Paul.

Eisenbud, J., 1970 : *Psi and Psychoanalysis.* New York and London: Grune & Stratton.

———, 1982 : *Paranormal Foreknowledge: Problems and Perplexities.* New York: Human Sciences Press.

———, 1983 : *Parapsychology and the Unconscious.* Berkeley : North Atlantic Books.

Estabrooks, G.H., 1957 : *Hypnotism.* New York: Dutton.

Evans-Wentz, W.Y., 1960 : *The Tibetan Book of the Dead.* London: Oxford University Press.

Fiore, E., 1978 : *You Have Been Here Before.* New York: Coward, McCann and Geoghegan.

Fisher, J., 1985 (1st publ. 1984 by William Collins Sons, Toronto). *The Case for Reincarnation.* London: Granada Publishing.

Fisher, J. and Commins, P., 1980 : *Predictions.* Toronto: William Collins Sons.

Fisher, S. and Cleveland, S., 1968 : *Body Image and Personality,* 2nd edn. New York: Dover Publications.

Fodor, N., 1959 : *The Haunted Mind.* New York: Garrett Publications.

———, 1966 : *Encyclopaedia of Psychic Science.* New Hyde Park, N.Y.: University Books.

Fortune, D., 1971 : *The Esoteric Orders and Their Work.* Minnesota: Llewellyn Publications.

Fox, O. (Pseudonym), 1962 (1st publ. 1939) : *Astral Projection: A Record of Out-of-the-Body Experiences.* Secaucus, N.J.: University Books.

Frazer, J.G. (Sir), 1968 : *The Belief in Immortality.* London: Dawsons of Pall Mall.

Frazier, K. (ed.), 1981 : *Paranormal Borderlands of Science.* New York: Basic Books.

Freemantle, F. and Trungpa, C., 1974 : *The Tibetan Book of the Dead.* Chicago: University of Chicago Press.

Friedmann, C. and Faguet, R. (eds.), 1982 : *Extraordinary Disorders of Human Behaviour.* New York: Plenum Press.

Fukurai, T., 1931/1975 : *Clairvoyance and Thoughtography.* New York: Arno Press.

Gabbard, G.O. and Twemlow, S.W., 1984 : *With the Eyes of the Mind.* New York: Praeger Publishers.

Gallup, G. and Proctor, W., 1982 : *Adventures in Immortality: A Look Beyond the Threshold of Death.* New York: McGraw-Hill.

Garrett, E., 1968 (1st publ. 1949) : *Adventures in the Supernormal. A Personal Memoir.* New York: Paperback Library.

Gauld, A., 1968 : *The Founders of Psychical Research.* London: Routledge and Kegan Paul.

Gauld, A., 1982 : *Mediumship and Survival: A Century of Investigation.* London: Heinemann.

Gauld, A. and Cornell, A.D., 1979 : *Poltergeists.* London/ Boston: Routledge and Kegan Paul.

Geley, G., 1927/1975 : *Clairvoyance and Materialisation.* London: T. Fisher Unwin. Reprinted by Arno Press, New York.

Geller, U. and Playfair, G.L., 1987 (1st publ. 1986 by Jonathan Cape in Great Britain). *The Geller Effect.* London: Grafton Books.

Gooch, S., 1984 : *Creatures from Inner Space.* London: Rider.

Goodman, J., 1979 : *Psychic Archaeology.* London: Panther.

Goss, M., 1979 : *Poltergeists: An Annotated Bibliography of Works in English, circa 1880-1975.* Metuchen, N.J., USA/London: The Scarecrow Press.

Green, C.E., 1968 : *Out-of-the-Body Experiences.* London: Hamish Hamilton.

———, 1971 : *Journeys Out of the Body.* New York: Doubleday. (Also publ. in 1972 by Souvenier Press, London).

Green, C.E. and McCreery, C., 1975 : *Apparitions.* London: Hamish Hamilton.

Greenhouse, H.B., 1972 : *Premonitions: A Leap Into the Future.* London: Turnstone Press.

Grey, M., 1985 : *Return from Death.* London: Arkana.

Grof, S., 1975 : *Realms of the Human Unconscious.* New York: Viking.

Grof, S. and Halifax, J., 1978 : *The Human Encounter with Death.* New York: E.P. Dutton.

Gurney, E., Myers, F.W.H. and Podmore, F., 1986 : *Phantasms of the Living.* London: Society for Psychical Research.

Hall, T.H., 1962 : *The Spiritualists.* London: Duckworth.

Hardy, A., 1965 : *The Living Stream.* London: Collins.

Hardy, S.A., 1979 : *The Spiritual Nature of Man.* Oxford: Oxford University Press.

Heron, J., 1987 : *Confessions of a Janus-Brain.* London: Tondymion Press.

Heywood, R., 1966 : *The Infinite Hive.* London: Pan Books. (publ. in 1964 by Chatto and Windus, London).

Hofstadter, D.R. and Dennett, D.C. (eds.), 1982 : *The Mind's I.* Harmondsworth, Middx. : Penguin Books/Basic Books.

Home, D.D., 1963/1972 : *Incidents in My Life.* Secaucus, N.J.: University Books.

Home, Mme D.D., 1988/1976 : *D.D. Home, His Life and Mission.* London: Trübner. Reprinted by Arno Press, New York.

Hurley, J.F., 1985 : *Sorcery.* London and USA: Routledge and Kegan Paul.

Hutchinson, M., 1986 : *Megabrain.* New York: Beech Tree Books.

Inglis, B., 1977 : *Natural and Supernatural.* London and USA: Hodder & Stoughton.

———, 1984 : *Science and Parascience: A History of the Paranormal,* 1914-39. London and USA: Hodder & Stoughton.

Jenkins, E., 1982 : *The Shadow and the Light: A Defense of Daniel Dunglass Home the Medium.* London: Hamish Hamilton.

Jenkins, S., 1977 : *The Undiscovered Country.* Suffolk: Neville Spearman.

Jinarajadasa, C., 1938 : *A Description of the Work of Annie Besant and C.W. Leadbeater.* India: The Theosophical Publishing House.

Judelson, C. (tr.), 1989 (1st publ. in Russian 1985) : *A Dictionary for Believers and Non-Believers.* Moscow: Progress Publishers.

King, C.D., 1963 : *The States of Human Consciousness.* New York: University Books.

Klate, J., 1980 : *The Tao of Acupuncture.* Amherst, Mass.:

Pioneer Valley Centre for the Healing Arts.

Knight, D.C., 1969 : *The E.S.P. Reader.* USA: Castle Books.

Kohut, H., 1971 : *The Analysis of the Self.* New York: International Universities Press.

Kohut, H., 1977 : *The Restoration of the Self.* New York: International Universities Press.

Krippner, S., 1980 : *Human Possibilities.* New York: Anchor Press/Doubleday.

Krippner, S. and Villoldo, A., 1986 : *The Realms of Healing.* California: Celestial Arts.

LeShan, L. 1969 : *Toward a General Theory of the Paranormal.* Parapsychological Monograph No. 9. New York: Parapsychology Foundation.

———, 1974 : *The Medium, the Mystic and the Physicist.* London/USA: Turnstone Press.

Loftus, E., 1979 : *Eyewitness Testimony.* Cambridge, Mass.: Harvard University Press.

London Dialectical Society, 1971/1976 : *Report on Spiritualism.* London: Longmans, Green, Reader and Dyer. Reprinted by Arno Press, New York.

Long, M.F., 1981 : *The Secret Science Behind Miracles.* California: DeVorss.

Lorimer, D., 1984 : *Survival, Body, Mind and Death in the Light of Psychic Experience.* London/USA: Routledge and Kegan Paul.

Lucas, J.R., 1973 : *A Treatise on Time and Space.* London: Methuen.

Ludwig, J. (ed.), 1978 : *Philosophy and Parapsychology.* London: Prometheus.

Luria, A.R., 1975 : *The Mind of a Mnemonist.* Harmondsworth, Middlesex: Penguin.

Mackie, J.L., 1974 : *The Cement of the Universe.* Oxford: Oxford University Press.

MacKenzie, A., 1987 : *The Seen and the Unseen.* London: Weidenfeld and Nicolson.

Malcolm, N., 1977 : *Memory and Mind.* Ithaca: Cornell University Press.

Maslow, A.H., 1970 : *Religious Values and Peak Experiences.* New York: The Viking Press.

Mauskopf, S.H. and McVaugh, M.R., 1980 : *The Elusive Science: Origins of Experimental Psychical Research.* Baltimore: The John Hopkins University Press.

Mavromatis, A., 1987 : *Hypnagogia.* London/New York: Routledge and Kegan Paul.

McDermott, J.J., 1967 : *The Writings of William James.* New York: Random House.

McKellar, P., 1979 : *Mindsplit.* London: J.M. Dent.

Merrell-Wolff, F., 1983 : *The Philosophy of Consciousness Without an Object.* New York: Julian Press.

Monroe, R.A., 1972/1977 : *Journeys Out-of-the-Body.* Garden City, New York: Anchor Press/Doubleday, London: Souvenir Press.

Moody, R.A. (Jr.), 1975 : *Life After Life.* Atlanta: Mockingbird Books/New York: Bantam Books (1981).

———, 1978 : *Reflections on Life after Life.* London: Corgi Books.

Moss, P. and Keeton, J., 1981 : *Encounters with the Past.* New York: Penguin.

Muldoon, S.J. and Carrington, H., 1968/1977 (1st publ. 1929) : *The Projection of the Astral Body.* New York: Samuel Weiser/London: Rider.

———, 1969 (1st publ. 1951) : *The Phenomena of Astral Projection.* New York: Samuel Weiser/London: Rider.

Müller, M. (ed.), 1880-1904 : *The Sacred Books of the East,* Vols. 1-49. London: Oxford University Press.

Murphy, G. and Ballou, R.O., 1960 : William James on *Psychical Research.* New York: The Viking Press.

Myers, F.W.H., 1903 : *Human Personality and Its Survival of Bodily Death,* 2 Vols. London: Longmans, Green. Reprinted in 1961 by University Books, New York.

Netherton, M. and Schiffrin, N., 1978 : *Past Lives Therapy*. New York: William Morrow.

Noakes, B. (ed.), 1986 : *Saw a Ghost*. London: Weidenfeld & Nicolson.

Ornstein, R.E., 1973 : *The Nature of Human Consciousness*. San Francisco: W.H. Freeman.

Osis, K. and Haraldsson, E., 1977 : *At the Hour of Death*. New York: Avon Books.

Ostrander and Schroeder, 1973 : *Psi: Psychic Discoveries Behind the Iron Curtain*. London: Sphere Books.

Pagels, E., 1979 : *The Gnostic Gospels*. New York: Random House.

Penfield, W., 1975 : *The Mystery of the Mind*. Surrey and New Jersey: Princeton University Press.

Perkins, J.S., 1982 : *Through Death to Rebirth*. Wheaton: Theosophical Publishing House.

Platt, C., 1987 : *Dream Makers*. London: Xanadu Publications.

Playfair, G.L., 1975 : *The Flying Cow*. London: Souvenir Press.

———, 1976 : *The Indefinite Boundary*. London: Souvenir Press.

———, 1980 : *The House is Haunted*. London: Souvenir Press.

Randall, J.L., 1982 : *Psychokinesis: A Study of Paranormal Forces Through the Ages*. London: Souvenir Press.

Rawlings, M., 1979 : *Beyond Death's Door*. London: Sheldon Press. (publ. in 1978 by Thomas Nelson, Nashville).

Research in Parapsychology, 1974. Metuchen, N.J.: The Scarecrow Press.

———, 1976. London: Scarecrow Press.

Rhine, J.B., 1971 rev. edn. (1st publ. 1934) : *Extra-Sensory Perception*. Boston: Society for Psychical Research/ Brandon.

———, 1937 : *New Frontiers of the Mind*. New York: Farrar and Rinehart.

———, 1954 (1st publ. 1947 by Morrow, New York) : *The Reach of the Mind.* Harmondsworth, Middlesex: Penguin Books.

Rhine, L.E., 1973 (1st publ. 1967) : *ESP in Life and Lab.* New York: Collin Books.

———, 1981 : *The Invisible Picture: A Study of Psychic Experiences.* Jefferson, N.J.: McFarland.

Richardson, A.L., 1969 : *Mental Imagery.* New York: Springer.

Richet, C., 1923 : *Thirty Years of Psychical Research.* New York: Macmillan/London: William Collins Sons. (Reprinted in 1975 by Arno Press, New York).

Ring, K., 1980 : *Life at Death: A Scientific Investigation of the Near-Death Experience.* New York: Coward, McCann, and Geoghegan.

Rogo, D.S., 1976 : *Phantoms: Experiences and Investigations.* Devon: David and Charles.

———, 1978 : *Mind Beyond the Body.* New York: Penguin Books.

———, 1987 : *The Infinite Boundary.* New York: Dodd, Mead.

Roll, W.G., 1972 : *The Poltergeist.* New York: New American Library.

———, (ed.), 1977 (1st publ. 1973) : *Research in Parapsychology.* Metuchen: Scarecrow Press.

Russell, P., 1979 : *The Brain Book.* New York: Hawthorn Books.

Sabom, M., 1982 : *Recollections of Death.* New York: Harper and Row.

Sagan, C., 1979 : *Broca's Brain.* New York: Random House.

Schilder, P., 1935 : *The Image and Appearance of the Human Body.* London: Routledge and Kegan Paul.

Shannon, B., 1974 : *Immortalism in a Temporary World.* London: Vision Press.

Sinclair, U., 1971 (1st publ. 1930) : *Mental Radio. Does It Work and How?* London: Werner Laurie/New York: Collier Books.

Singh, K., 1965 : *The Wheel of Life.* Delhi: Ruhani Satsang.

———, 1968 : *The Mystery of Death.* Delhi: Ruhani Satsang.

Smythies, J.R., 1967 : *Science and ESP.* London: Routledge and Kegan Paul.

Soal, S.G. and Bateman, F., 1954 : *Modern Experiments in Telepathy.* Lodnon: Faber.

Staal, F., 1975 : *Exploring Mysticism.* Harmondsworth, Middlesex: Penguin Books.

Steiner, R., 1975 : *Between Death and Rebirth.* London: Rudolf Steiner Press.

———, 1977 : *Reincarnation and Karma.* London: Rudolf Steiner Press.

Stevenson, I. (M.D.), 1966 : *Twenty Cases Suggestive of Reincarnation.* New York: American Society for Psychical Research.

———, 1974 : *Twenty Cases Suggestive of Reincarnation.* Charlottensville: University Press of Virginia.

———, 1975-83 : *Cases of the Reincarnation Type,* Vols. 1-4. Charlottensville: University Press of Virginia.

Targ, R. and Horary, K., 1984 : *The Mind Race.* New York: Villard.

Targ, R. and Puthoff, H.E., 1977 : *Mind Reach.* London: Cape/New York: Delacorte.

Tart, C.T., 1969 : *Altered States of Consciousness.* New York: John Wiley and Sons/Anchor Books.

Tart, C.T., Puthoff, H.E. and Targ, R. (eds.), 1979 : *Mind at Large.* New York: Praeger.

Taylor, J., 1971 : *The Shape of Minds to Come.* London: Michael Joseph.

Thakur, S. (ed.), 1976 : *Philosophy and Psychical Research.* New York: Humanities Press.

Thalbourne, M.A., 1982 : *A Glossary of Terms Used in Parapsychology.* London: Heinemann.

Thouless, R.H., 1972 : *From Anecdote to Experiment in Psychical Research.* London: Routledge and Kegan Paul.

Thurston, H., 1952 : *The Physical Phenomena of Mysticism.* Chicago: Henry Regnery Co.

———, 1953 : *Ghosts and Poltergeists.* London: Burns Oates and Washbourne.

Tietze, T.R., 1973 : *Margery.* New York: Harper and Row.

Tyrrell, G.N.M., 1961 (1st publ. 1938 in London). *Science and Psychical Phenomena.* New Hyde Park, N.Y.: University Books.

———, 1942/1961 : *Apparitions.* New Hyde Park, N.Y.: University Books. Published with Tyrrell 1938/1961.

———, 1947 : *The Personality of Man.* Harmondsworth, Middlesex: Penguin Books.

Vallee, J., 1979 : *Messengers of Deception.* USA: And/Or Press.

Van Dusen, W., 1974 : *The Presence of Other Worlds.* New York: Harper and Row.

Vasiliev, L.L., 1976 (1st publ. 1962). *Experiments in Distant Influence.* New York: E.O. Dutton.

Vaughan, A., 1980 : *Incredible Coincidence: The Baffling World of Synchronicity.* New York: Signet Books.

Volgyesi, F.A., 1966 : *Hypnosis of Man and Animals.* London: Bailliere, Tindall and Cassell.

Walker, B., 1974 : *Beyond the Body.* London: Routledge and Kegan Paul.

Walker, E.H., 1975 : "Foundations of Paraphysical and Parapsychological Phenomena", In L. Otera (ed.), *Quantum Physics and Parapsychology.* New York: Parapsychology Foundation.

Wambach, H., 1979 : *Life Before Life.* New York: Bantam Books.

Watson, D., 1991 : *A Dictionary of Mind and Spirit.* Calcutta: Rupa & Co. (1st publ. in 1991 by Andre Deutsch, London).

Watson, L., 1986 : *Beyond Supernature.* London: Hodder and Stoughton.

Watts, A.W., 1957 : *The Way of Zen.* Harmondsworth, Middlesex: Penguin Books.

———, 1972 : *The Supreme Identity.* New York: Pantheon Books.

Web, J., 1980 : *The Harmonious Circle.* London: Thames and Hudson.

Weed, J.J., 1968 : *Wisdom of the Mystic Masters.* New York: Parker Publishing.

West, L.J. (ed.), 1962 : *Hallucinations.* New York: Grune and Stratton.

Whatley, C., 1945 : *Telepathy.* London: Methuen.

Wheatley, J. and Edge, H. (eds.), 1976 : *Philosophical Dimensions of Parapsychology.* Springfield, Ill: C. Thomas.

Whitton, J.L. and Fisher, J., 1990 (1st publ. 1986) : *Life Between Life.* London: Grafton Books.

Wilber, K., 1980 : *The Atman Project.* Wheaton, Ill.: The Theosophical Publishing House.

———, 1982 : *The Holographic Paradigm and Other Paradoxes.* Colorado: Shambhala Publications.

Wilson, C., 1989 : *The Occult.* London: Grafton Books. (1st publ. 1971 by Hodder and Stoughton, London, and by Random House, New York).

———, 1986 : *Mysteries.* London: Grafton Books. (1st publ. 1978 by Hodder and Stoughton, London).

———, 1979 : *New Pathways in Psychology.* London: Victor Gollancz.

———, 1981 : *Poltergeist.* London: New English Library.

———, 1985 : *Afterlife.* London: Harrap.

———, 1988 : *Beyond the Occult.* London: Bantam Press.

Wilson, C. and Wilson, D., 1987 : *The Encyclopedia of Unsolved Mysteries.* London: Harrap.

Wolman, B.B. (ed.), 1977 : *Handbook of Parapsychology.* New York: Van Nostrand Reinhold.

Woods, R. (ed.), 1981 : *Understanding Mysticism.* London: The Athlone Press.

Zdenek, M., 1985 : *The Right Brain Experience.* London: Corgi Books.

Zohar, D., 1983 : *Through the Time Barrier.* London: Granada Publishing.

Zöllner, J.C.F., 1888/1976 : *Transcendal Physics,* trans., C.C. Massey. Boston: Colby and Rich. Reprinted by Arno Press, New York.

Science and Philosophy of Science

ABC's of the Human Mind, 1990 : New York: The Reader's Digest Association.

Anderson, A.R., 1964 : *Minds and Machines.* Englewood Cliffs, N.J.: Prentice-Hall.

Arey, L.B., 1954 : *Developmental Anatomy,* 6th edn. Philadelphia/London: W.B. Saunders.

Ashby, W.R., 1952 : *Design for a Brain.* New York: John Wiley.

Barrow, J.D. and Tipler, F.J., 1986/1988 : *The Anthropic Cosmological Principle.* Oxford: Clarendon Press.

Bergson, H., 1911a : *Creative Evolution.* London: Macmillan.

Best, C.H. and Taylor, N.B., 1966 (1st publ. 1937) : *The Physiological Basis of Medical Practice,* 8th edn. Baltimore: The Williams and Wilkins Co.

Blakemore, C. and Greenfield, S. (eds.), 1987 : *Mindwaves.* Oxford: Basil Blackwell.

Bohm, D., 1980 : *Wholeness and the Implicate Order.* London: Routledge and Kegan Paul.

Bonner, J.T., 1958 : *The Evolution of Development.* Cambridge: Cambridge University Press.

Bose, J.C., 1926 : *The Nervous Mechanism of Plants.* London: Longmans, Green & Co.

Bruner, J.S., 1983 : *The Search of Mind.* New York: Harper and Row.

Bünning, E., 1973 : *The Physiological Clock*. London: English University Press.

Capelin, S. and Davies, P.C.W. (eds.), 1986 : *The New Physics*. Cambridge, Mass: Cambridge University Press.

Capra, F., 1975 : *The Tao of Physics*. London: Wildwood House.

———, 1989 : *Uncommon Wisdom*. London: Flamingo (Fontana Paperbacks).

Carnap, R., 1967 : *The Logical Structure of the World: Pseudoproblems in Philosophy*. Berkeley, California : University of California Press.

Charlesworth, M., 1982 : *Science, Non-Science and Pseudo-Science*. Melbourne, Australia: Dankin University Press.

Chopra, D., 1989 : *Quantum Healing*. New York: Bantam Books.

Churchland, P.S., 1984 : *Matter and Consciousness*. Cambridge, Mass.: Bradford Books, MIT Press.

———, 1986 : *Neurophilosophy*. Cambridge, Mass.: MIT Press.

Crick, F.H.C., 1967 : *Of Molecules and Men*. Seattle: University of Washington Press.

Critchley, M., 1979 : *The Divine Banquet of the Brain*. New York: Raven Press.

Darwin, C., 1859 : *The Origin of Species*. London: Murray.

———, 1871 : *The Descent of Man*, 2 Vols., London: Murray.

———, 1880 : *The Power of Movement in Plants*. London: Murray.

———, 1982 : *The Movements and Habits of Climbing Plants*. London: Murray.

Davies, P.C.W., 1988 (1st publ. 1982) : *The Accidental Universe*. Cambridge: Cambridge University Press.

Dawkins, R., 1976 : *The Selfish Gene*. Oxford/New York: Oxford University Press.

———, 1986 : *The Blind Watchmaker*. New York: W.W. Norton.

Delafresnaye, J.F. (ed.), 1961 : *Brain Mechanisms and Consciousness.* Oxford: Blackwell.

Delbrück, M., 1986 : *Mind from Matter?* Oxford: Blackwell Scientific Publishing.

Dennett, D.C., 1978 : *Brainstorms: Philosophical Essays on Mind and Psychology.* Hassocks, Sussex: Harvester Press/Cambridge, Mass: MIT/Bradford Books.

D'Espagnat, B., 1976 : *The Conceptual Foundation of Quantum Mechanics.* Reading, Mass.: Benjamin.

Dixon, B. 1989 : *The Science of Science.* London: Cassell/ Equinos.

Dostal, R., 1967 : *On Integration in Plants.* Cambridge, Mass.: Harvard University Press.

Dreyfus, H.L., 1972 : *What Computers Can't Do: A Critique of Artificial Reason.* New York: Harper and Row.

———, 1979 : *What Computers Can't Do: The Limits of Artificial Intelligence.* New York: Harper and Row.

Driesch, H., 1914 : *History and Theory of Vitalism.* London: Macmillan.

Eccles, J.C. (ed.), 1966 : *Brain and Conscious Experience.* New York/Berlin: Springer.

———, 1973 : *The Understanding of the Brain.* New York: McGraw-Hill.

Eddington, A.S., 1928/1931 : *The Nature of the Physical World.* Cambridge: Cambridge University Press.

———, 1936 : *Relativity Theory of Protons and Electrons.* Cambridge: Cambridge University Press.

Edelman, G., 1987 : *Neural Darwinism.* New York: Basic Books.

Elsasser, W.M., 1958 : *Physical Foundations of Biology.* London: Pergamon Press.

———, 1966 : *Atom and Organism.* Princeton: Princeton University Press.

———, 1975 : *The Chief Abstractions of Biology.* Amsterdam: North Holland.

Emment, D., 1966 : *Whitehead's Philosophy of Organism.* London: Macmillan.

Feyerabend, P.K., 1981 : *Philosophical Papers,* Vols. 1 & 2. Cambridge, Mass.: Cambridge University Press.

Feynman, R., 1985 : *Surely You're Joking. Mr. Feynman.* New York: W.W. Norton.

Fisher, R.A., 1930 : *Genetical Theory of Natural Selection.* London: Clarendon Press.

Fodor, J.A., 1975 : *The Language of Thought.* New York: Thomas Y. Crowell/Cambridge, Mass.: Harvard University Press.

———, 1981 : *Representations: Philosophical Essays on the Foundations of Cognitive Science.* Cambridge, Mass.: MIT Press.

———, 1983 : *The Modularity of Mind.* Cambridge, Mass.: MIT Press.

Ganong, W.F., 1967 : *Review of Medical Physiology.* Los Altos, California: Lange Medical Publications.

Gardner, H., 1985 : *The Mind's New Science: A History of the Cognitive Revolution.* New York: Basic Books.

Gazzaniga, M.S., 1970 : *The Bisected Brain.* New York: Appleton-Century-Crofts.

———, 1985 : *The Social Brain.* New York: Basic Books.

Glass, A., Holyoak, K.J. and Santa, J.L., 1979 : *Cognition.* Reading, Mass.: Addison-Wesley.

Gleick, J., 1987 : *Chaos.* New York: Viking Press.

Good, I.J. (ed.), 1961 : *The Scientist Speculates.* London: Heinemann.

Goodman, N., 1984 : *Of Mind and Other Matters.* Cambridge, Mass.: Harvard University Press.

———, 1985 : *Fact, Fiction and Forecast.* Cambridge, Mass.: Harvard University Press.

Gould, S.J., 1977 : *Ever Since Darwin.* New York: W.W. Norton.

———, 1985 : *The Flamingo's Smile: Reflections in Natural History.* New York: W.W. Norton/Harmondsworth, Middlesex: Penguin Books.

Gregory, R.L., 1981 : *Mind in Science.* Harmondsworth, Middlesex: Penguin Books.

Griffin, D.R., 1984 : *Animal Thinking.* Cambridge, Mass.: Harvard University Press.

Guyton, A.C. (M.D.), 1966 : *Textbook of Medical Physiology,* 3rd edn. Philadelphia/London: W.B. Saunders.

Harth, E., 1982 : *Windows on the Mind.* Hassocks, Sussex: Harvester Press.

Hayes, J.R., 1978 : *Congnitive Psychology: Thinking and Creating.* Homewood, Ill.: Dorsey.

Heisenberg, W. and Others, 1961 : *On Modern Physics.* New York: Carkson Potter.

Hellemans, A. and Bunch, B. (eds.), 1989 : *The Time Table of Science.* London: Sidgwick and Jackson. (1st publ. in the USA in 1988 by Simon and Schuster).

Hempel, C., 1965 : *Aspects of Science Explanation.* New York: Free Press.

Hesse, M.B., 1961 : *Forces and Fields: The Concept of Action at a Distance in the History of Physics.* London: Nelson.

Hinton, G.E. and James, A.A. (eds.), 1981 : *Parallel Models of Associative Memory.* Hillsdale, N.J.: Erlbaum.

Hintzman, D.L., 1978 : *The Psychology of Learning and Memory.* San Francisco: W.H. Freeman.

Holton, G., 1973 : *Thematic Origins of Scientific Thought: Kepler to Einstein.* Cambridge, Mass.: Harvard University Press.

Hubel, D.H., 1988 : *Eye, Brain and Vision.* Scientific American Library Series No. 22.

Hunt, M., 1982 : *The Universe Within: A New Science Explores the Human Mind.* Brighton, Sussex: The Harvester Press.

Huxley, J., 1942 : *Evolution: The Modern Synthesis*. London: Allen and Unwin.

Jacobowitz, H. and Basford, L., 1982 (1st publ. 1967) : *Electronics Made Simple*. Calcutta: Rupa. (London: William Heinemann, 1981).

Jain, V.K., 1989 (1st publ. 1985) : *Computers for Beginners*. Delhi: Pustak Mahal.

Jaynes, J., 1980 : *The Origin of Consciousness in the Breakdown of the Bicameral Mind*. Harmondsworth, Middx.: Penguin Books.

Jennings, H.S., 1906 : *The Behaviour of the Lower Organisms*. New York: Columbia University Press.

Kandel, E.R., 1976 : *Cellular Basis of Behaviour: An Introduction to Behavioural Neurobiology*. San Francisco: W.H. Freeman.

Katz, B., 1966 : *Nerve, Muscle and Synapse*. New York: McGraw-Hill.

Klein, M., 1972 : *Mathematical Thought from Ancient to Modern Times*. New York: Oxford University Press.

Kosslyn, S.M., 1980 : *Image and Mind*. Cambridge, Mass.: Harvard University Press.

———, 1983 : *Ghosts in the Mind's Machine: Creating and Using Images in the Brain*. New York: W.W. Norton.

Kuhn, T.S., 1970 (1st publ. 1962) : *The Structure of Scientific Revolutions*, 2nd edn. Chicago: University of Chicago Press.

Lachman, R., Lachman, J.L. and Butterfield, E.C., 1979 : *Cognitive Psychology and Information Processing: An Introduction*. Hillsdale, N.J.: Lawrence Erlbaum.

Lashley, K.S., 1929 : *Brain Mechanisms and Intelligence*. Chicago: University of Chicago Press.

Leclerc, I., 1972 : *The Nature of Physical Existence*. London: Allen and Unwin.

Lenartowicz, P., 1975 : *Phenotype-Genotype Dichotomy*. Rome: Gregorian University.

Leslie, J. (ed.), 1990 : *Physical Cosmology and Philosophy.* New York: Macmillan/London: Collier Macmillan.

Lindauer, M., 1961 : *Communication Among Social Bees.* Cambridge, Mass.: Harvard University Press.

Lindsay, P.H. and Norman, D.A., 1977 : *Human Information Processing: An Introduction.* New York: Academic.

MacKinnon, D.C. and Hawes, R.S.J., 1961 : *An Introduction to the Study of Protozoa.* Oxford: Oxford University Press.

Maor, E., 1987 : *To Infinity and Beyond.* Boston: Birkhäuser.

Marais, E., 1971 : *The Soul of the White Ant.* London: Cape and Blond.

Marr, D., 1982 : Vision: *A Computational Investigation into the Human Representation and Processing of Visual Information.* San Francisco: W.H. Freeman.

Mayer, R.E., 1977 : *Thinking and Problem Solving: An Introduction to Human Cognition and Learning.* Glenview, Ill.: Scott, Foresman.

Mayr, E., 1963 : *Animal Species and Evolution.* Cambridge, Mass.: Harvard University Press.

Medvedev, Z.A., 1969 : *The Rise and Fall of T.D. Lysenko.* New York: Columbia University Press.

Mind's Eye, The Readings from Scientific American. New York: W.H. Freeman, 1986.

Minsky, M.L. (ed.), 1968 : *Semantic Information Processing.* Cambridge, Mass.: MIT Press.

———, 1986 : *The Society of Mind,* New York: Simon and Schuster.

Monod, J., 1972/1977 : *Chance and Necessity.* (Trans. A. Wainhouse). London: Collins/Fount.

Narasimhaiah, H. (ed.), 1987 : *Science, Nonscience and the Paranormal.* Bangalore: The Bangalore Science Forum.

Needham, J., 1942 : *Biochemistry and Morphogenesis.* Cambridge: Cambridge University Press.

Newell, A. and Simon, H.A., 1972 : *Human Problem Solving.* Englewood Cliffs, N.J.: Prentice-Hall.

Nicolis, G. and Prigogine, I., 1977 : *Self-Organization in Nonequilibrium Systems.* New York: Wiley Interscience.

Norman, D.A., 1969/1976 : *Memory and Attention: An Introduction to Human Information Processing.* New York: John Wiley.

Oakley, D.A. (ed.), 1985 : *Brain and Mind.* London and New York: Methuen.

Ozer, M.N. (ed.), 1978 : *Toward the More Human Use of Human Beings.* Boulder, Colo.: Westview.

Pagels, H.R., 1983 : *The Cosmic Code.* New York: Bantam Books.

———, (ed.), 1984 : *Computer Culture: The Scientific, Intellectual and the Social Impact of the Computer.* Publ. in NYAS Annals, Vol. 426.

———, 1986 : *Perfect Symmetry.* New York: Bantam Books.

———, 1989 : *The Dreams of Reason.* New York: Bantam Books. (Originally publ. in 1988 by Simon and Schuster, New York).

Pais, A., 1982 : *Subtle is the Lord: The Science and the Life of Albert Einstein.* Oxford: Clarendon Press.

Parsons, P.A., 1967 : *The Genetic Analysis of Behaviour.* London: Methuen.

Patten, B.M., 1968 : *Human Embryology*, 3rd edn. New York: McGraw-Hill Book.

Penfield, W., 1975 : *The Mystery of Mind.* Princeton: Princeton University Press.

Penfield, W. and Jasper, H.H., 1954 : *Epilepsy and the Functional Anatomy of the Human Brain.* Boston: Mass.

Penfield, W. and Roberts, L. 1959 : *Speech and Brain Mechanisms.* Princeton: Princeton University Press.

Penrose, R., 1989 : *The Emperor's New Mind.* Oxford: Oxford University Press.

Popper, K.R., 1959 : *The Logic of Scientific Discovery.* London: Hutchinson.

———, 1982 : *Quantum Theory and the Schism in Physics.* Totowa, N.J.: Rowan and Littlefield.

———, 1982 : *The Open Universe: An Argument for Indeterminism.* Totowa, N.J.: Rowan and Littlefield.

Popper, K.R. and Eccles, J.C. 1977 : *The Self and Its Brain* (Part I and II). Berlin/New York: Springer International.

Pribram, K.H., 1971 : *Languages of the Brain: Experimental Paradoxes and Principles in Neuropsychology.* Englewood Cliffs: Prentice-Hall.

Putnam, H., 1975/1985 : *Mind, Language and Reality, Philosophical Papers,* Vol.2. Cambridge: Cambridge University Press.

———, 1983 : *Realism and Reason,* Vol.31. Cambridge, Mass.: Cambridge University Press.

Pylyshyn, Z.W., 1984 : *Computation and Cognition: Toward a Foundation for Cognitive Science.* Cambridge, Mass.: MIT Press.

Radford, J. and Burton, A., 1974 : *Thinking: Its Nature and Development.* London: Wiley.

Raphael, B., 1976 : *The Thinking Computer: Mind Inside Matter.* San Francisco : W.H. Freeman.

Raven, P.H., Evert, R.F. and Curtis, H., 1976 : *Biology of Plants.* New York: Worth Publishers.

Reichenbach, H., 1951 : *The Rise of Scientific Philosophy.* Berkeley, Calif.: University of California Press.

Resnick, L.B., (ed.), 1976 : *The Nature of Intelligence.* Hillsdale, N.J.: Lawrence Erlbaum.

Resnik, M.D., 1980 : *Frege and Philosophy of Mathematics.* Ithaca: Cornell University Press.

Restak, R., 1979 : *The Brain: The Last Frontier.* Garden City, N.Y.: Doubleday.

Ricard, M., 1969 : *The Mystery of Animal Migration.* London: Constable.

Riedl, R., 1978 : *Order in Living Organisms.* Chichester/New York: Wiley Interscience.

Roitt, I.M., 1988 (Ist publ. 1971) : *Essential Immunology,* 6th edn. London: Blackwell Scientific Publications.

Rose, S., 1976. *The Conscious Brain.* New York: Vintage.

Rucker, R., 1984 : *Infinity and the Mind: The Science and Philosophy of the Infinite.* London: Paladin Books, Granada Publishing. (Originally publ. by Harvester Press, 1982).

Rumelhart, D.D., McClelland, J.L. and the PDP Research Group 1986 : *Parallel Distributed Processing, Explorations in the Microstructure of Cognition,* Vols. 1 & 2. Cambridge, Mass.: MIT Press.

Russ, M., 1979 : *Sociobiology: Sense or Nonsense?* Hingham, Mass.: Kluwer Boston.

Russell, E.S., 1945 : *The Directiveness of Organic Activities.* Cambridge: Cambridge University Press.

Satter, R.L., 1979 : "Leaf Movements Tendril Curling", In *Encyclopedia of Plant Physiology* (eds. A. Pirson and M.H. Zimmermann), New Series Vol.7, pp. 442-84. Berlin: Springer-Verlag.

Schank, R.C. and Abelson, R., 1977 : *Scripts, Plans, Goals and Understanding.* Hillsdale, N.J.: Lawrence Erlbaum.

Searle, J., 1984 : *Minds, Brains and Science.* Combridge, Mass.: Harvard University Press/London: BBC Publications.

Sheldrake, R., 1981/1985 : *A New Science of Life: The Hypothesis of Formative Causation,* new edn. London: Anthony Blond. (First publ. 1981 by Blond and Briggs, London.)

Shelley, J., and Hunt, R., 1986/1991 : *Computer Studies: A First Course,* 2nd edn. Allahabad: A.H. Wheeler/ London: Pitman Publishing, 1980.

Simon, H., 1981 : *Sciences of the Artificial.* Cambridge, Mass.: MIT Press.

Sinnott, E.W., 1963 : *The Problem of the Organic Form.* New Havan : Yale University Press.

Sloman, A., 1978 : *The Computer Revolution in Philosophy: Philosophy, Science and Models of Mind.* Hassocks, Sussex: Harvester Press.

Smith, S.B., 1983 : *The Great Mental Calculators.* New York: Columbia University Press.

Solso, R.L. (ed.), 1974 : *Theories in Cognitive Psychology: The Loyola Symposium.* Hillsdale, N.J.: Laurence Erlbaum.

——— (ed.), 1975 : *Information Processing and Cognition: The Loyola Symposium.* Hillsdale, N.J.: Laurence Erlbaum.

Sommerhoff, G., 1950 : *Analytical Biology.* Oxford: Oxford University Press.

Spear, N.E., 1978 : *The Processing of Memories: Forgetting and Retention.* Hillsdale, N.J.: Laurence Erlbaum.

Suppes, P., 1970 : *A Probabilistic Theory of Causality.* Amsterdam: North Holland.

Taylor, C., 1964 : *The Explanation of Behaviour.* London: Routledge and Kegan Paul.

Trigg, R., 1982 : *The Shaping of Man: Philosophical Aspects of Sociobiology.* Oxford: Basil Blackwell.

Uttal, W.R., 1978 : *The Psychobiology of Mind.* Hillsdale, N.J.: Laurence Erlbaum.

Vernon, P.E. (ed.), 1970 : *Creativity.* Harmondsworth, Middlesex: Penguin.

Vinacke, W.E., 1974 : *The Psychology of Thinking.* New York: McGraw-Hill.

Von Frisch, K., 1975 : *Animal Architecture.* London: Hutchinson.

Von Neumann, J., 1958 : *The Computer and the Brain.* New Haven, Conn.: Yale University Press.

Walker, E.H., 1970 : "The Nature of Consciousness", In *Mathematical Biosciences,* Vol.7.

Wann, T.W. (ed.), 1964 : *Behaviourism and Phenomenology: Contrasting Bases for Modern Psychology.* Chicago: University of Chicago Press.

Wardlaw, C.W., 1965 : *Organization and Evolution in Plants.* London: Longmans.

Wason, P.C., and Johnson-Laird, P.N., 1972 : *Psychology of Reasoning: Structure and Content.* Cambridge, Mass.: Harvard University Press.

Watson, J., 1968 : *The Double Helix: A Personal Account of the Structure of DNA.* London: Weidenfeld and Nicolson.

Weaver, J.H., Motz, L. and McAdoo, D. (eds.), 1987 : *The World of Physics,* Vols. 1-3. New York: Simon and Schuster.

Weinberg, S., 1993 : *Dreams of a Final Theory.* London: Vintage.

Weizenbaum, J., 1984 : *Computer Power and Human Reason.* Harmondsworth: Penguin Books.

Wheeler, J.A., and Zurek, W.H., 1983. *Quantum Theory and Measurement.* Princeton: Princeton University Press.

Whitrow, G.J., 1959 : *The Structure and Evolution of the Universe.* New York: Harper and Row.

Whyte, L.L., 1949 : *The Unitary Principle in Physics and Biology.* London: Cresset Press.

Wickelgren, W.A., 1974 : *How to Solve Problems: Elements of a Theory of Problems and Problem Solving.* San Francisco: W.H. Freeman.

Wigglesworth, V.B., 1964 : *The Life of Insects.* London: Weidenfeld and Nicolson.

Wigner, E., 1961 : "Remarks on the Mind-Body Question", In I.J. Good (ed.) *The Scientist Speculates.* London: Heinemann.

Wigner, E., 1967 : *Symmetries and Reflections.* Bloomington: Indiana University Press.

———, 1969 : "Epistemology in Quantum Mechanics", In *Contemporary Physics: Trieste Symposium 1968,*

Vol.2, pp. 431-38. Vienna: International Atomic Energy Authority.

Wilkins, M.B., (ed.) 1968 : *Physiology of Plant Growth and Development.* London: McGraw-Hill.

Wilson, E.O., 1975 : *Sociobiology : The New Synthesis.* Cambridge, Mass.: Harvard University Press.

Winson, J., 1986 : *Brain and Psyche: The Biology of the Unconscious.* New York: Vintage Books.

Winston, P.H., 1975: *Psychology of Computation Vision.* New York: McGraw-Hill.

———, 1977 : *Artificial Intelligence.* Reading, Mass.: Addison-Wesley.

Wolff, G., 1902 : *Mechanisms and Vitalisms.* Leipzig.

Woodger, J.H., 1929 : *Biological Principles.* London: Kegan Paul, Trench, Trubner & Co.

Wright, R., 1988 : *The Grand Design: Three Scientists and Their Gods.* New York: Times Books.

Zohar, D., 1991 : *The Quantum Self.* London: Flamingo. (Originally publ. by Bloomsbury, 1990).

Zukav, G., 1979 : *The Dancing Wu Li Masters.* London: Rider/Hutchinson. Fontana Paerbacks in 1980. (First publ. in the USA in 1979.)

Name Index

Subject Index